Eustace Mullins

BLOOD AND GOLD
The history of the CFR

OMNIA VERITAS.

Eustace Clarence Mullins
(1923-2010)

BLOOD AND GOLD
The history of the Council on Foreign Relations

1952

Published by Omnia Veritas Limited

© Omnia Veritas Ltd – 2024

⊘MNIA VERITAS®

www.omnia-veritas.com

CHAPTER 1 9

CHAPTER 2 20

CHAPTER 3 26

CHAPTER 4 34

CHAPTER 5 41

CHAPTER 6 46

CHAPTER 7 65

CHAPTER 8 72

CHAPTER 9 88

CHAPTER 10 105

CHAPTER 11 114

CHAPTER 12 123

CHAPTER 13 137

CHAPTER 14 148

CHAPTER 15 172

CHAPTER 16 179

CHAPTER 17 199

CHAPTER 18 229

CHAPTER 19 237

CHAPTER 20 273

CHAPTER 21 287

CHAPTER 22 293

CHAPTER 23 303

CHAPTER 24 311

CHAPTER 25 319

CHAPTER 26 330

CHAPTER 27 341

OTHER TITLES...349

CHAPTER 1

Revolutions are not made by the middle class. They are made either by dregs of a nation, that is, the Lenins and the Trotskys, or they are made by the oligarchy at the top. We in America are witnessing the latter, the members of an oligarchy who are promoting their ideal of a collectivist government. The immigrants who gained control of our monetary system, our heavy industry, and our labor force, are the oligarchy who are making the new society in America. It is a society planned by Marx and Lenin, a society in which our religion and our political institutions have no place.

The Council on Foreign Relations is that oligarchy. It is the policy-making group or Politburo for Marxist groups in the United States. Through the system of interlocking directorates, the same system by which they forced out competition in banking and industry, the emissaries and employees of the Frankfurt bankers have taken over the fields of education and propaganda. The members of the Council on Foreign Relations control a host of subsidiary political organizations devoted to Marxist propaganda, of which its principal offspring is the Institute of Pacific Relations.

The address of the Council on Foreign Relations for many years, 45 East 65th St., New York City, is also the address of the Woodrow Wilson Foundation, of which Alger Hiss was Director, the address of the American Association for the League of Nations, and the address of the American Association for the United Nations.

From the Council on Foreign Relations Handbook of 1936, we learn that

> "On May 30 1919, several leading members of the delegations to the Paris Peace Conference met at the Hotel Majestic in Paris to discuss setting up an international group which would advise their respective governments on international affairs. The United States was represented (unofficially, of course) by Gen. Tasker H. Bliss of

the banking family and Col. Edward Mandel House. Great Britain was unofficially represented by Lord Robert Cecil, Lionel Curtis, Lord Eustace Percy, and Harold Temperley. It was decided at this meeting to call the proposed organization the Institute of International Affairs. At a meeting on June, 5, 1919, the planners decided it would be best to have separate organizations cooperating with each other. Consequently, they organized the Council on Foreign Relations, with headquarters in New York, and a sister organization, the Royal Institute of International Affairs, in London, also known as the Chatham House Study Group, to advise the British Government. A subsidiary organization, the Institute of Pacific Relations, was set up to deal exclusively with Far Eastern affairs. Other organizations were set up in Paris and Hamburg, the Hamburg branch being called the Institut für Auswartige Politik, and the Paris branch being known as Centre d'Études de Politique Étrangère, at 13 rue du Four, Paris VI."

One of these founders of the Council on Foreign Relations, Dr. James T. Shotwell, was rushed into the breach to replace fellow-council-member Alger Hiss as President of the Carnegie Endowment for International Peace when Hiss was imprisoned for lying about his career as a Soviet spy.

The principal subsidiary of the Council on Foreign Relations, the Institute of Pacific Relations, was recently the subject of a full-scale investigation by the Senate Subcommittee on Internal Security, headed by Senator Pat McCarran. After months of investigation, and after the testimony of dozens of reliable witnesses had been taken, the Committee issued a 226 page report of its findings, to the effect that the Institute was a Communist-front organization devoted to the Marxist world revolution. It was proven to be the main factor in the surrender of China to Communism. Senator McCarran was interrupted by a determined and vicious personal attack on him in the yellow liberal magazines, *The Nation*, and the *New Republic*, and by the contribution of large sums to his opponent in the Nevada elections by Arthur Goldsmith of New York, head of the Anti-Defamation league of B'nai Brith. *The Nation* for many years was supported by money from Maurice Wertheim, senior partner of the international banking house of Hallgarten Co, New York, which originated in Frankfurt, Germany. The new republic's funds come from the fortune of the late Williard Straight, partner of JP Morgan Co. His son Michael Straight edits the magazine. Michael Strait is a member of the Socialist Group the Royal

Economic Society of London. Later, we shall show the role played by JP Morgan Co in supporting the World Revolution of Communism.

The Institute of Pacific Relations was set up according to the rules of the Communist International. It too had its international secretariat with branches in principal countries. In Russia, its branch is headed by A. S. Swandze. Its secretary general. Edward C. Carter notes in his who's who in America biography volume of 1946 that he has been awarded Russia's highest decoration, the order of the Red banner of Labor. Alger Hiss is a director of the Institute.

Such is the present power of the Council of on Foreign Relations that not once was it mentioned during the hearings on its subsidiary, the Institute of Pacific Relations. The institute numbers are among its members and financial supporters. John D. Rockefeller third, who carries on the family traditions of financing communist groups and the institutes leading intellectual is Philip C. Jessup, now alternate delegate to the United Nations from the US government. The well-known fellow traveler Joseph Barnes is also a member of the Institute. Barnes was revealed recently as the man who Ghost wrote General Eisenhower's profitable and tax evading million-dollar work of literature, "Crusade in Europe", in which the names of Eisenhower's chief aides in London, Rifkin, Schiff, and Warburg, are conspicuous by their absence.

In Paris in 1919, the guiding genius of the Organization of the Council on Foreign Relations was Baron Edmond de Rothschild, senior member of the Rothschild family. Then in his 80s, this organization was the crowning work of Baron de Rothschild's life. The directors. And members of the Council show his influence. The Council was grouped around the partners of Kuhn, Loeb Co., New York. Rothschild's principal agent in the United States. The Council on Foreign Relations Handbook for 1920 lists its officers as follows:

> ➤ Honorary Chairman Elihu Root. Senior partner of the firm of Root, Winthrop and Stimson, lawyers for Kuhn, Loeb Co. Root earned his place in the Communist Hall of Fame by his mission to Russia in 1918 with $20 million in cash for the Leninist Government.
> ➤ Treasurer Frank N Doubleday, president of Doubleday, Page publishers. This House, a principal agent of internationalism, employed the sons of ambassador to Britain Walter Hines Page. Arthur W. Page was editor of the magazine "World's Work",

and Frank C. Page later became a vice president of International Telephone and Telegraph Corporation.

> The chairman of the financial committee was Alexander Hemphill of the Wall Street bankers Hemphill Noyes. The executive committee consisted of Otto Kahn, partner of Kuhn, Loeb Co. Richard Washburn Child who was special assistant to Frank Vanderlip (president of the National City Bank) when Vanderlip was advisor on war finance to the US Treasury during the First World War. Child later became editor of Colliers magazine and F. Kingsbury Curtis, Wall Street lawyer.

These were the officers of the new enterprise, which was to advise the United States government on Foreign Affairs from New York. However, the Council did appoint a Washington representative in 1920, John Hays Hammond. Former chief engineer for the House of Rothschild and at that time advisory engineer to the Guggenheim Enterprises at a salary of $600,000 a year.

The Handbook for 1920s clearly stated the Council's intent as follows:

"The purpose of the Council is to stimulate international thought in the United States, to cooperate with existing international agencies and to coordinate their influence and activities."

The Council was so successful in stimulating international thought that the United States is now a member of the United Nations. What were the international agencies which the Council intended to coordinate? That question is easily answered. In 1920, there were only two international political agencies operating in the United States. They were the world Zionist organizations and the Communist International.

The Council on Foreign Relations creed of Internationalism was best expressed by its preceptor, Nikolai Lenin, dictator of Communist Russia, who wrote in volume ten of his selected works, page 4, as translated by J. Feinberg:

"There is one and only one kind of internationalism, indeed working wholeheartedly for the development of the revolutionary movement and the revolutionary struggle in one's own country, and supporting by propaganda, sympathy and material aid, such and only such a struggle and such a line in every country without exception."

Such influential members of the Council on Foreign Relations as Alger Hiss, Edward C. Carter and Frederick V Field have fulfilled Lenin's definition of internationalism. The Council's membership list of 1920 shows how Kuhn Loeb was the nucleus of the organization. Besides Otto Kahn on the Executive committee, other partners on the Council were Jacob Schiff, Mortimer Schiff and Paul Warburg. Partners who are known members include Lewis Lichtenstein Strauss of the US Atomic Energy Commission, John M Schiff, president of the Boy Scouts of America, and Benjamin Buttenwieser, assistant US High Commissioner of Germany.

The Frankfurt Banking House of Speyer and Co has been represented by James Speyer, head of the firm's New York Branch, and William F. Sands, who is now in charge of the historical section of the School for Foreign Service at Georgetown University, Washington, DC.

Frankfurt Bankers J and W Seligman Co have been represented by Earle Bailie, who won his fame when he gave $415,000 bribe to Juan Leguia, son of the President of Peru to encourage that nation to accept a loan during the orgy of the 1920s. Henry S. Bowers; Henry C. Breck of the American Society of International Law; Albert Strauss of the Peace Commission; Frederick Strauss, mastermind of the billion dollar holding company Electric Bond and Share. Norman H. Davis, president of the Council until his sudden death in 1944; Broderick Haskell; Alex I. Henderson; and the present scion of the house, Eustace Seligman, law partner of the Dulles brothers in the Wall Street firm of Sullivan and Cromwell.

The Banking House of Lazar Frere has been represented on the Council by Eugene Meyer, owner of the *Washington Post* and radio Station WTOP; George Blumenthal; Frank Altschul; and Thomas W. Childs, head of the British Purchasing Mission to the US during the Second World War.

The law firm of Cravath and Henderson succeeded Root, Winthrop and Stimson as legal counselors to Kuhn, Loeb Co when Root and Henry L. Stimson gave themselves to public service. Partners of Cravath and Henderson on the Council include Paul Cravath; S. Parker Gilbert; Russell C. Leffingwell, Thomas K. Finletter, who is now secretary of the Air Force; John J. Mccloy, former president of the World Bank and now US High Commissioner to Germany; and Nicholas Kelley, who was on the War Loan Staff of the US treasury from 1918–1920 in charge of loans to foreign governments, a matter of some $20 billion.

The International Banking House of Lehman Brothers has been represented on the council by Senator Herbert Lehman, Arthur Lehman, Robert Lehman, Arthur Bunker, brother of Ellsworth Bunker, (president of National Sugar Co and present U.S. ambassador to Italy) and Philip D. Wilson. The Lehman's giant holding company, the Lehman Corporation is represented by Thomas A. Morgan, who is chairman of the board of Vickers, Dorsey Richardson of the Peace Commission, Alexander Sachs, self-proclaimed originator of the atomic Bomb project, and John L. Simpson.

The membership list of the Council in 1920 included orders of the same banking clique such as Leopold Frederick, formerly Neuwirth, an immigrant from Yugoslavia, who was with the Ministry of Finance of Austria-Hungary until he decided to catch a fast boat for America. Here he became the treasurer of the Baruch-Meyer firm, the Yukon Gold Co. and treasurer of the Guggenheim Family biggest corporation, the American Smelting and Refining Co. A typical member of America's new oligarchy, he was also a director of the National City Bank of New York.

Henry Morgenthau, husband of Babette Guggenheim. A carrier has landlord of the Harlem slums, gave Morgenthau capital to buy into the Equitable Life Assurance Society with Jacob Schiff and Morgenthau became a director of the members of the Bamberger Del Mar Gold Mines, and treasurer of the Democratic National Committee. He gave enough money to Woodrow Wilson to receive the US ambassadorship to Turkey, while the Socialist Zionists were gathered in Istanbul for the completion of their plans to start the Bolshevik revolution in Russia.

Jacob Gould Sherman, ambassador to Germany from 1924 to 1933. Oscar Strauss of the family which owns R. H. Macy Co. Strauss had a distinguished career as a public servant in the democratic tradition. Morgenthau's predecessor as ambassador to Turkey, Strauss was appointed head of the US Immigration Commission in 1910. Soon after his appointment the immigration officials began to complain that whenever they rejected an immigrant on the grounds of illiteracy or mental condition, certain organizations, notably the American Jewish Committee, appealed the case to Washington, where orders would be issued to admit the rejected one. The immigration officials' protest were ignored by Strauss. As these immigrants began to be featured in the newspapers as the leaders of New York criminals, their affair threatened to become a nationwide scandal. President Wilson removed Oscar

Strauss and replaced him with Oscar Nagel, who continued to grant entrance to many of the rejectees. The long-range effect of the Strauss policy was shown by the Kefauver Crime Hearings.

Abraham I. Elkus, ambassador to Turkey from 1916–1919, trustee of the Baron de Hirsch fund, the basic capital of the Zionist movement.

Frank A. Vanderlip, president of the National City Bank.

Maurice Oudin, vice-president of International General Electric, and director of the National City Bank.

Edwin W. Price Jr. president of General Electric.

Thus, the 1920 Executive and membership of the Council on Foreign Relations show that it was founded by the most determined internationalists in the United States, Kuhn, Loeb Co. the Baruch interests, the Guggenheim interests, and their colleagues composed the Council, which was to assume the dominant role in US foreign policy after 1920. It is best known at present as the sponsor of the bi-partisan foreign policy, which has wrecked the two-party system of your Republic, and caused Colonel Robert McCormick to propose the American Party. Since both General Eisenhower and Adlai Stevenson were members of the CFR, Col. McCormick was correct in stating that they were agreed on all major issues.

The CFR was not long in obtaining a headquarters suitable to its important mission. The fabulous town house of Charles Pratt, treasurer of Standard Oil of New Jersey, 45 East 65th St. New York, was given to the Council by his son, Harold Pratt.

The list of men who have been directors of the Council since 1920 proves that it has maintained its mission as a Rothschild policy organization. The complete list is as follows:

1- Paul Warburg, director from 1921 until his death in1932.
2- Otto Kahn, director from 1921 until 1934.
3- Frank Altschul, of Lazard Freres, director since 1934.
4- Stephen Duggan, founder of the Institute for International Education, a mysterious group. Duggan has been a director since 1921. His son Laurence Duggan, prominent in Communist circles, died mysteriously in New York the day before he was to be questioned in Washington.
5- Paul D. Cravath, director from 1920 until 1932.

6- Isaiah Bowman, director since 1921. Chief of the Territorial Section of the Peace Commission in 1919, Bowman has been president of the John Hopkins University for many years.

7- Philip C. Jessup, director since 1934.

8- Hamilton Fish Armstrong, director since 1928, chief publicist for the Council. In 1950 he wrote a book glamorizing the Communist revolutionary Tito, dictator of Yugoslavia, "Tito and Goliath".

9- Norman H. Davis, director from 1921 until his sudden death in 1944.

10- Allen W. Dulles, director since 1927. Legal advisor to the American Peace Commission in 1919, he became Chief of the Department of State's Division of Near Eastern Affairs, and in 1926 resigned to join his brother John Foster Dulles in the law firm of Sullivan and Cromwell. One of the oligarchy with a passion for anonymity, metropolitan newspapers have standing order to avoid mentioning Dulle's name. He is deputy director of the Central Intelligence Agency and its real head, and President of the CFR. A director of J. Henry Schroder Co. the banking house whose Cologne branch handled Hitler's personal account throughout the 1930's, Allen W. Dulles was with the Office of Strategic Services throughout the Second World War, and conferred frequently with German business leaders in Switzerland. The CIA was reported in June of 1950 to have discharged two agents because they were caught forwarding information on Arab troop strength to the Israeli Government. The matter was hushed up, and only the John S. Knight papers carried the story, probably through an oversight on their part.

11- Russel C. Leffingwell, of Cravath and Henderson, with the US Treasury during "L'Affaire Meyer", and with JP Morgan Co. since the 1920s.

12- Walter Lippmann, columnist and propagandist for the Council.

This list of the Council's directors shows how Kuhn, Loeb has maintained tight control of the group since its inception. It was successful in one of its main objectives, the imposition of a decree of silence on the members of the American Commission to Negotiate Peace in 1918. All of them have had satisfactory careers in banking, education, and journalism since then, and they have been notably mute about what they did in Paris. The Council has been guilty of a criminal conspiracy to conceal the truth about the Treaty of Versailles and how it provoked the Second World War. Had that truth been given to the American people, we would never have been betrayed into the War to save Communism by Franklin D. Roosevelt.

In 1922, the CFR inaugurated its quarterly, "Foreign Affairs", which is required reading for university students of foreign relations. The pages of "Foreign Affairs" have been open to the views of the leading members of the Communist leaders of Russia, but they have always been closed to any critics of internationalism. Looking at a volume of "Foreign Affairs" at random, we find in the July 1932 issue an article, "The War in the Far East; a Soviet View" by Karl Radek, Chief of Propaganda for the Communist International. In the July, 1947 issue, there is an article by Eugene Varga, chief economist of the Soviet Union. Yet we look in vain for articles by American historians who criticized the internationalists such as the late Charles Beard, Harry Elmer Barnes, or Charles Gallan Tansill.

The CFR has had little contact with the hysterical comics who make up the lower echelons of the Communist Party of America. The Council is busy with intellectual propaganda and the dictation of US foreign policy, while the lower elements act as distractions from the work of the Council. The Council's present membership includes such well-known Communists or Communists sympathizers as the imprisoned traitor Alger Hiss, Frederick V. Field, who is also in jail, Owen Lattimore, now threatened with prosecution for perjury, Edward C. Carter of the Institute of Pacific Relations, as well as the late Laurence Duggan, the late Harry Dexter White, who also died suddenly while being questioned by the House Unamerican Activities Committee (Morgenthau's assistant in the US Treasury, he was implicated in giving the Treasury plates to Russia), Philip C. Jessup, General Dwight Eisenhower, who holds the Order of Suvorov from Stalin and is the only foreigner who ever stood by Stalin on Lenin's tomb during an annual Sports Parade, Lauchlin Currie, a leading Communist agent and personal assistant to Franklin D. Roosevelt, now fled the country, Corliss Lamont, and Cord Meyer, Jr.

After the Second World War, the Council considerably expanded its work. Leaving the 65th St. town house to Alger Hiss and the Woodrow Wilson Foundation, the Executive of the Council moved into elaborate and more convenient quarters at 1 East 68th St. across the street from the Russian Consulate. With its unlimited funds, the Council carries on long range propaganda projects, maintains a number of the old Paris crowd in comfortable sinecures, publishes "Foreign Affairs", and engages in other projects about which little can be discovered. Money is advanced from the international banking houses as it is needed, and the Council has never had to appeal to the public for funds.

To make certain that no unfriendly voices are heard in the universities and in the Government offices, the Council each year publishes a massive volume entitled "The United States in World Affairs", giving the Council's version of the political developments of the year. Another yearly volume is the "Political Handbook of the year", published by the Executive of the Council, which is furnished as the standard reference volume to all press associations, colleges, and government agencies. The publications of the CFR maintain a unique monopoly in the field of international information.

The New York critic, Dr. Emanuel Josephson, recently published an attack on the Council, called "Rockefeller International", which is excellent for the information on how much money the Rockefeller Foundation has spent to promote Communism in America. Josephson ignores the Kuhn, Loeb origins of the Council, nor does he seem to be aware that the Rothschilds and Jacob Schiff provided the money for the Rockefeller empire. Perhaps Rockefeller is to be the new Gentile scapegoat for the ills of the world, as JP Morgan was from 1900 to 1950.

I'm indebted to Mr Josephson for the story of Murray I. Garfein, a prominent member of the CFR. Although composed of the most dignified criminal lawyers and bankers of Wall Street, the Council also admitted Murray I. Garfein, the lawyer who arranged the release of Lucky Luciano from prison with Gov. Thomas Dewey, so that Luciano could go to Italy to direct the world's dope traffic from there. Dewey, however, remained here. Dope and homosexuality have been principal instruments of the Communist International, because of the hold which either vice affords over the habitue. Claude Cockburn has written of the clever use of dope in Berlin by the Communists during the Nazi-Communist battle for power in 1933, while the fairyland of the State Department under Welles, Biddle, and Acheson does much to explain that agency's limp-wristed attitude towards Soviet aggression.

The CFR has spawned a host of gatherings determined to destroy the American Republic. Some of these psycho-pathic alliances are the Institute of International Education, Atlantic Union, Inc. the Committee on the Present Danger, the Woodrow Wilson Foundation, the Twentieth

Century Fund, the World Peace Foundation, and the English-Speaking Union. The latest victory of the Council is the establishment of the Ford Foundation, with a fund of $500 million for the promotion of internationalism as called for by Lenin. Paul Hoffman, from the Lehman-directed Studebaker Corporation, and Robert Hutchins, from the Rockefeller-financed University of Chicago, are in charge of this fund. The fortune built up by the sturdy American patriot Henry Ford has been turned over to them to finance everything he most despised, the ambitions of the hateful crowd of immigrants who swarmed in from the Mediterranean slums and the stinking rat warrens of Central and Eastern Europe.

CHAPTER 2

The Hamburg branch of the Rothschild policy group, the Institut für Auswartige Politik, was placed in the hands of Dr. Albrecht Mendelssohn-Bartholdy, of the German Delegation to the Peace Conference in 1919. In 1933, the Nazi government decided that Dr. Mendelssohn-Bartholdy should find other and less dangerous work. Ambassador William Dodd, in his "Diary" published by Harcourt Brace, 1940 says,

> "Nov. 18, 1933: Dr Mendelssohn-Bartholdy, a great international lawyer and professor at Hamburg University, recently dismissed because his grandfather was a Jew, although he himself was a Christian, came to see me. When he left, I dictated a letter to the Carnegie Institution of New York, asking for an appropriation of the amount of his salary for two years"

Thus Dodd spreads the useful propaganda that Mendelssohn-Bartholdy was dismissed because of antisemitism, instead of the truth, that he was the head of a dangerous international organization which was a threat to the internal security of Germany. Hitler explained to the German people that their plight was due to the crime of Versailles. As a participant in that crime, Mendelssohn-Bartholdy was bound to be discharged. However, the Carnegie Institution, which devotes its funds to espionage and revolution, was glad to aid the good doctor.

The French branch was left to the direction of Baron Edmond de Rothschild. It is the British group, the Royal Institute of International Affairs, which concerns us here. The House of Rothschild associated itself openly with the Royal Institute. Not only did its largest investments appear regularly on the yearly list of corporate subscribers who gave $400,000 a year for its work, but N. M. Rothschild and Sons headed the list of those subscribers, one of the rare instances when that venerable name was allowed to appear before the public.

With the inauguration of the Royal Institute of International Affairs and its affiliates, the House of Rothschild took a great step forward to bring its long range plan of world domination to completion. Heretofore, the House had confined its influence to monetary affairs, with the adroit use of money behind the political scenes. Paul Emden writes in his laudatory history "Jews of Britain", Sampson and Low, 1944, page 357, that

> "At the International Monetary Conference convoked by America at Brussels in 1891, England was represented by Alfred de Rothschild. By a motion strongly directed against bimetallism he at once became a central figure among the delegates."

Not often did a Rothschild appear in public to gain the ends of the House. The fight against bimetallism was a desperate and successful attempt to preserve the control of monetary systems by holding nations fast to the gold standard of monetary issue, which was a Rothschild monopoly. This fight caused the panic of 1893 in the United States, and forced the Senate to abandon bimetallism in this country. The struggle continued on until 1896, when it dominated the campaign of that year. That was America's last chance to elect a President favorable to their interests. William Jennings Bryan made a noble campaign against the barbaric worship of the Golden Calf, but the agents of Rothschild defeated him. We have not had since 1896 a single candidate for the Presidency of the United States who was not passed upon by the House of Rothschild.

Corti's two volume biography of the Rothschild family is an admirable reference work which is more interesting than many adventure novels. Corti tells us how the old coin dealer Mayer Amschel Rothschild cringed before the Elector of Hanover, until he got his hands on the money left by the Elector of Hesse, the gold paid by England for Hessian mercenaries to fight against the patriots in the American Revolution of 1776. From this sordid barter in paid murderers came the impetus of the evil House of Rothschild. Old Mayer Amschel lent this money at usurious rates, and it increased so rapidly than in a few years he was court financier to the kings of Europe. He had five sons. Salomon Mayer stayed at the family house in Frankfurt, Germany, and his brothers emigrated to new opportunities. Mayer set up a bank in Vienna, where he dominated the Congress of Vienna in 1815, Nathan Mayer went to London, where he soon became the most prominent of the rascals of the Court, Karl Mayer went to Naples, and James Mayer went to Paris. Of James we have a note from Bray Hammond in the

Quaterly Journal of Economics of August 1947, quoting a letter from James de Rothschild to Nicholas Biddle of the Philadelphia family, saying that he was willing to advance seven million francs more to bolster up the tottering Second Bank of the United States, which had so nearly brought the young Republic to a civil war in 1830 when President Andrew Jackson withdrew the Government's funds from it, saying, "The safest place for the Government's money is in the pockets of the people."

A biography of James' son, Baron Edmon de Rothschild, who founded the Rothschild policy groups treated in these pages, is of great interest. "Baron Edmond de Rothschild", by David Druck, was privately printed in New York in 1928. Its introduction is written by Nathan Straus, of the diplomatic family which owns Macy's of New York. Straus was the mastermind behind the appalling flop of Senator Estes (Atlantic Union) Kefauver for the Democratic nomination for the Presidency.

> "In 1850, writes Druck, James de Rothschild's wealth had reached 600 million mark. Only one man in France possessed more. That was the King, whose wealth was 800 million. The aggregated wealth of all the bankers in France was 150 million less than that of James de Rothschild. This naturally gave him untold power, even to the extent of unseating governments whenever he chose to do so. It is known, for example, that he overthrew the government of Prime Minister Thiers."

It is also known that he tried to overthrow the American government of President Jackson, but in that hardy old pioneer he met his match, and retreated to his counting-rooms in Paris to plot the Civil War of 1860–1865. War, to the House of Rothschild, is monetary diplomacy by other means.

The Royal Institute of International Affairs has as its patron His majesty the King of England. All Prime Ministers and Viceroys of the colonies since 1923 have been Honorary Presidents of this Institute. The story of the Institute, "Chatham House", by Stephen King-Hall, 1933, says

> "The Prince of Wales graciously accepted the office of Visitor. This appointment secured that the Institute could never be perverted to party or propaganda purposes."

Its sister group, the Council on Foreign Relations, is also above party and partisan politics. The affairs of the international bankers are above the affairs of mere citizens and their political beliefs. King-Hall also tells us that

> "In 1926, the institute was granted a Royal charter, which was all important because it meant that no charter could in future be granted to any other institute for a similar purpose."

The monopoly on advising the government on its foreign policy was all important. Chaos would follow, if any, but the House of Rothschild told 10 Downing St what the foreign policy was to be. Good old windbag Churchill has been a good front for them.

Among the founders of the Royal Institute was Lt. Col. R. W. Leonard, who in 1923 gave his home, Chatham House, at 10 St. James Square, London, which has been the headquarters of the Institute ever since. It is one of the most important addresses in the world. Leonard had developed railways and electric power utilities in Canada for the Rothschilds. Other founders of the Royal Institute were Sir Otto Beit, of the banking family Speyer, who was a director of the Rothschild's British South Africa Co. and the Rhodesia Railways; P. A. Molteno, son of the Premier of the Cape Colony; John W. Wheeler-Bennett, who became political adviser to General Eisenhower in London from 1944–1945 (British Who's Who 1950); Viscount Astor, Chairman of the Times Publishing Co., director of Barclay Bank, and the Hambros Bank; Sir Julien Cahn; and Sir Abe Bailey, principal representative of the Rothschild gold and diamond interests in South Africa. The fabulous wealth of the Witwatersrand mines provoked the Boer War, gave us Winston Churchill, and financed the Rothschild foreign policy groups all over the world.

Stephen King-Hall tells us that Bailey Gave 5000 pounds a year. Beit and Molteno were heavy contributors, and the British Dominion and colonies found of the Carnegie Corporation of New York gave $3000 a year. But the largest single source of funds was the Rockefeller Foundation, which gave $40,000 a year over a period of years.

Donations by the corporate subscribers, which King Hall does not break down, make up the Royal Institute budget of $400,000 a year. The institute listed in 1936 corporate subscribers as Nathan Mayer Rothschild sons and its subsidiaries, among them the British South African Co., the Bank of England, Reuters News agency, Prudential Assurance Co, the Sun Insurance Office Ltd and Vickers-Armstrong Ltd. Other subscribers where the banking houses of J. Henry Schroder

Co., Lazard Freres Morgan Grenfell (JP Morgan), Erlangers Ltd and E. D. Sassoon Co. with its subsidiaries, which are given as the Chartered Bank of India, Australia and China., and the Ottoman bank. The list of subscribers remains much the same from year to year.

The alert observer cannot help but wonder why an organization of such noble origins and purposes, and financed by such unimpeachable banking houses, feels it necessary to clock its operations in international affairs in mystery. The Royal Institute gives little or no publicity to its meetings, which is true of its sister group, the Council on Foreign Relations, and their principal subsidiary, the Institute of Pacific Relations. Yet each of them has enormous influence in foreign affairs.

King Hall writes on page 85 of "Chatham House" that

> "The Institute of Pacific Relations conferences are entirely unofficial. Since 1927, Chatham House has sent a British group to each IPR conference. In 1931 its chairman was Archibald Rose, in 1933 Sir Herbert Samuel."

The betrayal of China was also unofficial. Owen Lattimore frequently traveled to England to speak before the Royal Institute. On May 5, 1936, he spoke on "Russo-Japanese relations" and on March 12, 1936, he spoke on "Japan's continental policy", which threatened the Rothschild investments in China. On October 9, 1936, Dr Chaim Weizmann lectured before the Royal Institute on Palestine today and on March 30, 1936 Maitre Rubinstein lectured on "The Refugee Problem", which was causing an economic crisis in Great Britain. One minority was emigrating from Germany and was landing in large numbers on the shores of England, who could in all goodwill, absorb only a percentage of them.

In 1946, with all of Asia directly under pressure from the Soviet empire and its program of hemispheric solidarity, the Royal Institute pooh-poohed the danger in the Far East. In its publication "The Pattern of Pacific Security, 1946, the experts of the Royal Institute declared that

> "The group regards as remote the danger of a pan-Asiatic movement specifically directly against the west"

Such propaganda, distributed as a working policy to Britain's foreign officials, effectively lulled their fears of communism in Asia. In 1952, Great Britain abandoned all her investments in China.

"Chatham House" defines the Royal Institute as "an unofficial and nonpolitical body founded in 1920 to encourage and facilitate the scientific study of international questions."

This is a more delicate statement than that of its sister group, the Council on Foreign Relations, which frankly desired to stimulate international thought and to coordinate existing international agencies. King-Hall does not bother to inform us that the Royal Institute has a sister group in America.

The Royal Institute sympathies lean to Russia, and the reason is given in its publication "International Trade" by A. J. Barnouw in 1943. On page 21, Mr Barnouw informs us that

> "The Union of Soviet Socialist Republics is the only nation likely to be potentially wealthy."

No wonder the Rothschilds are abandoning the western democracies.

CHAPTER 3

Frankfurt, Germany is the Rome of modern civilization. From Frankfurt have come the Great international banking houses which spread their influence across the world. The House of Rothschild and its subsidiaries Kuhn, Loeb Co. of New York, Lazard Freres of New York, London and Paris, and JP Morgan Co of New York, London and Paris. Other international banking houses originate in Frankfurt, were Hallgart Co, Ladenburg Thalmann, J. and W. Seligman and Speyer Brothers. These banking houses and their control of the world's gold supply gradually replaced the religion of Christ with the worship of the golden calf. The benignity of the face of Christ was vanished, and in its praise was the glare of the Horned beast of barbarism which initiated the era of World wars and mass slaughters of women and children. The Antichrist was returned to Earth.

The Frankfurt banking houses spanned the two dominant political movements of the 20th century, world Communism and World Zionism. Each of these movements claims democracy as its particular attribute, each of them functions on the gold standard of monetary issue, and each of them advocates on the tenet of internationalism. It may come as a surprise to those who consider communism as the enemy of bankers that Marxist economics are the most orthodox of contemporary systems. As Trotsky wrote in "The history of the Russian Revolution",

> "Gold is the only basis for money."

In the *Economic Journal* of March 1914, Israel Cohen wrote an article, "Economic activity of modern jewry", which is as follows,

> "Thanks to their dispersion in the various countries around the Mediterranean and the feeling of racial solidarity that united them, they had exceptional facilities for engaging in international trade. Jewish finance invested considerable in construction of railways in the latter half of the 19th century, the Pereire's in northern France, the Bischoffenheim's in Belgium, the Bleichroder's in Germany,

Baron de Hirsch in Turkey and Kuhn Loeb Co. in the United States, the Sassoons, the 'Rothschild of the East', created a network of banks from Baghdad to Shanghai. At present, the movement of precious metals throughout the world is mainly directed by Jewish bankers, who largely determined the rate of exchange between one country and another. Another important sphere of activity in which Jews are represented in increasing numbers is the liberal professions and government service."

The saying is often heard on the stock exchanges of the world that the Rothschild control gold, the Sassoons control silver and the Guggenheim control copper. This saying is confirmed by the volumes which list the director of corporations mining these metals.

The international bankers of Frankfurt rose to power at the same time that the Republic of the United States was born. The loans floated in Holland, which financed the American Revolution, can be given credit for the provision that all men are born free and equal in our Constitution. This was a notable departure from restrictions against Jews in Europe. The Treasury building was burned by the British in 1812, so that the origins of the loans cannot be traced in Washington, but it is it is safe to assume that they came from the same agencies which financed Robespierre and Mirabeau in the French Revolution. Both of these revolutionaries were outspoken advocates of Jewish rights. Jews at that time were not allowed to take part in the government or to engage in enterprises where they could take advantage of Christians. They have never been under any restrictions in America. Nevertheless, our Jewish citizens have always considered themselves a downtrodden minority, and they have roughly 350 organizations in the United States devoted to Jews, and as a pressure group having nothing in common with other citizens. Most of these organizations are run as profitable rackets by their entrepreneurs.

In 1837, August Belmont arrived in New York as the official representative of the House of Rothschild. In 1861, he revealed the Rothschild plan to Split America into two week democracies when he refused to lend Lincoln money for mobilization except at the unheard-of long-term interest rate of 25%. Lincoln's secretary of the Treasury Salomon P. Chase, financed the Union Army by issuing greenbacks, whereupon the New York Banks refused to honor them with gold, causing a crisis in 1863. The Rothschilds had another valuable ally in the person of Nicholas Biddle. Their most valuable agent, however, in 1869 began his career for the Rothschilds without revealing his backers.

He was JP Morgan. Gustavus Myers, in his "History of the Great American fortunes" Modern House, tells how Junius P. Morgan of George Peabody and Co, treasonably cooperated with the House of Rothschild in London throughout that war. His son, John Pierpont Morgan, made $30,000 profit selling faulty carbines to the US government during the Civil War, a feat which caused the House of Rothschild to appoint him their agent in the acquisition of US railroad properties. He subsequently became the chief international agent of the House, which was seldom mentioned after 1890. The branches of JP Morgan Co in Europe, Drexel Morgan Co of London, Morgan Harjes Co of Paris, as well as Drexel Co of Philadelphia and JP Morgan of New York, handled the large international transactions formerly the monopoly of the House of Rothschild. The reason for this is obvious. Morgan was a Gentile house. It has never had a Jewish partner. All of the other international banking houses were Jewish. Therefore, JP Morgan Co was allowed to make all the headlines in the international finance.

In 1828 the House of Rothschild appointed Samuel Bleichröder as their agent in Germany. Bleichröder became the financial adviser to Bismarck during the consolidation of Germany as a nation. His title was Prussian State Banker. During the Franco-Prussian War of 1870, Baron Edmond de Rothschild was the personal banker to Napoleon III of France, and his employee Samuel Bleichröder was personal banker to Bismarck of Germany.

When Bleichröder died, his place was taken by Max Moritz Warburg, who had three sons, Max, Paul Moritz, and Felix Warburg. Felix and Paul emigrated to New York, and Max stayed in Germany as banker to the Kaiser. F. W. Wile, Berlin correspondent of the London *Daily Mail*, in 1914 published his book, "When around the Kaiser", in which he said,

> "Ballin of Hamburg stands in the same relation the Kaiser as did those counselors of another generation to their sovereigns and governments—Rothschild of Paris to Napoleon III, and Bleichröder of Berlin to Emperor William I and Bismarck."

Actually, Ballin was only the front man for Max Warburg. Ballin was the head of the Hamburg-American Line and German Lloyd's, both of which steamship lines Max Warburg held the controlling interest. Max Warburg was the guiding influence behind the Kaiser during the First World War, but his could not be stated publicly, because his brother

Paul Warburg was in Washington as the Governor of the Federal Reserve Board. Therefore, Albert Ballin was publicized as the Kaiser's unofficial Prime minister. When Max Warburg came to the Versailles Pease Conference in 1919 as Chief of the German Financial Delegation, the newspapers were very considerate, and none of them printed the fact that Max's brother Paul had to stay home because it would never do to have one brother representing the Allies and another representing Germany.

When M. M. Warburg Co of Hamburg and Amsterdam succeeded to the stewardship of the Rothschild properties in Germany, they began to buy up railroad properties in the United States. *Newsweek* of Feb 1, 1936 noted

> "Abraham Kuhn and Solomon Loeb were general merchandise merchants in Lafayette Indiana in 1850. As usual in newly settled regions, most transactions were on credit. They soon found out that they were bankers, and they gradually forgot all about merchandise, and they moved west. In Cincinnati, they got considerable help from the Civil War; in 1867 they established Kuhn, Loeb Co in New York, and took in a young German, Jacob Schiff, as partner. After ten years, Jacob Schiff was head of Kuhn Loeb, Kuhn having died and Loeb retired. Schiff had important financial connections in Europe. Under his guidance, the house brought European capital into contact with American industry, which was then badly in need of it. The Union Pacific had used up a lot of funds. The railroad failed to earn a return. The panic of 1893 added the finishing touch. That failure was a boon to Kuhn, Loeb. By financing E. H. Harriman's plans for a new Union Pacific, the firm set itself up as the chief financial backer of American railways."

Jacob Schiff, of Frankfurt, had important financial connections, the House of Rothschild and M. M. Warburg Co. He took in Paul and Felix Warburg as partners, and Kuhn, Loeb became the largest owner of railways in the United States, still controlling 53% of total mileage in 1939, according to a TNEC report. Newsweek notes that Kuhn, Loeb got a considerable help from the Civil War, and that the Panic of 1893 was a boon to them. The history of the Rothschilds and Kuhn, Loeb is the history of wars and panics. Without the prospect of the world war or a great depression, Kuhn, Loeb would close its doors. The Panic of 1893 fixed upon the United States an inflexible gold standard, and delivered the Union Pacific into the hands of E. H. Harriman and his master, Jacob Schiff. How had this been accomplished? Simply by moving a hundred million dollars in gold from New York to Montreal at a critical moment on the New York Stock Exchange, and then Kuhn, Loeb called in their outstanding loans. Call rates on money jumped to 25%, a terrible money panic was precipitated, and Jacob Schiff got what he wanted. Then the hundred million dollars in gold was brought back from Montreal, and the market was normal again.

Many of our recent arrivals got considerable help from the Civil War, notably the family Lehman. The three Lehman brothers were living in Atlanta, Georgia at the outbreak of the Civil War. They strategically disposed themselves, one remaining in Atlanta while another moved to Montgomery, Alabama, and the third went to New York. Throughout the war the two Southern Lehmans shipped cotton to England, while the Northern Lehman collected for it in shipments of gold arriving in New York. After the War, the South seemed unprofitable, so all the Lehman went to New York. With their gold profits from the War, thy opened the banking house of Lehman Brothers. The scion of the house, Herbert Lehman, learned that war could be a very comfortable mission. During the First World War, he served daringly in Washington in charge of supplies, and won the Distinguished Service Medal for his valor in signing freight orders. He has been a prominent member of the American Legion ever since.

The Panic of 1893 was the signal to the rest of the Frankfurt bankers that they had won control of the American monetary system, and they rushed in for the profits. Lazard Freres, the family house of Eugene Meyer, established its New York office in 1893 at the height of the Panic, specializing in international gold movements. J. and W. Seligman opened its New York office in 1894. The Seligman firm seized its great opportunity in 1898, when the USS Maine blew up in Havana harbor, much to the surprise of the Spaniards. Theodore Roosevelt scurried off to Cuba to lead a charge which ended at the door of the White House, and when the smoke cleared, the house of J. and W. Seligman owned the railways and sugar plantations of Cuba.

It was about this time that a young man named Winston Churchill was fighting a ruthless war against the Boers in South Africa, who were defending their homeland against the Uitlanders, the horde of German Jews who were lusting for the rich diamond and gold mines of the Witwatersrand. The international news services devoted themselves to singing the praises of Roosevelt and Churchill, both of whom, under any moral or legal system of justice, would have been executed as bandits. With this publicity, these two aggressors began a lifelong career of service to the Jewish bankers. Such is the sordid basis of fame.

The news services were originated and controlled by the Frankfurt bankers as a business necessity. Kent Cooper, in *Life* magazine of November 13, 1944, wrote an article called "Freedom of Information" in which he said,

> "Before and during the First World War the great German news agency Wolff was owned by the European banking house of Rothschild, which had its central headquarters in Berlin. A leading member of the firm was also Kaiser Wilhelm's personal banker. What actually happened in Imperial Germany was that the Kaiser used Wolff to bind and excite his people to such a degree that they were eager for World War I. Twenty years later under Hitler the pattern was repeated and enormously magnified by DNB, Wolff's successors."

As the esteemed President of the Associated Press, it seems impossible that Kent Cooper should print publicly such a mass of errors. According to all authorities, the House of Rothschild never had its headquarters in Berlin. The Kaiser's personal banker, whom Cooper refuses to name, was Max Warburg, who was never openly know as a member of the Rothschild firm. More important, Cooper is accusing the Wolff agency of precisely the crime committed by the Associated Press, from 1933 to 1941, when the Associated Press created a war fever in the United States by its highly colored and often falser reports about the political intentions of Germany. All published plans of the Nazi Government, which were scrupulously followed by Hitler, called for a drive to the East, the Drang Nach Osten against Russia laid out by their science of Geopolitik. At this moment, Cooper was airing his propaganda in *Life*, a publication of *Time*, Inc, which was financed by JP Morgan Co in 1923 and run at a loos for five years, for its propaganda value.

Paul Emden, the English historian, and official biographer of English Jewry, published his definitive work, "Jews of Britain", Sampson Low, London, 1944. On page 357, he writes of Reuter,

> "Julius Reuter, who became naturalized in England, conducted his agency as a family affair until 1865, when he formed the Reuter Telegraph Agency. The Duke of Saxe-Coburg-Gotha had in 1871 given him the hereditary title of Baron; a special grant by Queen Victoria in 1891 gave him and his descendants permission to use it in the United Kingdom, and accordingly the man who by birth was

Israel Beer became Baron Julius de Reuter. It is only natural that in the development of news services all over the world the Jews should take a vital share—as financiers and merchants they had long recognized the immense value of early and reliable information. His astonishingly well-developed news service, one of the secrets of his continued success on the Stock Exchange, enabled Nathan de Rothschild to bring the British Government the first news of Waterloo. The Rothschilds liked to receive news before anyone else. One of the great features of Reuter's reports was that in 1865 they were two days ahead with the momentous news of the assassination of Abraham Lincoln. There were three important telegraph agencies in Europe, Reuters in London, Havas in Paris, and Wolff in Berlin. Havas was a French Jew, and Wolff is popularly supposed to have been Jewish."

Sir Roderick Jones, Chief of Reuters for many years, published his autobiography, "A life in Reuters", Hodder and Stoughton, 1951. He tells us that Reuter was born Israel Ben Josphat Beer, the son of Rabbi Samuel Beer of Cassel, Germany, and that in 1859 Reuter signed an agreement with is rivals, Wolff and Havas. Havas was to have South America, the three would share Europe, and Reuters was to have the rest of the world. This arrangement, providentially concluded just before the outbreak of the American Civil War, endured until 1914. During this time, Associated Press in America was under the control of Jacob Schiff, whose firm of Kuhn, Loeb handled all stock issues for Western Union Telegraph and always had three partners on its board of directors. Western Union in turn controlled Associated Press.

Sir Roderick got his training under Louis Weinthal, who writes at great length of how the House of Rothschild financed Cecil Rhodes and his empire in "The Story of the Cape to Cairo Railway". Jones tells us in "A Life in Reuters" that

"Towards the end of 1895, smoldering and unsubstantial fires of political discontent in Johannesburg were fanned by the Transvaal National Union and by the gold mine owners into an outwardly presentable flame of revolution. An Uitlanders Reform Committee was established, with an inner executive consisting of John Hays Hammond, Lionel Philipps (one of the heads of the gold and diamond mining firm of Eckstein—the Corner House), George Farrar, head of East Rand Property Mines, and Col. Frank Rhodes, brother of Cecil Rhodes, Prime Minister of the Cape. Percy Fitzpatrick was the Secretary. The general Committee consisted of sixty other prominent citizens, including Abe Bailey and Solly Joel."

John Hays Hammond was the chief mining engineer for the House of Rothschild. Paul Kruger, the head of the Boer Republic, sentenced him to death for plotting the violent overthrow of the government, and let him go with the payment of a fine of $120,000. He then became the chief engineer of the Guggenheim Properties at $600,000 a year, and subsequently Washington representative of the Council on Foreign Relations. His son. He's a notorious fellow traveler of Communists in New York.

The money for the Council and its affiliates came principally from the gold and diamond fields of South Africa. Sir Abe Bailey in whose name most of the Rothschild interests in the Witwatersrand were finally registered, was the principal Baker of the Royal Institute of International Affairs.

How Sir Roderick became head of Reuters is itself a gem. After serving faithfully under the Weinthal, he it tells us that

> "On April 28, 1915, Baron Herbert de Reuter, chief of the agency, shot himself. The cause was the crash of the Reuters Bank, which had been built up by Baron Julius de Reuter to handle foreign remittances secretly."

Since England was then at war with Germany, it was felt unwise to appoint another German Jew to head the agency, and so the directors appointed Sir Roderick Jones its chief. He finally resigned under circumstances which he says cannot be made public. That is very likely.

CHAPTER 4

Woodrow Wilson's twice elected president of the United States was one of the most unloved men ever to occupy that post. An arrogant campus dictator who was never able to deal with mature men. He attained esteem in the educational world and subsequently in the world of politics only by eagerly prostituting himself for the New York representatives of the Frankfurt bankers. As President of Princeton University, Wilson first attracted their favorable attention by his hysterical war on fraternities. The students believed that they had the right to choose their own companions, even if this meant excluding some of the scions of the immigrant bankers. Wilson went into a blind fury when the students opposed his principles of "equality", and banned fraternities from Princeton, a ban which lasts to the present day.

Frank Vanderlip, successor to James Stillman as President of the National City Bank tells us in his autobiography "From Farmboy to Financier", that he and Stillman had Wilson to launch in 1910 to look him over. Stillman, who had boasted to Carter Barron that he knew who blew up the USS Maine, said that Wilson would do, but that he was no great man. Wilson continued his campaign of cringing before the wealthy until he convinced them that he was trustworthy and would place their interests ahead of the rights of the people. During the Panic of 1907, he had declared allegiance to them when he proclaimed that we ought to turn the nation over to a Council of seven men headed by JP Morgan so that we wouldn't have any more panics. This was true. If Morgan could run the country the way he wanted to for the House of Rothschild, we would never have another panic. The fact that Morgan and Schiff had brought on the Panic of 1907 in a year of good crops and general prosperity for the sole reason of creating a climate in the economic world which would permit them to enact a "currency reform" bill giving them perpetual authority over the money and credit of the United States, was ignored by Woodrow Wilson.

In 1911, Woodrow Wilson was the first prominent educator to acclaim the Aldrich plan, written by Paul Warburg of Kuhn, Loeb Co and advanced in the platform of the Republican Party. In 1912, Woodrow Wilson was elected President to sign the Federal Reserve Act, the Democratic Party's edition of the Aldrich plan. Because there was public opposition to the Aldrich plan as a Wall Street Banking Act, Paul Warburg hastily revamped it, presented it as the Federal Reserve Act by the Democratic Party, and Wilson, the ardent proponent of the Republican Aldrich Plan, became the Democratic candidate for President and enacted the Federal Reserve Act into law.

At the Senate hearings of the Subcommittee on the Judiciary 1914, Senator Bristow asked of Paul Warburg.

> "I understood you to say Saturday that you were a Republican, but when Mr Roosevelt became a candidate, you then became a sympathizer with Mr. Wilson and supported him?"
>
> **Paul Warburg**, Yes.
>
> **Senator Bristow**, while your brother Felix Warburg was supporting Taft?
>
> **Paul Warburg**: Yes."

The presidential election of 1912 offers a beautiful laboratory case of the immigrant bankers operating the American democracy. Although President Taft was much more popular than the cold and cynical Wilson, Taft had incurred the enmity of Kuhn, Loeb Co, Archie Butt. White House aid to Presidents Theodore Roosevelt and Taft, describes the incident on page 625 of his "Letters", published by Doubleday Doran, 1930, as follows

> "Just now Schiff is demanding that President Taft abrogate the Treaty of 1832 with Russia and threatened him with the hostility of the Jews if he continued to refuse to accede to their demands. He and a number of Jews came to the White House a few evenings ago and practically told the President that unless he abrogate this treaty, the entire Jewish people of this country would not only oppose his renomination, but would support the Democratic candidate, whoever it might be."

This incident is described at greater length by B'nai Brith leader Simon Wolf in his autobiography, "Presidents I have known". Wolf, who was arrested in 1865 in connection with the death of Abraham Lincoln, was personally acquainted with all presidents from Lincoln through Wilson.

To ensure the election of Wilson, the divide and conquer technique was used. Theodore Roosevelt, the favorite of J&W Seligman Co, was dragged from retirement to run as a progressive candidate and split the Republican Party. In the end, Taft received six electoral votes. The shadow of B'nai Brith disapproval hung over is son Robert Taft at the Republican convention of 1952, when Rifkin and Warburg succeeded in getting General Eisenhower the nomination.

Although Wilson was publicized as the candidate of the common Man and dollar bills were solicited for his expenses, "the road to the White House", Princeton University Press 1951 gives Wilson's chief contributors as Jacob Schiff, Henry Morgenthau senior, Samuel Untermeyer and Cleveland H. Dodge of the National City Bank. Bernard Baruch handled the funds for Wilson and signed a number of checks for from $25,000 to $50,000 as they were needed during the campaign of 1912. This was not his own money, however. He was merely the head of the Wilson Trust Fund.

Second in importance to the Federal Reserve Act was Wilson's clearing up of the Mexican situation. The firm of Bleichröder of Berlin had been one of the earliest and heaviest investors in Mexican bonds, and Kuhn Loeb Co inherited their management. Mexico under Porfirio Diaz had gone bankrupt and a revolution was necessary to fund the debt and restore the dividends of the Bleichröder bonds. Consequently, the first successful communist revolution in history was executed in 1911 in Mexico. Properties owners were massacred and their land given to the peasants. However, the peasants needed mules and seed. They had no money, and so they mortgaged their land to the banks. Quite often they both tequila instead of mules, so that the land was rapidly concentrated into the hands of even fewer men than before the Revolution. This was communism. The peasants had less than ever, and worked harder than before the triumph of Marxism. Kuhn, Loeb received their dividends from the new government, and Porfirio Diaz was retired to Paris to live in luxury. Paul Warburg, Jacob Schiff and Jerome Hanauer became the directors of the National Railways of Mexico. Eugene Meyer junior developed large copper mines in Chihuahua and J&W Selligman Co developed public utilities there. (New York City directory of Directors, 1912.)

However, Jacob Schiff, the brains behind the Rockefeller expansion of Standard Oil, was worried about the future of Rockefeller properties in Mexico. Stern intervention was needed from Washington. Percy N.

Furber, President of Oil Fields of Mexico Ltd, told Carter Barron, the leading financial reporter of New York, that

> "The Mexican Revolution was really caused by H. Clay Peirce, who owned 35% of the Pierce-Waters Oil Co, of which Standard Oil held the other 65%. Pierce was a confidential Rockefeller henchman. He wanted to get my property."

Peirce demanded of Diaz that Diaz take the tax off of oil imports to enable Standard Oil to bring in products from the US for sale in Mexico. Diaz refused, and the Revolution followed. Peirce put up the money for Francisco Madero's successful revolution. Neither Peirce nor anyone else expected what happened afterwards. Madero was executed by Victoriano Huerta on February 18, 1913. Huerta was the pawn of British oil interests. Meanwhile, the revolutionary fever seized the whole country. Other revolutionaries, some with and others without the oil men's support, took to the field. In the north of Mexico, Carranza and Pancho Villa led armies against Huerta. It was a grand opportunity for salesman from Cleveland H. Dodge's, Remington Arms Co and Winchester Arms Co.

President Wilson had obligingly placed an embargo on arms shipments to Mexico, which created the chance to smuggle them at doubly high prices. This was too slow for Dodge, however, and on February 12, 1914, he got Wilson to lift the embargo and immediately shipped $1,000,000 worth of guns to Carranza, his choice for the successor to Huerta. From the outset, Wilson had steadfastly refused to recognize the Huerta Administration. But Dodge and others who had large stakes in Mexico were becoming alarmed at the magnitude of the revolutionary tide, and they proposed that Huerta be given American recognition if he promised to hold elections. This would give the oilmen a chance to buy some friendly local officials, which was all they wanted. A memo to this effect was relayed to Colonel house by Julius Krutschitt, Chairman of the Southern Pacific Railroad and House took it to Wilson. This memo was drawn up by D. J. Haff, a Kansas City lawyer, and was approved by Dodge's firm of Phelps Dodge before being sent to Washington, as well as by Greene Cananea Cooper, (Guggenheim) and E. L. Doheny of the Mexican Oil Co. Haff was then called in to confer with Wilson, and was introduced to him by Dodge, whose approval always went far with the president. There was one compelling reason why Huerta should be denied recognition if he refused to take orders from Washington, and he did refuse. The reason was simply that he had been violently installed in place of Standard

Oil's Madero by Lord Cowdray, head of British oil interests in Mexico, controlled by the Samuel family. Wilson, indeed, in the communication to Sir Edward Grey, then Britain's Foreign Minister, vowed that he would oust Huerta, whom the British government and various of its satellites had hastily recognized. Not until the early part of 1914 did Wilson give up hope of bringing Huerta under the thumb of Dodge and the National City Bank. Then a number of provocative acts disclosed the new temper in Washington. Besides the huge shipments of arms to Huertas's opponent, Carranza, there was the Tampico incident. A number of American sailors were landed at Tampico, ostensibly to replenish water and gas supplies. They were arrested by Huertas troops, but upon a violent protest from Washington, they were released. There was some astonishment in Washington. Then Wilson insisted that Huerta salute the American flag and apologize. Huerta refused. Under international law, there was no occasion for demanding a formal salute. Wilson arrogantly order the Navy out for Standard Oil and on April 21, 1914, American warships shelled Vera Cruz to prevent a German ship from landing supplies for Huerta. There was loss of civilian life and great property damage. On July 25, 1914, Huerta admitted that the odds were too great against him and fled to his bank accounts in, of all places, New York. Venustiano Carranza took office on behalf of the National City Bank. On the US border. General Pershing, related to Jules S. Bache of the New York Stock Exchange, held Pancho Villa at Bay while Carranza consolidated his power.

For the above account, I am indebted most to Ferdinand Lundberg's "America's Sixty Families", Vanguard Press, 1938, and Carter Baron's reminiscences of Wall Street. The episode could be repeated dozens of times in recounting the numerous revolutions of the 20th century, each of them historical evidence of J&W Seligman's protection of its billions of dollars of investments in Public Utilities and sugar in South America, the spoils of the Spanish-American War, and Samuel Zemurray of the Palestine Economic Cooperation protecting his United Fruit Co. interests in Central America. These episodes have created the legend of the United States "Dollar imperialism" in South America. Our Latin neighbors should be informed that most Americans deplore the arrogant exploitation of South America by the Zemurrays, Seligmans, and Warburgs.

No president before Woodrow Wilson showed such rank partiality to the minority which financed his campaign. The official appointments of Woodrow Wilson during his two administrations reads like Who's

Who in American Jewry, with the names of Morgenthau, Warburg, Meyer, Baruch, Brandeis, Frankfurter, Strauss, Nagel, Goldenweiser and hundreds of others. The history of Wilson's reign has been obscured over, and light upon his secret activities, the conspiracies of Colonel Edward Mandell House and Sir William Wiseman of Kuhn, Loeb Co, and the shady operations of the rootless immigrants to whom he gladly gave the highest offices in American government, is shed only occasionally by a bit of biography here and a stray page of information there. One of Wilson's most outrageous floutings of his oath of office was kept in absolute mystery for 26 years with the willing cooperation of the news services Paul Emden in his authoritative work, "Jews of Britain", says on page 310,

> "In April 1918, as a consequence of a large cotton speculation, a run had occurred on Bombay and cashed the value of a 1,372,000 pounds was drawned out. America alone could help but her vast stores of Silver had to be preserved as cover against her own paper dollar currency. In this appaling embarrassment, Lord Reading (Rufus Isaacs) came to the rescue. His powerful influence with President Wilson brought it about that the government at Washington and Congressional members of every party joined in the endeavour to meet this situation by passing an Act without discussion or practically no discussion, because any debate upon the subject would have been serious. The measure was passed in almost a record for shortness of time. It became law in a very few days, and vast millions of ounces of silver were sent across the ocean to India, simply because America saw how necessary it was at that particular moment to help the British Empire. Nothing was made known of this. Indeed, nothing appeared in the newspapers. Numbers of newspapers were aware of it, but they did not mention it. So far as I am aware, I have made the first public statement in regard to it."

Many questions spring to mind at this almost incredible story. The United States, in the midst of a Great War, stops all legislation to pass a secret bill to send silver to India because some speculators have caused a monetary crisis there. No congressman dares debate upon it or oppose it, no newspaper feels obliged to report such an exciting story, and the key figure is a shadowy alien was background will be given later. One would like a few moments with Mr Emden, to clarify this page. Why was it imperative that the law be passed without debate? Even our entry into the war was debated upon in Congress. Who were the speculators who caused the crisis in Bombay? And why should the monetary problems of India assume an absolute and secret priority over all matters pending before the Congress of the United States? But perhaps Mr Emden has told us too much already.

CHAPTER 5

Wars are made by men. The 20th century has been a disgraceful and nearly unanimous attempt by historians and economists, led by the rascals from Harvard and the University of Chicago, to avoid all personalities and facts in the accounting of contemporary history. These scoundrels have followed the line laid down by Karl Marx, that all events shall be reported in the abstract as the economic convulsions of the masses. While mass-history can be dealt with from the economic outlook, individual-history must use time, place and association, and it is these factors which the Marxist party-line historians are taught to avoid. Thus, the numerous books about the First World War, the Versailles Peace Conference, or the Great Depression of 1929–1933 contain an average of one fact per 10,000 words. The rest is a totally aimless mouthwash about social pressures, the "misdeeds of the capitalist" in which any mention of the Frankfurt bankers is conspicuous by its absence, and "the economic stresses of our time".

This drivel is spoon-fed by incompetence to our university students for four years. No wonder they never read another book. What is genuinely regrettable is the almost wholesale defection of the professors who deliberately pervert and perjured themselves in print with this slope, when they are aware of the facts. They are paid so little that it can hardly be said that they are bribed. Their self-debasement last only until someone is courageous enough to come up with the truth, and indeed that seems to be its only purpose, to conceal the facts until the criminals are beyond the reach of retribution. Harvard, Columbia and Chicago fighting a rear guard action in the protection of the international bankers who financed Nazism and Communism in order to make profits from world wars.

A young and confident German nation, made cocksure by an easy victory over a disunited France in 1870, dreamed of conquering Europe. At Kaiser Williams side, his personal banker Max Warburg encouraged that dream. Under Warburg's predecessor, Samuel Bleichröder, Germany had achieved the most centralized banking system in the world, the Reichsbank, which was in 1910 the only Central Bank capable of financing a large scale war. By 1914, Max Warburg's brother Paul Warburg, had centralized American finance into the Federal Reserve System so that the United States was able to finance all the nations composing the Allies in the First World War. The main job of a central bank is war finance.

As in 1939, Germany in 1914 dreamed of a lightning war, a blitzkrieg. The Kaiser knew he had the finest war machine in the world. Max Warburg assured him that he had the finest banking system in the world. Thinking in terms of a Pan-European Empire of which England was the only serious opponent, Germany in 1914, as in 1939, could not envision the possibility of the entry of the United States against her. Neither economically nor politically was America concern in a Pan-European Federation dominated by Germany. This receives decisive proof in Henry Morgenthau's "Secret of the Bosporus", the account of his experiences in Turkey as ambassador from the United States. He relates his conversation with the German ambassador, Baron Wangenheim, who in 1915 willingly told him as a neutral, how Germany had staked everything on the quick war. Should prospects of an early victory disappear, Germany would seek an armistice and arm for a better opportunity. Morgenthau mentioned the possibility of American participation against Germany. This stunned Wangenheim. "Why", he asked, "would America attack Germany?"

"For a moral principle", replied Morgenthau, the Harlem Slum King who fattened on tributes from poor Negroes. However, as always with the Morgenthau of the world, more practical considerations were at stake. Deserving primary consideration in 1915 was the problem of making the world safe for democracy of Communism and its twin, the democracy of Zionism.

The German Chancellor during the First World War was von Bethmann-Hollweg. Moritz Bethmann, his ancestor, had been the leading financier of Frankfurt during the time of Mayer Amschel Rothschild. The Bethmann and Rothschilds had intermarried to produce the German Chancellor. Germany had the gold, the armies and a highly productive industrial war machine. She lacked, however, certain vital chemicals, foodstuff and raw materials. At the beginning of the war, she had only six months supplies of such items as sugar, coal, tungsten and nitrates. Seeing that their plans could not be consummated by December 1916, the German General Staff advised the Kaiser to sue for peace. In August 1916, Max Warburg, then head of the German Secret Service, and Chancellor von Bethmann-Hollweg would not hear of suing for peace. America was coming in on Germany's side, they said, and pointed to the work of Jacob Schiff and James Speyer in New York to prove it. With her help, Germany could easily beat the Allies. As for the critically needed supplies, hundreds of tons of foodstuffs were coming in from Belgium. The results of Herbert Hoover's Commission for the Relief of Belgium operation, which should have been called the Hoover Commission for the Relief of Germany. Without the foodstuffs supplied by Hoover's Commission, Germany would have had to ask the armistice in 1916 and the war would have been over in two years instead of four.

A patriotic English nurse in Belgium, Edith Cavell, was horrified by the blatant treachery of the Hoover operation and she attempted to inform the British Government, which occasioned one of the saddest tragedies of the war. Billions of dollars had been staked on the war's continuance for another two years. Should Germany fall in the winter of 1916, it meant the loss of the major part of their fortunes for the Baruchs, Warburgs and Guggenheims, who had gambled everything on expanding for war production in the summer of 1916. Franklin D Roosevelt would have been indicted for doubling the amount of orders for the Navy, which was not authorized in the Congressional appropriation for that Department, and a budding political career would have been ended. Hundreds of men were making their fortunes out of smuggling coal and sugar to Germany. Sugar, paid for by American taxpayers was loaded secretly at night and shipped to Spain on the ships of the Royal Spanish line. From Spain it went by train to Switzerland, ostensibly for the manufacture of chocolate, and from Switzerland it went into Germany at $0.60 a pound.

One woman threatened this great fabric of treachery, and that woman, nurse Edith Cavell, was executed hastily by the orders of the German High Command by direct communication from Max Warburg, head of the German Secret Service. This execution was seized upon as an excellent opportunity for furthering the very war she had threatened Not only was information about the Commission for the Relief of Belgium cut off, but the newspapers in America headlined the atrocity for weeks. It was a heaven sent method of arousing the American people to a war fever.

Max Warburg was readying Lenin and Trotsky for their trip to Moscow and the Bolshevik revolution, which would knock Russia out of the war and leave Germany battling on one front against France and England. Even after Wilson brought America into the war, it would be months before she could mobilize her arms, and at least a year before she could send an army overseas. All of this was known in the offices of M. M. Warburg Co in Hamburg, at the offices of Baron Alfred de Rothschild in London, and in the offices of Kuhn, Loeb Co in New York. Heavy industry could be assured of two more years of war, and for that assurance Edith Cavell died.

While the German people settled down to endure two years of slow starvation, and while the armies of all the powers were stalemated in the trenches of France, a number of clever and ruthless men were arranging for America's entry into the war. An organization of Wall Street bankers headed by Isaac Seligman of. J. And W Seligman Co had formed in 1906 an organization called the American Association for International Conciliation. By 1915 this was known as the Carnegie League to enforce peace. Led by Kuhn, Loeb lawyer Elihu Root, the League was composed of Edward Filene, the Boston department store millionaire who left his fortune as the 20th Century Fund for the promotion of Communism, Rabbi Stephen Wise, the Zionist influence on President Wilson, John Hays Hammond, engineer for the Rothschild and Guggenheims, Isaac Seligman Perry Belmont, son of the official American representative of the House of Rothschild and Jacob Schiff of Kuhn Loeb Co. This group was the genesis of the Council on Foreign Relations. Its members use their influence in 1916 to devote the front pages of America's metropolitan newspapers and wire services to the exclusive use of professional war mongers. Most of the propaganda was provided by Cleveland H. Dodge, who organized the survivors of the Lusitania Fund (the Lusitania was loaded with ammunition from dodges Remington Arms Co) and Herbert Hoover, head of the Commission for the Relief of Belgium. Their propaganda was shamelessly childish. Between the stories of German submarines machine-gunning helpless swimmers in the water, and tales of the Huns' bouncing babies on their bayonets in Belgium, there is little to choose. Suffice it to say that Dodge and Hoover won the First World War for Zionism. America was inflamed, and when Wilson called for a declaration of war against Germany, it was given him by a Congress in which only a handful of Lafollettes, Norrises, and Rankins refused to sully their names forever.

Sir Roderick Jones, in "A Life in Reuters", give us on page 200 an intimate glimpse of history,

> "We dined in the private room at the Windham club (Jones General Smuts, Sir Starr Jameson and Walter Hines Page, who was then American Ambassador to Britain), the one in which twenty years later the terms of the abdication of King Edward VIII were settled. We drifted onto the question of the United States entering the war, for which Britain and France so patiently waited. Doctor Page then revealed to us, under seal of secrecy, that he had received from the President that afternoon, a personal communication, upon the strength of which he could affirm that, at last, the die was cast. Consequently, it was not without emotion that he found himself able to assure us that the United States would be at war with the Central Powers inside a week from that date. The ambassador's assurance was correct to the day. We dined on Friday, March 30. On April 2, President Wilson asked Congress to declare a State of War with Germany. On April 6, the United States was at war."

General Smuts, of the diamond fields of South Africa was a lifelong and consciousness advocate of the world state, so ardently desired by the House of Rothschild. In the last year of his life, he told Congressman George Holden Tinkham, himself heavy investor in South African gold mines, that his life had been wasted. Like other servants of the international bankers, notably the late Henry L. Stimson, Smuts went to his death sick with his guilt and the specter of a Third World War.

Sir Starr Jameson of this luncheon group represented the financial interest of the House of Rothschild in the British Government, and Sir Roderick Jones himself was the chief of Rothschild's information service. These were the men to whom Walter Hines Page first reported his success in betraying his people into the war.

CHAPTER 6

Throughout the First World War, a secret international government composed of Colonel Edward Mandel House, the personal emissary of Woodrow Wilson, Sir William Wiseman, partner in Kuhn, Loeb and then representing the British Government as liaison officer between America and England; and Rufus Isaacs, Lord Reading, Lord Chief Justice of England and subsequently ambassador to the United States from England, operated above and beyond all recognized parliamentary procedures. Colonel House remarks in his memoirs that he, Wisemen, and Isaacs considered themselves free to circumvent regular government channels, all of this, of course, in the interest of "winning the war".

Lt. Col. Norman Thwaites, former private secretary to New York publisher Joseph Pulitzer, was head of British Intelligence Service in the United States during the First World War. He writes in his memoirs, "Velvet and Vinegar", Grayson and Grayson, London, 1932, that,

> "Often during the years 1917–1920, when delicate decisions had to be made, I consulted Mr. Otto Khan, whose calm judgment and almost uncanny foresight as to political and economic tendencies proved most helpful. Another remarkable man with whom I have been closely associated is Sir William Wiseman, who was adviser on American affairs to the British delegation to the Peace Conference and liaison officer between the American and British governments during the war. He was rather more the colonel House of this country in his relations with Downing St. Wiseman and I were, I believe, a useful team when, in 1916 and onwards, we sought to curb the machinations of the enemy in America… As a partner in the banking House of Kuhn Loeb Co. this country has lost his services for a time… Let me mention here that whatever may have been the interests of the Jewish head of Mr. Kahn's firm of Kuhn Loeb Co, the international bankers, who was alleged to be definitely pro-German, and of the late Mr. Mortimer Schiff, who was

supposed to be on the fence awaiting the cat's jump, Mr. Otto Kahn made no mistake. He was definitely and wholeheartedly pro-Ally and especially pro-British. He knew that the side on which England ranged herself would win."

The offices of Kuhn, Loeb Co, New York, must have been the scenes of terrible quarrels, or so we might think, from the widely diverging and unalterably opposed political views of its partners. In 1912, we learned from the Senate hearings of 1914, Paul Warburg and Jacob Schiff were supporting Wilson's campaign, Felix Warburg was supporting Taft, and Otto Kahn was a fierce campaigner for Theodore Roosevelt. Kuhn Loeb during the First World War presents an even more amazing picture. Jacob Schiff and Paul Warburg were doing all they could to promote the interests of Germany. In 1915 and 1916, as governor of the Federal Reserve Board, Paul Warburg refused to let the Federal Reserve System accept discounts on munitions to be sent to Great Britain, a Federal Reserve Board decision of April 2, 1915. Otto Kahn and Sir William Wiseman were the most devoted adherents of the British Crown, while Felix Warburg was too concerned over the consolidation of the Zionist Organization of America to care who won the war.

Yet in the midst of all this tremendous partisanship, business was carried on as usual by Kuhn Loeb Co. None of the partners resigned. Indeed, it is not recorded that there was ever any real difference between them. The various nations and political causes espoused by the partners were more in the nature of investments. There might have been a friendly rivalry between Otto Kahn and Jacob Schiff as to which trained flea, Britain or Germany, would win the war, but the profits of Kuhn, Loeb Co, would be about the same in either case.

In his memoirs, Lloyd George, wartime Prime Minister of England, writes that,

> "Sir William Wiseman was a young officer who was attached to our embassy in Washington, where he developed remarkable ability as a diplomat. But this time was beginning to play a considerable part in smoothing over relations with the American government."

Sir Cecil Spring-Rice, British ambassador to the United States during the first years of the war, was a constant and accurate critic of Kuhn Loeb Co. In "The letters. Of friendships of Sir Cecil Spring-Rice", Constable, 1929, as quoted by Charles Callan Tansill in "America Goes to War", Little, Brown, 1938, we find that Ambassador Spring-Rice expressed his deep regret that Lord Reading, Rufus Isaacs, had been chosen to head the British Financial Mission to the United States in 1915. Because "he distinctly mistrusted Jews" and that "it would be necessary to save Britain in spite of herself". On page 122 of Tansill's book we find that,

> "On November 23, 1916, Colonel House had written him that Kuhn Loeb were considering a loan to certain German cities similar to those that had been advanced to cities in France. On the following day, the President sent a hurried letter to the Colonel in which he requested him to 'convey to Kuhn, Loeb Co through Mr. Schiff, who would be sure of my personal friendship, the intimation that our relations with Germany are now in a very unsatisfactory and doubtful state, and that it would be most unwise at this time to risk a loan'."

President Wilson in this instance is acting as a tipster to the international banker Schiff. He believes the loan would be a poor risk. That is the only factor which either Wilson or Schiff would consider.

From Spring-Rice's letters, also quoted by Tansill, is a letter to Sir Valentine Chirol, on November 3, 1914 as follows,

> "Paul Warburg, nearly related to Kuhn, Loeb Co, and Schiff, is a brother of the well-known Max Warburg of Hamburg, is a member of the Federal Reserve Board or rather THE member. He particularly controls the financial policy off the Yemeni stration, and page and Blacket had mainly to negotiate with him. Of course, it was exactly like negotiating with Germany. Everything that was said was German property. The result was that such arrangements as were made were thought to be for the advantage of the German banks, and the Christian banks were jealous and irritated."

Tansill also quotes a letter written by Spring-Rice to British Foreign Minister Sir Edward Grey, on August 25, 1914. The matter under discussion was a bold attempt to transfer the Hamburg American line to the United States flag, a proposition which seemed logical to his chief stockholder, Max Warburg. His brothers Paul and Felix in New York could take care of the business while Germany was at war with England. Spring Rice says,

> "It is not a very pleasant business. The company is particularly a German government affair... The emperor himself, is a large shareholder, and so is the great banking house of Kuhn Loeb, New York. A member of that House has just been appointed to a very responsible position, although only just naturalized. He is connected

in business with the Secretary of the Treasury, who is the president's son-in-law."

This was Paul Warburg of the Federal Reserve Board, naturalized in 1912 so that he could run the monetary policy from Washington. The president's son-in-law, William G. McAdoo, was an old Kuhn Loeb man, having been selected by them as first president of the Hudson Manhattan Railroad in 1904, for which they floated the entire issue of bonds.

Ambassador Spring-Rice's comments on Kuhn Loeb Co Caused consternation and bitterness in the British Foreign Office. In 1917, Rufus Isaacs, Lord Reading, headed another British purchasing mission to the United States. Spring-Rice was coldly shynted aside. Isaacs and Wiseman handled everything directly with Colonel House, and soon the axe fell; Isaacs, who arrived in Washington on September 1917 officially replaced Spring-Rice in January, 1918 as British Ambassador to the United States. A month later, Sir Cecil Spring-Rice died suddenly and unexpectedly in Ottawa, Canada on his way back to Britain. Had he lived, he could have told some interesting stories about Isaacs and Wiseman.

In Harold Nicolson's biography of JP Morgan partner "Dwight Morrow", Harcourt, Brace, 1935, we find that Lord Reading was sent to New York in 1915 on a financial mission "and many discussions took place between him and the Morgan partners in his apartment at the Biltmore Hotel." Unfortunately, we are not favored with any quotes from those discussions. Isaacs, Lord Reading, was one of those shadow and influential figures who have dominated English politics in the 20th century. Some attempts at a biography of him was made in these pages from "All These Things" by A. N. Field of New Zealand, from the Gift Copy of Field's book presented to the Library of Congress by H. L. Mencken.

"Rufus Isaacs' brother was managing director of Marconi Wireless Ltd. Isaacs was then Attorney General under Asquith. Immediately after the Marconi inquiry, Isaacs was appointed Lord Chief Justice and elevated to the peerage as Lord Reading. On January 25, 1910, Godfrey Isaacs had been appointed managing director of the Marconi Co. Doctor Ellies Powell, editor of the *London Financial News*, was aroused to conjecture, 'Isaacs has had no experience in wireless'. While L. J. Maxse, editor of the *National Review* wrote that 'There is nothing in his somewhat chequered career to suggest his suitability for such a high and responsible position; it is not easy to discover successful concerns with which he had previously been associated."

Godfrey Isaacs promoted the British Broadcasting Company in 1922, the outgrowth of his manipulations of Marconi. The other principals in the Marconi affair were Lloyd George, Sir Herbert Samuel of the family which conducts Samuel Montague Co, funded by Lord Swaythling, whose cousin Sir Edwin Montague while Secretary of State to India originated the plan to give India a democratic government. And Sir Matthew Nathan. The deal to handle the sale of the cooperating concerns, American Marconi Ltd and Canadian Marconi Ltd in the United States was effected by an agreement between Paul Warburg and Godfrey Isaacs in March 1912. Warburg, whose firm of Kuhn, Loeb handled all stock issues for Western Union Telegraph became the American agent for Isaacs. Harry Isaacs and Lloyd George were deeply involved. In October 1912, the scandal broke. Doctor Ellies Powell, editor of the *London Financial News*, made a speech at Queen's Hall, London, on March 4, 1917, regarding some aspects of the Marconi affair.

"At the beginning of the war, many thousands of German reservists were allowed to return to Germany Though our fleet could have stopped them. German individuals, firms and companies went on trading merely in British names, collecting their debts and no doubt financing German militarism. At the very moment when Germans were destroying our property by Zeppelin bombs, we were actually paying them money instead of taking their holding as partial compensation for damage done. In January 1915 came that vicious decision by Lord Reading and the Appeal court, according to which the Kaiser and Little Wilhelm Ltd. was a good British concern, capable of suing the King's own subjects in the King's own courts. Eighteen months elapsed before that monstrous judgment could be overruled by the House of Lords. Some lurking influence prevented the instantaneous passing of an Act to remedy the blunder of Lord Reading and his colleagues. The so-called 'British Company', composed of German components, was left in obscene triumph for eighteen months. Not until 1916, two years after the war broke out, was power given to wind up enemy business. The uninterrupted activity in this country of the Frankfurt Metal Octopus is not an accident. The late government bamboozled us with vain talk about 'eliminating' the German element from Merton's, one of the firms associated with the Frankfurt Metal octopus. Oscar Legendbach has only been replaced by Oscar Lang, and Heinrich Schwartz had only disappeared to give place to Harry Ferdinand Stanton—the same man under another name! Let me analyze one lurid case which has steered public indignation and anger to its depths. I mean the impudent survival of the German banks. We have now been at war nearly three years, yet their doors are still open. They sent large quantities of bullion to Germany after the war started... (Powell then criticizes the Marconi episode). The Marconi undertaking is the brains of the war. Through it there are traveling to and from all the myriad mandates from the center at Whitehall to every part of our interminable battle line. If Bernstorff had a secret wireless in Washington, do you think there is no secret wireless in England? If in the Marconi background we can discern either any German influence or any secrets capable of being used as means of German pressure upon any figure in English public life, we are in the presence of something that may be a source of the gravest peril. I tell you also that during the big gamble of 1912, no fewer than 50,000 American Marconi shares went to Jacob Schiff, the pro-German schemer in the United States, who has done everything in his power to bring about peace on German terms. With Schiff in this business there was involved one Simon Siegman. I said, deliberately and with full knowledge of my responsibility, that one-tenth of the Marconi dealings were disclosed to the bogus committee which sat in 1913 to investigate. At any rate, look at one feature of the picture—the existence of a common fund of 250,000 American Marconi shares for from which the participants in this huge gamble drew the numbers necessary for the completion of the transaction. Schiff and Siegman across the Atlantic made their deliveries from that fund. On this side it provided the shares dealt in by His Majesty's then Attorney General Isaacs, the present Lord Chief Justice. During the entire period of the negotiations between the government and Marconi, immense transactions in Marconi shares were being conducted by a Mr. Ernest Cameron of 4 Panton St. Haymarket. Notice that I give you a name and address. Cameron keeps a modest voice production Academy. At the end of April 1912, he had over 800 English Marconi shares open with various brokers. At the very first whiff that there were politics in the background, Cameron's huge account was taken over at a cost of 60,000 pounds by Godfrey Isaacs, the brother of the then Attorney General. None of the Cameron dealings were disclosed to the Marconi committee... The work of the dealings took place through Solomon and Co. The senior partner of Solomon and Co was a naturalized Austrian named Breisach. Those who were willing to further the peace schemes of Speyer and Schiff last December 1917, have lost none of their mischievous propensities."

This was the core background of the man who replaced Sir Cecil Spring-Rice as ambassador to the United States. One final honor remained for Isaacs, the position of Viceroy of India. Not once did any newspaper give the family name of Lord Reading during his presence in America. This was unbiased reporting that freedom of information which the Rothschild United Nations desires to give to the whole world.

As the first signed that he might be able to deliver America to N. M. Rothschild, Sons of London, Woodrow Wilson set up a Council of National Defense composed of seven men. Only three of them, amazingly enough, were Jews. They were Bernard Baruch, Julius Rosenwald, the multimillionaire head of Sears Roebuck, who set up the Rosenwald Foundation to promote racial agitation in the United States, and the radical Samuel Gompers, who did so much to deliver the American working man into the hands of dictatorial Jewish communist trade union leaders.

Since we were not attacked by anybody, the Council of National Defense did not last very long. Most of its functions were incorporated into the War Industries Board, which had absolute power over America's heavy industry. Bernard Baruch was appointed head of the War Industries Board by Woodrow Wilson. William L. White tells us in his recent biography of Bernard Baruch that Baruch had donated $50,000 to Wilson's 1916 campaign. It was logical that Wilson would turn over America's heavy industry to him. It was a good bargain and Baruch had a reputation for making bargains.

Carter Field, in his biography "Bernard Baruch, Park Bench Statesman", McGraw Hill 1944, says that Samuel Untermeyer, attorney for the Guggenheims, came around to ask Baruch his fee for obtaining Tacoma Smelting and Selby Smelting and Lad for American Smelting and Refining from Darius Ogden Mills. One million, said Baruch, and he got it. He, Jacob Schiff, Senator Nelson Aldrich, and John D. Rockefeller Jr. went in partnership to form the Continental Rubber Corp., which later became the Intercontinental Rubber Corp. Field says that Baruch and Eugene Meyer Jr. in 1915 advertised an offering of Alaska Juneau Gold Mining Co. prospectus of 400,000 shares, in which it was stated that "all stock not taken by public subscription will be taken by E. Meyer Jr. and B. Baruch." This profitable partnership was given official status during the First World War, when Wilson gave

Baruch the War Industries Board and Eugene Meyer Jr the War Finance Corporation, which loaned out $700 million. With Paul Warburg already governor of the Federal Reserve Board, Wilson completed the trio which actually ruled America during the First World War. Since all three were Jews, it is difficult to see how anyone could claim that Jews were being discriminated against in America. From the list of Wilson's appointments, however, one could easily say that native born Americans were discriminated against. They were eligible for cannon fodder in France, but there was no place for them in Washington. Wilson filled the government offices with his own tribe, the Lehmans, Frankfurters, Strausses and Baruchs.

Carter Field tells us that the personnel of the War Industries Board under Baruch became one happy family, which has held annual reunions through the years. It formed the nucleus of Baruch's personal entourage, from which he drew whenever he had to send somebody down to take over Washington. The Government paid for Baruch's building up of an intensely loyal personal staff. Eugene Meyer did the same thing with his staff of the War Finance Corporation, which went with him in to the Federal Farm Loan Board, and on into the Reconstruction Finance Corporation.

His personal view, says Field, is that "Baruch would have been tremendously important in the Hughes administration if Hughes had been elected in the close election of 1916, both in the conduct of the war and in the making of the peace." Field does not tell us how much Baruch contributed to the Hughes campaign. Baruch proved that the partners of Kuhn Loeb were not the only people who knew how to back both sides.

Of Wilson's regard for Baruch, Carter Field says "For one thing, Wilson not only admired Baruch, he loved him. Mrs. Wilson makes this specific statement in her memoirs. This was a generous regard of Mrs. Wilson for a rival. Of Baruch's unofficial power in the first Wilson administration, Field says, "Under this curious cloak of anonymity Baruch exercised a very unusual type of political power in those early Wilson days. He was cultivated by most of the Wilson lieutenants, who speedily found out that he could do more for them than they could do by directly appealing to Wilson. Naturally, there was no publicity for all this."

Certainly not. The news services have never shown any willingness to tell the people who was running the country. However, Carter Field must be a very naive man to think that this was an unusual type of political power. His admiration for Baruch leads him to believe that the Wall Street speculator originated the idea of putting up a stupid stooge to carry out his orders in a democratic manner. Field should read the Bible and find that Jews have been doing that ever since they hanged Haman for opposing them.

Carter Field also tells us that "Baruch finally approved the idea of a Reparations Commission for the American Committee to negotiate peace after the Armistice." It is certainly helpful to know who was responsible for that, since a number of historians, not the least of them Herbert Hoover, have firmly fixed upon the Reparations Commission the primary guilt for the Second World War.

Baruch started off as a humble "wash" man on Wall Street, fluctuating the prices of stocks up and down for the big operators by buying and selling on the London exchange, which opened four hours earlier than the New York Stock Exchange. To do this from New York, Baruch had to get up at 1:00 o'clock in the morning for years. There are still New Yorkers who remember seeing him creep off to work as they came in from a gay evening. Since the New York Exchange opened at the closing price of the London exchange, Barack had only to sell or buy a few shares in London to change the price in New York to what his employers wanted it. After some years of this, he worked in with Jacob Schiff, the Warburgs and the Guggenheims until he grew to their size.

At the Knee committee hearings in 1934, Baruch Gave the figures for his 1916 income as $2,301,028.03, On which he paid tax of $261,169.91. This is the last tax he is known to have paid. Since then, a bank in Holland and a bank in France have handled his immense transactions in foreign currencies, and their gains are not subject to income tax in the United States. Other international bankers operate in the same manner. Baruch has had some good years, since 1916, particularly 1923, the year of the mark inflation in Germany. Baruch now expresses his horror of inflation, but he has no reason to regret that one.

Baruch also testified in 1934 that "I carried through the war three major investments, Alaska-Juneau Gold Mining Co, Atolia Mining Co and Texas Gulf Sulphur." Atolia Mining was then the world's largest producer of tungsten, and Baruch virtuously told the Committee that the government never bought an ounce of tungsten. None of the correspondents reporting their hearings bothered to tell their readers that tungsten is the key metal used in the manufacture of steel. On every ton of steel or steel products purchased by the government during the First World War, Baruch got his share through Atolia. Sulphur is also a key chemical in heavy industry. As head of the War Industries Board, Baruch could see to it that is firms got preference. As for the gold mining company, it has long been known that gold is a key metal in wars. His partner, Eugene Meyer, was head of the War Finance Corporation, so Baruch was well covered on that investment.

"Joe Tumulty and the Wilson Era" by a Mr. Blum, published by Houghton Mifflin, 1951, is an attempt at a biography of Wilson's secretary, Tumulty. Blum mentions that the Republicans in Congress accused McAdoo, R. W. Bolling, who was Wilson's brother-in-law, and Bernard Baruch of profiting in stock market transactions because of their inside knowledge of government plans. Nobody could be found who dared to testify, and the charges were not pressed. Carter Field mentions the funny piece of 1916, which is also recorded in a *New Yorker* profile of Baruch. On December 12, 1916, Chancellor von Bethman-Hollweg transmitted a peace proposal to England, and on the 19th Lloyd George said there would be no peace negotiations as far as England was concerned. With this comforting information, prices rose on the New York Exchange. Nevertheless, Baruch was selling US steel short, gambling millions of dollars on a hunch that steel would drop. Of course, he had no inside information. On December 21st, Woodrow Wilson addressed a note to all the belligerents offering to act as mediator for peace talks. The world's press played up this stable dropping as meaning that peace was just ahead.

Steel took a terrific plunge of downward and Baruch made a profit of $750,000 in one day. According to his biographers, his total profit for the three days operation was $1,000,000. Carter Field blames the dirty work in this episode on Jacob Schiff and Otto Khan. After all, they are dead now and Baruch is still alive.

Bernard Baruch High handed methods of running the nation's industries caused widespread complaint. It did not own Congress then, and the Special House Committee was formed to investigate him. Baruch described himself to them as a speculator and said,

> "I probably had more power than perhaps any other man did in the war; doubtless that is true."

Of his rise to power with Woodrow Wilson, he said,

'I asked for an interview with the president. I explained to him as earnestly as I could that I was deeply concerned about the necessity of the mobilization of the industries of the country. The President listened very attentively and graciously, as he always does, and the next thing I heard, some months afterward, my attention was brought to this Council of National Defense.

Mr. Graham: Did the President express any opinion about the advisability of adopting the scheme you proposed?

Baruch: I think I did most of the talking.

Mr. Graham: Did you impress him with your belief that we were going to get into the war?

Baruch: I probably did.

Mr. Graham: That was your opinion at the time?

Baruch: I thought we were going to get into the war. I thought the war was coming long before it did.

Mr. Jeffries: Then the system which you did adopt did not keep the Lukens Steel and Iron Co, the amount of profit that the low-producing companies had?

Baruch: No, but we took 80% away from the others.

Mr. Jeffries: The law did that, didn't it?

Baruch: The government did that.

Mr. Graham: what did you mean by that use of the word "we"?

Baruch: The government did that. Excuse me, but I meant we, the Congress.

Mr. Graham: You meant that the Congress passed a law covering that?

Baruch: Yes, Sir.

Mr. Graham: Did you have anything to do with that?

Baruch: Not a thing.

Mr. Graham: Then I would not use the word 'we' if I were you.'

Although the Graham Committee administered a stiff rebuke to Baruch, there was little that could be done with him or with his partner Eugene Mayer, Jr.

Baruch's coterie of of the War Industries Board was built around that clique of Wall Street Jews who were pushing him forward as their leader, his personal assistant, and from then on his personal publicity man was Herbert Bayard Swope, executive editor of the *New York World*, which had been one of the finest newspapers in the country. It is now the *World-Telegram*. Some of the men Swope graduated to fame and fortune from the *New York World*, included Charles Michelson, speechwriter for the late Franklin Roosevelt, and Elliott Thurnston, chief of Public Relations for the Federal Reserve Board. At the same time, he was Washington correspondent for the world. Baruch's second assistant was Clarence Dillon, who, according to Who's Who in American Jewry was born the son of Samuel Lapowitz in Victoria, Texas. Dillon's International Banking House of Dillon, Reed became the chief agent for Baruch's mysterious operations. Also with Baruch on the War Industries Board were Isador Lubin, Chief of Production Statistics, who is now an important figure at the forum of Communist diplomats known as the United Nations; Leo Wolman, assistant chief of Production Statistics, Edwin F. Gay, Chairman of Planning and Statistics, later President of Schiff's *New York Post*, an important figure in the Council on Foreign Relations; and Harrison Williams, the millionaire front for Baruch's public utility holdings. Also worthy of mention in the War Industries Board are James Inglis, later head of the Security Exchange Commission, and General Hugh Johnson, later head of the National Recovery Administration under Roosevelt. Baruch also worked closely with Felix Frankfurter, the Viennese Jew who was chairman of the War Labor Policies Board and who represented the World Zionist Organization at the Peace Conference of 1918–1919. Frankfurter was another one of those aliens who didn't get to France until the slaughter was over, but they must have loved war, because they made sure there would be another one. Frankfurter was ineligible to serve in the Second World War because he was on the Supreme Court. I have not been able to find the name of a single important Zionist who was killed or even frightened in either World War.

Jacob Schiff had been awarded a decoration by the Mikado of Japan for his services in 1905 in financing Japanese war against Russia, when gold take from the US Treasury by Theodore Roosevelt to pay JP Morgan for the Panama Canal was shipped across the country and sent from San Francisco to Japan. The article in the *Quarterly Journal of Economic* describing this transaction does not tell us how Mr. Schiff got into the act, but it would have been difficult for anyone to fight a war in 1905 without calling on Kuhn Loeb Co.

Since the principal function of JP Morgan Co. has been to keep the name of Rothschild out of the financial news, the Morgan firm was made the scapegoat of the intrigues of the First World War. Since then, the communists have used the bloated figure of Morgan as the symbol of the capitalist warmonger. Of course, all capitalists and Communist propaganda are Gentiles. Kuhn, Loeb Co. has never been attacked in Communist publications, although it has been much more prominent in international finance since 1920 than JP Morgan Co. Harold Nicholson's "Dwight Morrow" quotes Thomas Lamont, senior partner of Morgan, as saying,

> "Our firm had never for one moment been neutral. From the very start we did everything we could to contribute to the cause of the Allies. At least the House of Morgan was free from those puzzling variations of political loyalties which characterized its sister House of Kuhn, Loeb Co, which, aside from playing both sides during the First World War, was at the same time financing revolution in Russia and counter-revolution in Poland. Nicolson tells us that Morrow was the chief supply agent for Pershing and was with him constantly in France, as was another Morgan partner, Martin Egan, who had a mysterious career in the Philippines with the British Secret Service agent Sir Willmot Lewis before the First World War and who rose suddenly to prominence in world finance. Egan became one of the first directors of Time, Inc.

At the Senate hearings of 1914, Senator Bristow had asked Paul Warburg,

> 'How many of these partners (of Kuhn, Loeb Co.) are American citizens? Or are they all American citizens?
>
> **Warburg**: They are all American citizens except Mr. Kahn. He is a British subject.
>
> **Senator Bristow**: He was at one time a candidate for Parliament, was he not?
>
> **Warburg**: There was talk about it. It had been suggested and he had it in his mind.'

It would be interesting to know why the British were deprived of the parliamentary brilliance of Otto Kahn. For some reason, he decided not to enter public debate. Paul Warburg mentioned at these hearings that M. M. Warburg Co. of Hamburg had been established in 1796, and about himself he said,

> "I went to England, where I stayed for two years, first in the banking and discount firm of Samuel Montague Co. After that I went to France, where I stayed in a French bank.
>
> **Senator Bristow**: What French bank was that?
>
> **Warburg**: It is the Russian Bank for Foreign Trade which has an agency in Paris."

Perhaps it was there that he made the contacts which enabled him to send Trotsky out of New York in 1916 with a sizeable purse and his blessing.

While Paul Warburg was governor of the Federal Reserve Board, his brother Max Warburg was head of the German Secret Service and personal banker to the Kaiser. Sir William Wiseman was liaison officer between the British and American governments. Otto Kahn was playing an unofficial role of political and economic adviser to the British officials in Washington and other partners of Kuhn, Loeb Co. and their employees were busy in the nation's capital with other affairs. Looking at the list, one is led to conjecture how we could have fought the First World War without Kuhn, Loeb Co. The answer to that is that not only would it have been impossible to fight the war, but had it not been for the able international intelligences, such a war could not have begun.

Besides the aforementioned partners, Kuhn, Loeb Co. was also represented in Washington during the First World War by partner Jerome Hanauer, who had been designated Assistant Secretary of the Treasury in charge of Liberty Loans. A director of Hudson Manhattan Railroad, Hanauer was also a director of the National Railways of Mexico, Westinghouse International Corp and dozens of other large firms. His son-in-law, Kuhn, Loeb partner Lewis Liechtenstein Strauss, was private secretary to Herbert Hoover, while Hoover was head of the US Food Administration during the war, and was the brains behind Hoover's return to respectability after an appalling foreign career which has been admirably documented by a number of biographers.

The firm of Cravath and Henderson had for some years been legal counsel to Kuhn, Loeb Co. Paul Cravath and Paul Warburg went on a special mission to England in 1917, while Cravath's two ablest men, S. Parker Gilbert and Russell C. Leffingwell rushed down to Washington to become under-secretaries of the Treasury in charge of War Bonds. Their work will be described in the House Report of Eugene Meyer. Both Gilbert and Leffingwell returned to Cravath and Henderson after the war, and were advanced to partnerships in JPMorgan Company. Both were prominent in the Council on Foreign Relations. Cravath and Henderson partner Nicholas Kelley was also with the Treasury during the war in charge of loans to foreign governments.

With Felix Warburg deep in consultation with Justice Brandeis over the future of Palestine, the offices of Kuhn Loeb must have been empty during most of the war, with the exception of Jacob Schiff and his son Mortimer, who were busy arranging loans to Germany and seeing that Lenin and Trotsky had enough funds to carry out a decent revolution. No doubt the incomes of Kuhn, Loeb's partners suffered from such devotion to the winning of the war. Certainly their contribution to the war effort has never been given sufficient recognition, but this is due more to modesty than to any other reason. There exists not a single biography of any of these self-effacing men. The information on their activities comes almost entirely from such dry volumes as Who's Who in American Jewry and the New York City Directory of Directors.

Herbert Lehman hurried down to Washington to offer his services when the United States stumbled into the war. He was promptly attached as a Colonel to the General Staff of the Army. He could not be sparred for the front, however. His administrative abilities demanded that he be given a desk job, and he became head of the Purchasing, Storage, and Traffic division of the American Expeditionary Forces were his stern courage won him the Distinguished Service Medal from a grateful Republic. He was in Washington when the AEF sailed for France, and he was there when they returned. This was heroism of a high order. His assistant was Sylvan. Stroock, the largest felt manufacturer in the world and a noted philanthropist to Jewish organizations. It was not Stroock's fault if some of these charities turned out to be communist fronts. Stroock describes himself in Who's Who in American Jewry as having been given the civilian rank of Colonel, whatever that is.

Warburg has been dealt with at greater length in "The Federal Reserve"[1], but no study of the First World War would be complete without the government Record of Eugene Meyer's activities as head of the War Finance Corporation. Now owner of the yellow liberal *Washington Post,* which still sheds tears over the persecution of Alger Hiss, Meyer is also the largest stockholder of Allied chemical and Dye Corp., one of the four great

---

[1] See *The Secrets of the Federal Reserve*, Omnia Veritas Ltd, www.omnia-veritas.com.

chemical concerns which control the trade by interlocking directorates, particularly with the Warburg-controlled firm of I.G. Farben. *Fortune Magazine* in an article on Allied Chemical and Dye stated that the firm has never had to offer its stock for sale to the public, so great is the demand for it from the operators in the know in Wall Street. *Fortune* also tells us that $93 million of its $143 million capital is in government bonds. This is most interesting information in view of the following quotations from House report No. 1635, 68th Congress, second session, March 2, 1925, "Preparation and destruction of government bonds", submitted by Louis McFadden, chairman of the House Banking and Currency Committee and chairman of the Select Committee to investigate the destruction of government bonds, page two of this report says,

> "Duplicate bonds amounting to 2314 pairs and duplicate coupons amounting to 4698 pairs ranging in denominations from 50 to $10,000 have been redeemed to July 1, 1924. Some of these duplications have resulted from error and some from fraud. This is indeed a serious charge that Eugene Meyer was head of an agency which committed fraud at the rate of $10,000 per piece of printed paper. Mr. Meyer, who owns the Washington television station WTOP, could present an interesting detective story about the duplicate bonds. On Page 6, he is more directly accused.

> "These transactions of the Treasury prior to June 30, 1920, including settlements for purchase and sales executed by the War Finance Corporation, were largely directed by the Managing director of the War Finance Corporation, and settlements with the Treasury were made principally by him with the assistant secretaries of the Treasury. And the books show that the basis of the price paid by the government for over $1,894 Million worth of bounds, which the Treasury purchased through the War Finance Corporation, was not the market price, was not the cost of the bond plus interest and the elements entering into the settlement were not disclosed by the correspondence. The Managing Director of the War Finance Corporation, Mr. Eugene Meyer Jr., stated that he and the Assistant secretary of the Treasury agreed to the price and it was simply an arbitrary figure set by an Assistant Secretary of the Treasury as to the bounce so purchased from the War Finance Corporation. During the period of these transactions and up until quite a recent date, the Managing Director of the War Finance Corporation, Eugene Meyer, Jr., in his private capacity maintained an office at No. 14 Wall Street, New York City and through the War Finance Corporation, sold about $70 million worth of bonds to the government and also bought through the War Finance Corporation about $10 million in

bonds and approved the bills for most if not all of these bonds in his official capacity as managing director of the War Finance Corporation. When these transactions just referred to, were disclosed to the committee in open hearing, the Managing director appeared before the committee and stated the fact that while the books of the War Finance Corporation disclosed the fact that commissions were paid on these transactions, they were in turn paid over to the brokers, selected by the managing director, who executed the orders issued by his brokerage house, and admitted after this disclosure to the committee that the managing director employed the firm of Ernst and Ernst, certified public accountants, to audit the books of the War Finance Corporations, who did, upon the completion of the examination of these books, report to the committee that all moneys received by the brokerage house of the managing director had been accounted for. While simultaneously with the examination being made by the committee, the certified public accountants heretofore referred to were nightly carrying on their examination, it was discovered by your committee that alterations were being made in the book of record covering these transactions, and when the same was called to the attention of the treasurer of the War Finance Corporation, he admitted to the committee that changes were being made. To what extent these books have been altered during this process the committee have not been able to determine. After June of 1921, about $10 billion worth of securities were destroyed."

Thus, Eugene Meyer employed a firm of accountants Ernst and Ernst, who busily changed the records at night to cover Meyer's misdeeds, while the House Committee was investigating during the day. The Congressmen should have known that checking up on the Meyers and Ernsts was a 24 hour a day job.

For small fractions of the sums misused by Eugene Meyer during his tenure as managing director of the War Finance Corporation, men have been publicly disgraced, dismissed from office, their property taken and sentenced to long terms in prison. The flagrancy of a man in public office buying and selling to himself in his private business $80 million in government securities has never been equaled in the chronicles of corruption in the world. It would tax the imagination to attempt to slander such a man. If the Secretary of Agriculture were discovered to be gambling $80 million or $8 million or $800,000 on the commodities exchange in the future of wheat or cotton, what would be the result? It would be a scandal which would unseat even the administration of a

Harry Truman who seems to be true only to thieves and traitors. Yet Eugene Meyer did it and with that self-same morality went on to become one of the most influential newspaper publishers in the country. The yellow liberal *Washington Post* has yet to discover a communist in Washington. Eugene Meyer was not even reproved from his mismanagement of public funds until seven years later, and then only because his greed for power caused him to disrupt the government by plotting to take over the Federal Farm Loan Board. A number of congressmen from farming districts, knowing his record, rightly feared that he would endanger the agricultural economy of the country if he obtained this position. Nevertheless, he got what he wanted and Coolidge placed the farmers of America in this man's hands. Since then, millions of farmers have been bankrupted and driven off their land to work in the factories. Was it because Meyer and the Warburgs wanted that cheap farm labor for their chemical factories?

In this face of this published evidence of unsurpassed corruption, which was never given notice by what is farcically known as the public press, President Coolidge appointed Eugene Meyer chairman of the Federal Farm Loan Board, President Hoover appointed him chairman of the Board of Governors of the Federal Reserve Board, Franklin Roosevelt kept him on the Reconstruction Finance Corporation, and in 1946 he was appointed the first President of the World Bank. Here is a recipe for success worthy of the attention of all young Americans, a career of public service covering 30 years during which time Eugene Meyer has become one of the 10 most powerful men in the world.

The summation of House Report No. 1635, page 14, follows:

> "Instead of buying the bonds directly, the treasury employed the War Finance Corporation for such purpose, and instead of promptly turning into the Treasury, the bonds purchased the War Finance Corporation accumulated great quantities of bonds, held them, and collected nearly 28 million in interest of them from the Treasury. And although the Ways and Means Committee in framing the Liberty loans Act changed the Treasury's billing over there to present the Treasury from selling bonds below par the War Finance Corporation carried on an extensive trading in these bonds on the market at less than cost and selling the same issue of bonds on the same day at several dollars less per 100 to others than they sold them to the Treasury, and furthermore often sold them to the Treasury at a higher price than what the bonds had cost. Mr. Eugene Meyer Jr. managing director of the War Finance Corporation, and Messrs.

Russell C. Leffingwell and S. Parker Gilbert, Assistant Secretaries of the Treasury, settled on the price which the Government paid for over $1 billion 894 million worth of bonds bought from the War Finance Corporation, the basis of which price was not the market price, was not the cost of the bond, and was not disclosed by the correspondence. Mr. Meyer stated that he and Mr. Leffingwell agreed to the price and it was simply an arbitrary figure set by Mr. Leffingwell (as to the bonds bought from the war finance Corporation prior to June 30th 1920, 99%). The managing director of the War Finance Corporation in his private capacity maintained an office at No. 14 Wall Street, New York City, sold about $70 million in bonds to the Government and also bought through the War Finance Corporation about $10 million in bonds and approved the bills for the same in his official capacity."

Chairman MacFadden's Committee Report is obviously antisemitic, since it exposes Eugene Meyer, the scion of the international banking house of Lazard Freres, chief French agent for the House of Rothschild. Current biography tells us that Eugene Meyer Senior came to the United States from France in the late nineteenth century and set up a New York office for Lazard Freres, in which Eugene Meyer Jr. was employed until 1901, when he set up the now famous office, Eugene Meyer Jr. Company, at No. 14 Wall St., New York City. Representative MacFadden and other Congressmen appeared at the Senate Hearings on the Fitness of Eugene Meyer to be a Governor of the Federal Reserve Board in 1931, and gave much more damaging testimony, which appears in "The Federal Reserve", but corruption is not a disqualification for public office in a democracy. President Hoover appointed him anyway. Hoover and Meyer had essentially the same background as far as handling other people's money was concerned. The nation's press, mindful of advertising revenue from the Allied Chemical and Dye Corporation and its affiliates maintained a discreet silence on the personal problems of Eugene Meyer in 1931, and he took charge of the Federal Reserve Board, duly confirmed by the Senate. Decency in public office no longer existed in our nation's capital. The scandals revealed in 1950 did not start in 1950, but in the flouting of every effort to put honest men in government from 1900 to the present day.

CHAPTER 7

Because of the centralization of American money and banking in the Federal Reserve System, because of the centralization of news in the wire services, and because of the centralization of heavy industry into huge interlocking corporations which could be maneuvered for international goals by the Frankfurt bankers who handled their stock issues, the American people were bamboozled into fighting the First World War. It was a war which did not affect them directly, a war which not conceivable threat to their political or economic system, and a war which never caused the death of an American in battle on American soil. The hysterical agitation for which Herbert Hoover and Cleveland H. Dodge were responsible worked the American people up into a frenzy against a nation which had never raised its hand against us, a nation which had provided a large percentage of the most stable and productive element of our population, the farmers of the agricultural heartland of our Middle West. The Germans who had pioneered in settling the Indian Territories now found themselves the object of hatred and suspicion in areas where they were the first white settlers.

In retrospect, the First World War seems to have been one of the most ludicrous chapters in our history. Certainly it earned for America the contempt of every nation in Europe. That war was run like a state college football game, and it was no accident that a nearsighted college professor was put in the Presidency to umpire the game. While Kuhn, Loeb. Co. and Eugene Meyer and Co. grabbed the savings of the American people for war bonds and Liberty Loans which could well be termed Warburg Bonds and Meyer Loans, other immigrants piled up fortunes in the goldrush to supply the armed forces. As head of the War Price-Fixing Committee, Bernard Baruch, what price should set for the tungsten of Atolia Mining Co. in which Bernard Baruch was the principal stockholder.

Besides being profitable venture, heavy industry found the First World War its unsurpassed opportunity for the perfecting and consolidation of international agreements. Throughout the war, German industrialists met with French, English, and American industrialists, in Sweden and Switzerland and America. French businessmen travelled in the Ruhr, German bankers travelled in France, and more than half of the Frankfurt speculators migrated to England during the war. As one historian has remarked ironically, "Only the soldiers were at war."

For four years Germany received coal through Belgium, sugar through Switzerland, and chemicals through Sweden, while France received steel from Germany, and England refinanced German industry. Not until 1932 did much of this material come to light, when most countries of the world had been bankrupted by the intrigues for the gold standard which brought on the collapse of 1929–1933, and Russia witnessing the dismal failure of the First Five Year Plan. None of the Western nations had money to spend for armaments, and Russia was barely able to provide the necessities of life for her Commissars. A disarmament fever swept the world. Pease movements occupied the energies of the nervous crackpots who later were exposed as Communists. Pacifist literature was published in many languages. The scandals of the First World War were dragged out by dozens of eager and ambitious journalists, most of whom made a better living writing war propaganda after 1936. Disarmament was the party line of the Communist Party, the Council On Foreign Relations, and other groups financed by the international bankers.

The influence of these books and of public opinion may be judged by the fact that by 1935, when the last of them were shocking the simple taxpayers, the world was already well-embarked on a program of rearmament. Nevertheless, these books contain useful facts. Because of the Communist background of most of their authors, the racial identity of the war criminals is carefully ignored. However, Paul Emden, in his book, "Jews of Britain", tells us on page 232 that

> "The first important capital of the Royal Dutch Shell Corporation was furnished by Samuel Bleichroder. The Asiatic Petroleum Co. was subscribed by Royal Dutch Shell and the Rothschilds in equal part. Viscount Bearsted (Walter H. Samuel) succeeded his father as Chairman of the Shell Trading and Transport Co., in which he represented forty subsidiaries. He was also a director of the Alliance Assurance Co. with Baron Antony de Rothschild."

The Samuel family, Emden tells us, has retained total control of Shell, the second largest oil trust in the world, which on the world press has persistently referred to as being controlled by the late Sir Henri Deterding, who managed it for the Samuel family. The Samuels remained unnoticed by the public, although they were the second most powerful family in England in the twentieth century, being surpassed only by the Rothschilds. Churchill has long been a favorite of the Samuels. When he was First Admiral of the Fleet in 1915, he changed the British Navy from coal to oil.

Emden also mentions Lord Melchett, Sir Alfred Mond, and Lord Reading in the formation of the Imperial Chemical Industries of Great Britain, one of the Big Four which controls the world's chemical industry. The others are Meyer's Allied Chemical and Dye, Warburg's I. G. Farben, and Dupont. Two World Wars have had little effect on the close relationships and interlocking directorates and trade agreements of these four corporations and their myriads of subsidiaries. No doubt they will survive the Third World War with mutual esteem and regard for each other's interests. Imperial Chemical combined the Brunner Mond Chemical Co. with the Nobel Industries, the international explosives trust in 1915. Since this was done in the midst of the war, it necessitated one of the most amazing and documented evidences of international cooperation in business between belligerents. The Hamburger Fremdenblatt, on May 15, 1915, advertised an exchange of shares in Nobel Ltd of England for shares in Nobel Co. of Hamburg. 1,500,000 pounds were paid by English shareholders for the exchange of stock, involving 1,800,000 shares. The advertisement, as quoted in George Seldes' "Iron, Blood, and Profits" Harpers, 1934, states that

> "An announcement of exchange of ordinary shares of Nobel Dynamite Trust Ltd of London for shares of Dynamit Aktiengesellschaft, formerly Alfred Nobel Co. of Hamburg. This agreement is to be retroactive to Jan. 1, 1914."

Seldes' book also describes the formation in 1916 of the Harvey Armorplate Cartel, with Leon Levy as the largest stockholder and director, others were the Deutsche Bank of Berlin, Edouard Saladin of France, and Baron Oppenheim of Cologne, another instance of international amity in the midst of bloodshed. Seldes also criticizes other aspects of the conduct of the slaughter for profit. On page 88, he notes, "the uneasy rumor that the Foch, Haig, Pershing, the Crown Prince Wilhelm, and other Headquarters were listed on maps and notes exchanged by the enemies during the war. Generals die in bed."

Skoda of Czechoslovakia, Schneider Creusot of France, Vickers of England, and Loewe's of Germany were the European munitions firms which cooperated to each other's satisfaction during the First World War. Schneider Creusot was controlled by the Bank of France, which in turn was controlled by the de Wendel family, and the House of Rothschild. In 1914 Schneider Creusot caused a general alarm all over Europe when it purchased the Russian munitions firm, the Putiloff works of St. Petersburg. The trustee for the debentures involved was the Royal Exchange Assurance Ltd of London, one the oldest Rothschild insurance firms, on which Thatcher Brown, of Brown Brothers Harriman, partner of Secretary of Defense Robert A. Lovett and Mutual Security Administrator W. Averell Harriman, has been listed as a director for many years.

Richard Lewinsohn, in his excellent biography "Zaharoff, the Mystery Man of Europe", Lippincott, 1929, says that,

"On the board of the Nickel Co. Zaharoff sat next to the representatives of the House of Rothschild."

Zaharoff was the best salesman for the Big Four of the munitions world. He had nothing to do with their finance, and little to do with their organization. He was the greatest warmonger in the world, and he was paid millions by the Rothschilds as a salesman for Vickers and its subsidiaries. He became the scapegoat for the disarmament furor, and received a great deal of free publicity, which no doubt increased his value to his employers. It is difficult to find anyone employed by the Rothschilds who has ever been injured by scandals being published about them.

Richard Lewinsohn, in his retrospective book "The Profits of War", E. P. Dutton, 1937, says that the Rothschilds attained international influence principally from their profits from the Napoleonic Wars, a point made clear by the work of Corti but not so pointedly expressed. Lewinsohn also says,

"Under Metternich, Austria after long hesitation finally agreed to accept financial direction from the House of Rothschild."

Like other empires which accepted the financial direction of the Rothschilds, the Austro-Hungarian Empire has ceased to exist. Metternich was the first prominent statesman of Europe to succumb to the attraction of Rothschild money, one of a long list which now includes Wilson, Churchill, and Roosevelt.

"The Secret International" a definitive pamphlet published by the Union for Democratic Control, London, 1934, states that Vickers in 1807 bought the Naval Construction and Armament Co. and Maxim Nordenfeldt Guns and Ammunitions Co. This combination, then known as Vickers Sons and Maxim, supplied both sides during the Russo-Japanese War of 1905. They then combined with S. Loewe Co. the largest manufacturer of ammunition in Germany, and Loewe became a director of Vickers. The Rothschild control of Vickers is revealed by the interlocking of the directors of Vickers with directorships in other Rothschild enterprises. Sir Herbert Lawrence, director of Vickers in 1934, was also a director of the Bank of Rumania Ltd, the Sun Assurance Office Ltd the Sun Life Assurance Co. and the Ottoman Bank (Sassoon-controlled) of which Sir Herbert was Chairman of the London Committee. Sun Life was one the earliest Rothschild ventures, into insurance and still has two Rothschilds on the board of its Baltimore incorporation. The Bank of Rumania also is a longtime affiliate of N. M. Rothschild Sons of London. Another director of Vickers was Sir Otto Niemeyer, director of the Bank of England and of the Anglo-Iranian Bank (Sassoon). The Bank of England, of which Alfred de Rothschild was director for thirty-two years, is synonymous with the House of Rothschild. A third director was Sir Vincent Caillard, President of the Ottoman Debt Council and financial expert on the Far East. He was one of the principals in the negotiations between Theodor Herzl, Zionist leader, and the Sultan of Turkey for funding the Turkish Public Debt in exchange for a Zionist state in Palestine. (*Theodor Herzl*, by Jacob DeHaas). However, the World War came along before the negotiations were concluded, and the Zionists waited for the Balfour Declaration.

Among the international bankers who decided to leave forever feudal Germany at the onslaught of the war was Baron Edgar Speyer of the Frankfurt banking house of Speyer Brothers. Edgar Speyer went to New York in 1915, came back across the Atlantic to Britain, where he learned that his thick accent wouldn't do him any harm in the more affluent circles of Great Britain, and made his home in London after 1916. In New York at this time his brother James Speyer had working in his office the son of Count Bernstorff, German Ambassador to the United States. Speyer and Schiff were the two most indefatigable pro-Germans in New York.

Baron Bruno von Schroder also made his home in England as a safer place than Germany, during the war. His family house J. Henry Schroder Co. set up offices in London and New York. It kept its German branch as the J. Stein Bankhaus of Cologne, which became personal banker to Adolf Hitler after he became dictator of Germany. The House of Schroder, one of the four most important international banking firms, has until recent years escaped notice entirely. James Stewart Martin has written much about its influence and about one of its directors, Allen W. Dulles, now head of the Central Intelligence Agency and the Council On Foreign Relations.

Fortune Magazine of March, 1945, gives us an insight into how the international elements travelled about, seizing upon every opportunity afforded them by the war. "L'affaire Dreyfus", reprinted in its entirety, as follows:

> "In 1938 the London Stock Exchange made the rule that dividends and profit statements must made simultaneously. It was flagrantly violated by British Celanese, 60 million dollar brother of American Celanese manufacturer of synthetic yarns and of all-important chemicals. Last December 1, its directors announced a 15% dividend on ordinary shares; its first payment on common stock. The stock, which had been climbing steadily, climbed still higher. Then on December 11, the company issued a profit statement showing that 1944 earnings were only a fraction of this dividend money, which came largely from tax reserves available a the result of a tax adjustment with the British Government. The stock dropped sharply. Such was the outcry from anguished investors that the venerable Stock Exchange Committee felt constrained to issue an unprecedented public reprimand. At the height of *l'affaire Dreyfus*, old Henry Dreyfus, co-founder of the company, died at his London home. A native of Switzerland, he came to England in 1916 at the invitation of the British Government to supervise the making of non-inflammable cellulose acetate for airplane wings. He remained and organized British Celanese, which in 1924 produced the first successful synthetic yarn. At about the same time brother Camille Dreyfus led in the organization of American Celanese Corporation."

The Dreyfus family, with the help of the British Government, became one of the big three of the international rayon industry, the other two being Dupont and Bemberg. In *Who's Who in American Jewry*, Camille Dreyfus identifies himself as President of American Celanese, now called Celanese Corporation of America, and director of Canadian Celanese Corporation.

The Bemberg family settled in Argentina, where Otto Bemberg died leaving an immense fortune. Peron finally made some inroads upon it with inheritance taxes, and a widespread campaign against him, notably in the Luce publications, *Time*, and *Life*, caused him to ban them in Argentina. The Bemberg case was not taken up by Luce. It was merely that all at once he took a violent dislike to Peron's government. Their influence continued through Dr. Gainza Paz, editor of the Buenos Aires paper *La Prensa*. At last Peron was forced to close the paper down, to put an end to the diatribes against him, and the American press, if it can still be described as American, put on a day of mourning. Dr. Paz is now enjoying a lucrative lecture tour in the United States.

CHAPTER 8

While the international bankers were strengthening their holdings in the heavy industries of many countries during the war of 1914–1918, they also were consolidating the influence of the two new philosophies of government, international Communism, and international Zionism, which they had been promoting as the answer to the twentieth century. Either one would serve their interests well, since both of them were devoted to the subversion of all existing national governments in the world.

Consequently, the agents of Communism and the agents of Zionism, who often were the same people, took no part in the First World War as far as the national interests of the belligerents were concerned. They travelled freely back and forth, between, and across the warring nations, intent upon their long range plans for world power. The World Zionist Organization, in particular, had been presuming upon an approaching world war for some time, as the article "When Prophets Speak", by Litman Rosenthal, American Jewish News, September 19, 1919, bears witness. Rosenthal describes an episode at the Sixth Zionist Congress in August of 1903, at which Max Nordau, second-in-command of the Zionist movement, told Rosenthal,

> "Herzl knows that we stand before a tremendous upheaval of the whole world. Soon some kind of world congress will be called and England will then continue the work it has begun with its generous offer to the Sixth Congress; let me tell you the following words as if I were showing you the rungs of a ladder leading upward and upward; Herzl, the Sixth Zionist Congress, the future world war, the peace conference where with the help of England a future Palestine will be created."

Nordau's prophecy came out exactly as he foretold it, but it was not so remarkable, because it was entirely foreseeable to the political strategist. It was apparent to many observers who travelled in Europe from 1885 to 1914 that the tremendous pressures created by the Industrial Revolution could only be discharged by a world-shaking conflict, just as the pressures of 1952 can only be discharged by the inevitable Third World War. At the turn of the century, the peoples of Europe were deriving little benefit from the great forward strides in technology, because their monetary systems, still strangled by the gold standard which was the monopoly of the House of Rothschild, could devise no way in which to distribute the mass-produced goods to the population. Consequently, heavy industry had to turn to the production of war goods, because they could be distributed by a war economy. In "The Federal Reserve", I reprinted an article from the Quarterly Journal of Economics which proved that Europe was ready for a continental conflict as early as 1887. The fact that it had to be postponed until 1914, when the Federal Reserve System was able to finance the Allies, only made it worse when it came.

Moreover, at the Peace Conference of 1919, the war-wearied and demoralized peoples of the belligerent nations did not want anything except peace. They desired an impossible peace, whereas the Zionists were there en masse with a number of specific demands for Jewish rights in European countries and for the establishment of a Jewish National Home in Palestine. They wanted something which it was impossible to get, and they got it.

Israel Cohen, in his definitive book, "The Progress of Zionism", published in the fateful year of 1929, gives us the two objectives of the Zionist movement, which he claims is as old as the Jewish people. First, Zionism must prevent the assimilation of the Jews into any other people, maintaining the positive national identity of the Jewish nation until they got their own country, and the second objective was the establishment of a Jewish national state. The anti-assimilation stand is also part of the official Communist program, and it is based upon the understanding that the Jew's first allegiance is to world Jewry, and his second allegiance is to whatever nation he happens to be residing in at the moment. This is an important definition, because Cohen thus defines as perjurers the late Justice Brandeis and the present Justice Felix Frankfurter of the Supreme Court of the United States. Both of them were prominent Zionists leaders when they took their oaths of office; indeed, both of them were but professional Zionists. Yet they both swore to abide by and uphold the laws of the United States without mental reservation. Brandeis states repeatedly in his papers and speeches that nothing is more important to the Jew than Zionism. This meant that the laws and customs of the United States took second place to the future of Israel.

There is a great deal of evidence to prove that Zionism was the force which provided the pressure to get the United States into the First World War. American Zionists leaders made the bargain with England that in exchange for the Balfour declaration setting up a Jewish National Home in Palestine, America would be brought into the war. England was glad to make this bargain, because she was having a hard time winning the war, particularly because of the numbers of Speyers, Schroders, and lesser Germans in England who were maintaining daily contact with their homeland.

In 1919, the Zionist Organization of America published a book called "The American War Congress and Zionism", containing the outspoken and positive partisanship for the Zionist movement if many of our top Government officials, including statements from sixty-one Senators and two hundred and thirty-nine Representatives, a total of three hundred men who voted for war with Germany in 1917. Each of these three hundred members of your War Congress expressed his extreme personal interest in and admiration for the world Zionist movement. This book alone indicts the Zionists for our involvement in the bloody conflict of 1914–1918, but there is much more evidence from the Zionist leaders themselves. The most prominent spokesman for the Zionist Organization of America for many years was Rabbi Stephen Wise, the personal friend for Presidents Woodrow Wilson and Franklin Roosevelt. In his autobiography, "Challenging Years", Putnams 1949, page 186 he writes that,

> "Reinforced by the boundless generosity of Baron Edmond de Rothschild, the Palestine colonies developed. Our government, thanks to President Wilson and Secretary of the Navy Josephus Daniels, made it possible to assure money and food to the Jews in Palestine, even permitting the use of battleship for that purpose."

This was logical enough. Why shouldn't we use our battleships to send supplies to Palestine, even though we needed them for the war? One cannot help but wonder why Josephus Daniels hasn't been made President. His assistant Secretary of the Navy in this operation was Franklin Roosevelt, who reaped the benefits of this aid to Palestine in four Presidential elections.

Rabbi Wise says that Wilson addressed a letter to him on August 31, 1918, saying,

> "I welcome an opportunity to express the satisfaction I have felt in the progress of the Zionist movement in the United States and the Allied Countries."

The phrasing here is important. Wilson mentions the Allied countries because, as Frank E. Manuel reveals in his "Realities of American-Palestine Relations", Germany was bidding for the support of the Zionists with several offers. She lost Zionists, and lost the war.

In the "Eighth Crusade", we are told that in 1916 the Zionists secretly transferred their headquarters from Berlin to London, and gave up the Germans. Rudolf Steiner, an important emissary of the movement, passed to and between London and Berlin throughout the war, despite police regulations. Professor Otto Warburg, cousin of the banking family, had become President of the World Zionist Organization in 1911, when it still looked as though Germany might achieve her Pan-European Empire. As soon as it became apparent to the internationals that Germany could not supply herself during a protracted war, the Zionists began the shift to London. Under Warburg, Cologne had been for a time the headquarters of the movement. Jessie Sampter, in the "Guide to Zionism", page 80, says of Jacobson, one of the directors,

> "When he saw that Cologne could no longer be the center of Zionist policy, Jacobson left and went to Copenhagen, where in a neutral country he could be of practical use to the Zionists by transmitting information and funds."

Oblivious of the millions of men locked in a death grip on the battlefronts of Europe, the Zionists moved in and out of the beleaguered capitals, attending to their lust for power. Although they did not participate in the fighting, the Zionists won the peace, which should be a lesson to all warriors.

In 1914, the Zionist Inner Action Committees had spread around the world. One of the founders of the movement, Dr. Schmarya Levin of Berlin, came to the United States to reside during the War, where he instructed Louis Brandeis in the faith. Brandeis then educated Woodrow Wilson, who reciprocated by making his teacher Justice of the Supreme Court.

Rabbi Wise, on page 186 of "Challenging Years", says,

"I had taken occasion to give to President Wilson, even before his inauguration, a rather full outline of Zionism. From the very beginning of his administration, Brandeis and I knew that in Woodrow Wilson we had and would always have an understanding sympathizer with the Zionist program and purposes. Brandeis, particularly after his assumption of the leadership of the Zionist Provisional Committee, together with myself and others, contrived to discuss Zionist problems with the President. Throughout, we received warm and heartening help from Col. House, close friend of the President and his unofficial Secretary of State. House not only made our cause the object of his very special concern, but served a liaison officer between the Wilson Administration and the Zionist movement."

Wise has given us a real paragraph of history. At last, we find something that Woodrow Wilson really believed in, Zionism, and we discover the true role of the ubiquitous Col. House, the liaison officer between Wilson and the World Zionist Organization.

Most of the public official class of Great Britain jumped on the Zionist bandwagon during the War, and those who didn't were either quickly forgotten by the public, for their names and pictures no longer appeared in the newspapers, or, if they were too influential to be disposed of by the silent treatment, they suddenly passed away, as did the late Ambassador to the United States, Sir Cecil Spring-Rice.

Foreign Minister Arthur Balfour was one of the most ardent Zionists in England. One might have thought it the new Christianity, judging from the number of his appearances on Zionist platforms, and the fervor of his zeal. At last he published a book of his Zionist speeches, "Great Britain and Palestine", although Palestine actually should have come first in the title as it did with him. On July, 12, 1920, at a speech given at a public demonstration held by the English Zionist Federation whose Chairman was Lord Alfred de Rothschild, Balfour,

"For long I have been a convinced Zionist."

This was exactly as though our present Secretary of State, Dean Acheson, should stand up and say publicly, "For long I have been a convinced Zionist", as indeed he might, for he was private secretary to Justice Louis Brandeis in 1921–1922 when Brandeis was head of the Zionist Organization of America. Zionists have a way of getting on in foreign affairs. Balfour also made a speech "Ten Years After", given before the officials of the Anglo-Palestine Bank at the Hotel Cecil in London on Nov. 10 1927, in which he said,

"It is quite true that I am one of the oldest British Zionists"

This is a most damning statement, since Zionism, like Communism, demands absolute allegiance. Members of either movement cannot be loyal to the nation of their birthplace of their residence. Yet such a man in charge of the Foreign Affairs of a great Empire. In the hands of the Zionists, it is easy to understand why Britain, in the space of a few years, has lost most of an empire which she built over a period of centuries.

The pernicious evidence of Zionist influence in the United States is obvious, and much evidence of the guilt of the Zionists in involving us in the First World War is available in the biography, "Brandeis, A Free Man's Life", by Alpheus T. Mason, Viking Press, 1946. Mason, a professor at Princeton University, tells us that Brandeis' father was an immigrant who carried a letter of introduction from the Rothschilds, looking over possible investments in America, in 1848; that he became wealthy from selling grain to both sides during the Civil War, when he had established his business in the border zone of Louisville, Kentucky; and that his son was able to afford an expensive Harvard education.

Mason quotes *Truth magazine*, edited by George R. Conroy in Boston, from the issue of Dec. 165, 1912, as follows,

"Mr. Schiff is head of the great private banking house of Kuhn, Loeb, which represents the Rothschild interests on this side of the Atlantic. He has been described as a financial strategist and has been for years the financial minister to the great impersonal power known as Standard Oil. He was hand-in-glove with the Harrimans, the Goulds, and the Rockefellers in all their railroad enterprises, and has become the dominant power in the railroad and financial world of America. Brandeis, because of his great ability as a lawyer and for other reasons which will appear later, was selected by Schiff as the instrument through which Schiff hoped to achieve his ambition in New England. His job was to carry on an agitation which would undermine public confidence in the New Haven system and cause a depression in the price of its securities, thus forcing them on the market for the wreckers to buy. The New England fight is simply part of a world movement. It is the age-long struggle for superiority between Jew and gentile. Schiff is known to his people as a 'Prince in Israel'. He has given millions to Jewish charities, and in keeping in mind always the Yiddish proverb 'He who has the money has the authority', is ever solicitous for the progress of his race along financial lines, confident that in the end it will control the world."

Of Brandeis' opportunistic adoption of Zionism, after his trimming in his desire for public recognition in the New Haven conspiracy, Mason says,

"It was not until DeHass' South Yarbrough visit in August, 1912 that Brandeis' interest in Zionism was fully awakened. They were consulting at William G. McAdoo's request about funds for the Democratic campaign. DeHass made some mention of Louis Dembitz as a 'noble Jew', a prominent Zionist and Brandeis' uncle and namesake, and then launched into the subject nearest his heart, Zionism. He told the story of his British birth and of the influence he had been able to exert on Senator Henry Cabot Lodge. That an obscure London-born Jew could gain the sympathy of the stiff-necked Senator piqued Brandeis' curiosity. In 1912 Brandeis made cross-country tours speaking in favor of Zionism."

It is interesting that the subject of Zionism came up in connection with the problem of raising funds for the Wilson campaign of 1912, and that Samuel Untermeyer, the prominent Zionist leader, was one of the heaviest contributors to Wilson's fund. At any rate, the die was cast. The Zionists needed Brandeis to give the movement some respectability in America. Although he was considered a dangerous person by Democratic politicians because of his willingness to espouse antisocial causes, he had attained the respect of America's Jewish population because of his huge income from the practice of corporation law. His espousal of Zionism meant the turning point in its fortunes in America. Mos Jews had considered it only as a movement, which, because of its radical plans and the publicity-seeking nature of it roaming adherents, would be more likely to cause anti-Semitism than to help the Jews, who were prosperous and happy in America. However, Brandeis seized upon Zionism as his chance to gain the political power which had been denied him by the stable society of New England. His domineering leadership gradually forced into the Zionist movement against their better judgment, the majority of American Jews.

Although Brandeis was unable to attend the Eleventh World Zionist Congress held in Vienna, he sent a message urging Jewish immigration into Palestine in anticipation of the backing of the American Government. This message, and his tours, led to his election as

Chairman of the Provisional Zionist Organization of America, later the Zionist Organization of America. Mason quotes a letter written by Brandeis to his brother Alfred on April 15, 1915.

"Zionist affairs are the really important things in life now."

At this time he was being considered for the Supreme Court, thanks to Samuel Untermyer. The son of Wilson's mistress had gotter into an embezzling scape, and, after some negotiations, Untermeyer put up the necessary $150,000 with understanding that Brandeis would get the next vacancy on the Court. Since Rufus Isaacs was Lord Chief Justice of England, Wilson would show them that we were as democratic as the English. This appointment meant that the Zionist Organization of America would become respectable.

On page 448, Mason writes that,

"In May, 1915, Brandeis heard that Rufus Isaacs and Sir Herbert Samuel were considering Zionism, and that Lloyd George and Balfour were distinctly favorable."

Since Lloy George would favor anything that Isaacs favored, or lose his Marconi shares, it is not puzzling that he favored Zionism. Balfour, of course, like Franklin Roosevelt, based his entire political career on a fanatical adherence to Zionism.

Mason quotes a letter from Brandeis to Abram I. Elkus, U.S. Ambassador to Turkey, in December 1916 (page 452).

"Zionism is taking its place in public consideration, and is one of the problems the war is likely to settle for us."

The Zionist plan hinged on getting America into the war.

On the same page, Mason quotes a letter from Col. House to Rabbi Wise on February 7, 1917.

"I hope the dream we have may soon become a reality."

This was a matter of weeks before Wilson declared war on Germany.

Mason tells us that on January 28, 1916, Wilson appointed Brandeis Justice of the Supreme Court. This appointment, given to an opportunistic corporation lawyer who had never looked askance at any method of furthering his political and financial fortunes, had only one purpose, the establishment of a firm Zionist movement in America. It aroused nationwide dismay among Gentile lawyers, for tit was rightly foreseen as the beginning of the end for one of the checks and balances in our government as said by Thomas Jefferson. It was a deathblow to our constitution and legal system. What Wilson began, Franklin Roosevelt completed, so that the time Truman got around to appointing his mediocre party hacks, Tom Clark and Fred Vinson, to the Supreme Court, the public no longer cared.

Brandeis, writes Mason, was not considered a good citizen by the business community. He was known as a professional agitator and professional Zionist, nor had his considerable fortune served to make him worthy of respect in New England, where money was not yet everything. Consequently, a great deal of criticism was levelled at Wilson for his choice of an undignified man for a very dignified office. The yellow liberal press, just getting its voice, sprang like a hungry cat to Brandeis' defense. Both Frances Perkins and Walter Lippmann got their start in this foray. They filled the columns of the New Republic of March, 18, 1916, with their syrupy worship of millionaire Brandeis. It was a golden opportunity for many breast-beaters for Zionism to declare themselves, and to begin a long and prosperous career with favourable publicity.

The Senate was placed in a very awkward position by Wilson's treasonable action. That body was still capable of manifesting a sense of public responsibility, and so the appointment was debated for some months. To approve the appointment meant that the Senators would earn the opprobrium of every decent person in the country, but decent people do not swing elections. Fear won out. Should they refuse, every Senator denying the appointment would face the concentrated virulence of the Jewish population in his next election, and it is wellknown in American politics that "Hell hath no fury like Hebrew scorned". Moreover, it meant the automatic alienation of what is jokingly termed the public press, and so, on June 5, 1916, the Senate approved the appointment of Brandeis.

The same day, Wilson wrote Henry Morgenthau Sr., as quoted by Mason,

> "I am relieved and delighted at the Senate confirmation. I never signed any commission with such satisfaction as I signed his."

Throughout the Senate debate on his nomination, Brandeis was travelling about the country to speak on Zionism, this strengthening support of his nomination to the Supreme Court.

Mason says that the only Jew previously offered a seat on the Supreme Court was Judah P. Benjamin. President Fillmore offered the appointment to Benjamin, who declined because he was already committed by the Rothschilds to be treasurer of the Confederacy during the approaching Civil War.

"At the news of his confirmation", says Mason on page 452 "Brandeis resigned as Chairman of the Provisional Zionist Organization, but this withdrawal was far more apparent than real... He resigned his membership in the National Economic League and all his Harvard law school connections. His most recent interest—Zionism continued... Zionists came to see him singly and in groups from all over the world. His daily mail brought him news from Palestine, reports and more reports. He kept a captain's hand on the tiller of American Zionism, and warmly supported the Mack-Brandeis group, led by Judge Julian Mack and Robert Szold, when they wrested leadership from the Lipsky clique."

Mack's law secretary at that time was a young man named Max Lowenthal, who heads the Zionist Inner Mission at the White House during the Truman occupancy.

On page 595, Mason again positively identifies Brandeis as the leader of the Zionist movement throughout the years he was sitting as Justice of the Supreme Court of the United States. Mason says,

> "Brandeis was now the elder stateman of Zionism in America."

Mason remarks on page 452 that,

> "America's entry into the war seemed to clinch the case for Zionism in the minds of its leaders here."

With America delivered as called for, Britain went ahead with the plans for a Jewish National Home in Palestine, ignoring the fact that this would surely wreck the British influence in the Near East, as it has done. Mason says,

> "On April 25, 1917, James de Rothschild cabled from London that the plans called for a Jewish Palestine under British protection."

Brandeis had Arthur Balfour to a White House luncheon in May of 1915. "You are one of the Americans I had wanted to meet", said Balfour to Brandeis. The White House at this time was the official headquarters of the Zionist movement in America, with House, Wilson, Wise, and Brandeis dashing in and out in the hectic days of the Balfour Declaration. Brandeis cabled Louis de Rothschild,

> "Have had a satisfactory talk with Mr. Balfour, also with our President. This is not for publication."

Mason then tells us that Brandeis lunched in Washington in mid-September with Lord Northcliffe and Rufus Isaacs Lord Reading, "with whom he undoubtedly talked Zionism".

Mason remarks that Norman Hapgood wrote Brandeis from London on Jan. 10, 1917,

> "Hoover is the most interesting man I know. You will enjoy his experience in diplomacy and finance."

Later, Mason tells us that,

> "By the end of January, Hoover was in the United States asking funds to aid starving Belgium, and in early February he talked with Justice Brandeis. Brandeis arranged a conference with Senator Bristow and Secretary McAdoo which led to Hoover's appointment as U.S. Food Administrator."

For Brandeis' position on Zionism and the problem of his mythical loyalty to the United States, we have ample material, a book of his speeches, published by the Zionist Organization of America, "Brandeis on Zionism."

Speaking on "The Jewish Problem", in June of 1915, as quoted in his book, Brandeis said before the Eastern Council of Reform Rabbis,

> "Organize, organize, organize, until every Jew in America must stand up and be counted with us."

On page 74 of this book, Brandeis writes that "Democracy is a Zionist concept". Oddly enough, Lenin and Marx considered democracy to be the peculiar attribute of Communism. However, Brandeis clarifies his idea by his following sentences, "Socialism is also a Zionist aim."

On page 75, Brandeis says, "The Zionist movement is essentially democratic": Only Jews need apply.

Brandeis reminds us on page 80 that "Zionism has not sprung out of the war. It was vital and active before."

On the eve of his appointment to the Supreme Court, on Jan. 2, 1916, Brandeis told the Knights of the Zion Club in Chicago,

> "There isn't a thing that should be more interesting to a Jew today than the events of Zionism. Your own self-respect, your own duty demands that you join a Zionist organization."

On July 7, 1916, after his confirmation by the Senate, Justice Brandeis told the Federation of American Zionists in Philadelphia,

> "Our work can be accomplished only if we recognize and live up to the fundamental basis of Zionism, the democracy of the Jewish people. Upon them rests the duty to spread the Zionist movement."

Brandeis' activity at any time during the many years of his tenure on the Supreme Court was sufficient grounds for his removal from office, had there been any force in America strong enough to oppose Zionism. This can also be said of his successor in Zionism and on the Supreme Court, Justice Felix Frankfurter. The Frankfurters emphasize the importance of being on both sides, for, while the good Justice has been sitting augustly on the bench, his brother Otto has been an habitual criminal, who resided for some years as a guest of the State of Iowa in the State Prison at Anamosa. Upon his graduation, Otto was deemed sufficiently trained for government service, and he was promptly appointed to an important post in Paris in the Economic Co-Operation Administration under Senator Lehman's stooge Paul Hoffman.

The Balfour Declaration, the result of many years of international intrigue, called for the establishment of a Jewish National Home in Palestine with the official protection of Great Britain. Much more was promised the Zionists behind the scenes, but Britain was unable to live up to those unwritten promises, causing Zionists to score her for her failure throughout the 1930s. In Sampter's "Guide to Zionism", pages 85–86, is reported that

> "The wording of the Balfour Declaration came from the British Foreign Office, but the text had been revised in the Zionists' offices in America as well as England. The Balfour Declaration was made in the form in which the Zionists desired it."

For the most accurate account of this tale of international bribery against the background of a world war, I must turn to "The Realities of

American-Palestine Relations". By Frank E. Manuel, Public Affairs Press, 1949. On page 116, Manuel says,

> "Wilson's interest in Zionism was being slowly nurtured by Louis Brandeis, one of the men who stood closest to him in the early years of the Administration and who became the key figure in future American intervention in Palestine."

On page 117,

> "Brandeis was not a man of half-measures. 'Zionist affairs are the really important things in life now,' he wrote his brother Alfred on April 25, 1915. He thrust aside arguments about dual allegiances and proclaimed categorically that loyalty to America demanded that each American Jew become a Zionist."

Here was a reasoning process worthy of being enshrined on the Supreme Court. Loyalty to America demanded that its citizens embrace an alien philosophy, which took precedence over American ideals. It is unfortunate that most of Brandeis' more violent letters preaching Zionism have been called in and destroyed.

On page 136, Manuel tells us that,

> "Salonika Jews played a role in the uprising of the Young Turks, and the Minister of Finance Djavid was a Jew by race though a Mohammedan by religion."

Thus Jew considers another Jew as still a Jew even though he has embraced a different religion. Should a Christian refer to a Jew as a Jew after becoming a Mohammedan or whatever religion is necessary for him to adopt in order to get ahead in the world, it would be rank anti-Semitism.

On page 154, speaking of the First World War, Manuel says,

> "The American State Department began to use the outrages against the Jews in a psychological warfare offensive. At first they had a limited objective, concentrating on the moral of the Jews in Austria and Germany. With this aim in mind they discreetly suggested to Britain that the facts about the Palestine atrocities be communicated to the Jews of the Central Powers through the Jews in neutral countries like Switzerland."

Manuel noted that our State Department for many years had follows a distinctly anti-Palestine policy, but under Wilson all this was changed.

It should be unnecessary to add to Manuel's observation the fact that the State Department, until the unhappy advent of Wilson the most respected of the Government agencies, soon went to seed, and became filled with various foreign-born species of radicals, a process which culminated in its systematic reorganization as a Communist cell under Roosevelt from 1933 to 1945.

On page 160, Manuel tells us that,

> "During the years 1916 and 1917, members of the British War Cabinet represented by their Director for Near Eastern Affairs, Sir Mark Sykes, and English Zionists, grouped around Dr. Chaim Weizmann, an émigré from Russia then lecturer in Chemistry at the University of Manchester. During the War American Zionists grouped around Brandeis were kept informed of the progress of the London talks between Zionists and the British War Cabinet. They accepted Weizmann's de facto leadership in the negotiations, even though he had no official status on the Executive of the World Zionist Organization. Prior to 1917, this American support bestowed upon Weizmann great worth in the eyes of the British hoping for the participation of the United States in the war; even after America's entry the development of enthusiasm in the United States for the European War was still a major concern of British leaders. Lloyd George, who was Prime Minister at the time, testified before the Royal Commission in 1937 that stimulating the war effort of American Jews was one of the major motives which, during a harrowing period in the European War, actuated members of the cabinet in casting their votes for the Balfour Declaration. T. E. Lawrence refers to the Balfour Declaration as payment for the support of American Jews and Russian revolutionaries."

Paul Emden has pointed out that Weizmann's power in Zionism came from his support by Mond and Melchett of Imperial Chemical, for whom he had developed a highly profitable poison gas.

Manuel also quotes Rabbi Wise as saying that in June, 1917, President Wilson told him that the Jews and the Armenians were two nations certain to be reborn after the war. This statement is also printed in slightly different form in the May 5, 1920 issue of the Zionist Bulletin:

> "At a meeting held on Sunday May 2, in New York, Rabbi Stephen Wise said that shortly before the United States entered the war, President Wilson told him that two lands should never go back to

the Mohammedan Apache, Christian Armenia, and Jewish Palestine."

Christian Armenia is at the present writing a highly industrialized state of atheist Russia, but Jewish Palestine, we are happy to report, is more Jewish than ever.

On page 166, Manuel tells us that,

> "During his trip to the United States in May, 1917, Balfour had discussed Zionism and its prospects with Brandeis. In one of his private talks with Wilson, Balfour informed the President as a 'personal' not an official capacity, of secret treaties among the Allies respecting Palestine. On May 15, Brandeis cabled Louis de Rothschild in London that he had had a satisfactory talk with Balfour and with the President, but that this news was not for publication. Whatever discussions about a Jewish Palestine went on were arranged directly between members of the Brandeis group and the President, or through the intermediary of Col. House, without the knowledge of Secretary of State Lansing. It was not unusual for Wilson to formulate international policy without consulting his Secretary of State."

This was a precedent earnestly followed by Wilson's understudy, Franklin Roosevelt. It has been pointed out that Roosevelt's Secretary of Sate Hull often did not know what our policy on a certain question was until he read Eugene Meyer's Washington Post, which always received advance news on foreign policy from Roosevelt. Treated with such ignominy, the decent members of the State Department got out and left it to Roosevelt and his Communist proteges, Currie, Lattimore, and Hiss.

"The Realities of American-Palestine Relations" includes one of the extremely absorbing aspects of history which the Marxist party-line historians prefer to ignore. On page 170, we find that,

> "Edelman learned that the Zionists had even tried to bargain with the Vatican, offering to use Jewish financial and political influence to arrange for Vatican representation at the Peace Conference in exchange for Catholic support of the Zionist program. On February 13, 1918, British Intelligence prepared a Memorandum on the Attitudes of Enemy Governments towards Zionism, which outlined the Karasso Scheme, a competitive bid by the Turks at German instigation to grant certain autonomous rights to the Jews of Palestine. The memo concluded that British Zionist policy still had

a distinct edge over Turkish and German attempts to woo the Jewries of the world."

How the Jews must have laughed to see the great nations of the East and of the West rushing forward with proposals to win their favor. After centuries of ghetto life, this must have been balm of Gilead to the wounded Hebrew spirit.

Manuel tells us on page 168 that,

"Earlier in the year House had written ecstatically to Rabbi Wise, 'I hope the dream we have may soon become a reality.' For the President's Zionist friends Col. House had always a pleasant mien."

The trade union movement came to power in the democracies at the same time as the rise of Communism and Zionism. Dubinsky took hundreds of thousands of dollars from the helpless workers in the garment unions, and sent it to Palestine. Arthur Creech Jones, Under Secretary of State of Britain, wrote in "British Labor and Zionism",

"For many years I have been very closely associated with the Zionist movement in Britain."

CHAPTER 9

L ike the prophets of Zionism, the exponents of Communism for many years had been looking forward to a world war as their opportunity to seize power in many countries. The Marxist dialectic had been preached for decades that a universal conflict would be the signal for the workers of the world to refuse to fight each other, to throw down their arms, and to turn upon their capitalist oppressors. In 1914, however, at the crucial moment the workers of the world were still influence by such old-fashioned concepts as race and nationality, and the Communist resolved to burrow into the educational systems of all countries to eradicate these heretical beliefs. Meanwhile, the First World War was an excellent chance to put into effect some of their ideas of totalitarian state control over the people. The rationing techniques and other police state methods directed by Bernard Baruch in America and by Max Warburg in Germany provided good training for the bureaucracy of the future World Socialist State.

Political changes are expensive. Sometimes they are costly in lives, sometimes they cost only property, but always they are costly in money. Therefore, it has ever been the task of the money lords to anticipate and control political movements which have a potential success. An investment in a new political movement is both insurance on present property and a speculation on acquiring more. In "The Federal Reserve", I described the manner in which the reform movement in the United States was bought out and corrupted in the early years of the twentieth century.

Since Communism front ally attacked the princes of finance and property, the more progressive of those princes became the chief fund-raisers for the new movement, and of these princes the lords of the House of Rothschild led all the rest. The task of supplying capital for the Communist agitators fell to the firm of Kuhn, Loeb Co. New York, and M. M. Warburg Co. of Hamburg, Germany.

A party which attacks bankers can be used by one banker to subordinate and control his rivals, and, in effect, this is what the Rothschilds did with Communism. For all his ranting, Hitler made no changes in the banking system of Germany from 1933 to 1945.

At its inception, the Communist Party was an evening discussion group of French workers in Paris, a club similar to the Juntos begun in this country by Benjamin Franklin, and in every way typical of the enlightened and self-questioning aftermath of the eighteenth century rationalists. Into this group came the embittered and disowned son of a Frankfort banker, Karl Marx. Marx was disgusted with capitalism, with Judaism, with his wife, and with society in general. Indeed, no one has yet discovered anything which pleased him. This disgruntled psychopath found in the French workmen's group a chance to spread out his discontent, and, by setting them at each other's throats, he soon became the leader of the workmen's discussions. The technique of divide and conquer had had its first Communist success.

A second Marxist technique was soon invoked in Paris, the outpouring of bitter and hysterical invective towards anyone who criticized the leader. This was a development of Marx' paranoiac belief that the rear must be secured, which Lenin invoked by concluding the war with Germany in 1917 as soon as the Bolsheviks seized power.

Marx was soon joined in Paris by an old acquaintance, the never-do-well son of a German manufacturer, one Friedrich Engels. An indolent anthropologist and ideological revolutionist, Engels had made prolonged studies of the history of the family as a social group. He had determined that the family must be abolished, which intrigued Marx, for this meant that the State could assume complete control over the child. In 1848, Marx and Engels published a Communist Manifesto, a program of ten points. Point Two of this program, a heavy of graduated income tax, was signed into the law of the United States by President Woodrow Wilson, who also signed on December 23, 1913, the Federal Reserve Act, which fulfilled Point Five of the Communist Manifesto, calling for a centralized State Bank. The other points were put into effect by Franklin Roosevelt during the 1930s, camouflage under his measures for "social security".

The Communist movement was largely ignored in Europe for many years, except by social misfits of the lunatic fringe, until the First Zionists Congress at Basle, Switzerland on August 29, 1897. Two hundred and six delegates came from all over the world to hear Theodor

Herzl lay down his program. Within a matter of months after this meeting, the Communists began a hectic program of expansion, with plenty of funds. Although Marxism was mainly concerned with the problems of the modern industrial state, it was Russia, the least industrialized member of the European community, which became its prime target. This was because Russia had the world's largest Jewish population, and the historical unrest of that minority has always been fertile ground for any revolutionary movement. Also, the Warburgs and the Rothschilds had been pouring capital into Russia in the last half of the nineteenth century, financing the building of railroads and factories, and at the turn of the century, Russia was an economic colony controlled by Frankfort bankers. Her oilfields were divided between the Nobels and the Rothschilds, Kalonymous Wolf Wissotsky was known as the Russian Tea King, and Baron Guinzburg, the patron of Litvinoff, had obtained a monopoly on sugar. The aristocracy of Russia was well aware that their rule was threatened by the rise of a new trust aristocracy, but they had no answer to the question "Whither Russia?"

Communism is trust government. This aspect of the present political system of Russia has been given the silent treatment by our economists, because a parallel development has been occurring in the United States. In Russia there is a Gold Trust, a Steel Trust, etc. and the heads of these trusts are the real powers in the Soviet Government. The problems of public administration are handled by designated public officials, who have a direct authority over Russian citizens, but only a constitutional authority over the trusts. Such constitutional authority, as Americans have learned to their sorrow, is a luxury to be invoked only at the pleasure of those who have power.

Of the role played by Kuhn, Loeb Co. in the Communist Revolution in Russia, there is considerable documentation. A United States Naval Secret Service Report of December 12, 1918, identified Paul Warburg as one who had handled large sums of money for Lenin and Trotsky.

Cholly Knickerbocker, society columnist syndicated in many papers, wrote in his column of Feb. 3, 1949, appearing in the Hearst chain,

> "Today it is estimated even by Jacob Schiff's grandson, John Schiff, a prominent member of New York society, that the old man sank about $20 million for the final triumph of Bolshevism in Russia."

This grandson of the financier of the Russian Revolution is now President of the Boy Scouts of America, which has recently been criticized for its Communist infiltration.

Another member of Kuhn, Loeb, Otto Kahn, born in Mannheim, Germany, with the Deutsch Bank in Berlin and with Speyer Brothers in London before he came to the United States, became a partner of Kuhn, Loeb, in 1897. He is regarded with a peculiar reverence in Russia today. Nobody has ever been able to find out what country or countries could, if they wished, claim him as a citizen. The journalist Hannen Swaffer wrote in the *London Daily Herald* of April 2, 1934,

> "I knew Otto Kahn, the multi-millionaire, for many years. I knew him when he was a patriotic German. I knew him when he was a patriotic Briton. I knew him when he was a patriotic American. Naturally, when he wanted to enter the House of Commons, he joined the 'patriotic' party."

The English diplomat, Lord D'Abernon, wrote in his "Memoirs" that Kahn's brother-in-law, Herr Felix Deutsch, was the head of the German Electric Trust, A.E.G., which had financed the Bolshevik revolutionist Krassin, and with which Walter Rathenau had been associated before his assassination. After the mark inflation of 1923, A.E.G. fell into the hands of Bernard Baruch, whose International General Electric Corporation, under Gerard Swope, continued to control A.E.G. throughout the Hitler regime. Lord D'Abernon also claimed that Otto Kahn's house was a meeting place for Bolshevik agents.

The French newspaper *Figaro*, in its issue of June, 1931, described the magnificent treatment accorded Mrs. Otto Kahn when she visited Russia that month. She was acclaimed as visiting royalty, troops of the Red Army line the road at present arms as she entered Moscow, and the highest officials of the Soviet Government vied with each other in doing her honor. A grand diplomatic dinner was given her, and several brilliant diplomatic receptions enlivened the usually dull social season in Moscow. Notice was thereby given Europe that Communism too had its international aristocracy, whose members claimed for themselves the graces and airs of the lords and ladies whom they had murdered.

On the occasion of Mrs. Otto Kahn's subsequent visit to Russia, the *London Star* noted on July 23, 1935,

> "After her visit to Russia a few years ago, a sinister political significance was alleged by a French newspaper. The truth is that

Mrs. Kahn is interested in Russia, and when she goes to Leningrad is officially welcomed by the great Stalin himself."

Col. Ely Garrison, in his book "Roosevelt, Wilson, and the Federal Reserve Act", says that Max Warburg met the Russian minister Protopopoff in Stockholm in February of 1917 to complete plans for the Revolution. For some reason which he does not disclose, Leon Trotsky goes out of his way to deny that Kuhn, Loeb, Co. had anything to do with the Russian Revolution. This statement, which appears in Trotsky's "History of the Russian Revolution", is a direct contradiction of many newspapers and periodicals which reported the facts, among them, the *New York Times*, which, in its issue of March 24, 1917, presented a front-page story on the mass meeting of the Friends of Russian Freedom the previous evening at Carnegie Hall in New York City. This meeting was called to celebrate the revolution in Russia, and was presided over by Rabbi Wise, who divided his time equally between Zionism and Communism. It was a tumultuous and joyous affair, at which it was difficult to keep order. The principal speaker was George Kennan, who told his excited audience how he had distributed tons of Communist literature to Russian officers held prisoner by the Japanese in 1905. "That literature", he said, "was paid for through the generosity of a man whom you all know and love, Jacob Schiff." Kennan then read a telegram from Jacob Schiff, sent from White Sulphur Springs, West Virginia, where Schiff was taking the waters at an expensive resort. The telegram expressed Mr. Schiff's joy at the occurrence of the event for which they had striven so long, and sincerely regretted that he was unable to be there with them.

The man on the front page of the *New York Times*, George Kennan, was to die before his namesake, protégé, and nephew was appointed U.S. Ambassador to Russia. *Who's Who in America*, 1922-23, lists George Kennan as manager of the Western Union office in Cincinnati during the Civil War, went to Siberia as explorer and telegraphic engineer in 1965, was superintendent of the construction of the Russo-American Telegraph Line from 1866-68, manager of the Washington office of the Associated Press from 1877-86, investigated the Russian exile system in Siberia from 1885-86, covered the Russo-Japanese War for Outlook Magazine in 1905, author of "E. H. Harriman's Far Eastern Relations," and a two-volume biography of E. H. Harriman.

Harriman was Jacob Schiff's front man for Kuhn, Loeb's acquisition of the Union Pacific railroad and other properties. As previously mentioned, Kuhn, Loeb controlled Western Union, which in turn controlled the Associated Press. What George Kennan did not put into *Who's Who* was the fact that he had been Jacob Schiff's personal agent in Russia from 1885 to 1916, after he had proven his loyalty to Kuhn, Loeb in the Washington office of the Associated Press. He made numerous trips to Russia for Schiff, handled large sums of money which he delivered to revolutionary groups in Russia as it was needed, and even put himself on record in the *New York Times* as having been Schiff's emissary on a Communist mission.

His nephew, George Kennan, was well-thought-of in Russia, and it is small wonder that the news of his appointment was noted by a headline in the Washington, D.C. Evening Star, December 26, 1951, "Russia Approves Nomination of Kennan as Ambassador".

The inside story of the international Communist Party from the year of the Zionist Congress, 1897, to the year of their success in Russia, 1917, is the history of the power of money to corrupt and overthrow popular governments. Feudal though he was, the Czar of Russia was deeply loved by his subjects, and the Communists brutally murdered him soon after their seizure of power, for they knew that as long as he lived, their revolutionary conspiracy had little chance of retaining its victory.

In 1905, the Communist nearly brought off their revolution in Russia. They failed because they had not prepared themselves for power, rather than because of the concerted opposition of the Czar's Government. The influence of German money in Russia had divided the country so that the Czar really never ruled after 1900. He held power in a half-world of court intrigue in St. Petersburg which had little connection with what was going on in the rest of the country. The wreckers, left to their own devices, were able to build the background for the October Revolution, and one of these saboteurs was Maxim Litvinoff. The later appeared in those glorious days of the Russo-American coalition, when Zionists and Communists all over the world had everything they wanted from the American people, and still they were not satisfied. American boys were being slaughtered on farflung battlefields to advance the imperialist dreams of Joseph Stalin and the vision of world empire which haunted Chaim Weizmann, but, so long as the American Republic remained as a political entity, Stalin and Weizmann would be discontent.

Litvinoff, says Pope, was born Meer Wallach, son of Moses Wallach and Anna Perlo. In 1881 his father was thrown into prison for conspiring with foreign elements who were hostile to Russia. Although

Pope does not identify them, we can imagine what these foreign elements were. Young Wallach's incipient revolutionary tendencies were encouraged by the Russian Sugar King, Baron Guinzburg, who made him manager of one of his factories, and then sent him to Great Britain. Here, Wallach was introduced to Lenin in the British Museum by one Blumenfeld.

Pope tells us that the guns for the 1905 Revolution were provided by Schroeder Co. of Germany. Wallach, now Litvinoff, had married Ivy Low, niece of the English journalists, Sir Sidney and Sir Morris Low.

Another mysterious figure in the early days of world Communism was one Ashberg. The *London Evening Star* of September 6, 1948, described this man as follows,

> "There was recently a visit by Mr. Ashberg at a secret meeting in Switzerland with Swiss Government officials. Diplomatic circles describe Mr. Ashberg as the Sovied banker who advanced large sums to Lenin and Trotsky in 1917. At the time of the revolution Mr. Ashberg gave Trotsky money from the Nya Banken of Stockholm to equip the first unit of the Red Army."

Mr. Ashberg has been one of the four of five top people in the Soviet Government, although his name has not appeared in the world press a dozen times in the last thirty years. The most recent occasion in which his name was kept out of print involved his attempt to get a permit to travel in the U.S. Zone of Germany in 1950. Even Assistant High Commissioner Benjamin Buttenweiser of Kuhn, Loeb Co. didn't dare issue such a permit, and Ashberg had to be content with sending his emissaries into our zone.

The background of the Russian Revolution of 1917 reads like a cheap novel. The bankers Ashberg, Warburg, and Schiff, ordinarily the most cautious of men with their investments for years had been handing out funds to undistinguished rabble which roamed about Europe with vague dreams of establishing a Communist State in Russia. Often, by the merest chance, Lenin and Trotsky missed being imprisoned for years in one country or another, but, had this occurred, the bankers would have written them off and gotten someone else, for there were plenty like them in Europe. They could be picked up on the waterfront of any big seaport, or in the slums of any industrial city.

At least once, a high Government official saved Trotsky from prison. In 1916, Trotsky, born Lev Bronstein, was thrown into prison in

Halifax, Nova Scotia, for inciting to riot. He was on his way to New York for a final conference with Warburg and Schiff before re-embarking for Europe with the East Side oiled-hair contingent which was to be the Parliament of the new Russia. Frantic telegrams were exchanged between New York and London, and the pitiful creation of Rufus Isaacs, Prime Minister Lloyd George, wired a direct executive order to the Halifax authorities commanding them to release Trotsky and send him on his way. It is not too much to say that this order changed the political complexion of the world as we know it. Trotsky trained and led the troops of the Red Army whose guns at a critical moment made possible the seizure of the Ministries in the October Revolution.

This amazing cooperation of important officials marked the slow progress of the homeless revolutionaries across warring Europe to their goal. Vernadsky, in his "Life of Lenin, the Red Dictator", Yale University Press, 1931, page 140,

> "In the autumn of 1915 the German Russian Social Democrat Parvus (Israel Lazarevitch) who had formerly been active in the Revolution of 1905, announced in the paper published by him in Berlin 'The Bell' his mission 'to serve as an intellectual link between the armed Germans and the revolutionary Russian proletariat."

On page 151, Vernadsky says,

> "During the war Helphand Parvus was engaged in furnishing supplies to the German armies in huge quantities, and so considerable amounts of money passed through his hands."

On page 155, Vernardsky tells us that,

> "A railway car in which were Lenin, Mertov, and other exiles was attached to the train leaving for Germany from Switzerland on April 8, 1917. On April 13, Lenin embarked on the steamer sailing from Sassnotz to Sweden. So the trip through Germany took at least four days."

Because of his high contacts with the military authorities, Parvus was given the delicate task of handling the military clearance for Lenin's car through wartime Germany. When Lenin reached Russia, the Kerensky Government at once proclaimed him an outlaw, and he went into hiding. While the Provisional Government floundered along, Lenin remained a fugitive and perfected his plans for the October Revolution. In

September, 1917, he published an article "The Threatening Catastrophe", outlining his plans for setting up a totalitarian state. This article rallied the radicals around him. Trotsky arrived with Ashberg's money to equip the Red Army, Stalin assured the support of Russian Jewry, which he had been organizing through the years Lenin and Trotsky were wandering over Europe, and the stage was set for the most unscrupulous band of men in modern history.

The October Revolution in Russia was a seizure of power characterized by little fighting or bloodshed. Trotsky tells us that few of the street-cars stopped running that day. A group of men who knew what to do occupied the State Bank, the Ministry of Propaganda, the Telephone Agency, and the Telegraph Agency; that was all that needed to be done.

It was after the October Revolution was consummated that the bloodshed started. Lenin, Trotsky, and Stalin were determined to hold their power, and they did this by exterminating anybody who could offer any competition. After wiping out all their potential opponents, they started in on each other, a gory process which ended with Stalin as the lone survivor of the October Revolution.

The most sordid event in the program of planned mass murder was the cooperation of the Jewish peers of England with the brutal slaughter of the Czar, his wife, and little daughters, in Ekaterinburg. None of the revolutionists felt secure as long as the Czar was alive. Lenin was well aware of the reverence felt by the Russian peasant for the "Little Father of all the Russias". Many diplomats in America and England knew Lenin's intention, and they tried to save the Czar and his family, only to meet a stone wall in their own governments. Congressman Louis T. MacFadden of the United States, Wickham Steed, editor of the *London Times*, and Sir George Buchanan, British Ambassador to Russia, were among those who left us records of their attempts to save the Czar and how they were thwarted.

At the first onset of the revolutionists, Prime Minister Lloyd George extended an invitation on March 23, 1917, to the Czar and his family to seek asylum in Britain. The Czar was a cousin of the British Royal Family. The story of how Lloyd George was forced to rescind this invitation upon pressure from Sir Herbert Samuel and Rufus Isaacs Lord Reading, is told in Buchanan's daughter's book, "Dislocation of an Empire", and corroborated by Kerensky's "Murder of the Romanov", in 1935. The British Royal Family could not protest, and mutely waited until their cousins were massacred by the revolutionaries. In a hundred years of the Rothschild dynasty, Britain had come a long way down.

In a special interview given to a *New York Times* reporter on March 19, 1917, the prominent Zionist lawyer Louis Marshall hailed the Russia Revolution as the greatest world event since the French Revolution. This was followed by the celebration of Rabbi Wise, George Kennan, and the other Friends of Russian Freedom in Carnegie Hall.

President Woodrow Wilson greeted the revolutionists on the floor of Congress on April 2, 1917, with the statement,

"Here is a fit partner for a league of honor."

However, his open-mouthed admiration for the terrorist leaders of Russia was not shared by the country at large, and Kuhn, Loeb had to wait sixteen years for the election of Franklin Roosevelt before they could gain official recognition from the United States for their fair-haired child, Communist Russia.

Wilson also hailed the Russian Revolution as a triumph of freedom. How he could make this statement of an event whereby a nation lost its native government and was given over to the ruthless tyranny of an alien minority is difficult to understand, since he was well-acquainted with the facts.

One of the most peculiar episodes in American history inadvertently came to light, and was promptly closed again, in the Congressional Hearings On Russian Bonds, 1919, Library of Congress listing HJ 8714.U5. These Hearings contain the financial statement of Woodrow Wilson's expenditure of the $100,000,000 voted him by the War Congress as a Special War Fund. The statement, given by his secretary, Joseph Tumulty, also was recorded in the Congressional Record of September 2, 1919. The amounts are given in round figures, and contain items totalling twenty million dollars which was spent in Russia by Elihu Root's Special Mission to Russia in 1918.

This mission was one of the dark pages of our history. The Leninists had squandered their funds, and they needed dollars to stabilize their rule. To whom should they turn, but their powerful friend in the White House, Woodrow Wilson? He dispatched Elihu Root, Kuhn Loeb's legal counsel and former Secretary of State, at once with $20 million of his Special War Fund for the Leninists. Although there was some grumbling in Washington that the taxpayers' money should be given to the world's most famous revolutionary, it was a democratic procedure. Congress had voted Wilson the money to spend as he saw fit, and what could be more important than the Russian Revolution?

Another gentleman who has never been given sufficient credit for his support of the Leninist Government in its crucial hour is the late Col. Raymond Robins, head of the Red Cross Mission to Russia in 1917 and 1918. Under Henry P. Davison, partner of J.P. Morgan Co. the Red Cross raised $370 million in cash during the First World War. Robins was in Russia with millions of that money when Lenin needed it, as admirably documented by Ferdinand Lundberg in "America's Sixty Families", as well as by Kahn and Seghers in "The Great Conspiracy Against Russia", 1946.

Lenin, Trotsky, and Stalin knew how to attain power by bombs and by ideas. They successfully used both in the long years of their march to victory, but revolution had to come to and end sometime, and Stalin was the only one stable enough for administrative work. The hysterical intellectual Trotsky and the neurotic rabblerouser Lenin, were of little use after the dust settled in Russia. Stalin employed Trotsky's military ambitions to build up the Red Army, and Lenin's talents as an orator served to put across some of the more important items at the early Soviet Congresses, but when these things were done, it was seen that Stalin was giving the orders to the Soviets. It was not long before Stalin decided that Lenin would be of more use to Russia dead. Trotsky directly accuses Stalin of slowly poisoning Lenin to death, and there is no reason to doubt it. The Communists have been known for years to employ drugs and poisons to attain their ends, notably in the Cardinal Mindszenty case. At any rate, Lenin mysteriously withered and died, and Trotsky saw the handwriting on the wall, and escaped to the Black Sea. So great was his terror that he dared not come back for Lenin's funeral, and in the eyes of the Soviet leaders this meant that his power was ended.

Nevertheless, Trotsky was not to be gotten rid of so easily. He had been one of the Big Three, and he controlled the Red Army. Stalin had the Soviets firmly in his power, and he foiled Trotsky's petty intrigues one after another, until Trotsky gave up and fled to the Island of Prinkipo, where he received notice of his banishment from Russia. Thus he began that strange trek from continent to continent which ended in 1940 in Mexico with an axe in his skull. Always well-financed, Trotsky travelled with a sizeable entourage, causing great controversy wherever he landed. His brief stay in Norway, which offered him refuge in 1937, had its effect on history, for Norway's Minister of Justice, if he deserved the term, was Trygve Lie. Stalin expressed his displeasure at having Trotsky harbored so close to Russia, and Lie, who was identified by Trotsky as a former member of the Communist International, readily expelled the homeless revolutionary. Lie was finally rewarded for this good deed by being presented with the Secretary-General/Ship of the United Nations.

There was a considerable outcry by diplomatic and political leaders in Europe who knew the background of the Communists. Many of them were not slow to stand up and express their feelings, and of these one the most outspoken was Senator M. Gaudin de Villaine, who spoke in the Senate of France on May, 13, 1919, as follows,

> "The Russian Revolution and the Great War of 1914–1918 are only phases of the supreme mobilization of the cosmopolitan powers of money, and this supreme crusade of Gold against the Christians is nothing more or less than the furious aspiration of the Jew for domination of the world. It is the High Jewish Bank which has fomented in Russia the Revolution prepared by the Kerensky and finally perpetuated by the Lenins, Trotskys, and Sobelsohns, as was yesterday the Communist coup d'État in Hungary, for Bolshevism is nothing but a Talmudic upheaval. The Russian Revolution was a Jewish Revolution, supported by Germany, the cradle of modern universal Jewry, and the Bolsheviks, the executioners of the bloody Russian agony, are all, more or less, of the race of Judas. Journals the least suspect of antisemitism have recognized this fact. By a combination of Big Capital and Bolshevism, Judaism is getting ready to conquer the world—such is the prevision of a German journal, the *Deutsche Tagezeitung,* which writes, 'With the possible exception of Lenin, Bolshevism is directed by Jews'. In whatever country it is found, revolution reinforced Jewish influence. The Jews are exploiting with adroit vigor the Bolshevik anarchy. When Revolutionary Russia capitulated to Germany, Germany made it give up Russian gold. Why since the Armistice have we not taken the same precautions? In view of Spartacist menaces, the gold of the German banks was collected at Frankfurt. Always the same mysterious influences! Frankfurt! This is the Sacred Ghetto, where there still exists the old and leprous hovel with the sign of the Red Shield! (Rothschild)"

French newspapers reported that at the conclusion of this speech the French Senate dissolved in a tremendous uproar, such a melee as all the turmoil of the War had not been able to cause in that legislative body. The speech was ignored by the international news services, and was not known in England or in America. This was the last notable public utterance of Senator Villaine.

Official documents of the United States Senate prove Senator Villaine's statements. U.S. Senate Document 62, 66th Congress, 1st session, presents hundreds of pages of testimony from American witnesses of the Russian Revolution which go further than the Senator's speech. Outraged and courageous Americans did not hesitate to place their lives in their hands by testifying as to the real forces at work in Russia. Rev. Charles A. Simons, Minister of the Methodist Episcopal Church of Petrograd from February, 1907, until October 6, 1918, testified on Feb. 12, 1919 before the Senate Committee on the Judiciary,

> "There were hundreds of agitators who followed in the trail of Trotsky-Bronstein, these having come over from the Lower East Side of New York. A number of us were impressed by the strong Yiddish element in this thing right from the start, and it soon became evident that more than half of the agitators in this socialist Bolshevik movement were Yiddish."

> SENATOR NELSON: Hebrews?

> SIMONS: They were Hebrews, apostate Jews. I do not want to say anything against Jews, as such. I am not in sympathy with the anti-Semitic movement, never have been, and do not ever expect to be. But I have a firm conviction that this thing is Yiddish, and that one of its bases is found in the East Side of New York.

> SENATOR NELSON: Trotsky came over from New York during that summer, did he not?

> SIMONS: He did. In December, 1918, under the Presidency of a man named Apfelbaum (Zinoviev), out of 388 members, only ten happened to be real Russians, with the exception possibly of one man who is a Negro from America, who calls himself Professor Gordon, and 265 of the Northern Commune Government that is sitting in the Old Smolny Institute came from the lower East Side of New York, 265 of them. I might mention this, that when the Bolsheviki came into power, all over Petrograd we at once had a predominance of Yiddish proclamations, big posters, and everything in Yiddish. It became very evident that that was now to be one of the great languages of Russia, and the real Russians, of course, did not take very kindly to it."

William Chapin Huntingdon, commercial attache of the U.S. Embassy in Petrograd, testified that,

> "The leaders of the movement, I should say, are about two-thirds Russian Jews. The Bolsheviks are internationalists, and they were not interested in the particular national ideals of Russia."

Not all of the American officials in Russia during the Revolution volunteered testimony at the Senate Hearings. Those who maintained a discreet silence stayed with the State Department and became highly favoured and important administrators, as well as being admitted to the Council on Foreign Relations. Such were Norman Armour, Secretary of the U.S. Embassy in Petrograd from 1917 to 1918, who was appointed Ambassador to Spain, and Dewit C. Poole, chargé d'affaires in Russia from 1917 to 1919, who was appointed head of the Foreign Nationalities Branch of the Office of Strategic Services from 1941 to 1945, and Chief of the Division of Russian Affairs of the State Department. He was Chairman of the Advisory Board of the School of Public Affairs at Princeton, and was appointed a member of the top-secret Mission to Germany in the spring of 1945. A member of the Institute of Pacific Relations as well as the Council On Foreign Relations, he is an editor of Bobbs-Merrill Publishing Co.

The Senate Hearing of 1919 contained hundreds of pages of sensational material, which should have been given the widest publicity because of the peril to our religion and to our Republic. Yet they were given the silent treatment by the press. Is there any reason to doubt who controls that press?

At the beginnings of theses Senate Hearings, President Woodrow Wilson, fearful of light being brought to bear upon the crucial role he had played in the success of the Bolsheviks, had a fit of hysteria, and telephoned Baruch that he intended to have the Hearings halted. Baruch, always the spine of the nervous weakling who is now enshrined as a great man, warned Wilson to do no such thing. He convinced Wilson that such an action would only draw attention to the Hearings, which were going to get the silent treatment, and so they did, so successfully that there are only two places in this country where they can be found.

The magazine, *Asia*, in its issue of March, 1920, commented that,

> "In all the Bolshevik institutions the heads are Jews. The Soviet Commissar for Elementary Education, Grunberg, can hardly speak

Russian. The Jews are successful in everything and obtain their ends. They know how to command and get complete submission. But they are proud and contemptuous towards everyone, which excites the people against them. At the present time there is a great national religious fervor among the Jews. They believe that the promised time of the rule of God's elect on earth is coming. They have connected Judaism with a universal revolution. They see in the spread of revolution the fulfilling of the Scripture: Though I make and end of all the nations whither I have scattered thee, yet will I not make end of thee."

The *American Hebrew*, in its issue of September 10, 1920, featured an editorial which was a warning and a threat to America, as follows,

"The Jew evolved capitalism with its working instrumentality, the banking system. One of the impressive phenomena of this impressive time is the revolt of the Jew against the Frankenstein which his own mind conceived and his own mind fashioned. That achievement, the Russian overthrow, destined to figure in history as the overshadowing result of the First World War, was largely the result of Jewish thinking, of Jewish discontent, of Jewish effort to reconstruct. The rapid emergence of the Russian Revolution from the destructive phase and its entrance into the constructive phase is a conspicuous expression of the constructive genius of Jewish discontent. What Jewish idealism and Jewish discontent have so powerfully contributed to accomplish in Russia, the same historic qualities of the Jewish mind and heart are tending to promote in other countries. Shall America, like the Russia of the Czars, overwhelm the Jew with the bitter and baseless reproach of being a destroyer, and thus put him in the position of an irreconcilable enemy? Or shall America avail itself of Jewish genius as it avails itself of the peculiar genius of every other race? That is the question for the American people to answer."

Yes, *American Hebrew*, that is the question for the American people to answer. Shall we accept the terrorism of your police state, or shall we defend the heritage of liberty and our fierce pride in the freedom of the individual which is the characteristic of our race?

The Russian paper, *On To Moscow*, carried an article in its issue of September, 1919, stating that,

"It should not be forgotten that the Jewish people, who for centuries were oppressed by kings and czars, are the real proletariat, the real internationale which has no country."

For further light on the Russian Revolution, we turn to the *Zionist Bulletin*, official publication of the World Zionist Organization. On Oct. 1, 1919, the *Zionist Bulletin* reported that,

> "Meir Grossman, member of the Zionist Central Committee and Jewish National Assembly in the Ukraine, stated that the majority of the Jewish people were behind the Zionists. The Jewish masses stood firmly behind the Zionist Organization. At the end of 1918 the elections in the Ukraine led to such Jewish successes that the administration of the central autonomous bodies had to pass over to the Zionists. The Jewish Committees, then, have won a great victory. We need not be troubled as to the future of Zionist Organization in Russia and in the Ukraine. It has outlived the dictatorship and the rule of violence of the Czars; it will find new ways and means to continue working for Palestine. The heroic deeds of the Jewish Communists will be recorded in the history of the Jewish people."

The Jewish Communists were quite frank in stating that they were working for Palestine. During the glorification of Marx, the ideological leader of political Zionism, Dr. Nathaniel Syrkin, has remained unknown to Gentile students. Syrkin, whose writings on Socialist Zionism and Nationalist Socialism at the turn of the century provided much of the government structure adopted by Russia in 1918, Germany in 1933, and Israel in 1950, published his definitive work, "Essays on Socialist Zionism", in 1898. The introduction to this work stated that,

> "To Syrkin, Socialism and Zionism were two aspects of the same thing-Jewish nationalism."

The history of the twentieth century bears out this statement. On page 15, Syrkin gives warning to those who oppose the coming world state,

> "At least one part of Ludwig Berne's famous saying that anti-Semites will in the future be candidates either for the workhouse or the insane asylum has been realized."

This was the impetus of the Jewish science of psychiatry, which analyzed opponents of Zionism as hopeless neurotics who must be confined for their own safety. At the same time, their criticism of the new world force could be discounted, because the author was out of his mind. Those opponents of Zionism who did not get a room in the asylum could be prevented from earning a living, and sent to the workhouse. Such is to be the fate of patriots the world over, until the new world power is strong enough to execute them openly.

"The Essays on Socialist Zionism" are very explicit as to the part the Jew is to play in twentieth century. Syrkin says,

> "The Jew must become the vanguard of Socialism. The Socialism of the Jew must truly become a Jewish Socialism... Zionism is a creature work the Jew, and is not in contradiction with the class struggle. Zionism must of necessity fuse with Socialism. Fusing with Socialism, Zionism can be raised to a great national passion."

These instructions, which have been carried out, explain Brandeis and Frankfurter to America, Trotsky and Apfelbaum to Russia, and Samuel and Isaacs to England.

One final poignant passage from Syrkin, the father of Socialist Zionism. On page 15 of the *Essays*, he says,

> "Anti-Semitism helps the Jews maintain their national solidarity."

Solidarity for many years has been a key rallying word in the world Communist movement.

CHAPTER 10

T he Communist Revolution in Russia materially benefitted one group more than any other, the members of the Jewish minority. The April Revolution was a convulsive and short-lived attempt to pull together the tottering government of the Czar, and Trotsky is correct when he describes it in his "History of the Russian Revolution" as no revolution at all. The October Revolution, however, which followed the April Revolution, was a genuine overthrow dedicated to the violent seizure of power by a determined and cohesive group. That that group was Jewish cannot be denied.

The *Chicago Jewish Forum* of Fall 1946, contains an article by Edward W. Jelenks, as follows,

> "Recognizing anti-Semitism as the most vicious and dangerous of chauvinistic outbursts, the Soviet leaders did not wait long after their ascending to power to put their ideas regarding free development of minorities into effect. On November 15, 1917, one week after the October Revolution, the Declaration of Rights Peoples of Russia was issued in the name of the Russian Republic by the Council of People's Commissars over the signatures of V. Ulyanov (Lenin) and J. Djugashvili (Stalin), who signed it as People's Commissar of Nationalities. The Red Army men were soon taught to consider anti-Semitism as a symbol of counter-revolution and to root out of their own ranks those guilty of this form of reaction. The War Commissariat maintained a special section for anti-pogrom propaganda. Lenin and Stalin were not satisfied with their formal statement of policy, and amplified their action by a special statute; Decree of the Council of People's Commissars on the Up-Rooting of the Anti-Semitic Movement: 'The Council of People's Commissars declares that the anti-Semitic movement and pogroms against the Jews are fatal to the interests of the workers and peasants revolutions, and calls upon the toiling people of Socialist Russia to fight this evil with all the means at their disposal. The Council of People's Commissars instructs all Soviet deputies to take

uncompromising measures, to tear the anti-Semitic movement out by the roots. Pogromists and pogrom-instigators are to be placed outside the law.' Chairman of People's Commissars V. Ulyanov (Lenin), August 9, 1918"

This order is also reprinted in its entirety in the September 1941 issue of *Jewish Voice*, a periodical published by the National Association of Jewish Communists in New York. The Soviet leaders, who did not hesitate to murder millions when it suited them, were especially concerned that not a single Jew was to be harmed in democratic Russia. The July-August 1941 issue of *Jewish Voice* contains an editorial entitled "Anti-Communism is Anti-Semitism", which seems to be the case.

Jewish Voice of June, 1941 contains an article, "The Renaissance of the Jews in the Soviet Union", by the Soviet economist L. Singer, reprinted from the Soviet Yiddish Quarterly Forepost, published in Birobidjan, the autonomous Jewish state in Russia. It is as follows,

> "In advanced branches of industry, such as metallurgy, Jews were rare. The great Socialist Revolution brought about a complete change in this respect. The statistics of the first Soviet census, in 1926, showed that vast transformations had already taken place among the Jewish people. The fulfillment of the First Stalinist Five Year Plan basically transforms the social composition of the Jewish population. The number of metal workers doubled and the number of chemical workers tripled. Over one-half of the Jewish workers in the Soviet Union are classified as highly qualified, or qualified, specialists."

Part 2 of Singer's article appeared in the July-August 1941 issue of *Jewish Voice*,

> "Jewish Soviet culture is growing national in form and Socialist in content. The Jewish intelligentsia of the Soviet Union is very intimately associated with the development of cultural life. During the past Five Year Plan alone the number of Jewish primary and secondary schools increased by 30%. As a result of the application of the Leninist-Stalinist national policy, the social reconstruction of the Jewish population was completed by the Second Five Year Plan."

Thus, from an official Communist publication, we learn that the Leninist-Stalinist policy had as its goal the social reconstruction of the Jewish population. This was splendid for the Jews, but what about the rest of the peoples of Russia? There is little information concerning their reconstruction.

The scholar Avrahm Yarmolinsky, America's leading authority on Russia, published in 1928 "The Jews and Other Minor Nationalities", Vanguard Press, one of a series called Studies of Soviet Russia, edited by Jerome Davis of Yale University, outgrowing from the desire of Kuhn, Loeb to explain the new democracy of Russia to the American people. Yarmolinsky's first sentence is striking:

> "The French Revolution proclaimed the liberty, the equality, the fraternity of all men; the Russian Revolution proclaimed the liberty, the equality, the fraternity of all peoples, that is, of peoples led by the workers and peasants. As long as the nations of the Soviet Union are loyal to the new social order, they are free to realize their separate potentialities... During the last half-century of its existence, the St. Petersburg administration pursued a narrow, coercive, illiberal policy which was bound to cause profound discontent among non-Russian elements of the population, particularly those bent upon maintaining a distinct group life of their own."

Thus, Yarmolinsky tells us that the non-Russian elements of the population were the ones who were discontented and fomented revolution. On page 3, he says,

> "The idea of a super-national state failed to take root in Russia (under the Czars). The intolerant aggressive nationalism of the administration increased, and under the last two Romanovs it was erected into a system."

Nationalism was the crime of the Czarist Government. Communist dialectic has always condemned nationalism, and promoted the super-national state. On page 17, Yarmolinsky says,

> "It was especially the Jews' participation in the liquor traffic, in the towns as well as in the villages, that brought upon them the accusation that they were ruining the peasantry."

On page 32, he tells us that,

> "In 1906 the Russian Zionists decided to supplement work for the restoration of Jewry in Palestine with a struggle for national rights in the Dispersion. In 1897, the year of the 1st Zionist Congress, a dozen people, representing the scattered groups of propaganda and

the trade unions, came together secretly in a room at Wilno and founded the General Jewish Workers Union, the Bund of Russia, Poland, and Lithuania, commonly styled the Bund."

From Pope's biography of Litvinoff, we learn that this Bund was the chief revolutionary agency in Czarist Russia.

Yarmolinsky observes on page 39 that,

"On August 23, 1915, the Czarist Government issued and order in which the phrase occurred, 'In view of the fact that the majority of Jews are suspected of participation in espionage'." We pointed out that the international news services were founded by Jews, and the relationship between the professions of journalism, espionage, and propaganda, are so close that they are synonymous terms."

On page 48, Yarmolinsky says of the Revolution,

"When the autocratic regime fell, the crash reverberated in Jewish ears as though all the bells of freedom were ringing. With a stroke of the pen the Provisional Government abolished the whole complex network of laws directed against Jews."

As Trotsky complains, however, the Provisional Government was not strong enough to implement these changes, and in the vacuum created by Kerensky's hesitancy, he and Lenin seized power. Their years of sullen intrigue in the capitals of Europe and their experiences as homeless revolutionaries had emphasized their tendencies toward destruction, and such tendencies were needed to bring about the turning upside down of the Russian social structure. What Lenin and Trotsky accomplished was not only the defeat but the annihilation of an entire governing class in a longrange plan of mass murder. A comparable event in the United States would be the execution of all business and government officials and schoolteachers in the towns and counties of our nation. That was the identical program put into action by the Communists in Spain during the Civil War of the 1930s.

Yarmolinsky notes on page 67 that,

"What is deadly to the Jewish trader is the development of consumers' and producers' cooperatives. Even before the war they were taking business away from the private trader."

This is of particular interest to Americans, because certain interests are waging an undeclared war against consumers' and producers' cooperatives in this country. Full-page ads have been appearing in the newspapers, urging the abolishment of or increased taxation of cooperatives. As the Jews rapidly increase their number in our retail trade, it can be seen that the cooperatives are their only real competition.

On page 79, Yarmolinsky writes that,

> "The law of 1847 allowed all jews to enter the agricultural class. Over 10,000 families registered as wishing to settle on the land, but because of their resistance of the kahals, only two hundred families made the move."

The Czarist Government tried to solve the Jewish problem peacefully, but the kahals, the Jewish elders, would not let them.

The contemporary Russian scene is described by Yarmolinsky on page 105,

> "Jewish soviets exist wherever there is a considerable Jewish group. In the Jewish soviets practically all the transactions, both oral and written are in Yiddish. It is the language of the sessions, of all instruments, and of the correspondence. In some cases, the soviets use Yiddish in their communications, so that the executive committees of some non-Jewish regional soviets have to maintain a special department to handle Jewish business. Last spring plans were underway for the establishment in Kiev of courses which would train clerks for the Jewish soviets. There are also a number of courts (36 in the Ukraine and 5 in White Russia) where the business is conducted entirely in Yiddish. Marriages, births, and deaths may be registered at the Government Bureau of Records in Yiddish. An inscription in Yiddish appears for the first time in history on the coat of arms of a State, namely on that of the White Russian Republic. Yiddish is also, of course, the language in which Jewish children get their schooling, and is also employed in a number of homes where Jewish children are cared for."

On page 110, Yarmolinsky tells of Jewish predominance in the Party,

> "The Communist rule among the Jews, as elsewhere, is the rule of a well-organized and purposeful minority. The members of the race who belong to the Party have been growing in number. On Oct. 1, 1926, the Communist Party of the Soviet Union counted over 47,000 Jewish members and candidates. The respective members for the Jewish membership of the Communist Union of Youth, a sort of

Bolshevik Boy Scout organization, were 100,000 as of December, 1926, and 125,000 on July 1, 1927."

On page 111, returning to the events of the revolution, we learn that,

"At the outbreak of the Bolshevik revolution there were groups of active Jewish Communists in Great Russia, chiefly in Moscow and Leningrad. On March 7, 1918, there appeared in Leningrad the initial issue of the first Yiddish Communist newspaper. A few months later it changed it place of publication to Moscow, and its title, *Der Wahrheit*, to the less literary *Der Emes*, under which it has been appearing ever since."

On page 112,

"By the end of the Civil War, the Jewish Sections of the Communist Party, where the former Bundists had found their places, were in sole possession of the field. The Jewish Communists were perhaps more intolerant than their Gentile comrades. The left wing of the Poale-Zion, known as the Jewish Communist Party and subscribing to the tenets of the Third Internationale, is allowed to work in the open."

On page 124, Yarmolinsky says,

"It must be borne in mind that the Yiddish schools form an integral part of the Sovied educational system, and are wholly supported by the State. There is a central Jewish Bureau in the Commissariat of Education, and Jewish instructors in the local bureaus. The largest collection of Jewish books is in the Central Jewish State Library of Kiev, which bears the name of Morris Winchewsky, the Russian-American poet and publicist who is the father of Socialist Litterature in Yiddish. The tenth anniversary of the revolution was marked by the opening at Odessa of a State Museum of Jewish Culture, named for 'grandfather' Mendele Mocher Sforim. The Jewish Section of the Institute of White Russian Culture came into being in 1925, and has already set up several commissions of inquiry into matters of literary, historical, and linguistic significance. Work has begun on an academic dictionary of Yiddish. Similar work is being done under the auspices of the Chair of Jewish Culture at the Ukrainian Academy of Sciences at Kiev. In 1925 almost as many Yiddish titles were published in the Soviet Union as in all the other countries taken together. During 1927 the number reached 294. By 1927 there were six Yiddish dailies in the Soviet Union, and periodicals were not lacking. One of the several Yiddish weeklies is gotten out by the

Central Commissariat of the Communist Party of the Ukraine. The Yiddish monthlies include an educational journal and a general review, the *Red World*, which is issued by the Ukrainian State Publications Board. As Jewish culture gains strength, the arts are bound to assert themselves."

Hollywood has proved that to Americans, Yarmolinsky makes an interesting statement on page 130.

"The social landslide was far less destructive to Jewish literature than it was to Russian, since the Yiddish authors had always written, not for the doomed middle class, but for the common people."

The phrase "the doomed middle class", is particularly illuminating. It is one of those rare instances where the Communist desires are nakedly exposed. They aim to eliminate entirely the intelligent middle class, and to create a two-class society, one class of the masses of workers and peasants leading a slave existence, and a small class of rulers, a self-perpetuating elite. On page 130, Yarmolinsky says,

"Assimilation is frowned upon on all sides. The Communists are working, as stated elsewhere, toward the consolidation of the Jewish nationality. The assimilation program is definitely rejected by the official policy of the Communist Party."

This is in exact accord with one of the two principles of the Zionist movement, which, according to Israel Cohen, is devoted to preventing assimilation and setting up a Jewish State. On page 136, Yarmolinsky says,

"At a conference of the Jewish Communist Sections a resolution was offered which indicated the possibility of assimilation for the Communists outside of the main Jewish centers. Its was objected to on the ground that it was a tactless move and one which would offend the people. The Jewish Soviet Republic envisaged by the orthodox Communists differs fundamentally from Herzl's polity in Zion. Within its local scope it would afford Russian Jewry a basis for a full national life. The Jewish Republic is a matter for the future. Unless all signs fail, the future will witness the rise of a distinct Jewish culture on Russian soil."

Page 136 continues,

"February of 1928 witnessed the appearance of a rabbinical periodical in Hebrew under the imprint of a Communist firm in

Moscow. It is perhaps too early to judge the results of the Russian Revolution, but it would seem that its chief effect upon the Jewish people is to have freed them not merely as individuals, but as a group having the potentialities of nationhood."

A further selection from the immense amount of evidence concerning the enormous direct and longrange benefits derived by Jewry from the Russian Revolution brings us to the Zionist Bulletin. In the issue of March 17, 1920 is the following item,

"The Weiner Morgenzeitung has received the first number of the Jewish newspaper Naschy Slowo, published in Harbin, Siberia by the Jewish democracy. The communist government has been democratized since April, 1919, and contains a large number of Zionists on its council. Reports of the suffering of Jewish fugitives in Siberia would seem to have been exaggerated, as most of them have found a means of livelihood. There is a Yiddish Culture League of Siberia, with branches in all the chief towns, which is very active. There have been frequent communications between the Jews of Siberia and America, where many of them propose to settle."

The issue of March 24, 1920 states that,

"A paper on Jewish literature in Russia under the Bolshevik regime was read by Mr. Efroikin at a conference of Jewish Literacy Men recently held in Vilna, Poland. A list of Jewish publications was read, concluding with the announcements that the Petrograd society Mefizeh Haskalah is preparing for the press a series of economics works in Yiddish, and the society Oze a series of medical works. More important than all these, however, is a projected Yiddish Encyclopaedia, for which the Commissariat of Popular Education is furnishing two million roubles."

The purpose of these Yiddish schools and Yiddish medical books and encyclopaedia was to gradually eliminate Russians from the Professions and close all but Yiddish universities, arriving at the entirely Jewish ruling class of officials and professional men which is inherent in the idea of Syrkin's Socialist Zionist World State.

Hamilton Fish Armstrong, director of the Council On Foreign Relations, writes on page 240 of his glowing praise of the Communist revolutionary Tito, "Tito and Goliath", Macmillan, 1951, that,

"So many Jews held office in the first Communist-dominated cabinet in Hungary that it was said that the one or two so-called

Christian members had been included in order to make sure that there might be someone to countersign decrees of execution on Saturdays."

Armstrong is correct in saying "so-called Christians", for no real Christian would be involved with the bloody mass-murderers of Jewish Communism.

CHAPTER 11

Because of the many striking parallels between those government techniques developed by the Franklin Roosevelt Administration and the program outlined by the Communist Manifesto of 1848, the Manifesto will be discussed in the Roosevelt chapter. An examination of the works of Lenin is more pertinent to the study of the Russian Revolution, for the October Revolution was the Leninist Revolution. In the 1935 edition of "The State and Revolution", published in English in Moscow, and written by Lenin in 1918, he quotes at great length from Friedrich Engels' "The Origin of the Family". On page 16, he quotes Engels as follows,

> "As against the ancient gentile organization, the primary distinguishing feature of the state is the division of the subjects of the state according to territory. Such a division seems natural to us, but it cost a prolonged struggle against the old form of gentile society."

Again and again Lenin and Marx stressed the importance of destroying the gentile society, which is based on the family. By wiping out family ties allegiances, the Communists hoped to set up a state of totally obedient subjects whose only loyalty would be to their rulers. They considered the parents as physical necessities for bringing the child into being, but demanded that the State have the child as soon as it was weaned.

This development in Russia has been accelerated by the Communist attack on religion. It is unfortunate that opponents of Communism in the English-speaking countries have not seen fit to employ Lenin's outspoken position on religion in their battle. A volume of his statements on religion was published by International Publishers, New York, the official publishers for the Communist Party of America, in 1933, the year that the party came out into the open here following the election of Roosevelt. The first sentence of the Introduction to Lenin's "Religion", follows,

> "Atheism is a natural and inseparable part of Marxism, of the theory and practice of scientific Socialism. Engels and Marx agreed 'All religious bodies without exception are to be treated by the state as private associations.'"

This meant that churches would no longer be tax-exempt, and they would have to show a profit to survive in a Communist State. It was the death-blow to the concession as the State had afforded religious bodies. The Introduction continues:

> "From the writings of Lenin the following four principles stand out as the most important: 1. Atheism is an integral part of Marxism. Consequently a class-conscious Marxist party must carry on in favour of atheism. 2. The demand for the complete separation of the church and the state, and the church and the school, must be made. Note: This is one of the constant points of agitation carried on by Eleanor Roosevelt in her daily newspaper column 'My Day'. She is satisfied with the atheist United Nations, to which she is delegate, because it operates without any religious influence or guidance whatever. 3. The winning-over of the proletariat is accomplished principally by dealing with their everyday economic and political interests; consequently the propaganda in favour of atheism must grow out of, and be carefully related to, the defense of these interests. (Note. In the recent controversy over whether the government should provide transportation to parochial schools for children, Eleanor Roosevelt in her column attacked the proposal on the ground that it placed an unwarranted tax burden upon citizens whose children did not go to parochial schools. Her arguments closely followed the official Marxist-Leninist line. However, she does not attack the Marxist income tax as an unwarranted burden upon the citizen.) 4. The final emancipation of the toiling masses from religion will occur only after the proletarian revolution, only in a Communist society. This however, is not a reason for postponing the propaganda for atheism. Rather does it emphasize its urgency in subordination to the general needs of the workers' class struggle."

This book also quotes from the Programme of the Communist Party in March, 1919, commenting that in the battle between the church and the state for men's minds, the workers have obtained and advance without revolution.

> "With regard to religion the Communist Party of the Soviet Union does not confine itself to the already decreed separation of church and state, and of the school and the church, i.e. measures advocated in the programmes of bourgeois democracy, where the mater has nowhere been consistently carried out owing to the diverse and actual ties which bind capitalism with religious property. The Communist Party of the Soviet Union is guided by the conviction that only the conscious and deliberate planning of all the social and economic activities of the masses will cause religion prejudices to die out."

The only religious prejudice in Russia was against the Jews, and that was mostly economic resentment of Jewish domination of the liquor industry, wholesale trade, and other large industries. There was some suspicion among the peasants of the mysterious rites of Judaism and the odd dress and behaviour of orthodox Jews, which caused tales of blood rites and ritual murder of Christian children in their religious orgies to be circulated.

Lenin's book, "Religion", on page 28, quotes the Communist Program of the Sixth World Congress,

> "One of the more important tasks of the cultural revolution affecting the wide masses is the task of systematically and unswervingly combating religion, the opium of the people. The proletarian government must withdraw all state support from the church, which is the agency of the former ruling class; it must prevent all church interference in state-organized educational affairs, and ruthlessly suppress the counter-revolutionary activity of the ecclesiastical organizations. At the same time, the proletarian state, while granting liberty of worship and abolishing the private position of the formerly dominant religion, carries on anti-religious propaganda with all the means at its command and reconstructs the whole of its educational work on the basis of scientific materialism."

The formerly dominant religion, Christianity, was the real target of the Jewish Communist Party. On page 7 of this volume, we find an Editorial Note on Marx's statement that "Religion is the opium of the People," as follows,

> "This aphorism was employed by Marx in his criticism of Hegel' Philosophy of Law. After the October Revolution it was engraved on the walls of the former City Hall in Moscow, opposite the famous

shrine of the Iberian Virgin Mother. This shrine has now been removed."

Yet the agent of the Straus family, Bardsley Ruml, treasurer of Macy's says, in *Fortune Magazine*, March, 1945, page 180 of his visit to Russia in 1936 that

"In Kazan, off the Intourist route, Mr. Ruml concluded that, from the splendid condition of a Byzantine church and its priest, the Kremlin did not propose to ignore the political possibilities of eastern orthodoxy."

Since few Americans are permitted to travel about Russia as they wish, we must accept Mr. Ruml's conclusion that all is well with religion in Russia with some reservation as to the source.

On page 14 of Lenin's "Religion", we find that

"Marxism is materialism. As such it is relentlessly opposed to religion as was the materialism of the Encyclopaedists of the 18th century... The fight against religion must not be limited or reduced to abstract, ideological preaching."

On page 18,

"The Marxist must be a materialist, i.e., an enemy of religion."

On page 17,

"If a priest comes to cooperate with us in our work—if he conscientiously performs party work, and does not oppose the party programme—we can accept him into the ranks of Social Democracy."

On page 20,

"Our fraction acted quite correctly when it declared from the Duma tribunal that religion is the opium of the people, and in this way they created a precedent which should serve as the basis for all speeches delivered by Russian Social-Democrat fraction in the Black Hundred Duma had to do was done with honor."

On page 32 and 33, Lenin makes a statement which has been followed by the leftwing intellectuals in New York for many years,

"We trust that the magazine which desires to be the organ of militant materialism will give our reading public reviews of atheist literature and in what relation particular books are generally suitable."

Elsewhere we will show how this has been done by the *New York Times* and *New York Herald Tribune* book reviews for the past thirty years. The American Communist does not have to go to the *Daily Worker* to find what books are recommended by the party. He has only to go to the Saturday Review of Literature or the above-named newspaper reviews.

Lenin's moral and religious views find their highest expression on page 48, from a speech delivered to the Third All-Russian Congress of the Young Communist League on October, 2, 1920.

"We deny all morality taken from superhuman or non-class conceptions. For us morality is subordinated to the interests of the proletarian class-struggle."

This statement appears again and again in Communist literature. It is drilled into young Communists, and explains the sexual activities of such Jewish Communist spies as Judith Coplon.

Lenin is a forceful and constant exponent of democracy. In "The State and Revolution", page 86, he states that,

"Democracy for the vast majority of the people means suppression by force, i.e. the exclusion from democracy of the exploiters and oppressors of the people—this is the change democracy undergoes during the transition from capitalism to communism."

Lenin and the Warburg intend democracy for everybody except those who oppose government by and for Kuhn, Loeb Co. Such opponents are guilty of oppressing the people, and, of course, they are guilty of anti-Semitism.

On page 96, Lenin writes,

"Democracy is of great importance for the working class in its struggle for freedom against the capitalists. Democracy means equality."

We find more of the same in the writings of James Paul Warburg.

In September of 1917, Lenin published an article, "The Threatening Catastrophe", reprinted in *Selected Works*, volume X, translated by J.

Fineberg, on page 185, Lenin outlines his plans for the seizure of financial power. These plans have been followed by the Labor Government of England by the Truman Socialism of the American postwar government, following the precedent of the Roosevelt Socialism of the 1930s. Lenin calls for

"1. Nationalization of the banks. Ownership of capital which is manipulated by the banks is not lost or changed when the banks are nationalized, and fused into one state bank, so that it is possible to reach a stage where the state knows whither and how, from where and at what time millions and billions are flowing. Only control over bank operation providing they are merged into one state bank will allow, simultaneously with other measures which can easily be put into effect, the actual levying of income tax without concealment of property and income. The state for the first time would be in a position to survey all the monetary operations, then control them, then to regulate economic life. FINALLY, to obtain millions and billions for large state operations, without paying the capitalist gentlemen sky-high commissions for their services. It would facilitate the nationalization of syndicates, abolition of commercial secrets, the nationalization of the insurance business, facilitate the control of and the compulsory organization of labor into unions, and the regulation of consumption. The nationalization of the banks would make circulation of checks compulsory by law for all the rich, and introduce the confiscation of property for concealing incomes. The five points of the desired program then, are nationalization of the banks, nationalization of the syndicates, the abolition of the commercial secrets, compel labor to join trade unions, and the compulsory organization of the population into consumer associations."

Lenin's program is the most vital page in all Communist literature for those who are interested in preserving the American Republic. Here is the inner dictum, the program which the NRA of Roosevelt and the Political Economic Planning of Moses Sieff in England, attempted to foist on the Anglo-Saxon citizens. These five points embrace all segments of the population, and give absolute control over all elements of society. The Labor Government of England proved that the ownership of capital is not affected by nationalization of the banks, when they nationalized the Bank of England. The stockholders continued to receive their dividends, and most important, the list of stockholders remained a secret.

The historical significance of this article is this: With the publication of this single statement, "The Threatening Catastrophe", Lenin assumed leadership of the Bolsheviki. Its announcement of a desperate determination to seize and hold absolute power rallied around Lenin the discontents of the April Revolution. For the October Revolution, Trotsky furnished the guns, courtesy of Ashberg, and Stalin assured Lenin the support of Russian Jewry. Vernadsky, in his *Life of Lenin*, points out that until the Russian Revolution and the advent of the Provisional Government, Lenin had never reached the public consciousness. Among the revolutionists themselves, he was but one of many nervous and eager opportunists in whom breath was sustained wholly by the lust for power over his fellow-men. It was the hesitancy of the Kerensky Government which created the necessary climate for the fanatical murderers of the Party, and made it possible for them to seize the machinery of government. And at this moment, what was the attitude of President Woodrow Wilson? Vernadsky quotes him on page 211. The President made a public statement in which he said,

> "The whole heart of the people of the United States is with the people of Russia in their attempt to free themselves forever from autocratic government and become the master of their own life."

This is the most cynical statement in our political literature. Woodrow Wilson knew that the native government of Russia was being overthrown by an alien minority, and he knew that the funds for that revolution came the same gold bank which had furnished him his campaign money. The following year, Wilson sent Lenin $20 million from the Special War Fund which the Congress had given him to pursue the war against Germany. Like his understudy, Franklin Roosevelt, Wilson never lost an opportunity to affirm publicly his faith in and admiration for the most vicious regime in modern history, the totalitarian dictatorship of Bolshevik Russia.

Lenin himself gives the explanation of his victory. In volume X of his *Selected Works*, translated by J. Fineberg, page 284, he wrote,

> "We achieved victory in Russia, and achieved it so easily, because we prepared for our victory during the imperialist war."

While Paul Warburg and the Federal Reserve Board avowedly were doing their best to prevent monetary stability in the United States, Lenin wrote, on page 324 of volume X,

"If we succeed in stabilizing the ruble for a long period, and then permanently, we shall have won."

Monetary stability is the test of all governments. The downfall of most revolutionary governments, including the classic example of the French Revolution, was the dreaded inflation of money pas the point where it was a useful medium of exchange. The banking brains behind Lenin, however, successfully guided the Communist government past the pitfalls of money.

Moscow itself continued to be an armed camp for many months after the October Revolution. In the official *Communist Life of Lenin*, by Kerzhentsev, page 244, is related the story of how the great dictator and his sister were stopped by bandits and their limousine taken from them on a main avenue of Moscow in January, 1919. As a symbol of their release from Czarism, the Bolsheviks had decreed that policemen should not wear uniforms. Consequently, anyone could hold a gun on a passerby and the crowd would consider him a policeman. Now, of course, Communists police wear uniforms like other nations.

In April, 1918, Lenin published a volume showing the new democracy in action. "The Soviets at Work", is translated by Anna Louis Strong, late famed as one of the harmless agrarian Chinese Communists. On pages 24 and 25, Lenin writes that,

> "We must strengthen the People's Bank as a step toward nationalizing all banks as centers of social book-keeping. We are backward in our collections of tax on wealth and income, this must be better organized. To become stronger, we must substitute for the contributions exacted from the bourgeoisie (requisitioned property) steadily and regularly collected wealth and income taxes. The delay in introducing obligatory labor service is another proof that the most urgent problem is precisely the preparatory organization wok which on one hand is necessary to prepare the campaign to 'surround capital' and to 'compel its surrender'."

In the space of a few months, the Leninist Government had come to the rude awakening that a government cannot exist for long on the wealth which it seizes from one class of its citizens. Surrounding capital and compelling its surrender is apt terminology for the greatest mass burglary in modern history, the early days of the Bolshevik regime when the Communist leaders drove out or killed the property owners and seized the palaces and estates for themselves, always in the name of the state, of course. Thus the little group of fanatic calling themselves the "dictatorship of the proletariat" wallowed in the luxury they had envied for so long without being able to attain it in stable society.

Woodrow Wilson, in his Annual Message to Congress on January 8, 1918, included several paragraphs assuring the Bolsheviks of the "great sympathy of the United States for Russia" and boldly promising the Russian people active assistance in their struggle for "freedom". Nor was this an idle promise, for within six months he dispatched Elihu Root to Moscow with $20 million of desperately needed capital for the Revolutionary Government. Who in America took notice of this? Our people were deeply involved in the First World War, which, as both Lenin and Trotsky have pointed out, was the golden time for revolutionary movements all over the world.

CHAPTER 12

The Paris Peace Conference of 1918–1919 resulted in the formation of the Council On Foreign Relations, the organization of the League of Nations, and the Second World War. The conferees, or rather, the conspirators, made the Second World War inevitable by their punitive reparations against Germany, which effectively alienated the German people from the Concert of Europe, and by the arbitrary redistribution of minorities in the explosive countries of Central Europe. Versailles was a successful conspiracy against peace. The creation of Czechoslovakia, the Polish Corridor, and the special privileges given certain minorities, notably the Jews, were factors which made a lasting peace impossible. Some correspondents and delegates left the Peace Conference in disgust, declaring that "The Paris Conference does not mean peace, it means war."

The facts about the Paris Peace Conference are elusive. Many of the delegates wrote their memoirs of that event, and more boring or more disappointing books it would be difficult to find. Of one of the most important gatherings in the history of the world, we find no records of the discussions, save in the vaguest terms, by the participants. The following few pages are the digest of sixty-odd books on this Conference.

The representatives of many peoples, of the conquerors and vanquished, came to the Versailles Conference full of hope for the future. They left with their hearts filled with foreboding. All of the little peoples wanted peace, but they discovered that all of the big interests were looking forward to another war. That was the climate of the proceedings, and in the midst of this soul-searching and looking into the dark future, only one group had everything to gain and nothing to lose. That was the Jewish people.

Dr. E.J. Dillon, one of our most uncompromising historians, published his last work, "The Inside Story of the Peace Conference", in 1920. His publisher was Harpers. Now Harpers is controlled by the Council On Foreign Relations. The Chairman of Harpers is Cass Canfield, its Editor-in-Chief is John Fischer, Henry J. Fisher is on the Executive Committee, Frederick Lewis Allen is editor of *Harper's Monthly*, and George L. Harrison of the New York Federal Reserve Bank is a director of Harpers. All of these men are prominent members of the Council On Foreign Relations. Needless to say, Harpers does not publish Dr. Dillon or anyone of like courage today.

On page 12 of the "The Inside Story of the Peace Conference", Dr. Dillon writes that,

> "Of all the collectivities whose interests were furthered at the Conference, the Jews had the most resourceful and certainly the most influential exponents. There were Jews from Poland, Palestine, Russia, the Ukraine, Rumania, France, Britain, Holland, and Belgium; but the largest and most brilliant contingent was sent by the United States."

On page 496–497, Dr. Dillon tells us that

> "A considerable number of delegates believed that the real influences behind the Anglo-Saxon peoples were Semitic. They confronted the President's proposal on the subject of religious inequality, and, in particular, the odd motive alleged for it, with the measures for the protection of minorities which he subsequently imposed on the lesser states, and which had for their keynote to satisfy the Jewish elements in Eastern Europe, and they concluded that the sequence of expedients framed and enforced in this direction were inspired by the Jews, assembled in Paris for the purpose of realizing their carefully thought-out program, which they succeeded in having substantially executed. The formula into which this policy was thrown by the members of the Conference, whose countries it affected, and who regarded it as fatal to the peace of Europe, was this, 'Henceforth the world will be governed by the Anglo-Saxon people, who in turn are swayed by their Jewish elements.'"

> "A lack of reserve and moderation was displayed by the promoters of the minority clauses. What the Eastern delegates said was briefly this:

> "The tide in our countries was flowing rapidly in favor of the Jews. All the Eastern European governments which had wronged them were uttering their mea culpa, and had solemnly promised to turn over a new leaf. Nay, they had already turned it. We, for example,

altered our legislation in order to meet and anticipate the pressing needs of the Jews. Poland and Rumania issued laws establishing absolute equality between the Jews and their own nationals. Immigrant Hebrews from Russia received full rights of citizenship and became entitled to fill any office in the state. The fervent prayer of Eastern Europe was that the Jewish members of their respective communities should be gradually assimilated to the natives and become patriotic citizens like them. But in the flush of triumph the Jews were not satisfied with equality, what they demanded was inequality to the detriment of the races whose hospitality they were enjoying. They were to have the same rights as the Russians, the Poles, and other peoples among which they lived, but they were also to have a good deal more. Their religious autonomy was places under the Protection of the League of Nations, which is but another name for the Powers which have reserved to themselves the governance of the world.

The method is to oblige each of the lesser states to bestow on each minority the same rights as the majority enjoys, and also certain privileges over and above them. The instrument imposing these obligations is a formal treaty with the Great Powers, which Poland, Roumania, and other small states were summoned to sign. The second clause of the polish treaty enacts that every individual who habitually resided in Poland August 1, 1914 becomes a citizen forthwith. On August 1, 1914, Numerous German and Austrian agents and spies, many of them Hebrews, resided habitually in Poland. Moreover, the foreign Jewish elements there, which had immigrated from Russia, had definitely thrown in their lot with the enemies of Poland. Now to put in the hands of such enemies constitutional weapons was already a sacrifice and a risk. The Jews in Vilna recently voted solidly against the incorporation of that city in Poland. Are they to be treated as loyal Polish citizens?"

Thus President Wilson, who spoke so eloquently and so sincerely for the rights of small nations, forced those little nations to accept into their bosoms alien revolutionaries, agitators, and espionage agents who could not become decent citizens of any country. The Jews in particular, even when their hosts desired most honestly to accept them as full-fledged and assimilated citizens, had no intentions of becoming such. Their religious and political philosophy, Socialist Zionism, expressly prohibited them from becoming assimilated in any country. Yet this aspect of the Jewish problem was ignored at Versailles. Dr. Dillon quotes a speech of M. Bratianu, Premier of Roumania, at the Conference,

> "Roumania conferred full rights of Roumanian citizenship on 800,000 Jews. If, however the Jews are now to be placed in a special category, Kept apart from their fellow citizens by having autonomous institutions, By the maintenance of the German-Yiddish dialect, which keeps alive the Teutonic anti-Roumanian spirit, and by being authorized to regard the Roumanian state as an inferior tribunal, from which appeal is always to be had to a foreign body—the Governments of the Great Powers-this is calculated to render the assimilation of the German-Yiddish speaking Jews to their Roumanian fellow-citizens a sheer impossibility. The majority and the minority are systematically and definitely estranged."

Dillon says that

> "President Wilson rejoined Bratianu lengthily, saying that the Great Powers were making themselves responsible for the permanent tranquility of the smaller states. The treatment of the minorities, unless fair and considerate, might produce the gravest troubles and even precipitate wars."

Implied in Wilson's speech was the threat that if the smaller States allowed a hair to be harmed on a Jew's head, the Great Powers would declare war on that state. Here at least is one explanation of why the United States went to war with Germany in 1941.

However, the future of Zionism was not Woodrow Wilson's only concern in Paris. He also had an intense and burning desire to rush to Moscow and extend his congratulations to the Red Dictator Nikolai Lenin. His opening address to the Peace Conference declared that

> "There is moreover a voice calling for these definitions of principles and of purpose which is, it seems to me, more thrilling and more compelling than any of the moving voices with which the troubled air of the world is filled. It is the voice of the Russian people. There are men in the United States of the finest temper who are in sympathy with bolshevism because it appears to them to offer that regime of opportunity to the individual which they desire to bring about."

This speech, quoted in the Communist apology, "The Great Conspiracy Against Russia", by Michael Seghers and Albert Kahn, Steinberg Press,1946 is the explanation of the present enshrinement of Woodrow

Wilson as the Abraham Lincoln of Communism. This speech was official warning to all the nations of Europe that the Government of the United States was sympathetic to Communism, and was a green light to every Communist agitator in the Balkan countries.

The memory of Woodrow Wilson is kept alive by the most subversive elements in America. Isaiah Bowman, Chief of the Territorial Section of the Peace Conference, and a founder of the Council on Foreign Relations, was made president of Johns Hopkins University, and set up the Woodrow Wilson School of Foreign Affairs there. He placed in charge of that school the most indefatigable Communist agent in America, Owen Lattimore. Johns Hopkins also graduated and sent out to the world one of the most despised Americans since Benedict Arnold, the perjurer and traitor, Alger Hiss.

At the library of Congress, the Communist admirers of Woodrow Wilson had one of that building's largest and most elaborately furnished rooms set aside for his papers, a sanctum sanctorum into which the gullible citizens might stare but could not enter. As for seeing Wilson's papers, that is forbidden. Should his correspondence with Jacob Schiff or Rufus Isaacs come to light, a god would fall.

Many or our universities, such as the university of Virginia, when they set up schools of foreign relations, named them after the Bolshevik financier Woodrow Wilson. The memory of Presidents, who had helped build America, Washington, Jefferson, Adams, Jackson, and Lincoln, was put aside to honor a servile half-man who did so much to further the cause of World Communism.

In the records of Woodrow Wilson's speeches at Versailles, we look in vain for any reference to the nation which had given him her highest honors. Not once did he ever mention or show concern for the future of the American people while he was in Paris. Surrounded by the Baruchs, Warburgs, and Frankfurters, he expressed his deep interest in world Zionism and world Communism, but he never evinced any interest in the American Republic.

No sooner did President Wilson arrive in Paris than he sent as his personal envoy to Lenin the Department of State attaché William C. Bullitt, with his warmest expression of personal regard to the Red Dictator. This junket turned out to be one of the strangest episodes in our diplomatic history. Bullitt went to Moscow, had his interview with Lenin, Who was, as always, pleased to hear from his admirer Woodrow

Wilson, and returned to Paris. Then Wilson refused to see him. This caused the wildest speculation among the press corps in Paris, but none of them came up with the explanation of Wilson's action. Years later, we learn from Col. House what had happened.

Col. House, who often took Wilson's foot out of his mouth for him was horrified, when he found out that Wilson had sent a personal envoy to Lenin. House was at that moment deep in the plans for the League of Nations, of which Wilson was intended to become the symbol and Chief advertisement. This meant that Wilson had to give up his most passionate interest, Communism, lest he, and indirectly, the League of Nations become identified as Marxist in the minds of many peoples. With such a Dream at stake, Wilson reluctantly made an end to his oft-expressed admiration of the Soviet Leaders, and, while the world waited to see how he would receive Bullitt on his return from Moscow, Wilson resolved not to admit him. As always, Wilson did the wrong thing. It would have been far Less damaging to him had he made a more sensible move, but this inexplicable action, coming hard after Wilson's pro-Communist speech at the Conference, was such a complete reversal of policy that it caused the wildest rumors. It was said that Wilson had made a secret pact with Lenin, and as secretly abrogated it, that Lenin had refused to see Bullitt because no more funds had been forthcoming from Wilson, and that Bullitt and Lenin Had made an agreement to which Wilson refused to be part. None of these speculations was true, and none of them was necessary. Had Wilson had the slightest sense of public relations, this faux pas would never have occurred. Ever since the first property-owner had been murdered in Russia In the spring of 1917, President Woodrow Wilson had been making speech after speech proclaiming his sympathy and admiration for the murderers, who, in the dark reaches of his mind, were somehow connected with his conception of "freedom". He could hardly expect to reverse such a long-standing and publicly known sentiment without arousing a great deal of curiosity.

Little admiration, however, was wasted on Woodrow Wilson by his colleagues of the Supreme Council, Orlando of Italy, Clemenceau of France, and Lloyd George of England. They knew him for what he was, and they delighted in humiliating him. Particularly did Clemenceau, the Tiger of France, see in Wilson an object of disgust. In "The Eighth Crusade", on page 183, we read that

> "Clemenceau made no secret of his contempt for President Wilson.
> At The peace Conference he treated him with studied insolence,

affecting to Fall asleep while the President was speaking, and, waking up at the end of The speech, he would ignore Wilson's statement altogether, and merely reaffirm what he himself had said prior to the President's pronouncement, and then resume his slumbers."

Wilson deserved the contempt of his confreres because he was the most servile to the Zionists. Although all of them had their Jewish secretaries With the night and day, Clemenceau with his Georges Mandel, Orlando With his Baron Sonnino, and Lloyd George with his Sir Philip Sassoon, Wilson was always surrounded by a bevy of chattering Zionists, such as Louis Marshall, Justice Brandeis, or Felix Frankfurter, and no oiled-pig-Tail from the ghettoes of the Near East was too greasy to be refused an Audience with the President while he was in Paris.

In his autobiography "challenging Years" on page 196, Rabbi Wise tells us that

> "During the Paris Peace Conference of 1919 Wilson's influence for Zion's good made itself felt in the conduct of Secretary of State Lansing. When Dr. Weizmann, President of the World Zionist Organization, Appeared before the delegates to the Peace Conference to make his classic Presentation of the Zionist case, Lansing, tested friend of the Zionist Cause, was presiding officer of the session."

John Foster Dulles, whose first taste of international intrigue was at The Hague Peace Conference of 1907, was at the Paris Peace Conference as The secretary to his uncle, Robert Lansing, the tested friend of the Zionist Cause. Thomas Lamont, senior partner of J.P, Morgan Co., in his privately Printed autobiography "across World Frontiers" wrote that

> "All of us placed great reliance upon John Foster Dulles."

His brother Allen Dulles was there as legal adviser to the American Delegation. The Dulles brothers learned then that Zionism was the coming Thing.

The staff of the American Committee to Negotiate Peace was a bad joke On the American people. Frank E, Manuel, in his "Realities of American-Palestine Relations", writes on page 206,

> "In the fall of 1918, while the American delegation to the Peace Conference was assembling its staff, the American Zionists conducted a thorough preliminary campaign of 'predisposing'

members of the delegation to The Zionist program. In addition to predisposing the members of the American Committee to negotiate Peace, the Zionists associated themselves with The aspirations of all the subject nationalities which were clamoring for Independence."

Woodrow Wilson had with his as his personal financial adviser Norman H. Davis, of J. and W. Seligman Co. As special financial representatives from The U.S. Treasury, he had Albert Strauss of J. and W. Seligman, and Thomas Lamont of J.P. Morgan Co. Col. Edward Mandel House was there with his personal staff, consisting of Arthur Frazier, Gordon Auchincloss, and Whitney H. Shepardson. Auchincloss was a Wall Street lawyer. Shepardson devoted the Rest of his life to the Council on Foreign Relations. When Lansing returned to the United States on May 5, 1919, the Chairmanship of the U.S. Delegation was assumed by Frank Polk, whose law partner, John W. Davis then Ambassador to England, came over to help at the Conference. Davis, Polk, Gardiner, and Reed were the lawyers for J.P. Morgan Co. The distinguished American diplomat, Henry White was there. White is described by his biographer, Allan Nevins, as a lifelong friend of the Rothschild family. Other American representatives were General Tasker H. Bliss, Joseph Grew, a nephew of J.P. Morgan, prof. Archibald Coolidge, Philip Patchin, then Assistant Secretary of state, now a director of Standard Oil of California, Carter Glass' son, Major Powell Glass, Sidney E. Mezes, brother-In-law of Col. House and President of Baruch's alma mater, city college Of New York, William C. Bullitt, Dr. Isaiah Bowman, Capt. Simon Reisler, Capt. James Steinberg, Capt. William Bachman, Lt. W.G. Weichman, Lt. J.R. Rosengarten, Lt. E.E. Wolff, Lt. J.J. Kaths, Hyman Goldstein, A. Schach, Edith C. Strauss, and clerk Louis Rosenthal. We repeat, this was the American Delegation to Paris, from the official State Department list given to the Senate in accounting for expenditures.

The press corps from American newspapers also was carefully chosen for their devotion to certain ideals. Their chairman, unanimously elected, was Herbert Bayard Swope of the New York World, Baruch's favorite newspaper, which had by three the largest delegation, the others were Charles M. Lincoln, Samuel S. McClure, Ralph Pulitzer, and Louis Seibold. David Lawrence represented the Schiff paper, the New York post. Lawrence is now the Publisher of US. News and World Report. The Negro agitator William E.B. Dubois was there representing the Crisis. Abraham Cahan represented the Jewish Daily Forward, and Lewis Gannett represented the Survey.

The German Delegation, although from an enemy country, contained friendly elements. Its head was Mathias Erzberger, the German deputy who had helped Lenin across Germany in 1917, and the American found old friends with Erzberger. Thomas Lamont writes in "Across World Frontiers" on page 138 that

> "The German Delegation included two German bankers of the Warburg firm Whom I happened to know slightly and with whom I was glad to talk informally, for they seemed to be striving earnestly to offer some reparations compromise that might be acceptable to the Allies."

International bankers always talk "informally". Wars and panics are always planned at little gatherings of influential men where they speak casually, off the record, and no notes are taken. The two un-named bankers from the Warburg firm were its head Max Warburg, and his assistant, Carl J. Melchor. Lamont brought greetings to Max from his brothers Paul and Felix Warburg of Kuhn, Loeb, New York, who were unable to be present because some critics might have commented on the fact that one family was representing both the Allies and the Central Powers at the peace table.

The principal author of the reparations clauses in the Peace Treaty, Which are now decided upon as being one of the two causes of the Second World War, was a man who had much to gain from world rearmament, Bernard Baruch. The draft of the economic clauses of the Treaty of Peace with Germany were presented to the Senate Foreign Relations Committee in the summer of 1919 by their author, the Hon. (with rank of Minister) Bernard Baruch. Baruch testified before the Graham Committee that

> "I was Economic Advisor with the Peace mission.
>
> GRAHAM: Did you frequently advise with the President while there?
>
> BARUCH: Whenever he asked my advice I gave it. I had something to do with the reparations clauses. I was the American Commissioner in charge of what they called the Economic Section. I was a member of the Supreme Economic Council in charge of raw materials.
>
> GRAHAM: Did you sit in the council with the gentlemen who were negotiating the treaty?

BARUCH: Yes, sir, some times.

GRAHAM: All except the meetings that were participated in by the Five?

BARUCH: And frequently those also."

This was an interesting statement, because Dr. Dillon tells us in "The inside Story of the Peace Conference" that

"The Council of five was a superlatively secret body. No secretaries were admitted to its gatherings and no official's minutes were recorded. Communications were never issued to the press. When misunderstandings arose as to what had been said or done, it was the official translator, M. Paul Mantoux—one of the most brilliant representatives of Jewry at The Conference—who was wont to decide, his memory being reputed superlatively tenacious. In this way he attained the distinction of being the Sole available record of what went on at the historic Council. He was the Recipient and is now the only repository of all the secrets of which the Plenipotentiaries were so jealous, lest they should be used one day for Some dubious purpose. It was affirmed that, being a man of method and foresight, M. Mantoux committed everything to writing for his own behalf. Doubts were expressed as to whether affairs of this magnitude, involving The destinies of the world, should have been handled in such secret and unbusinesslike fashion."

The future of two billion people was decided at the most important Gathering in history, and that meeting was conducted like a gang of thieves planning a bank robbery. In the larger sense, that was all that it was. Desperate and determined men were conspiring as to how they could derive the most profit from the further slaughter of the excess population of the twentieth century. Dillon, also points out that

"Never was political veracity at a lower ebb than during the Peace Conference. It was characteristic of the system that two American citizens, both of them Jews, were employed to read the cablegrams arriving from the United States to French newspapers. The object was the suppression of such Messages as tended to throw doubt on the useful belief that the people of the great American Republic were solidly behind the President. Not until several months had gone by did the French public become aware of the existence of a strong current of American opinion highly critical Of Mr. Wilson's policy."

President Wilson sabotaged his chances of getting the abortive League Of Nations proposal adopted by Congress because of the high-handed manner in which he left the business of the American people and sailed off to Europe to further the interests of the Zionists and the Communists in Paris. The motley crew of the American delegation, chosen for their adherence to a World State? Did little to placate American opposition to Wilson. Indeed, members of Congress at this time, fully aware of the peril to their own reputations if the truth about the war should come out, were in rebellion against Wilson. Its members lost no opportunity to criticize the lack of news from Paris, and the tremendous daily expense of the merry Andrews of the American delegation, while month after month passed with no concrete results. The New York Times of July 4, 1919, carried the description of a gay champagne party at the Hotel Crillon, while American waited for news of the peace. The New York Times of August 29, 1919 Said that President Wilson begged for money for the American delegation, Saying that $1,500,000 for their expenses was really very moderate. He had originally asked for $5,000,000 to pay for the pleasures of his Zionist Adherents in Paris, but the Senate ignored him. $105,000 was spent to send mysterious Committee into the Balkans, and it was widely reported that these Committee, whose findings were shrouded in secrecy, were Estimating the possibility of encouraging Communist movements in Central Europe.

Senator Norris was one of the most outspoken critics of Wilson's extravagant demands for the American delegates. Norris pointed out that they had rented the entire Hotel Crillon, with 280 rooms, 201 servants, and 156 doughboys assigned to fetch and carry for the regal Zionist agitators. A fleet of seventy limousines was at the disposal of House and his crew.

Carter Field, in his biography of Baruch, notes on page 186,

> "Nearly every afternoon Baruch had a pleasant session at the Crillon With three or four of his old cronies from the War Industries Board."

Life in Paris must have been delightful. The blood, sweat, and tears Of the War were forgotten as soon as the Baruchs and Frankfurters came in.

The people of Central Europe were alarmed by the American Committees Circulating among them, and they were even more alarmed by the overtly Pro-Communist attitude of the Supreme Council of the

Conference. Dr. Dillon Writes in "The Inside Story of the Peace Conference" that

> "The Israelite Bela Kuhn, who is leading Hungary to destruction, has been heartened by the Supreme Council's indulgent message. People are at a Loss to understand why, if the Conference believes, as it has been asserted The Bela Kuhn is the greatest scourge of latter-day humanity, it ordered The Roumanian troops when nearing Budapest for the purpose of overthrowing Him in that stronghold, first to halt and then withdraw. The clue to the Mystery has at last been found in a secret agreement between Kuhn and a certain financial group."

> "An influential French press organization wrote: The names of the new Commissars of the people tell us nothing, because their bearers are unknown. But the endings of their names tell us that most of them, like those of the preceding government, are of Jewish origin. Never since the Inauguration of official Communism did Budapest better deserve the appellation of Budapest. That is an additional trait in common with the Russian soviets."

When the short-lived Communist government of Bela Kuhn was overthrown by Admiral Horthy, hordes of Jews fled Hungary to escape justice and were welcomed by their co-religionists in America. The Hungarian Jew Anna Rosenberg is now Assistant Secretary of Defense.

The three architects of the reparations clauses which caused the second World War were M. Klotz, French Minister of Finance, Bernard Baruch of The United States, and Max Warburg of Germany. M. Klotz and risen to an Easy victory in French politics by shouting to all France through-Out the War that Germany would have to pay every franc of the cost of France's defense. One can only conclude that Hitler's speeches, translated into English by the Royal Institute of International Affairs, were incredibly mild. It is noteworthy that Hitler, while informing the German People that the Jews were responsible for the reparations clauses, never Named those Jews, and Max Warburg stayed in Germany until 1941, when he calmly embarked for New York City.

The reparations Commission, which during the 1920s provided a comfortable post for incompetents from the J.P. Morgan family, also shrouded its Operations in mystery. The French writer Andre Tardieu complains that in His book, "The Truth About The Treaty" that no one could learn what amount Had been paid by Germany, and today there is no figure available from the Thousands of pages of economic studies of the reparations, and the debt System which resulted from the war. The Treaty of Versailles provided That Germany should pay before May 1, 1921 twenty billion gold marks, But this sum was impossible for the wrecked economy of Germany, and was never taken seriously by anybody at the Conference except M. Klotz, Who proposed it. The reparations Commission called for thirty annual installments, and it was the pressure for these payments which forced Germany to go to Kuhn. Loeb Co. Otto Kahn testified before the Senate Committee on Foreign Bonds in 1933 that at that time Kuhn, Loeb held $600Million of German short-term credits.

Lenin, in volume X of his selected works, translated by J. Finberg, Says on page 325,

> "By the Versailles Peace Treaty the capitalist countries created a financial system that they themselves do not understand."

By capitalist countries, Lenin certainly did not mean Baruch, Klotz, and Warburg, who did understand what they had created. Lenin meant the Simple taxpayers of the capitalist countries, who would pay the debts and then go out to be slaughtered in the creation of more debt.

Herbert Hoover, in "The Problems of Lasting Peace", says that Germany Was asked to pay reparations of forty billion dollars. What she actually paid was only a fraction of this sum the exact amount of which is known only in the offices of Kuhn, Loeb Co. When Hitler seized the government of Germany, all the German records of reparations mysteriously disappeared. Government upsets have their purposes.

Hoover also criticized the purposeful alienation of the German people by making the democratic government which replaced the Kaiser sign a war Guilt clause proclaiming that the entire German people were responsible for the war. No one has yet been able to suggest a satisfactory method of any people not fighting a war. The young men have the choice of choosing between public denunciation and imprisonment, or a long trip in a cattle-Boat to the slaughter-pits. Few adolescent candidates for massacre have the shamelessness of the young Jews of Britain, who by the thousands in The First World War refused to go into the Army, an attitude in which they were encouraged by their rabbis and by Jewish publications.

Hoover in his book deplores the blockade of Germany, which was continued for five months after the signing of the Armistice on

November 11, 1918 until late in March of 1919. One of the worst war crimes in History, this callous act directly caused the death of two hundred thousand German children from starvation during that period, and malnutrition permanently crippled millions of others. This excessive brutality, which would not have been condoned by any decent elements in the Allied countries, was the result of secret orders given the British Admiralty by the Privy Council to the King of England, which was composed of Sir Herbert Samuel, Rufus Isaacs Lord Reading, and Lord Alfred de Rothschild. The Orders continuing the blockade were countersigned by then Secretary of War for Great Britain, Winston Churchill, former First Lord of the Admiralty.

CHAPTER 13

W orld Jewry had been planning for the centuries for a League of Nations which would unite them in their dispersion over the nations of the world. The Versailles Peace Conference climaxed one hundred years of such negotiations in Europe. That century of intrigue was inaugurated by the Congress of Vienna, which is described by Max J. Kohler in "Jewish Rights at the Congress of Vienna 1814–1815, and at Aix-La-Chapelle 1818," American Jewish Committee, 1918. On page 2, Kohler writes,

> "The conditions that confronted Europe at the Congress of Vienna were, in important respects, similar to those that are likely to confront the Peace Conference to meet at the close of the present war. The Napoleonic Wars, like the one in which civilization is now involved, saw material improvement wrought in the civil and political condition of the Jews. It is to the credit of the greatest of the statesmen assembled at Vienna that they adopted a resolution restraining individual German states from curtailing Jewish rights."

> "The French Revolution, consciously to a great extent following our American precedent, had emancipated the Jews in French and Holland, and its influence in Italy, Germany, and Austria, had also been strongly in favor of abolishing Jewish disabilities. Karl von Dalberg the Prince primate of the Confederation of the Rhine, had greatly alleviated Jewish Disabilities in Frankfurt, and granted enlarged rights, on Dec, 28, 1811, In consideration of large payments of money and bonds, though his edict Was repudiated by the municipality in 1814. The Jews of Frankfurt were officially represented at the Congress by Jacob Baruch and GGG. Uffenheim. Prince Hardenberg and Wilhelm von Humboldt were the leading advocates Of Jewish rights at the Congress and Metternich aided their efforts. Of Course, unofficially, many other Jewish communities and leaders were Active at the Congress in the cause of Jewish emancipation, particularly Individuals like the Rothschilds and the Arnsteins, and the Herz and the Eskeles families

of Vienna. Nor should I overlook the brilliant group of Salon leaders of the day, Fanny von Arnstein, Cecilie von Eskeles, Madame Pereyra and Madame Herz of Vienna, and Dorothea Mendelssohn von Schlegel, With whom so many of those assembled were on intimate terms. Nearly all of the work was done at conferences of four or five of the Great Powers, the great majority of envoys never being admitted to any formal Session." This is 1814, not 1919, but it is the same machinery.

On page 19, Kohler tells us that

"Most prominent among the social festivities during the Congress were those given by Baroness Fanny von Arnstein, wife of the wealthy banker Nathan von Arnstein, of the firm of Arnstein and Eskeles, her sister Madame Eskeles being a close second. They were the daughters of Daniel Itzig, and all the prominent statesmen of the Congress were their guests from time To time. Other brilliant Jewish salons of the period were those of Madame Pereyra, Ephraim, and Levy. Of course, all this social influence was potent upon the deliberations of the Congress."

Kohler writes on page 48 that

"The Rothschilds became potent factors in enlisting Metternich's aid On behalf of the Jews."

He quotes from Friedrich von Gentz diary, Tagebucher, vol. 2, as follows:

"Nov. 6, 1817. Worked on an important memorial On behalf of the Jews in Austria. Nov. 9, 1817. Visit from Moritz Bethmann of Frankfurt who held some of the bonds given by the Frankfurt Jews to Archduke Karl von Dalberg, in payment for their grant of civil rights. His firm was one of the most prominent banking houses of the day. Dec. 10, 1819. Salmon and Karl von Rothschild from Frankfurt called, and the next Evening, Baruch."

On March 14, 1821, von Gentz reported that Rothschild was with him, and he said that he dined on March 16, 1821 at Eskeles' house, where Rothschild was present. On May 1, 1822,

"Baruch and Rothschild excite me with an account of the deplorable Frankfurt Jewish matter. Nov. 23, 1825, conferred with Baron Rothschild regarding Roman Jewish matters."

Kohler's book could have been written about the Versailles Peace Conference. Only the dates needed to be changed.

Against the knowledge that the Jews were a sore spot in every Community in Europe, Woodrow Wilson threw the potential vengeance of the Great Powers. In "The Stakes of the War", by Lothrop Stoddard and Glenn Frank, Century, 1918, we find that

> "There was no middle class in Poland because retail trade was controlled by the Jews. In Roumania, both peasants and nobles were so thriftless that, but for the restrictions, it is feared the Jews would soon own the Whole country. The Jews are only five per cent of the population, but they Control Roumania's retail trade, and the liquor traffic, and they are usually the overseers of the estates of the nobles, who are absentee landlords."

The terrible fact was that the proponents of Jewish rights were usually the most ruthless terrorists and revolutionaries. In the Southwest Review, of Southern Methodist University, July, 1950, Shelby T. Mosloy writes that

> "Robespierre and Mirabeau were ardent proponents of Jewish rights."

These were two of the greatest mass murderers in history. The massacres of The French Revolution were repeated in Russia in 1917, in Hungary in 1919, And in Spain in 1936. Woodrow Wilson was in good company when he defended the terrorists and bank robbers of the Bolshevik regime.

Lloyd George writes in his "Memoirs of the Peace Conference", Yale, 1939, vol. 2, page 725, that

> "The Germans were alive to the fact that the Jews of Russia wielded considerable influence in Bolshevik circles. The Zionist movement was exceptionally strong in Russia and America."

Frank E. Manuel, in "The Realities of American-Palestine Relations" Tells us on page 206 that

> "The pro-Zionist spokesmen at Paris were numerous and influential, Rabbi Stephen Wise, Mrs. Joseph Fels, wife of the soap manufacturer and Socialist, Bernard Flexner, Jacob DeHaas, Felix Frankfurter, Howard Gans, Benjamin Cohen, Judge Julian Mack, Justice Brandeis, and Horace Kallen. At Paris in 1919 the balance

of world power was shifted across the Atlantic. With Wilson in the Peace Conference Chair, American Jews assumed primacy. When President Wilson, during his pre-conference tour though England, received the freedom of the City of London, Rabbi Wise was in his entourage. The President introduced him to Balfour, and the next day he was invited to a luncheon at Downing Street with Lord Walter Rothschild of Britain."

On page 252, Manuel tells us that

"Professor Frankfurter had assumed active leadership of the American Zionist delegation to the Peace Conference, under the remote control of Justice Brandeis. He knew many of the American professors on the Peace Commission, and he participated in the drafting of a number of non-Zionist Projects at the Conference, such as the International Labor Office He was possessed with Zionism as Brandeis at this period. He accepted The Zionist solution with implicit faith in its outcome."

Although all was going well for Zionism, not everyone at the Conference was so pleased with the turn of events. The New York Times of May 22, 1919 carried a story that of the members of the American Commission were Resigning, and quoted the Paris correspondent of the Westminster Gazette As follows:

"With every day that passes the dislike which some members of the American Commission feel for the Peace Treaty grows into open opposition. One Member said, 'The treaty does not mean peace. It means war.' The correspondent added that he is greatly concerned with the evidence of a changed Feeling in American quarters regarding President Wilson."

The only people at the Conference certain of victory were the Zionists. Mason writes in his life of Brandeis that

"In Paris in June of 1919, Brandeis conferred with President Wilson, Col. House, Lord Balfour, the French cabinet, the Italian Ambassador, Louis Marshall, and Baron Edmond de Rothschild. On June 25, Brandeis left for Palestine."

On page 529, Mason tells us that

"Brandeis himself gained knowledge Of certain international complexities during the summers of 1919 and 1920 When he went abroad on Zionist missions, making short stays in London and Paris."

The Zionist Bulletin on August 26, 1919, reported that

> "Under auspices of the English Zionist Federation, a large gathering was held on August 21 at the Finsbury Town Hall to welcome the Hon. Louis D. Brandeis of the Supreme Court of the United States. Dr. Weizmann presided, and among those present were Felix Frankfurter and Messrs. Ussishkin, Rosoff, and Isaac Goldenberg of Russia. Dr. Weizmann said that they had assembled there to meet a man who had for the past four or five years devoted himself to building up the Zionist movement. He did not propose to speak about Brandeis the Great Magistrate. They were there to welcome Brandeis the Jew and the Zionist. From a small Zionist organization in America he had built up the present structure. With the entrance of Brandeis into Zionism, a new era had commenced in America Jewry. In no country was the conquest of the community by Zionism so complete as in America. Dr. Schmarya Levin welcomed Mr. Brandeis in the name of the Inner Executive. Mr. Boris Goldberg welcomed Justice Brandeis on behalf of Russian Jewry."

The use of the phase "the conquest of the community by Zionism" is not accidental. The Zionist Bulletin reported on Sept. 2, 1919 that

> "A dinner in honor of the Hon. Justice Louis D. Brandeis, prior to his return to America, was given by the Executive of the World Zionist Organization on August 26 at the Ritz Hotel. Dr. Weizmann said that it was impossible as yet to appreciate the significance of the work accomplished by Mr. Brandeis; that remained for future historians to estimate. Prof. Frankfurter, in proposing the toast to His Majesty's Government, referred to the months of hard work in which he and the other Jewish delegates had been engaged in Paris. They often spoke in different tongues, but they were all animated by a single sentiment-the welfare of Israel and the good of Zion. Both Britons and Jews were dependent upon a common understanding and a common belief in the realization of their ancient hopes and the attainment of yet higher glories. (Cheers from audience)."

It is interesting to learn that Justice Frankfurter is animated by a Single sentiment, the welfare of Israel and the good of Zion. That is why Roosevelt appointed him to the Supreme Court.

An observation on contemporary journalism appears in the Zionist Bulletin, On May 4, a meeting of the Shanghai Zionist Society was held at which a resolution was passed expressing profound joy at the triumph of The Zionist ideal at the Peace Conference in Paris. The speakers were

Messrs. N.E.B. Ezra and Goerge Sokolsky. This is Sokolsky, the political Columnist, then the associate of Borodin and other Communist leaders in China. He later became a member of the Institute of Pacific Relations.

On page 31 of the Jewish Yearbook on International Law of 1948, we find more Zionist diplomacy, as follows,

> "The secret treaties, which could not have been unknown to leading American Jews, had disposed of almost the whole of the Turkish Empire. Nothing short of the promise to transform Palestine into Jewish State Could be expected to win over the decisive influence of American Jewry. It has been argued that the assimilated Jews could hardly have been Interested in pro-Zionist pronouncements. But the most influential Jewish Leader, Mr. Justice Brandeis, President Wilson's trusted advisor, was an Ardent Zionist and the President of the Zionist Organization of America. Furthermore, the non-Zionist Jews were greatly impressed by the fact that For the first time in history one of the Great Powers had openly proclaimed a Pro-Jewish policy."

The creation of the League of Nations was one of those mysterious Events brought about by mysterious people. A.W. Smith in his biography "Mr. House of Texas", says that Col. House wrote the first draft of the League Covenant on July 16, 1918, and immediately rushed it over to Herbert Bayard Swope for approval.

Walter Lippmann, in who's Who in American Jewry, says that he was a Captain in the U.S. Intelligence Service attached to the Conference. And that he was secretary of an organization which was directed by House to prepare data for the American Commission, including the League Covenant.

The Zionist had been holding World Conferences for twenty-two years, and the League of Nations was made to order for their peculiar international Qualities. Jessie Sampter, on page 21 of "Guide to Zionism", says

> "The League of Nations is an old Jewish idea."

Avrahm Yaxmolinsky, on page 48 of "The Jews under the Soviets". Tells us the startling news that

"The Jews looked upon the Russian Revolution as a steppingstone toward A World Congress, which would create a permanent body capable of requesting From the Entente a mandate over Palestine."

This was one more proof of the Jewish investment in the future known as the Russian Revolution of 1917.

Jewish Comment, published by the World Jewish Congress of New York, Says in the issue of August 27, 1943,

"The American Jewish Congress convened after the Armistice from Dec. 15–18, 1918. Upon arriving in Paris for the last Peace Conference, the American Jewish delegation cooperated with European Jewry, and with the Palestine and Canadian Jewries to from the Committee of Jewish Delegation. The efforts of the Jewish delegation at the Peace Conference were crowned with a high degree of success. After the peace conferences were completed, The Committee did not disband, but it continued for sixteen years to watch over the implementation of Jewish rights in Europe. The Committee was Active in numerous international conferences of organizations grouped Around the League of Nations."

The President of the Committee of Jewish Delegation at Paris was the millionaire Zionist Lawyer, Louis Marshall, who had hailed the Russian Revolution as the greatest world event since the French Revolution. The Committee finally was incorporated into the League against War and Fascism under the Leadership of Marshall's law partner, Samuel Untermeyer, and became the center of radical pro-Communist groups in the United States. The legal counsel for the Committee in Paris was Benjamin Cohen, one of the founders of the present United Nations. He is not to be confused with the notorious Benjamin Cohen who is the lawyer for the Florida gangsters.

Rabbi Wise, on page 196 of "Challenging Years" comments that

"Our battle did not end with the ceremonial of Versailles. Every moral Gain achieved at Paris was scrupulously safeguarded at all subsequent Meetings of the powers. We Zionists found in landing's successor, Bainbridge Colby, an equally sympathetic furtherer of the cause supported by his Chief."

The League of Nations in operation turned out to be another one of those sacrosanct gathering with which Europe had periodically been affected since the Congress of Vienna. It was composed of well-dressed gentlemen who had no visible means of support, who enjoyed life, and who had no recognizable ambitions. They sat and talked with each other for hours at a time, they had an eye for a well-turned ankle on the boulevards of Geneva, and they were typical remittance men, favorite sons whose families sent them away with an allowance because they were of no foreseeable use on the estate or in the business. They are sometimes known as diplomats. As for the business of the league, "There is no business." One correspondent disgustedly cabled his paper after weeks of sitting and drinking coffee in Geneva.

The Zionist Bulletin of March 17, 1920 reported that

> "In the course of a lecture on the league of Nations to the Cambridge University Zionist Society, on the 11th inst. Mr. S. Landman stated that it was to the interests of the Zionists that the league should be a strong Body. He also remarked, 'The Jewish people has quite a particular occasion To congratulate today the philosopher of the Prague Palace. Masaryk is one of the few politicians in Europe who has grasped the significance of The Zionist idea."

Early in life, the "philosopher of the Prague Palace" decided to throw in his lot with the Jews. Masaryk's biographer tells us that as an obscure Young lawyer in 1899, he defended one Hillel in a case involving the Ritual murder of a Christian girl, a case which rocked Central Europe. Masaryk got Hillel acquitted, and was amazed to find himself world famous. Nor was he slow to follow up his advantage, and he soon became known as Europe's foremost exponent of Jewish rights. His reward was extraordinary.

The Jews had long since been accustomed to make their allies among the Gentiles the heads of the State, but in Masaryk's case a special dispensation was made. No State existed for him, and therefore one was carved out Of Central Europe for his leadership.

Czechoslavakia was to be the antidote for the excessive nationalism which, so the Zionists said, was the curse of Europe. Czechs, Slavs, Jews, Germans, all the most explosive racial components of Central Europe, Were crammed into a little state surrounded by Great Powers. Everything was done to make the new nation's path easy. The League of Nations considered it a special pet, and the international bankers overextended themselves to make it financially secure. Paul Einzig says in "Finance and Politics" that

"The fact that Czechoslavakia was able to stabilize her currency as early as 1922 was largely due to the loans raised in London and New York."

I pointed out in "The Federal Reserve" that the league was mostly interested in restoring the gold standard and setting up central banks in every country. Its political negotiations were never of any consequence. Its chief value lay in its precedent of world government, and its training for the bureaucracy of the future World Socialist State.

It was a foregone conclusion by the admirer of Lenin, Woodrow Wilson, That the United States would become the partner of Russia in the League of Nations. Being of recent immigrant stock, of uncertain origin, Wilson Was oblivious of a chapter of history known as the American Revolution, Which was fought by sturdy individualists to free themselves from foreign taxation. The League of Nations, of course, would levy upon its Members for its far-flung and vague projects, such as the development of Palestine, unfortunately, the only country which had any money, the United States, did not join, and the league was never able to do very much.

Wilson's proposal that we join the League of Nations met with almost Unanimous opposition in Washington and then throughout the United States. The swift disillusion following the Armistice, the widespread feeling that we had been tricked into war, and the growing dislike of the cynical Wilson, as well as our unwillingness to give up our nationhood, erected a stone wall before Wilson and his international friends. The Jewish sponsorship of the league aroused conjecture as to its real purpose, and our Congress made it known that they were not convinced of the necessity for our involvement in such a project.

Woodrow Wilson, still rankling from the sneers of the European Leader and the jibes of the peoples of France and England, made one last Effort to exert his will upon the American people. He made a cross-country Tour, speaking everywhere for his project, the League of Nations. It was the crux of his political career, and as he saw the people silently turn Away from him in town after town, his reason tottered. The crowning blow fell on him in San Francisco. The Irish had always disliked Wilson, and they were ready for him there. He was not able to complete a sentence. They hooted and jeered every time he opened his mouth, and, sick at heart, He left the platform and took his train for Salt Lake City, where he was to speak. He never made that speech, nor did he ever speak in public Again. One reporter said that after San

Francisco, Wilson would come out to meet people gathered by the tracks in a small town, dance a little Jig, grin foolishly, and be led in again by his aides. Veteran reporters, who had watched him for years, recorded that he was not himself. Others cruelly commented that he had slipped a cog. At any rate, the word was sent out that he had suffered a breakdown, and he returned to Washington to take to his bed, a broken man.

In the nation's capital, surrounded by the Baruchs, Warburgs, and Strausses during two terms in the White House, Wilson had come to fancy Himself an omnipotent prince. Now, for the first time, he realized that what had been done throughout his Presidency had only been effected through the sovereign power of international gold. He had no political influence, nor did his people have any affection for him. His carefully nurtured Illusion of himself was shattered, and so he did behind drawn curtains in His sickroom while Col. House carried on as President of the United States. There was little change in the administration of national affairs.

The defeat of the League of Nations proposal by the Senate Opened floodgates of invective from the yellow liberal press which Continues to the present day. Even after they had the United States safely locked up in the United Nations, the Socialist Zionists still lost no opportunity to revile the memories of those Senators who had beaten those Twenty-five years before. The News Republic and The Nation snarl and Spit like slum cats on a garbage can whenever they have occasion to recall the names of Norris, Lafollette, and Lodge.

A university professor anxious to get ahead in the world could always grind out another book about the awful effects of the defeat of the League of Nations proposal. In some perverted manner, it was decided upon as the Cause, and the sole cause, for the Second World War. The League of Nations Argued the longhaired nitwits of City College, could have been strong enough to stop Hitler and Mussolini without war if the United States had been a member. We could have gone to war with them to prevent war, as we are doing for the United Nations in Korea. Since we have already proved that the Second World War was made inevitable by the reparations policy and by the redistribution of minorities in Europe, we leave the University fuddle brains to their self-delusions.

The latest of these libels on the dead is a book called "Woodrow Wilson and the Great Betrayal", ground out by Thomas A. Bailey and published

By Macmillan in 1945. I seized upon it with interest, thinking it was an Account of how Woodrow Wilson had financed the Communist Government Through its formative years. However, it turned out to be a repetition of the tired folktale that the United States was responsible for everything that was wrong in the world, because our people legally and constitutionally demonstrated that we did not want to pay the bills for the League of Nations. The Senators who voted against it, have, through some twist of reasoning, have become traitors. I wonder how Mr. Bailey would classify Alger Hiss. No doubt he would refer to Hiss as a world patriot.

Bailey's discussion of the event is significant. He terms the outcome of the league proposal a "betrayal of the masses", a phrase he must have picked up from an old volume of Lenin. He runs on about the ideals of Woodrow Wilson, without being very specific about what they were. The Present writer has endeavored for some years to discover any ideals of Mr. Wilson's. He exemplified and faithfully executed the desires of Kuhn, Loeb Co., but desires are not ideals.

CHAPTER 14

The background of the political development in Europe during the 1920's is explained by a quote from Paul Einzig's book, "France's Crisis", Macmillan, 1934,

> "The fatal errors of the Allied statesmen at Versailles were the origin of most of the economic troubles from which the world has been suffering for the past fifteen years. The political provisions of the Peace Treaty Were mild, but the financial clauses were impossibly severe."

Knowing Messrs. Warburg, Baruch, and Klotz as we do, there is no Reason to suppose that the financial clauses were errors, although they were Fatal to the cause of peace. The reparations demands by this unholy trip were mathematically impossible of fulfillment, as they well knew.

The excess, then, had a purpose, for these men did not come to Paris to amuse themselves. Their purpose was the further economic demoralization Of Europe, to the point where a Second World War was the only way out.

In "World Finance, 1914–1935" Macmillan, 1935, Einzig comments that

> "The history of postwar finance constitutes a study of the ways in which the various countries tried to pay for the war."

The young men of Europe were dead. France had lost a generation which removed her from the scene of world power, the officers who Administered Britain's empire were blown to bits at Ypres and Verdun, And the governing class of Germany died in the drivers against Paris. Yet the bankers rubbed their hands together and demanded that they be paid for what they had brought. They had risked the money, they had Held their international conferences within sound of the battlefields, and they had withstood the galling criticism of patriots wherever they had been unable to buy the mortgages of the newspapers. Now they wanted to be paid. No wonder Ezra Pound was imprisoned as a madman when he went on the Air to inform the American people that

"Wars are made to create a debt."

Mr. Pound also writes from the madhouse that "Debt is slavery", a Statement which infuriates his Jewish keepers. Ludwig Berne said, "Put them in the insane asylum or the workhouse." At the end of every war, the peoples of the earth have lost more and more of their freedoms. They Are in debt, and that debt demands of them that they sacrifice their sons to the maw of war and lower their standard of living. (America 1950).

Einzig chortles that "The financial system today is much more interwoven than it was before the war." As the chief writer for the London financial Paper "The Economist", the principal Rothschild organ, Einzig ought to know how it is interwoven.

His" World Finance 1914–1935" continues,

"The cessation of hostilities found the world amid the biggest movement of international inflation that has ever yet occurred. In Germany, Russia, Poland, Austria, and Hungary, inflation practically wiped out the public debt, but experience Has proved that this method of paying for the war is unsatisfactory in the long run, For not only is it the public debt that is wiped out, but every form of capital and Savings which is not invested in real wealth. This destroyed capital had to be restored In order to secure a normal existence to these countries, and it could Only be restored through the creation of new indebtedness, which, in the Case of Germany, Austria, and Hungary, assumed the form of external debts."

The economist who is not on the payroll of the House of Rothschild Might be moved to inquire why it is not a healthy thing for every form of Capital and savings not invested in real wealth to be destroyed every Generation or so. It is this demobilized and parasitic capital, desperately seeking a return, which is responsible for so much iniquity, for it is this capital, not invested in real wealth, which makes up the Public debts of the world.

The restoration of this destroyed capital, forced upon the defeated Nations by the international bankers, merely prolonged their economic Difficulties. Consequently, as Paul Einzig so complacently remarks, these Nations had to assume an external indebtedness. A nation in debt cannot call its life its own. Yet Russia, whose economy was as disrupted as any In Europe, did not have to assume any external Indebtedness, because the Leninists, when they destroyed capital, destroyed its owners at the same Time. Thus, there was nobody to restore it to.

The complexities of modern Europe and the states encroaching upon one Another in an era of international trade created problems which could be exploited by the agile few. In "World Finance 1935–1937", MacMillan, 1938 Paul Einzig tells us that

> "Ever since 1914, Holland and Switzerland have fulfilled the roles of the world's gambling dens in exchange. Every currency in turn was attacked by one or more of these countries. Amsterdam and Zurich played a Prominent part in the mark gamble of 1923 (Led by the Baruch-Franklin Roosevelt group of New York, United European Investors Ltd.), in the Attack on the franc in 1924 and subsequent years; bears in Lira and Belgian francs were welcomed with open arms by Swiss and Dutch bankers, Who regularly acted as agents for the speculative operations of countries Where the existence of exchange restrictions recluded the possibility of Gambling in the open market. Neither the Swiss nor the Dutch bankers not their presidents, nor the Central Banks nor the Government of the two countries found any fault with these subversive activities, nor with Pocketing the handsome profits derived from them."

The Amsterdam branch of M.M. Warburg Co., of which Paul Warburg was A director, and the Zurich office of J. Henry Schroder Co. Led in these Manipulation of international currencies, an immensely profitable poker Game for which the bankers always stacked the deck. Besides these Adventures on the exchanges, Zurich and Amsterdam and Stockholm have always been the centers of international espionage. The spies always gather near the centers of exchange.

Furthermore, says Einzig,

> "The French War Office supplied the Government of Poland and of the States of the Little Entente with armaments on a credit basis. It was a Very convenient way of getting rid of old supplies for which France had no further use. Ammunition left over from the Great War, too old to be kept much longer without risk of explosion, was sold to these Governments, who were only too glad to take them over so long as there was no need to pay Cash. On more than one

occasion the ammunition thus sold duly exploded Soon after its arrival at its destination, leaving destroyed depot buildings And an increased external indebtedness behind. One of the reasons Why Poland, Yugoslavia, and Roumania found it difficult to raise loans for constructive purposes was the large amount of indebtedness arising from such transactions."

It would be difficult to imagine a chapter more depressing than that Paragraph. Impoverished nations were unable to raise money for Constructive purposes because the Zaharoffs, the Schneiders, and The Rothschilds, had unloaded their worthless ammunition on them after the war.

The Frankfurt bankers continued to consolidate their gains throughout The 1920s. An excellent illustration of their method of gaining control of an industry is given by John K. Winkler in his "Dupont Dynasty", Reynal Hitchcock, 1935, page 254. He is writing about William Durant, The founder of General Motors, a brilliant organizer, but no financier.

> "To get the money, Durant had to create a five-year voting trust under The laws of New York, under which two banking firms, Lee Higginson of Boston and J. and W. Seligman of New York, agreed to loan $15,000,000 for Five years, with the understanding that they would have control of the Board of directors."

The Seligmans would lend the money, but they wanted to run the Business. The foregoing paragraph explains the fact the 1950 issue of Poor's Directory of Directors lists 117 directorships in America's heavy Industry held by the partners of Senator Herbert Lehman's family banking House. This is how the Lehmans control Studebaker, Climax Molybdenum, Continental Can, and dozens of other huge corporations. They were able to give General Lucius Clay the Presidency of Continental Can when he returned from enforcing a "hard peace" upon the German people.

The Wall Street bankers attempted the same holdup on Henry Ford in 1920. Ford was the sharpest economist produced by America. It was he who Originated the practice of paying workers higher wages so that they would Have money to purchase the products of heavy industry, and ushered in the Present era of prosperity. Old Henry wanted twenty million to retool for Civilian production after the war, and New York was willing to lend it, if they could name Ford's board of directors. Henry refused, and refinanced his company from his own fortune. This was anti-Semitism, a crime which was erased after his death, when the soft thing named Henry II turned over the Ford fortune to the promotion of the dubious Aims of world Jewry.

The international cartels strengthened their ties during the war, and the monetary manipulations throughout the 1920s enormously increased their value, on paper. Inflation does not hurt the manufacturer or the Property-owner. The 1920s saw the great game of juggling the prices of Currencies and stocks on the world exchanges, a game which achieved its Purpose in 1929, when the citizens were cleaned out, and holding companies Such as the Lehman Corporation got everything they wanted for a fraction of its value.

One of the principal evidence of international amity in 1925 was Paul Warburg's organization of American I.G. Chemical, a branch of his Family concern, I.G. Farben of Germany. Warburg's assistant was Walter Teagle of Standard Oil, and DuPont was browbeaten into accepting the Presence of a dangerous and powerful ally on her own territory. Eugene Meyer's Allied Chemical and Dye Corporation, with its treasury filled With Government bonds, was able to take care of itself, and Baruch was handling the electricity of the world. Frank A. Southerd, in "American Industry in Europe", Houghton Mifflin, 1931, gives an excellent account Of International General Electric's octopus sprawling out under Baruch And Gerard Swope's guidance, reaching into Europe and Russia during the 1920s. Some American businessmen have always done business with Russia. Dr. Josephson gives a good history of the Rockefeller contracts with the Communist Government.

The League of Nations, and its successor, the United Nations, were the inevitable outcome of the internationalization of industry and finance. I. G. Farben was a family of nations in itself, thanks to the strategic Dispersion of the brothers Warburg. Sooner or later they had to have some Sort of forum for their intrigues which would present a show of legality. At some time or other, every criminal longs to be respected, and will do anything to gain it, except to become respectable. The Federal Reserve System and the League of Nations were Kuhn, Loeb's attempts at Respectability, but they soon degenerated into the same old gang plotting For the fast dollar. Thus, the 1920s, which started as a crusade for peace, Soon became an era of inflation, the golden age of the Wall Street Speculators, who erected a fabulous pyramid of credit on whose crest Rode Paul Warburg and Otto Kahn like conquerors of the storied past.

The economist Frederick Drew, in "Stock Movements and Speculation", D. Appeleton Co. 1928, says,

> "A great rising market such as that of 1924 onward is under the in- and Out direction of powerful industrial and financial interests operating For the rise almost always in concert with groups and cliques directed by Single managerial minds."

The single managerial mind during the 1920s, as I proved in "The Federal Reserve", was Paul Warburg. He and his cohorts modernized the Technique of buying favorable reviews of a new stock issue, which had been done by presenting the financial writers with a number of shares. The Warburgs simply purchased the newspapers.

Robert Liefmann emphasizes that cartels have their origins in the large risks peculiar to modern enterprise, in either raw materials or finished products, but these large risks are the creations and the Frankensteins of the cartels themselves. The desire to make the profit from the stock issue, and to let the victim, or purchaser of the stock, Worry about whether the corporation would ever show a profit, has caused much of the disturbance in our economic structure. The looting of the Railroads by Kuhn, Loeb and then wishing to turn the bankruptcies over to the Government by Socialism is only one small chapter of the tale of intrigue which will change the economy of our nation during this generation. Recognizing what they have done, and seeing the cracks in the wall, Kuhn Loeb have decided that their only chance is to finance Communism, the new System of trust capitalism. That is the history of the twentieth century to 1950.

One of the best investments Kuhn, Loeb ever made in a second-rate man was their purchase of Henry L. Stimson, long-time law partner of Felix Frankfurter. Stimson once publicly bemoaned the fact that he was racially excluded from joining the Zionist Organization of American. His biographer, The Council on Foreign Relations propagandist McGeorge Bundy, says in "On Active Service in Peace and War", page 108,

> "This book is a record of Stimson's public service, and we unfortunately cannot stop to consider the ins and outs of even his major law cases. He defended the makers of cement against an anti-trust suit; he was retained by the bituminous coal experts to file a brief before a Government commission investigation the coal industry. Both the cement case and the coal case were affected with public interests, and in both Cases Stimson found his basic opinion

reinforced by his experience. The cement case was an excellent illustration of the dangers of government by indictment; the cement companies were guilty, but what they had done had been part of the war effort, with direct encouragement of the Government."

The fact that "the government" during the war was Baruch, Meyer, and Warburg, and that the government had encouraged any company to evade the Law, should not surprise anyone, much less lawyer Stimson, who first Crawled out into daylight during the Kuhn, Loeb seizure of the Union Pacific Railroad. Most important is Bundy's determination not to discuss Stimson's source of income. In 698 pages of drool about Stimson's Sacrifice for the American people, Bundy cannot tell us about a single one of the hundred thousand dollar fees which were standard at Winthrop and Stimson. The "public service" we can get in one paragraph in Who's Who in America. What we want to know is, who was paying him off, and how Much, and that the Bundys of biography never tell us. We can obtain an Odor of Stimson's background from the following paragraph, also from the Bundy masterwork,

> "As Secretary of State under Hoover, Stimson acquired a group of Assistants who served under him with distinction in the following years. The first step had been taken with the appointment of Allen M. Klots as Special assistant to the Secretary. Klots had made a distinguished record In college, in war, and in Winthrop and Stimson. Stimson appointed Harvey H. Bundy, a Boston lawyer with some experience in finance, as Assistant Secretary, and Herbert Feis, a distinguished New York Economist as Economic Adviser to the Secretary."

It was democratic of Stimson to help his law partners get ahead. As for Bundy, it explains biographer McGeorge Bundy, who is the issue of the Boston lawyer with Stimson. McGeorge Bundy recently appeared on the Bookstalls with a book of Dean Acheson's public breast-beating for communism, Which Bundy somehow transforms into a plea for democracy, whatever that is. It has already been defined as "the fight to pay taxes." I claim no ability To probe the minds of the Bundys. Perhaps they are only guilty of contempt for the public's intelligence. I dare not imagine that they believe the Sewage which they pour into the propaganda trough.

With an elephantine attempt at flippancy, Bundy tells us how the public Servants of Kuhn, Loeb Co. manage to live so well. He says:

"When Stimson arrived in Washington in 1929, the most difficult problem was in finding a house. It was not until midsummer that the Stimsons Decided to buy an estate called Woodley. At the time it was an expensive Decision ($300,000) but, as it was done by the sale of some wonderfully High-priced stocks, which were radically devalued by the market crash a little later, it was probably a profitable investment."

The scrapers and bowers before the Warburgs were well rewarded in 1929. When the Crash came, these scum had sold all their stocks and put their money in property and Government bonds. While decent Americans were starving, the Stimsons were clipping coupons.

The Council on Foreign Relations exposed its sluttish morality during The 1920s. Its Publication No. 28 is the report of a banquet at the Hotel Astor on Jan. 6, 1922, entitled "Mineral Resources and their Distribution as Affecting International Relations". Dr. J. E. Spurr, President of the Mining and Metallurgical Society of America, said,

"One basic principle, covering the whole world, the committee declares for. It says: Any restrains, national or international, which interfere with the necessary searching of the earth, are in principle undesirable."

Thus, the Council on Foreign Relations declared its intentions of violating the borders of any nation on its missions for the Warburgs and The Guggenheims. Baruch's handmaiden of the mineral world, both in Washington and Paris, Dr. Charles K. Leith, of the War Industries Board, and The Paris Peace Conference, stated at this banquet that

"Only one kind of entente or alliance can survive the commercial Alliance. We suggest the right of stronger government to bring pressure up on weaker governments in the interest of developing minerals which the World needs."

Dr. Leith is right. Military alliances have been abrogated by the dozen during the twentieth century, but the commercial alliances of I.G. Farben Have survived two world wars. His statement of principle, if Chile didn't want the Guggenheims to take out her copper and nitrates, then the Guggenheims have the right to order out the U.S. Marines against her, was made history when the Marines landed in Nicaragua to protect the Right of J. and W. Seligman to issue the money of Nicaragua. Troops were landed in other and similar cases. This is what was going on while the idiots over in Geneva were boring each other to drink in the League of Nations.

The classic instance of such an operation is the Panama Canal. Since the Law firm of Sullivan and Cromwell is the governing body of the Council on Foreign Relations, its prominence in the Panama Canal history is worthy Of our attention. The family Pulitzer, which fled a pogrom in Hungary to become the press agents for democracy in America, quarreled with President Theodore Roosevelt, and spilled the Panama story. We quote From

> "The Roosevelt Panama Libel Case against the New York World (U.S. Vs. the Press Publishing Co.) A brief history of the attempt of President Roosevelt by executive order to destroy the freedom of the Press in the United States, together with the text of the unanimous Decision of the United States Supreme Court handed down by Mr. Chief Justice White affirming the action of Judge Hough of the U.S. District Court in quashing the Indictment. Printed For the New York World, 1911."

> "On. Oct. 3, 1908, the Democratic National Committee was considering The advisability of making public a statement that William Nelson Cromwell In connection with M. Bunau-Varilla, a French speculator, had formed a Syndicate at the time when it was quite evident that the United States Would take over the rights of the French bondholders in the DeLesseps Canal, and that this syndicate included among others Charles P. Taft, Brother of William H. Taft, and Douglas Robinson, brother-in-law of President Theodore Roosevelt. These financiers invested their money Because of a full knowledge of the intentions of the U.S. Government to Acquire the French property at a price of about $40 million and thus Because of the alleged information from Government sources—were Enabled to reap a rich profit. The World tried to ascertain if any facts could be discussed in Addition to those dragged to light by Senator Morgan in 1906, in the Course of the investigation of the Panama Canal matter by the U.S. Senate, Which investigation had been thwarted by Mr. Cromwell's refusal to answer The most pertinent questions put to him on the ground that as counsel For the New Panama Canal Co. his relations with the canal vendors Were private and confidential.

> "Unsuccessful attempts were made to get at the records in Paris and Washington. The World retained an eminent English lawyer, a Member of Parliament, who went to Paris. He reported, 'I have

never known in my Lengthy experience of company matters, any public corporation, much less One of such vast importance, having so completely disappeared and removed All traces of its existence as the New Panama Canal Co. The stock of the New Company was originally registered, but power was subsequently obtained to transform it into 'bearer' stock which passed from hand To hand without any record. There is nothing to show who received the Purchase money paid by the United States.

"Under instructions from President Roosevelt, U.S. Attorney Henry L. Stimson, who was Mr. Roosevelt's unsuccessful candidate for Governor of New York, obtained further indictment for criminal libel. On Jan. 3, 1911, The Supreme Court threw it out.

"On Aug. 29, 1908, the Democratic National Committee issued a Statement from its headquarters in Chicago identifying Cromwell as 'William Nelson Cromwell of New York, the great Wall street lawyer, attorney for The Panama Canal combine, Kuhn, Loeb Co. the Harriman interests, the sugar Trust, the Standard Oil trust et al.

"On Oct. 4, 1908, the World printed a story that Cromwell had the run Of the White House and the War Department after the sale of the Panama Canal to the United States. Mr. Cromwell took an active part on promoting The revolution on the Isthmus which took the canal territory from Colombia And created the Republic of Panama and that the Roosevelt Administration Had advance knowledge of the manufactured revolution and took steps to Make it a success by having warships near at hand. The revolution occurred at the time set. On May 9, 1904, the Secretary of the Treasury Shaw signed the $40 million warrant, the largest ever drawn by the Government, in Payment for the canal property. What Mr. Cromwell got out of this has always been conjectural. He was to get a 5% commission and pay all the expenses Himself. 5% of 40 is two million, but it costs something to manufacture a Revolution. On Jan. 2 last a cablegram from Paris to the New York Newspapers stated that Mr. Cromwell's bill to the Panama Canal Co. was $742,167.77. The bill was finally arbitrated at $125,000. The arbitrators In looping $600,000 from Mr. Cromwell's bill took into consideration That for nine and a half years the Canal Co. had paid him an annual Retainer of $10,000.

"In 1891 the great firm of Decker, Howell, and Co. went under, owing $10 million. Mr. Cromwell was made assignee and in six weeks the affairs Of the firm had been straightened out. The court awarded him a fee of $260,000, the largest of its kind up to that time. At the time of the life Insurance scandal (involving Jacob Schiff and

James Speyer) Mr. Cromwell Spent two hours in District Attorney Jerome's office, with the Avowed purpose of telling Mr. Jerome all the inside secrets of the 'yellow Dog fund' in the Equitable Life. After Mr. Cromwell had left, Mr. Jerome Admitted that he had not been able to get a fact out of him.

"In Sept. 1904, during the absences of Secretary Taft from Washington, Mr. Cromwell, a private citizen, practically ran the War Department, John F. Wallace, Chief Engineer of the Panama Canal, testified before the Senate Committee on Feb. 5, 1905, 'Cromwell appeared to me to be a dangerous man.' Wallace testified that he looked over the report of the Panama Railway (a Canal subsidiary) and discovered that its Board of Directors and Declared a dividend of more than $100,000 in excess of what the road had Earned, and afterwards sold bonds for money with which to repair its Rolling stock. 'I reached the conclusion', said Mr. Wallace, 'that a man who would thus advise the Government is a dangerous man.' Mr. Cromwell helped E.H. Harriman knock Stuyvesant Fish out of the Illinois Central and also helped Harriman beat down the minority stockholders Of the Wells-Fargo Co. when they tried to get a small share of the enormous Surplus of its company.

"On Oct. 19, 1908, the World pointed that 'The members of the American Syndicate found it necessary to raise only $3 million to get a substantial share Of the securities of the French company. There was also a large subscription To the Republican national campaign fund by which the support of Gen. Mark Hanna was won over to the Panama route as against the Nicaragua route, which many engineers considered to be more feasible and cheaper. Mr. Cromwell was not idle. He had a literary bureau at work, and checks were sent every month to 225 newspapers in the interior of the country in payment for printing the product of the literary bureau. This product showed the advantages of the Panama route over The Nicaragua route and built up public sentiment in favor of the former.

"The World continued, on Oct. 19, 1908, 'That Mr. Cromwell contributed Funds to the revolutionary party in Panama was admitted by Mr. Cromwell Himself in the presence of Secretary Taft. This admission was made at a Banquet given in the Isthmus in December, 1904. In his speech Cromwell referred to a provision of the Constitution of Panama which gave all financial Contributors to the revolution the right of citizenship. Cromwell declared that He had contributed largely to the revolutionists' treasury and was therefore entitled to citizenship. $40,000 was given to the son of President of Panama, $35,000 in silver to the Admiral in charge of the Colombian garrison. If the canal costs between $400 and $500 million as engineers expect, Its earning power is, it is declared, largely insufficient, even under favorable Conditions, to pay the interest on the bonds issued by the Government to Defray the cost of construction, says Rep. Henry T. Rainey of Illinois. At this time President Roosevelt was also involved in a scandal concerning His granting a franchise to Standard Oil in Oklahoma, as also reported in the New York Sun of Nov. 26, 1908 His private secretary in this affair was William Loeb."

Cromwell was the legal counsel to all of the Rothschild interests, Kuhn, Loeb, Standard Oil, and the Panama Canal combine. Naturally he had the run Of the War Department and the White House. He was senior partner of the Firm of Sullivan and Cromwell, which now includes the Dulles brothers. The Senate investigation of the Panama affair in 1906, stymied by Cromwell, Was reopened after the Roosevelt-Pulitzer battle by the House of Representatives, and in 1913 the House made an 800 page report of its Investigation, a volume more exciting than most novels. The Panama story, A tremendous scandal involving the highest government officials of the United States was of such proportions that ever since, a politician who had A shady financial chapter of his life has been said to have a "Panama".

The House Hearings revealed that the American syndicate's financial Affairs were handled by J.P. Morgan Co. and J. and W. Seligman Co. of New York. The Bunau-Varilla interests, representing the French shareholders, were in the charge of Heidelbach, Ickelheimer and Co. New York. The French shares had been peddled in France originally with great ballyhoo and at a high price by a syndicate headed by Cornelius Herz. The shares dipped to a hundredth of their cost, and that nearly unseated The French Government. After the French purchasers were using them for Wallpaper, the scheme to get the U.S. Treasury in on it was hatched by the Relatives of the Presidents and the aforementioned banking houses. Two Obstacles were in their path. The government had already decided to build A canal through Nicaragua, whose rocky soil provided a much better siding For a canal than Panama, where, forty years later, the sides still roll down, And second, even if public opinion could be swung to Panama, there Remained the necessity of paying Colombia a large sum for the right-of-way.

Cromwell solved both problems. He purchased enough public opinion through the newspapers, which will accept a check from anybody, and convinced the voters that Panama was the best route, in the face of engineering opinion to the contrary. Then he went down to Panama, by Bribery brought about a revolution, and the cost was clear. The French shares were purchased from their disappointed holders for three million dollars. Cromwell spent two million in bribes, and the syndicate sold the package To the U.S. Government for $40 million in gold from our Treasury. The arithmetic of the case, aside from ideological interpretations, shows a Profit of $35 million on a $5 million investment.

Philip Bunau-Varilla, described by the World as a speculator, was a Professional engineer for the House of Rothschild. He built railways for The House in Spain and in the Congo, and finally was selected for the Panama fiasco by DeLesseps.

The U.S. House of Representatives Hearings on Panama, 1913, were the result of the diligence of Congressman Henry T. Rainey of Illinois. We quote As follows,

> "The New York Sun carried a story 'The Battle of the Routes' on Jan. 2, 1902, to the effect that the Hepburn bill for a Nicaragua Canal had passed the House of Representatives amid great applause by a vote of 308 To 2. On March 17, 1903, the New York Sun reported that the Colombian Treaty for a Panama Canal was ratified by the Senate by a vote of 73-3. This remarkable change of policy and of national opinion occurred within Fifteen months."

On page 29 of the Hearings,

> "The story of Mr. Cromwell's encouragement of the revolutionists and Then of his cold-bloodedly abandoning them to their fate was told in detail By Jose Augustin Arango in a pamphlet entitled 'Datos historicos para la Independencia del Istmo', dated Nov. 28, 1905. It is perfectly accurate in all the details."

On page 61 Congressman Rainey testifies that

> "The revolutionists were in the pay of the Panama Railroad and Steamship Co. a New Jersey Corporation. The representative of that Corporation was William Nelson Cromwell. He was the revolutionist who Promoted and made possible the revolution on the Isthmus of Panama. At that time he was a shareholder in the railroad and its general counsel In the United States. William Nelson

Cromwell—the most dangerous man This country has produced since the days of Aaron Burr—is a professional Revolutionist."

Does anyone wonder that Wall Street promoted the Bolshevik Revolution in Russia? Next to war, revolution has been the most frequently employed Weapon of the Frankfurt bankers to gain their ends. The New York branch Of J. and W. Seligman Co. has promoted literally hundreds of revolutions in The Latin-American countries to protect its monopoly of public utilities In those countries. On page 53, Rainey tells us that

> "The declaration of independence which was promulgated in Panama on The 3rd of November of 1903 was prepared in the office of William Nelson Cromwell of New York. Our State Department was a party to the agreement That a revolution should occur on that date, the 3rd of November, 1903, And that day was selected for the reason the papers of the United States Would be filled with election news and would not give much attention to News from Panama."

This maneuver was recalled in the appointment of Anna Rosenberg as Assistant Secretary of Defense on Nov. 3, 1950, in the hopes that Anti-Communists would overlook the appointment.

Mr. Hall of the New York World testified, as reported on page 135,

> "The Government of France—and this is important because Mr. Roosevelt Is on record as saying that he paid the $40 million direct to the French Government—the Government of France formally disavowed all connection With the Panama Canal Co. and all responsibility for it through its Ambassador In Washington. The $40 million was paid to the Bank of France by J.P. Morgan Co. who got the money from the American Government."

It was no novelty for Theodore Roosevelt to perjure himself before the American public. He knew that the government of France did not receive a cent from him or from anybody else in the sale of the canal.

To understand the power of John Foster Dulles, the present Republican Advisor to the Department of State on foreign policy, it is but necessary To turn to page 206 of these Hearings. There is reprinted in full the Brief submitted by Cromwell to the New Panama Canal Co. We quote

> "As far as the business of the great corporations is concerned in the United States, the general counsel is, as a rule, the guiding spirit and has control. The law firm of Sullivan and Cromwell occupies a

recognized Position among the great legal corps of the Nation. In the course of a Very active thirty years the firm of Sullivan and Cromwell has found itself Placed in intimate relations, susceptible of being used to advantage, With men possessing influence and power everywhere in the United States; They have also come to know, and be in a position to influence, a considerable number of men in political life, in financial circles, and on the press, and all these influences and relations were of great utility in their performance of their duties in the Panama matter. Public opinion demanded the Nicaragua Canal. The daily press and the magazines of this country were entirely favorable to the Nicaragua Canal, and it was only by the greatest special personal efforts that it was possible to get them to take interest in Panama."

Cromwell's special efforts consisted of signing checks to the newspapers in payment for their featuring of his Panama propaganda. His brief, one of the most brazen revelations of skullduggery in our language, was priced at about five dollars a word, and was worth every cent of it. I am particularly pleased by Cromwell's delicacy in referring to his revolution as "the Panama matter". On page 462 of these Hearings we find that

"Bribes were paid through drafts on J.P. Morgan Co. through Isaac Brandon and Brothers. Colombian officers received in bribes $1,270,000 through this Panama house."

Cromwell's designation as "the most dangerous man in America" is a little now strongly competed for by the brothers who succeeded him in Sullivan and Cromwell, Allen W. Dulles and John Foster Dulles, either of whom could be described as the most sinister behind-the-scenes influence In Washington.

It was Sullivan and Cromwell's inheritance of the legal guardianship Of the House of Rothschild's major investment in America which accounted For Cromwell's ability to commit major crimes, both national and international, and yet stay out of prison and in the Social Register. This immunity from prosecution can best be explained by a few quotes about the Rothschild family. Picciotti, in his "Anglo-Jewish History" says

"Nathan Mayer Rothschild has participated in most of the great financial affairs of America, France, England, and of nearly every other Country ... Another event by which he would have been exposed to great Danger was the conversion of French rentes projected by M. Villele. Fortunately for Mr. Rothschild the measure was lost by a single vote in the Paris Chamber of Peers. Had it been carried out, the convulsion that shortly followed in the money markets of Europe would probably have proved fatal to his position, notwithstanding his vast resources. Another Perilous contract was the 4% loan made by M. de Polignac prior to the celebrated three days of July 30 which heralded the fall of the Bourbons in France. The stock went down from 20 to 30%, but, luckily for Mr. Rothschild, the greater part of the loan had been distributed among the Subscribers, who suffered more or less severely." We may depend on it that the Rothschild would not take the loss.

Paul Emden writes of the Rothschilds and of the other influences behind The downfall of the British Empire in "Behind the Throne", Hodder and Stoughton, London, 1934, as follows,

"Edward's preparation for his metier was quite different from that of His mother, hence he 'ruled' less than she did. Gratefully he retained around Him men who had been with him in the age of the building of the Baghdad Railway; the range of his advisers had to be broadened by the inclusion of Men who were in constant touch with business; so there was added to the Family advisory staff the brothers Loepold and Alfred de Rothschild, various Members of the Sassoon family, and above all his private financial adviser Sir Ernest Cassel."

Old Victoria must have writhed in her tomb while Edward was bringing in this horde of Jewish bankers to run the British Empire. On page 294, Emden tells us that

"The enormous fortune which Cassel made in a relatively short time gave Him an immense power which he never misused. He amalgamated the firm of Vickers Sons with the Naval Construction Co. and the Maxim-Nordenfeldt Guns and Ammunition Co., a fusion from which there arose the worldwide Firm of Vickers Sons and Maxim. He organized the great undertaking, which was the foundation of the Central London Railway Co. which built the London Railway tube. On an entirely different capacity from Cassel, were businessmen Like the Rothschilds. The firm was run on definite principles, and the various Partners all had to be members of the family. With great hospitality and in a princely manner they led the lives of Grand seigneurs, and it was natural that Edward the Seventh should find them congenial. Thanks to their international family relationships and still more extended business connections, they knew the whole world, were Well-informed about everybody, and had reliable knowledge of matters which did not appear on the surface. This combination of finance and Politics has been a tradition with the Rothschild from the very beginning. The House of Rothschild always knew more than could be found in the papers, and even more than could be read in the reports which arrived At the Foreign Office. In other countries also the influence of the Rothschilds extended behind the throne."

Of Alfred de Rothschild, Emden tells us that he was a director of the Bank of England from 1868 to 1890, and adds,

"Not until numerous diplomatic publications appeared in the years After the War did a wider public learn how strongly Alfred de Rothschild's Hand affected the politics of Central Europe during the twenty years Before the War."

In his book "Randlords", Hodder and Stoughton, 1935, Paul Emden writes of the diamond and gold kings of the Witwatersrand of South Africa,

"The House of Rothschild was inclined to become interested in the Kimberley domain, and Sir Carl Meyer, their official representative, had already gone into London with his report. The way to the large shareholders Had already been smoothed with the Rothschilds as partners, and with de Crano and Harry Mosenthal of the Exploration Company on his side, Cecil Rhodes (task in Paris was not difficult. A syndicate was formed in August Of 1887 with N.M. Rothschild Sons at the head, which advanced the sum of 1,400,000 pounds for the purchase of the shares bought in Paris, and took up the new DeBeers shares. From now on, Cecil Rhodes had in the House of Rothschild an ally who willingly interested himself in any business which Rhodes proposed."

This passage gives some light on the always mysterious activities of The Rhodes Scholars, American boys who are educated in England with funds From the Cecil Rhodes fortune. Rhodes, like his American counterparts, J.P. Morgan and John D. Rockefeller, was a Gentile stooge for the House of Rothschild, and his fortune was willed to the promotion of treason. The Rhodes Scholars have been criticized as being pro-British, but it would be far more apt to say that they are pro-Socialist and pro-Zionist.

Emden also tells us that arms were smuggled into the goldfields for the rebellion against the Boers by the German Jewish Uitlanders, marked as mining machinery consigned to DeBeers. In his book, "Empire Days", Hutchinson, London, 1942, Emden writes on page 153,

> "The DeBeers Mining Co. was founded in 1880 with a capital of 200,000 pounds, which steadily increased until 1888, when it had become So strong that Rhodes, backed by the Rothschilds and Alfred Beit of Wernher Beit and Co., could carry through the amalgamation of all Diamond mines in Kimberley."

This is confirmation of the fact that the worldwide diamond trust of DeBeers is a Rothschild interest. The Suez Canal is also a Rothschild Venture, and the House may claim an important part in the recent unseating Of King Farouk in Egypt. All biographies of Disraeli confirm the interest Of the Rothschilds in the Suez Canal. I have selected one note on this, from the "History of the Cape to Cairo Railway" by Reuters Correspondent Louis Weinthal. On page 633,

> "In 1875 Disraeli induced N.M. Rothschild Sons to advance approximately Four million sterling for the purchase of 176,602 deferred shares in the Suez Canal Co. standing in the same of His Highness the Khedive Ismail, Which secured for Great Britain a predominance in the administration of The Canal. The whole transaction stands on record as a deal of the Utmost patriotic value and farsighted diplomacy, apart from its financial Aspect, the interest and dividends on which in the financial year 1921-22 amounting to pounds 1,094,303."

Nevertheless, Mr. Weinthal, it was a deal, and not a treaty. Thanks to Her business advisers, the Rothschilds, Cassels, and Sassoons, the international Relations of Great Britain had taken a new tack.

How the Rothschilds extended their influence in America is described By James W. Gerard, in "My First 83 years in America". Mr. Gerard, former Ambassador to Germany, has seen all forms of matter in his long life;

> 'August Belmont had come to America in 1837, when he was twenty-one, As the representative of the Rothschilds, whose riches and interests in Europe were all-embracing... The first of society's hierarchy (in New York) Was the elder August Belmont. Despite the fact that he spoke with a thick German accent, he ruled as an absolute social arbiter.'

Mr. Gerard's publishers with difficulty restrained him from writing That Belmont spoke with a thick Yiddish accent, for Belmont had started From Germany as a Schoenberg. When he crossed the border, this financial Chameleon took on the protective coloration of the Gallic countryside, and the beautiful mountain became Belmont. The largest single influence In the Democratic Party during the last half of the 19th century, Belmont Was a great racing promoter (the Belmont Track), and the builder of The New York City subways system. His son August Belmont Jr. carried on with the subways. For a century there always seemed to be an August Belmont, just as there always seems to be a Eugene Meyer or Henry Morgenthau in the twentieth century.

Old August's son Perry Belmont did not soil his hands with money. He Went into public service and became Chairman of the House Committee on Foreign Relations, the ideal spot for a Rothschild representative. In the Great gold bond deal of 1895, Perry received a two million dollar cut, but his role remains conjectural.

At any rate, the reason for all this muck about the Rothschilds is to Explain the frantic campaign by their representatives in New York, Kuhn, Loeb Co. during the 1920s to get the United States to recognize the Socialist Zionist nation, Communist Russia. One of the reasons Trotsky was shunted aside was his reputation as a frantic, which endangered the press Campaign of Kuhn, Loeb from 1918 to 1933 which presented Russia as An experiment in harmless agrarianism.

One of the results of universal education has been the utter inability of the ordinary citizen to believe that bankers would promote a revolution. "Why", openmouthed,

> "bankers are steady, conservative people, who would be the last ones in the world to get mixed up in a revolution."

That may be true of the bankers in your small town, Mrs. Williams, but it is not true of the international Frankfurt crowd. Revolutions are not accidental. Like wars and panics, they require the conferences of Experts and a sizeable amount of cash. A revolution is a political investment The Rothschilds and Schiffs poured their money into Russia in 1917 to protect their investments there. That protection money was the cash which put Lenin and Stalin in power.

Isaac Seligman, elder of the House of J. and W. Seligman, said during a Speech given before the American Association for International Conciliation In January 1912, published as Pamphlet No. 50, that

"The Russo-Japanese conflict of 1904-05 was halted because bankers refused to float loans at anything like ordinary terms, after probably A half billion dollars had been wasted in the contest. The interests of Commerce have thus put into the hands of international bankers a powerful Weapon to use in the interests of conciliation and peace. France today Holds one billion worth of Russian securities, and it can be readily understood that Russia would not engage in any war without the consent of France."

Isaac's boat of the power of international bankers to stop war if they chose looks pretty bad, since his speech was made only two years before the outbreak of the First World War. The Second World War also was a matter of orthodox finance, which could not have caused the death of a Single youth if the bankers had not worked for thirty years to bring it about.

Chief among the numerous and determined agencies working in the United States during the 1920s for official American recognition of the Communist Government in Russia was the League of Free Nations Association, Which, in its pleas for public support, advertised that its sole purpose Was that recognition, and boasted that it was well on its way to Achieving its objective. The Chairman of the Executive Committee of This organization was James Grover McDonald, who has made a dubious Living all of his life out of such enterprises, always for the same Socialist Zionist crowd. He was rewarded by being appointed the first U.S. Ambassador To the newly stolen State of Israel. His assistant in this Communist Endeavour during the 1920s was Stephen Duggan, President of the Institute Of International Education. Both of these groups, of course, were financed By the Council On Foreign Relations.

The June, 1920 Bulletin of the League of Free Nations Association Proclaimed that it was "actively working for the to build up of a country-wide demand for the restoration of trade with Russia". Kuhn, Loeb and J.P. Morgan Anxiously watched the reception accorded this feeler group, and proceeded toward their goal when it became apparent that Duggan and McDonald were not going to be locked up as agents of a foreign power.

On page 193 of Pope's biography "Maxim Litvinoff" we find that

"On July 7, 1922, Litvinoff stated in conversation that the Russian Delegation at the Hague Conference was expecting to negotiate with an important group of financiers which included Otto H. Kahn of

Kuhn, Loeb Co. New York. A week later Otto Kahn, who had arrived in the Hague, Declared that "The conference with Russia will bring useful results and Will lead to a closer approach to unity of views and policies on the Part of England, France, and the United States with respect to the Russian situation."

This accounts in some small way for the fact that Mrs. Otto Kahn was always received by the great Stalin himself when she visited Russia. Otto Kahn worked very hard to achieve "a unity of views and policies" in his adopted countries of England, France, and the United States, with respect to his latest and most fervent allegiance, Communist Russia. The last passion is always the fiercest, and Kahn's love for Mother Russia Seems to have supplanted all of the patriotic fires which burned in his Breast in rapid succession for Germany, England, and America.

Although the firm of Kuhn, Loeb was able to weather the stress of half A dozen conflicting allegiances during the First World War, there is no Record of a division of opinion among its partners on the question of Russian recognition. Their attitude towards Communism reflects a singular and an admirable harmony. (To attack Kuhn, Loeb in the presence of a Communist is like spitting on Lenin's tomb.) Capitalists were all bad, of Course, but the "financial irrigaters" of Kuhn, Loeb were world patriots, not to be confused with the wicked bankers who bore Gentile names.

Pope's biography of Litvinoff also reveals that

"In 1925 W. Averell Harriman had undertaken to organize American Participation in financing Russo-German trade, and Felix Warburg and Other outstanding bankers stood ready to cooperate in the project, while Ivy Lee of Standard Oil promoted Russian recognition, aided by such well Known American firms as General Electric, Vacuum Oil, International Harvester, and New York Life Insurance."

Despite his quarter-century of distinguished service to Communist Russia, W. Averell Harriman was not a Communist. He was the largest American Shareholder in Germany's heavy industry during the 1930s, but he was not A Nazi. He was only a representative of Kuhn, Loeb Co.

The Rockefellers were not idle in promoting Russian recognition. The Rockefeller Foundation had millions at the disposal of anyone who could present a workable plan for furthering Communism in America, as Dr. Josephson has proved. It granted millions to the London School of Economics, which trains the bureaucracy for the future World Socialist State, and which has graduated such great Americans as Dean Acheson's brother. Edward Campion Acheson, who has been an important behind-the-scenes figure in Washington.

Most noteworthy was Rockefeller's dispatching his personal publicity Man, Ivy Lee, who was in charge of public relations of the Standard Oil Corporation of New Jersey, to Russia to bring back a favorable report On the Communist police state. Lee would have come back bubbling Over with enthusiasm even in Stalin had thrown him into a dungeon and Beaten him three times a day. It's hard to discourage a man who's getting paid so much a word. Ivy Lee is not to be confused with the Virginia Family, who have ALWAYS been named Lee. His junket was made late in 1926, and in 1927 Macmillan Co., the propaganda house for international Bankers, published" Present Day Russia", which presented Russia as a Chamber of Commerce country like America, with members of the Communist Hierarchy who were like our young, businessmen, progressive, dynamic, And charming. Lee neglected to point out that American businessmen do not throw their competitors into concentration camps. Lee, the chief of Propaganda in America, had long talk with Karl Radek, chief of Propaganda for the Communist International. On page 125 of his book, Lee tells us that

> "Radek said that Bolshevik propaganda has little intention of influencing the masses of the peoples of the world, but attempts to train a hard core of revolutionists. The object of Communism, he declared, was to gain control of the hordes of Asia, as the first and most important Step in world conquest."

Besides Kuhn, Loeb, Standard Oil, and the Harrimans, the rest of the Rothschild crowd in America were not dragging their feet. While the Paunchy figure of J.P. Morgan was being berated as the official target of Communist propaganda, the firm of J.P. Morgan was working behind the Scenes for Russia, Harold Nicolson, in his biography "Dwight Morrow", tells us that

> "Morrow's interest in Russia dated from 1917, when Thomas D. Thacher, His law partner, had been a member of the American Red Cross mission During the Revolution. It was strengthened by his friendship with Alex Gumberg, who had come to New York as the representative of the All-Russian Textile Syndicate. 'I have felt', wrote Morrow in 1927, 'that the time would come when something would have to be done for Russia.' He was himself active in

furthering unofficial relations between Soviet Emissaries and the State Department, and he provided Maxim Litvinoff With a warm letter of introduction to Sir Arthur Saler and others and Geneva. Nor was this all. When in Paris in the spring of 1927 he gave a dinner party at Foyot's to which he invited M. Rakovsky and other Soviet representatives."

Thus, while the Communist sheets of the world devoted page after page to diatribe and invective against Morgan, a Morgan partner was throwing Dinner parties at expensive restaurants in Paris for Communist officials, and when the Commissar for Foreign Relations of Soviet Russia, Maxim Litvinoff, went to the League of Nations, he had a letter from a J.P. Morgan partner.

The full truth is that J.P. Morgan Co. has done almost as much to Promote Communism as has its sister banking house of Kuhn, Loeb Co. The senior partner of J.P. Morgan between the two world wars, Thomas Lamont, financed the leftist Saturday Review of literature to gather American writers into the fold, at one time owned the leftwing New York Post, now owned by Mrs. Dorothy Schiff, and was a director of Collier's Weekly, whose political hatchet man, Walter Davenport, reserves his most vicious barbs for patriots. Mrs. Thomas Lamont was a trustee and director of several Communist Fronts, and their son, Corliss Lamont, has been a tireless fellow-travelers, Being the Chairman of such notoriously Communist enterprises as the Council Of American-Soviet Friendship and others equally well-known to the FBI.

Dwight Morrow had been the law partner of Thomas Thacher, a Wall Street lawyer, before graduating to J.P. Morgan Co. Thacher had been a Member of the infamous Red Cross Mission to Russia during the Revolution. The Chief of that Mission, Col. Raymond Robins, in the 1930s suffered a Change of hearts, broke off with all of his Wall Street intriguers, changed His name, and went to live in a small town South Carolina, and died there A few years later.

Harold Nicolson, on page 28 of his chatty biography "Dwight Morrow" Tells us that at Amherst College, Morrow, the son of poor parents, wore The castoff silk shirts of his older fraternity brother, Mortimer Schiff, Son of Jacob Schiff, with MLS embroidered on the front. Morrow wore the colors of Kuhn, Loeb all of his life.

Although the lunatic fringe of the Communist Party of America was Noisy and absurd during the hysterical decade of the 1920s, it was an excellent cover-up for the serious Communist work being done by the Members of the Council on Foreign Relations. The 1920s were the halcyon Days of American Communists, when the Owen Lattimore could travel back And forth between Washington and Moscow without hindrance or criticism. Indeed, it was difficult to get a post as professor of government or History unless one had made the pilgrimage to Moscow or had a few articles published in The Nation or the New Masses. The 1920s were also the golden Days of the trade unionists. Walter Reuther, now the emperor of the CIO Automobile Workers Union in Detroit, was a prominent and well-received Visitor to Moscow, and is said to have been a star student at the top-flight Lenin School of Revolution. The FBI refuses to release its information on Him to Congressmen.

CHAPTER 15

M y book, "The Federal Reserve"[2] relates the immediate monetary negotiations Responsible for the Crash of 1929, from the Congressional Hearings which Exposed the meeting of the European Central Bankers with the Governors Of the Federal Reserve Board in Washington in 1927, at which the Decision to raise the bank rate and precipitate the Crash was made. The Present work gives the ideological background of that decision. The idea Was to deflate the prosperous United States and pull gold from this country to the poorer European countries, and to help Russia overcome her Economic crisis. Trotsky had written in his "History of the Russian Revolution" that

> "Gold is the only basis for money. All other money is but a substitute."

Trotsky did not tell us that money itself is only a substitute. At any rate, we cannot expect anyone born Bronstein to want any kind of money except gold. That was the revolutionary economic doctrine of Communism, and, since the Federal Reserve System and the Bolshevik Revolution both sprang from the agile minds of Paul Warburg and Baron Alfred De Rothschild, it is not surprising that there was a community of interests Between the Crash of 1929 and the welfare of Communism.

On page 123 of "Present Day Russia", Macmillan 1927, Ivy Lee writes that Karl Radek, Chief of propaganda for the Communist International, told him,

> "He despaired of making headway in the United States because of the Prosperity of the working people, and suggested that a

---

[2] "The Secrets of the Federal Reserve – The London Connection", Omnia Veritas Ltd, www.omnia-veritas.com.

depression would be the only thing which would spread Communism in America."

That prosperity, as I pointed out, was due to Henry Ford's revolutionary Innovation of paying his workers five dollars a day when everybody Else would pay only three. When the union racketeers, all from a certain Racial minority, moved in and tried to take credit for what Ford had done For his workers, Ford ran them out, and kept them out years after every other American manufacturer had surrendered to the Marxist trade unionists, The parasites feeding off of the American workingman.

The Federal Reserve System was always willing to oblige Mr. Radek, Just as the pages of the Council On Foreign Relations' magazine "Foreign Affairs" were always open to Radek's Communist propaganda.

Nikolai Lenin, on page 127 of Vol. X of his Selected Works, as translated By J. Fineberg, says

> "Revolution is impossible without a national crisis affecting both the Exploiters and the exploited, to make the lower classes refuse to want the old way, and impossible for the upper classes to continue in the old Way."

Our Crash of 1929, the worst calamity ever inflicted upon the American People, was brought about according to the precepts of Lenin and Radek. It was just the shot in the arm needed by Stalin's Five-Year-Plan. Paul Einzig, in "France's Crisis", Macmillan, 1934,

> "The dumping of commodities by Soviet exporting organizations had a share in the fall of world prices, and accentuated the crisis. This Dumping of commodities is part of the much-discussed Five-Year-Plan... Should the Five-Year-Plan succeed, the power of Soviet authorities to carry on dumping will increase to no slight extent, which is calculated to make men pessimistic about the prospects of industry in other Countries. The world crisis left the Soviet Union practically unaffected."

In "The World Economic Crisis", Macmillan, 1934, Einzig writes that

> "The Soviet Union has benefitted by the crisis. They find it easier to obtain credits than at any time during their existence, because every Country had become more anxious to sell its good."

Although she was on the gold standard, the Soviet Union, strangely Enough, did not suffer the calamity which befell the other gold standard Countries. This immunity has yet to be explained by our economists. That the brains behind the Soviet Union understood the fine art of money as Well as the fine art of revolution is illustrated by Einzig's comment in His book "France's Crisis",

> "The Soviet bought various goods on credit and resold them at once for Cash. In doing this, they suffered substantial losses, but it enabled them to acquire machinery for the carrying out of the Five-Year-Plan. Expensive As this method of borrowing appears, it is in fact cheaper that the rate at which the Soviets could borrow in the open market."

It is odd that fanatic revolutionaries could understand that deft Art of such financing, but any displaced person who opened a retail Clothing store in New York and sold his goods below cost could explain It to him.

Bruce Hopper, a top-level contact man between New York bankers and the Soviet leaders, who replaced George Kennan in the 1920s, wrote in the April, 1932 issue of "Foreign Affairs", an article called "Soviet Economy In a New Phase", in which he said,

> "Ironically enough, the capitalist countries have obligingly tobogganed into the depths of the depression just in time to give the Bolsheviks A breathing spell when needed it most."

My record is full of odd things which happened just when Communists and the international bankers desperately needed them to happen. The Crash Of 1929 did not occur in one day, nor was it an accident that it happened Just in time to help the Soviet Union. Hopper also remarks that the Soviet Foreign trade monopoly by the State shuts off the planning system from the Disastrous effects of currency exchange. This does not mean that the State Monopoly is better, but that it has mechanisms which protect it as a State Monopoly from the ills of the free-enterprise system. Obversely, the free-enterprise system has checks which protect it from the Disasters of the State monopoly system, and it is these checks which the Council crowd wants to get rid of. Hopper also points out that the continuous week of five days was adopted in 1929 in atheist Russia to abolish Sunday, as in integral step in the Leninist program. He notes that the State Bank Issues funds to the factories only when the contracts have been fulfilled. This is a development of the "Work or starve" philosophy of Communism, Point 8 of the Communist Manifesto.

One of the major causes of the debacle of 1929-33 was the systematic Bleeding of the American public by their purchase of foreign bonds from The international banking houses, a crime which netted the bankers two Billion dollars in profit, and caused a Senate Investigation of that racket, so it Now has to be done by Government agencies, such as the Economic Co-Operation Administration, which functioned so well under Herbert Lehman's front, Paul Hoffman.

Lothrop Stoddard, in his book, "Europe and Our Money", Macmillan, 1932, Writes that Paul Mazur of Lehman Brothers, Eugene Meyer, and Paul Warburg Were the three masterminds who promoted these worthless bonds in the United States. Stoddard also says that the public realization that 45 billion dollars was gone was one of the psychological factors behind the panic.

The sinister Allen W. Dulles, now President of the Council On Foreign Relations, is rather put out at the complaints from people who were swindled By the international bankers. Dulles writes in the April, 1932 issue of "Foreign Affairs", an article entitled "American Foreign Bondholders", Page 479, in which he says that only one billion dollars out of eight billion Held in America have defaulted. A billion dollars lost is nothing to complain about, says Mr. Dulles, to whom such sums are meaningless. He comments that

> "Holders of defaulted bonds readily become critical, and in many cases Unfairly so, of the banking house which sold the bonds … Despite the blow Which foreign financing in the New York market has received in consequence Of recent events, we shall again be lending money abroad before many years. A reversal such as we are now witnessing is not a permanent deferral to foreign investment."

Allen W. Dulles does not believe the swindled Americans ought to complain about the crooked bankers who sold them the phony bonds. Anyway, he consoles The Frankfort confidence men, the suckers will be back in a couple of Years. This is the sort of morality which endows churches and universities, And it the money behind this morality which has kept out churchmen and Our professors from criticizing the triumphal march of Socialist Zionism, And, indeed, purchased many of them for the fifth column of Marxism.

October 29, 1929, Black Thursday on the New York Stock Exchange, when so many Gentile businessmen jumped out of their office windows, was a Day of rejoicing for the immigrants who had planned it all. Carter Field, In his biography of "Bernard Baruch", writes that

> "Baruch got out of the market just before the Crash. But what made Baruch sell stocks and buy tax-exempts at such a favorable time? Always studying the value of securities he held, Baruch reached the conclusion that most stocks were selling for far more than they were worth."

This is sheer nonsense. Stocks had been enormously over-priced for More than two years. Baruch, on the eve of the Crash, suddenly sells out, Buying Government bonds. So do the stockholders of the Federal Reserve System. So do the Lehman brothers. So do the partners of Kuhn, Loeb Co. So do the partners of all the international banking houses. The origins Of the Crash may be surmised from the fact that not a single partner of any Of the Frankfort-originated banking houses lost by it. On the contrary, their fortunes were doubled and tripled. When they had the suckers where they wanted them, they pulled the props out from the market, just in time to prevent a collapse in Soviet Russia, and the American people entered into four years of misery.

Where were the Rothschilds when all this was going on? Time Magazine of the August 18, 1952, page 28, remarks that

> "The failure of the Austrian-Creditanstalt, controlled by the Rothschilds, in 1929 sparked the worldwide depression."

Many of our oldest families lost their stocks and their property to the Lehmans and the Warburgs. The Crash was an economic disaster to our Native-born citizens, but it was a boon for others. Herbert Lehman and Frederick M. Warburg formed their giant holding company, the Lehman Corporation, to buy up whole industries for a fraction of their value. Eugene Meyer Expanded his already huge Allied Chemical and Dye Corporation, James Paul Warburg increased the branches of his Bank of Manhattan Company, while Samuel Zemurray of the Palestine Economic Corporation and others of his species formed another big holding company, the Atlas Corporation. The partners of Sullivan and Cromwell and of Lehman Brothers formed the Marine Midland Company, which controlled the Niagara power interests and the industry of Upper New York State.

Amadeo Giannini, of the Bank of America, nearly lost his holdings to the National City Bank, and waged a strong fight throughout the 1930s to save His bank from National City (Rothschild) domination. An honest Italian, Giannini had built up the largest bank in the West, and the New York crowd Seized 1929 as their chance to break him. He made a brilliant comeback, and in 1951 Wall Street finally enlisted the Federal Reserve Board in an All-out attack on the Bank of America, ordering it to dissolve its holdings In the Transamerica Corporation. This was an action so blatantly prejudiced that it would have aroused widespread resentment among the American People had the public press bothered to inform them of the issues at stake.

The Crash of 1929 was an excellent chance for the radical Marxist Trade unionists to consolidate their hold on the union movement in America, And to beat down the factory owners, of whom many went broke. The leader of the Marxists was the notorious Communist Sidney Hillman. The Biography "Sidney Hillman", by Jean Gould, Houghton Mifflin 1952, relates on page 276 that

> "Sidney Hillman incorporated the Amalgamated Bank of New York and Chicago on April 14, 1923. This bank was unaffected by the depression and had $11,000,000 in cash at the time of the crash. A. D. Marimpetri 'was happy to be able to report that they had operated without so much as a single dollar' Loss throughout one of the greatest market breaks in the history of the Stock exchange."

Not only was Soviet Russia unaffected by the Crash, but the principal Capital of Marxism in America, Communist Sidney Hillman's Amalgamated Bank, also was unaffected.

I noted in "The Federal Reserve" that, of the 106 firms which founded The New York Cotton Exchange in 1870, only two have survived to the present Day, Baruch's banking house of Hentz and Co., and Herbert Lehman's family House of Lehman Brothers.

No scoundrel was too reprehensible to be refused employment in the great war On the wealth of the American people if he had a good scheme, and so a European adventurer named Ivar Kreuger was backed in a $250 million swindle by Three New York and Boston banking houses, Lee Higginson Co. Dillon Read Co. And Brown Brothers Harriman. One of the worst financial scandals in modern History, it was criticized on the floor of Congress on June 10, 1932 by Rep. Louis

MacFadden, Chairman of the House Banking and Currency Committee, As follows:

> "Every dollar of the millions Kreuger and his gang drew out of this country On acceptances was drawn from the Government and the people of the United States through the Federal Reserve Board and the Federal Reserve banks. The credit of the United States was peddled to him."

CHAPTER 16

The three most important dictators of the twentieth century, Lenin, Mussolini, and Hitler, all knew the workings of international finance capital. Mussolini defeated the Banca Commerciale in Italy and made himself a leader, Hitler is supposed to have beaten the Rothschilds in Germany, and Lenin, Of course, spearheaded the new development of international finance capital, now known as Communism.

The international spider of finance which had spun its web out from Frankfort and over Europe and America did not fail to reach into Italy, with such success that before the First World War Italy was in the hands of The German bankers. Dr. E.J. Dillon, in his history, "From the Triple to the Quadruple Alliance", Hodder and Stoughton, 1915, writes that

> "Italy was become a commercial colony of Germany. Prof. Pantaleoni Early saw the evil influence which was being exerted by the Banca Commerciale, Which had its headquarters in Milan, and which had been founded in 1895 By Herr Schwabach, the Chief of Bleichröders, and other German Jews such as Joel, Weil, and Toepliz. The Banca Commerciale controlled the Italian economy By a system of interlocking directorates."

Lehman Brothers is doing the same thing in the United States. Benito Mussolini freed Italy from the Banca Commerciale, and earned for himself the epithet "dirty Fascist" which became standard in our controlled press.

Another reason for the press campaign against Mussolini is given by Paul Einzig in "World Finance 1914–1935",

> "In Italy Signor Mussolini placed a ban on loans issued abroad, and the extent to which Italy participated as a borrower in the orgy of International lending was moderate."

Mussolini broke the power of the Banca Commerciale by showing the utmost Determination that Italy should find her own destiny in Europe, without knuckling to the dictation of the Rothschilds. After the March on Rome, Mussolini proved that He was more than a dramatist, when he overvalued the Lira, which effectively weakened the influence of the international bankers and their interlocking assets In Italy. At this time, the German bankers were helpless to do anything about it. They had wrecked Germany, and they had to wait until Hitler came along to pull that nation back on her feet. Meanwhile, the Frankfort boys were pushed out of Italy by a former mineworker who earned the admiration of the world. He stood for Italia Irredenta, a renascent Rome. No wonder that the Jewish Sentinel in its issue Of November 26, 1920 complained that

> "Our only great historical enemy, our most dangerous enemy, is Rome in All its shapes and forms, and in all its ramifications. Whenever the sun of Rome begins to set, that of Jerusalem rises."

That Mussolini was Rome is proven by his writings, which are as forthright as the statements of Cincinnatus. In starling contrast to the vindictive anti-Christian writings of Marx and Lenin, which I have already quoted, and which express a racial attitude, the religious spirit of Benito Mussolini is expressed in his most important book, "The Doctrine of Fascism", Firenze 1936, which became the principal guide of the Italian Fascist Party. On page 44, Mussolini tells us that

> "The Fascist State is not indifferent to religious phenomena in general nor does it maintain an attitude of indifference to Roman Catholicism, The special positive religion of Italians. The State possesses a moral Code rather than a theology. The Fascist State sees in religion one of the deepest of spiritual manifestations and for this reason it not only Respects religion but defends it and protects it. The Fascist State does not attempt, as did Robespierre at the height of the revolutionary delirium Of the Convention, to set up a god of its own, nor does it vainly seek, As does Bolshevism, to efface God from the soul of man."

Instead of finding out what Mussolini stood for, The American people were treated to a steady diet of Walter Lippmann and Walter Winchell, whose rabbinical loyalties prevented either of them from Mentioning Mussolini's Christian program. Nevertheless, Mussolini was able to effect vast reforms in Italy, nor were the international news services Able to keep that information from the American people. Hundreds of thousands of tourists visited Italy during the 1930s, and saw the new state which Mussolini Had raised from the poverty of an Italy which had been dominated by the International bankers. American officials were impressed by Mussolini's Leadership, although they were careful to avoid stating this publicly. One such opinion comes to light years after Mussolini's brutal murder By Communist partisans, from Stimson's biography, "On Active Service In Peace and War, by McGeorge Bundy, page 268,

> "As Secretary of State, Stimson visited Italy in 1931. In Italy were Benito Mussolini and Count Dino Grandi, his youthful Foreign Minister. It Seems ironical, but in this period Mussolini was one of the most ardent and least inconsistent advocates of disarmament in all Europe … A few Days later, he took the Stimsons for a motorboat ride. 'He showed his Attractive side, and we both liked him very much.' From a Memo, July, 9, 1931, 'He was emphatic that Italy stood for disarmament and for peace.'"

Although the international bankers were disgruntled over being driven Out of Italy, such temporary setbacks were not new to them. It meant that Italy would be on the wrong side during the next war, and then they could do what they pleased with her. The vindictive murder of Mussolini would discourage other Italians from his boldness.

One reason the bankers were not too unhappy about being pushed out Of Italy for the time being was pointed out by Paul Warburg in one of his Cynical asides to financial reporter Carter Barron. "Why," sneered Paul, "should we bother about a country which has no gold?"

Paul Einzig (half of these creatures seem to be named Paul) in his book "Finance and politics", Macmillan, 1932, remarked that

> "The Bank of Italy had never been in a position to accumulate a gold Reserve comparable with that of France, or even, comparatively speaking, With that of Holland, Switzerland, or Belgium."

Italy's lack of gold was a challenge to Mussolini which he accepted. He Developed a strong internal economy which was not dependent upon the Vagaries of Paul Warburg or Sir Ernest Cassel, as Einzig points out in "World Finance, 1935–1937" Macmillan, 1938,

> "By 1927, drastic exchange restrictions were adopted in Italy, and By this action it virtually ceased to be a member of the Gold Bloc."

Einzig suggested in "World Finance 1938–1939" that

> "A friendly Italy would find no difficulty in obtaining the participation of British or other foreign capital in exploiting Abyssinia's natural resources. The termination of the civil war in Spain might lead to such developments."

Since Einzig is the publicist for the House of Rothschild, this suggestion could mean only that the Rothschild were making Mussolini one last Offer before the outbreak of the Second World War. It was probably an Attempt to break up the Rome-Berlin Axis, but Mussolini ignored both the Promise and the threat implicit in the bribe.

Mussolini's offenses against the international bankers, however, are Mild compared to those of Adolf Hitler. A smalltime rabblerouser, Hitler Was mouthing around Germany about the Jews after the First World War, When the Socialist Zionists decided that he would be a good man to enforce Dr. Nathaniel Syrkin's admonition that "Anti-Semitism helps the Jews Maintain their national solidarity."

All at once, Hitler's little group had large sums advanced to them From London and New York, and the agitators blossomed forth as a Full-fledged political party. In "Merchants of Death", by H.C. Engelbrecht and Frank C. Hanighen, Dodd, Mead, 1934, we find on page 243,

> "The Man behind Hitler is Thyssen, the steel magnate of the Ruhr. Thyssen supplied more than three million marks in campaign funds to the Nazis in the critical years 1930 to 1933. He brought about the short-lived Hitler-von Papen-Hugenberg alliance and the fall of von Schleicher, and thus paved the way for Hitler's rise to power. For this aid Thyssen demanded and received control of the German Steel Trust, which is the Heart of the arms industry."

This is documented by many sources, such as Ernest's article in "Living Age", October, 1933, entitled "The Man Behind Hitler". However, there is no Story entitled "The Man Behind Thyssen". Fritz Thyssen was not a banker, he was one of those perennial organizers of heavy industry who are so useful to the bankers.

The man behind Thyssen was Bernard Baruch's chief financial agent, Clarence Dillon, senior partner of the international banking house of Dillon, Read. Dillon is listed in Who's Who in American Jewry as the son of Samuel Lapowitz; the name Dillon is gratuitous, a gift from democracy. Dillon had been Baruch's Assistant Chairman of the War Industries Board, when Baruch consolidated his control of United States Steel, and set about forming an international steel Cartel.

Germany after the First World War had the greatest efficiency and largest Potential of any steel industry in Europe, and, very considerately, it had not been damaged by the war. It was a rich prize, and it fell into Baruch's hands as booty from the mark inflation of 1923. For the job of refinancing it, Baruch selected his Right-hand man, Clarence Dillon. There is plenty of documentation for the fact that Baruch was the man behind Hitler. We quote from one of the most widely Distributed books of, its time, "Iron, Blood, and Profits", by George Seldes, Page 252,

> "Of the $200,000,000 in bonds listed in New York as having been issued By Dillon, Read in the past ten years, until 1934, for German clients, about $124,000,000 has been poured into the Vereinigte Stahlwerke (German Steel Trust), $48,000,000 for Siemens and Halske (General Electric affiliate) and $12,000,000 for the Ruhr Gas Corporation. The gold which made possible the Hitler march to power has been American bankers' gold."

However, Mr. Seldes, all of these "American bankers" are listed in Who's Who in American Jewry. Dillon Read refinanced Germany's rearmament program, And Baruch was behind Dillon Read. Having fathered an undying resentment In the German people by his reparations claims against them, and having Driven the German people into debt to Kuhn, Loeb to pay installments on Those reparations, Bernard Baruch recreated the German Army to give voice to That resentment, and picked up from the gutter a leader who would call the Germans to war, Adolf Hitler. This was inevitable. The bosses of heavy industry Always talk peace, but they always look forward to war. When they see the garages beside the homes filled with cars, they begin to dream of manufacturing a Million tanks and three million airplanes. Hitler was the answer to their dreams.

In the early days of the Nazi Party, Hitler's money had come directly From the Cassel-Rothschild-Loewe armaments trust, Vickers-Armstrong of England. In 1924, Dillon Read got behind him, and there was never any real Doubt after that as to whether he would become the master of Germany. The Strange patterns of the First World War were repeated in the Second, with The President of Dillon Read, James Forrestal, as Secretary of the Navy, And with Allen W. Dulles, a director of Hitler's personal bankers, J. Henry Schroder Co. as Chief of the Office of Strategic Services. Throughout the War, Dulles met constantly with German representatives in Switzerland.

The historian Otto Lehman-Russbeldt noted in his book, "Aggression" Hutchinson, London, 1942, page 44, that

> "Hitler was invited to a meeting at the Schroder Bank on January 4, 1933. He promised to break the power of the trade unions."

After 1933, Hitler's personal account, according to James Stewart Martin, was handled by the Schroder bank, J. M. Stein Bankhaus of Cologne. The formal alliance between the German General Staff and the Nazis was Concluded when General Kurt von Schroder, of the international banking Family, became the liaison between these two forces which controlled Germany. The alliance between the Schroders and the Rockefellers was concluded with the establishment of Schroder, Rockefeller Co. of New York, An investment concern which handles joint interests of the two families.

The third hand behind the throne of the Nazi leader was that of Max Warburg. George Sokolsky, in his book, "We Jews", points out that

> "Even in Hitler Germany the firm of Max Warburg Co. has been exempt from persecution."

The two biggest corporations in Germany backed the Nazi Party. The Steel Trust has already been discussed. The second was I. G. Farben Co. the Biggest chemical concern in the world. Fortune Magazine of September, 1942 Remarked on page 107 that

> "It is now historical fact that the steel and chemical cartels financed Hitler's early political adventures."

The hand of I.G. Farben has been omnipresent in the United States since the First World War Edward T. Clarke, private secretary of President Coolidge, registered himself as the Washington representative of I.G.'s biggest American subsidiary, Drug, Inc. which owned Sterling Drug, Inc. the firm producing Bayer Aspirin, and headed by Dr. William Weiss, one of the most sinister figures in the 1920s. On April 26, 1929, on the eve of the Crash, Paul Warburg and Walter Teagle of Standard Oil Launched I.G. Farben's American branch, American I.G. Chemical Corporation, The stock issue of $30,000,000 being handled by the National City Bank and by Warburg's International Manhattan Co. In 1939, its name was changed to General Aniline and Film Corporation. At that time it owned $17,500,000 in Dupont and Standard Oil stock, in accordance with the Rothschild system of interlocking directories. I.G.'s importance today is measured by the relationship of its chief representative in Washington, George E. Allen, to President Truman. Allen, a white House adviser who also represents I.G. Farben's interest in the giant Hugo Stinnes Industries of Germany and the United States, was appointed Chairman of the Reconstruction Finance Corporation by Truman. Allen was the go-between in the negotiations Between Truman and General Eisenhower preceding Eisenhower's acceptance Of the Republican draft. Shortly after Allen's trip to Europe to see "Ike", Truman's Daughter Margaret appeared on a Sunday night nationwide television show with the printed message "I Like Ike".

The importance of the 1929 floating of the $30,000,000 stock issue of American I.G. Chemical by Warburg was that it provided $30,000,000 of ready Cash for the Nazi Party of Germany, which needed huge sums to carry on its National program of anti-Semitic propaganda. More than $100,000,000 was provided for the Nazi Party during the crucial years from 1929 to 1933, before it was strong enough to gain power. Of this sum, General Ludendorff's Wife testified that Paul Warburg headed a New York syndicate which provided $34,000,000. The rest came from the Bank of England and other Rothschild Concerns, and this entire $100,000,000 was handled by the banking house Of Mendelssohn and Co. of Amsterdam, which conveniently failed in 1939.

To conclude the list of Jewish international bankers behind the successful Bid for power of Adolf Hitler, I quote I.F. Stone. Writing in PM, a newspaper now Defunct, of July 26, 1944, Stone said,

> "John Foster Dulles, of Sullivan and Cromwell, America's greatest corporation Law firm and prewar counsel for many of the great Nazi-dominated cartels, is believed to have inspired Tom Dewey's stand some years ago on The Anglo-American alliance. J. W. Beyen was head of the Bank of International Settlements at the time it transferred Czech gold holdings to the Reich after Munich. Another member of the Dutch delegation (to the Bretton Woods Conference) is D. Crena de Longh, who was with the Mendelssohn bank of Amsterdam, which was a financial collaborator of the Nazis and which acted As a dummy to hide German influence in the American Bosch Corporation. One member of the British delegation, Robert H. Brand, representative Of the United Kingdom Treasury in Washington and longtime partner In Lazard Brothers of London, is believed in part to be at least favorable to the idea of an Anglo-American monetary condominium. Lazard Brothers is one of the four London banks which were members of the notoriously pro-Nazi Anglo-German fellowship before the War."

Rep. Louis MacFadden, former Chairman of the House Banking and Currency Committee, testified that Lazard Brothers was the family banking house of Eugene Meyer.

Sumner Welles, in "Seven Decisions That Shaped History", Harpers, 1950, says on page 214,

> "We Americans poured hundreds of millions of dollars into Germany in the Form of loans. It was those policies which were directly responsible for the Second World War."

I do wish that Sumner Welles and George Seldes would stop whimpering that "we Americans" and "American bankers' gold" were responsible for the rise of Adolf Hitler. The American bankers involved were Baruch, Dillon, and the partners of Kuhn, Loeb Co. In 1933 the Senate Committee investigating Foreign Loans heard Otto Kahn testify that Germany at that time owed Kuhn, Loeb Co. $600,000,000 in short-term loans. Paul Einzig, in "Finance and politics", Macmillan, 1932, says that

> "In the past it has been the bankers' loans which have kept the uneconomic system of reparations in existence."

At least Einzig does Not say "American bankers' gold". Under the Roosevelt law, Americans do not have any gold. The authors of the uneconomic system of reparations were Messrs. Baruch, Warburg, and Klotz, who very definitely knew what they were doing.

The German upper class despised Adolf Hitler, whose greatest attraction to the Warburgs lay in the fact that he could become a symbol of the impotence Of the German Junker class. The Junkers had to let Hitler have Germany because they had no choice in the matter. They had been bankrupted by the war and by the mark inflation of 1923. As payment for stepping aside for Hitler without making a fuss about it, von Hindenburg and other prominent Prussians were allowed to retain their heavily mortgaged estates.

Hitler, the guttersnipe, hysterical and undetermined, came forth in 1933 with a well-integrated corps of political planners who had a definite Program of action. How did this come about? For the answer, we must turn to the people against whom Hitler shouted the loudest, and to whom He owed everything, the Jews.

Unlike Mussolini in Italy, who concerted his political program with Christianity, Hitler's system took its inspiration directly from Socialist Zionism. Dr. Nathaniel Syrkin, father of that movement, wrote in his Last work, "Nationalism and Socialism", 1917, that

> "Out of the War will appear a purified humanity and a new Socialism."

Syrkin's National Socialism became the program of Adolf Hitler's Nazi Party. It was a National Socialism which Syrkin propounded, as opposed to The international Socialism of Karl Marx. For nationalism, Hitler found His greatest inspiration in the most fiercely nationalistic of all Peoples, the Jews. Joseph C. Harsch of the Christian Science Monitor, Wrote in his book, "Pattern of Conquest", that

> "The basic racialism and mystic authoritarianism of Nazism are not really new. The concept of a special race divinely ordained by a tribal God for conquest and exploitation at the expense of others comes straight From the Old Testament. No other race in history but the Jews of the Old Testament ever achieved such complete confidence in its supernatural Selection for a private status. The parallelism between Nazism and Judaic Racialism is too near to rule out a strong suspicion that those who erected Modern German racialism were students of the motivating impulse which Swept the walls of Jericho and the Philistines from the path of triumphant Judaic tribalism."

Certainly the Jews had had several thousand years successful practice Of "triumphant Judaic tribalism", whereas the Nazis were novices at it.

Jewish World of September 22, 1915, declared that

> "Nationality is not determined by the place in which a person is born, but by the race from which that person springs."

This is only one of many Jewish precepts which Hitler adopted. He claimed as German nationals all Persons of German descent born in other countries. Our own patriotism in America is provincial, rather than racial. We give our loyalty to our state and To the United States.

The battle of race overshadows all wars. The Jews were aware of its Importance. In *Jewish World* of January 15, 1919, we find that

> "As a people, we Jews have not been at war between ourselves, the Jews In England against the Jews in Germany, or the Jews in France

against the Jews in Austria; and to sectionalize Jewry in obedience to international Differences seems to us to give away the whole principle of Jewish nationalism. Jewish nationalism is a Jewish question which must be governed by Jewish Principles, and not made subservient to the convenience or exigencies for the Time being of any government."

According to Jewish World, the spokesman for English Jewry, the Jews Owe allegiance to nothing but Jewish nationalism. Nations and governments May fall, but the Jews go on forever. That is the basis of their attitude towards Whatever nation they happen to be living in.

Adolf Hitler paraphrase this Jewish idea when he wrote that

"All that is not race is dross."

Hitler's idea on labor also were taken from Jewish writers. Solomon Schiller, in his book, "Principles of Labor Zionism", published by the Zionist Labor Party of America, 1928, writes that

"Labor Zionism is a synthesis of Zionist social ideas, nationalism, and Socialism."

The Nationalist Socialist Party of Hitler was known as the Nazi Party.

In view of these political origins of Nazism, why was Hitler anti-Semitic? And how anti-Semitic was he? Douglas Reed states in "Lest We Regret" Johnathan Cape, London, 1943, that Hitler got his start with the short-lived Communist Government in Germany from November 1918 until May, 1919, Under Prince Minister Eisner and Levine of Moscow. The biographies of Hitler Have never revealed what post Hitler had under the Eisner Government, But it was during those months that he began to devote all of his time to Politics.

Most estimates of the percentage of German real wealth owned by Jews After the mark inflation of 1923 agree on eighty per cent. Five years After Hitler came to power, by 1938, they still owned at least thirty per cent. Jews who lost their property were those who were opposed to Zionism, or Those who had incurred the dislike of the international banking crowd. Even Ambassador Dodd noted that Max Warburg had nothing to fear.

The official listing of the American Jewish Community, "Who's Who In American Jewry", edited by John Simons, in its volume for the years 1938–1939, lists Gerard Swope as Director of Allgemeine Elektricitat

Gesellschaft, of Berlin, Germany, the German Electric Trust. Swope was then the President of Baruch's power trust, International General Electric. The German combine had fallen into his hands after the mark inflation.

In his book, "Unfinished Victory", Arthur Bryant tells us that

> "According to the *London Times* correspondent in Berlin, even in November Of 1938, after five years of anti-Semitic legislation, the Jews still owned something like a third of the real property of the Reich. Most of it came into their hands during the inflation."

The attitude of Jewish bankers towards outwardly anti-Semitic governments makes for some puzzling chapters in history. I have pointed out the backing which Hitler received from Baruch, Dillon (Lapowitz), Max Warburg, Paul Warburg, and Mendelssohn Co. Jacob Marcus, in his definitive book, "The Rise and Destiny of German Jews", published in 1934 by the Union of Hebrew Congregations, Remarks that Mendelssohn of Berlin was the financier of the Russian Czars Through some of Russia's worst pogroms. He also gives us some information on the development of Germany's heavy industry. The vast Hugo Stinnes Works were financed by Jakob Goldschmidt, and Max Warburg controlled the Reichsbank, the Hamburg-American Lines, and German Lloyd's, which steamship lines made much of their fortune from transporting Immigrants to the United States during the early years of the twentieth century. The third largest bank in Germany, the Disconto Gesellschaft, was owned by the Solomonsohn family, who, Marcus says, have now become Christians and are Named Solmssen. Finally, Jacob Marcus tells us that the Warburgs financed I. G. Farben Co. the largest cartel in the world, which, with the German Steel Trust, backed Hitler's rise to power.

One of the most revealing books about Nazi Germany is "Ambassador Dodd's Diary", published by Harcourt Brace in 1941. Although openly Unsympathetic to the Nazis, Dodd does not cite a single case of persecution of Jews during his eight years in Berlin as U.S. Ambassador. The Washington story is that Roosevelt intended to name a party hack, William Dodd, to the Ambassadorship in Germany in 1933. The only William Dodd his secretary had listed was Professor William Dodd of the University of Chicago, who was telephoned that he had been appointed to the diplomatic post, much to his surprise. Roosevelt was so amused by the mistake that he left Professor Dodd go ahead with the job. If this seems irresponsible, it should be remembered that Roosevelt was elected President because he WAS irresponsible. The Baruchs and Warburgs wanted a man in the Presidency who was so irresponsible that he would embark on a crusade to save Russian Communism without a second thought of the cost in American lives.

On June 16, 1933, Dodd records in his diary" that

> "I had a conversation with Roosevelt. Schacht president of the Reichsbank, was threatening to cease paying both interest and principle on bills due American creditors in August. Roosevelt said, 'I know our bankers made exorbitant profits when in 1926 they loaned huge sums to German corporations and cities and they succeeded in selling bonds to thousands of our citizens with interest at six or seven per cent. But our people are entitled to repayment, and while it is altogether beyond governmental responsibility, I want you to do all you can to prevent a moratorium'."

On July 3, 1933, Dodd says

> "I went at ten to a conference at the National City Bank, where State Department people had asked me to review the financial problems of German and American banks, including payment of one billion two hundred million dollars to American creditors who had been hoodwinked by bankers into making loans to German corporations. The National City Bank and the chase national held more than one hundred million dollars worth of German bonds. Then came a prearranged conference with Judge Julian Mack, Felix Warburg, Judge Irving Lehman, Rabbi Stephen S. Wise, and Max Kohler, who is writing a biography of the Seligman family. The conference had been arranged by George Gordon Battle, a liberal lawyer."

On July 4, 1933, Dodd says

> "Col. House's car met me as I walked out of the railway station. We talked two hours about my 'difficult mission'."

And on September 1, 1933,

> "Henry Mann of the National City Bank spoke of the conversation he and Mr. Nelson Aldrich had had some ten days before with the Chancellor of the Reich at his summer palace. Despite Hitler's attitude, these bankers feel they can work with him."

On December 4, 1933,

"John Foster Dulles, legal counsel for associated American banks, called at noon to give an account of claims being urged on behalf of bondholders against German cities and corporations. He seemed very clever and resolute."

Dulles had been serving on the Reparations Commission before promoting himself into the job of collecting debts owed by Germany.

On January 19, 1934,

"My wife and I attended a party of Baron Eberhard von Oppenheim, who is a Jew still living in style near us. Many Nazi Germans were represented there. It is reported that Baron Oppenheim has given the Nazi Party 200,000 marks, and has been given a special party dispensation which declares him an Aryan."

On March 12, 1934,

"Stephen P. Duggan of the International Institute of Education called."

Dodd returned to the United States for a visit in the spring of 1934.

He notes on March 23, 1934,

"Col. House sent his handsome limousine with a friend to meet me when the Manhattan docked, to take me quietly to his house. He gave me valuable information about unfriendly officials in the State Department with whom I would have to deal."

On May 8, 1934,

"At dinner tonight at Col. House's, soon after we sat down to the table, we talked intimately about the groups in the Cabinet. This reminded me of the pressing invitation I had had from Gerard Swope to take luncheon with him, Herbert Bayard Swope, Owen D. Young, and Raymond Moley while I was in the city. Gerard Swope is head of General Electric; Herbert Bayard Swope figured in a doubtful capacity at the London Economic Conference; and Owen D. Young I have never regarded with any enthusiasm. I declined the invitation mainly because of the feeling that some sort of game was in mind. I distrust every one of the four."

Since his appointment was a mistake, Dodd was honest. Evidently he did not know that Baruch's private brain trust, Swope, Young, and Moley, wanted to explain some things to him about the anti-Semitism of the Nazi Party. Dodd does not record that he never spoke with

Baruch, and the fact that he distrusted all of Baruch's lieutenants speaks very highly for his personal integrity. There are still men who cannot be bought, even if they do get into government by accident.

On July 24, 1934, Dodd writes that

> "James Lee, son of Ivy Lee, who for months has been trying to sell the Nazi regime to the American public, came to see me."

On several occasions, Dodd records his disgust with the Lee, who was Rockefeller's, Hitler's, and Stalin's agent in America. A House Investigating Committee found that Ivy Lee had been receiving $33,000 a year from the Nazi Government. However, it was not of his major accounts.

On July 28, 1934, Dodd says,

> "Max Warburg, eminent Hamburg banker and brother of Felix Warburg of New York (the third brother, Paul, died in 1932), came to see me. He thinks Rabbi Wise and Samuel Untermeyer of New York have done the Jews of both the United States and Germany great harm by their craving for publicity. He said Felix Warburg was of the same opinion. Both of them were fully in sympathy with Col. House in his efforts to ease off the Jewish boycott and reduce the number of Jews in high positions in the United States, Before leaving, Warburg indicated that he doubted the wisdom of James McDonald's activity in his position at Lausanne. That has been my attitude from the beginning. Warburg suggested that Lazaron, living quietly in Berlin, might do more with the German Government than McDonald, and I agreed with him. Any man who would take a big salary for such a service, all from people who give for the relief of suffering fellowmen, is not apt to appeal strongly to other givers, and McDonald has shown so much self-esteem on different occasions that I fear these traits have become too well-known in Berlin official circles."

This was James McDonald, the former Soviet publicist, who had promoted himself into a plush and important job as refugee administrator, operating on a big expense account out of Lausanne, Switzerland. He later became the first U.S. Ambassador to Israel, which did little to raise the prestige of our diplomatic corps.

On August 23, 1934, Dodd writes,

"In the afternoon Ivy Lee came to see me with his smooth young son."

On August 28, 1934, he says

"Dr. Max Ilgner of the I.G. Farben concern and President of the Carl Schurz Foundation, came to see me. He did not mention Ivy Lee, who received a large fee from his concern. He did talk a good deal about a business trip to Manchuria, where he said his company had bought 400,000 bushels of soy beans. I suspect he is on a mission to exchange poison gases and explosives for Japanese products."

And on December 4, 1934,

"Col. Deeds called. He represents the National Cash Register Co., and also the National City Bank. His son was brought before the Nye Committee last September to explain sales of arms to Germany by a company of which he is an officer, allegedly in violation of the American Treaty with Germany. He told me that National Cash Register is doing a vast business with Krupp's, which receives 20% of the sales to Germany."

On March 8, 1935, Dodd records that at a party,

"Max Warburg seemed quite secure this evening."

What did a Warburg have to worry about in Hitler Germany?

March 31, 1935, Dodd writes

"Poor Lazaron revealed great concern because so many wealthy Jews have surrendered to the Nazi leadership and are influential financial aides to Dr. Schacht, who thinks their assistance is very important in the present economic situation."

On June 8, 1935, he says

"Lochner (Louis Lochner, CBS correspondent in Berlin) showed me a copy of secret instructions sent to the German press about the necessity of conciliating the Jews, who have the world film business in their control. Lochner said he could not send the report over the AP wire because it was so confidential."

Yes, indeed, that one was kept confidential.

On September 14, 1935, Dodd writes

"Mr. S. R. Fuller called. Mr. Fuller, who is a friend of President Roosevelt, owns large rayon interests in Tennessee, is connected with Dutch and Italian interests manufacturing rayon, and is part owner of similar corporations in Germany, including an industrial plant in Hanover."

On October 14, 1935, he records that

"Dr. Jacob Gould Schurman, the former Ambassador, brought a friend, Ben Smith of New York City. Smith quite frankly remarked, 'I am a New York speculator, but also a close friend of President Roosevelt.' Dr. Schurman told me in an aside that his friend Smith was a clever speculator who violated all bankers' advice in 1929 and sold stock short in such enormous amounts as to make many millions."

Nearly all the bankers I have studied, including the Governors of the Federal Reserve Board, warned members and friends in advance that the break was coming. Smith was only one of a number who sold stock short in expectation and inside knowledge of the Crash of 1929. On January 24, 1935, Dodd tells us that

"John Foster Dulles, a New York lawyer from Sullivan and Cromwell, reported his difficulties in financial matters here."

Dodd records on October 20, 1935 that

"I asked a lawyer why Standard Oil sent millions over here in December of 1933 to aid Germany in making gasoline from soft coal for war emergencies? Why do the International Harvester people continue to manufacture in Germany when their company gets nothing out of the country and when it has failed to collect its war losses?"

Dodd seems to be quite naïve. Does he really think that International Harvester, which is controlled by J.P. Morgan Co. lost anything in the war? It would have been impossible to have a Second World War unless industrialists and bankers in England, France, and America helped Germany rearm just as it is impossible to have a Third World War until we rearm Russia, which is the *raison d'être* for the Marshall Plan, the Economic Co-Operation, and the Point Four program inspired by Communist Earl Browder. They are intended to get machine tools and power equipment to Russia to aid her in rebuilding her war potential.

The case of Dr. Hjalmar Schacht, President of the Reichsbank and Finance Minister of the Hitler Government, is an interesting one. Schacht was the first to be denazified after the surrender of Germany. This was made much easier by the gracious admission from Dr. Schacht that he really had never been a Nazi. According to our own bankers, Hitler's entire program would have failed in the 1930s had it not been for the financial genius of Dr. Schacht, but he was never a Nazi.

Schacht had travelled about the world, held conferences with other Central Bankers at their "Club", the Bank of International Settlements in Switzerland, and particularly was most cordial to his opposite number in Great Britain, Sir Montagu Norman of the Bank of England. He alone of the top Nazi officials had such freedom. The others spied, interpreted, and misinterpreted each other's doings to Hitler, while Schacht paid no attention to any of them, and even dared to insult the great Goring to his face.

One of the outstanding facts about the supposed seizure of the German Government by the Nazis, publicized in America as a radical overthrow, was the Adolf Hitler made no changes in the German banking system. The Warburgs kept control through Dr. Schacht, who was there when Hitler came in. Paul Einzig, in "World Finance 1935–1937" says,

> "Dr. Schacht was not a Fascist, but an orthodox banker. Mr. Montagu Norman's friendship with Dr. Schacht played an important part in the shaping of the Bank of England's policy throughout the postwar period.

> Norman displayed his friendship by making an eleventh—hour attempt to strengthen his friend's position in the Nazi regime. This opportunity was provided by the deeply deplored death, though a bathing accident, of the French General Manager of the Bank of International Settlements, M. Auhein."

Although banking is supposed to be a very stable business, one cannot help but be struck by the number of events in international banking which are extremely accidental. Some deeply desired and immediate objective is obtained, not by a successful devising of strategy for it, but by the hap chance dropping of some obstacle out of a tenth-floor window, or into sixty feet of water. The passing of James Forrestal, President of Dillon Read banking house, and Secretary of Defense, is a case in point. Forrestal plummeted to his death from one of the highest points in the Washington area, the Navy hospital tower at Bethesda,

Maryland. When his mind had begun to slip, and his conscience had tortured him to the point where he felt that he had to bring certain matters to the attention of the American people, notably the influence of Zionism in Washington, he was rushed off to Florida and kept in seclusion in the custody of Brown Brothers Harriman partner Robert Lovett, now Secretary of Defense. From there he was transferred to the Naval Hospital, a prisoner, and not even his priest was allowed to talk to him. The word was given out to the press that he had attempted suicide, yet he was taken to the highest point around Washington, the Bethesda Hospital Tower, and placed by an open window, and at last he went out of it, whether or not by his own power.

Hitler carefully outlined his proposed program, step by step, in his book, "Mein Kampf". It seemed a desirable aim, to the international bankers, that he set up a pan-European Confederation which would make a suitable opponent for a Second World War. Consequently, as he made each of the moves which he had outlined in his prospectus for the investment bankers, mysterious influences in the capitals of the world kept down opposition to him, until his training period was over, and the fight went on in 1939.

Paul Einzig points out, in "World Finance 1935–1937", that

> "It was the mistake deflationary policy pursued under the Government of Dr. Bruning during the depression and more especially after the crisis of 1931 that was largely responsible for the advent of Hitler ... It was because the energies of France were focused on the defense of the franc that Hitler took his chance and reoccupied the Rhineland in March, 1936."

It is absurd to pretend that Hitler took any chance, as if the fate of a billion dollar investment was decided by a reputed madam stepping across a border. Hitler actually had to be coaxed into reoccupying the Rhineland. He knew that he wasn't strong enough for such a step at that time, and so did everybody else. At the slightest show of protest from England or France, he would have scurried back across the Rhine like a frightened water-rat. However, he had received assurance that no protest or resistance would be forthcoming.

In "World Finance 1938–1939", Paul Einzig writes that

> "We now discover the close connection between the weakness of the franc under Chautemps and Hitler's decision to invade Austria in 1938. With France paralyzed in the throes of a monetary crisis,

there was no chance of an assistance to Austria from either Great Britain or Italy."

As Hitler made each of his advances, the lords of money, like the gods of the Iliad, hovered over him, watching in approval or disapproval of the manner in which he executed their will. Einzig continues in "World Finance 1938–1939", as follows:

"It is worth pointing out that the gold taken over from the Austrian National bank never appeared in the Reichsbank return. Toward the end of 1938 it was spent on imports of raw materials for rearmament... Austria's short-term credits were defaulted upon, immediately after the Anschluss by the Germans."

Without wishing to praise Hitler, it must be pointed out that he was largely responsible for the economic recovery of France, England, and the United States, from 1935 to 1940. It was his war scares, ably publicized by the international news services regularly from 1935 to 1939, which stock prices of heavy industry bounding up and up, and his large orders for raw materials and finished products re-employed millions of workers in these countries during these years while Japan was carrying out the same useful function for the world munitions industry in the Far East.

In "World Finance 1935–1937" Einzig wrote that

"M. Sarraut intended to mobilize when Hitler reoccupied the Rhineland, but Gen. Gamelin informed him that it would cost 6 milliard francs. He consulted the Finance Minister, who said he would have to devalue, if that sum were expended at that time. Rather than devalue, M. Sarraut left Hitler in possession of the Rhineland."

The above paragraph may be classified as science-fiction. Although Einzig habitually resides in the vest pockets of the Finance Ministers of Europe, that passage could have been overheard only in a pipedream. However, he does give us some accurate reporting in the following excerpt from "World Finance 1939–1940",:

"After the invasion of Czechoslovakia, the Bank of International Settlement cheerfully surrendered to the German authorities the six million pounds of gold it held on behalf of the Czechoslovakian National Bank. Gold and foreign assets held by the Bank of England, thanks to the firm British character. German politicians were understandably perplexed by this unusual display for firmness and swiftness, for the possession of those assets running to tens of millions of pounds, would have enabled Germany to import substantial reserves of raw materials before the outbreak of the war."

It is amusing to read that "firm British character" had anything to do with the disposition of a large sum in gold. The fact was that the great double-cross was now being out into effect. After rearming Germany, and letting Hitler believe that he was God, or at least a new Attila, the international bankers shut off his credits and waited for him to take the only possible step, the touching off of the Second World War. It was a perfect job of casting, even though the plot of the melodrama was a very ancient and obvious one.

CHAPTER 17

Franklin Delano Roosevelt died thinking that the world would never forget him because he saved Communism, but today it seems more likely that his real memorial will be the Third World War. Carter Field notes, in his biography of "Bernard Baruch". That

> "Franklin D. Roosevelt personally got tremendous credit in 1917 for his daring in having ordered, prior to the declaration of war, far and away in excess of the authority granted the Navy Department by Congress."

He was upholding Cousin Theodore's precedent of not waiting for a declaration of war. As Assistant Secretary of the Navy, Franklin Roosevelt placed many large orders with heavy industry for which there was no authority, and if the Hoover-Dodge propaganda machine had failed to get us in the war, young Roosevelt's political carrier would have ended. At that time, he was still a struggling young lawyer, with little more than a famous name and a toothy smile. Baruch paid him off in 1923 by cutting him in on the mark inflation in Germany. Roosevelt was the front for United European Investors, Ltd. whose prospectus avowed that it intended to speculate in the mark. With the profits from this gambling venture, Roosevelt was able to afford a front as a Wall Street lawyer, as the firm of Roosevelt and O'Connor.

How much money they made, if any, is open to speculation, but the fact is that Roosevelt turned back to politics. His name got him elected Governor of New York, with a good bit of help from the Communist Party. He helped to sabotage the campaign of Al Smith for President, in favor of the gold standard bearer from London, Herbert Hoover. In 1932 Roosevelt turned on Hoover by waging a campaign of utter falsehood against him as regards his political career, while persons interested in the recognition of Communist Russia circulated the stories of Hoover's successful campaign to keep out of jail in England over a period of years while promoting a number of fast-dollar propositions in mining stock.

The stories about Hoover were true, but the stories about Roosevelt were worse. He too had blood on his hands from the First World War, when he had been one of Baruch's Inner Circle, he had made a shady living on Wall Street since then, and he had been struck down with a crippling disease which left him a prematurely hateful and morbid old man. It needs no psychiatrist to deduce why this miserable human wreck in his wheelchair sent millions of stalwart young men out to face death, nor do we need Freud to tell us how Roosevelt was comforted when he saw them come back by the thousands from Anzio and Guadalcanal, still in their teens, as crippled and hopeless as himself.

Roosevelt's campaign against Hoover was characterized by the open deceit and deliberate lying which marked his public utterances throughout his career. The most cynical liar in America's political history, Franklin Roosevelt sincerely believed that our people were too stupid to believe anything but lies. His contempt for our citizens was such that time after time he stood before them and cheerfully told them obvious lies, and laughed in their faces while they applauded him.

While scrupulously avoiding the part which Hoover had played in getting us into the First World War, or his feeding Germany, or his pre-War career as one of the most scandalous operators in London, Roosevelt tried to make Hoover responsible for the Depression. Hoover, in the third volume of his Memoirs, which forget a great deal, says,

> "To Roosevelt's statement that I was responsible for the orgy of speculation of the 1920s, I considered for some time whether I should expose the responsibility of the Federal Reserve Board by its deliberate inflation policy from 1925 to 1928 under European influence, and my oppositions to these policies."

Four times Roosevelt took the oath of office as President, and four times he perjured himself, for each time that he laid his hand on the Bible and swore to uphold the Constitution of the United States, his mind was filled with the schemes of his alien-born advisers for subverting and evading its principles. Future generations will curse the citizenry which sat by while Woodrow Wilson tore up the Constitution and Franklin Roosevelt threw the pieces away. Roosevelt had been Wilson's understudy in Communism and Zionism during the First World War, but, like his mentor, Roosevelt did not live to see the moment of triumph, when the flag of Israel billowed above New York City at the United Nations Headquarters.

Roosevelt had announced himself as material for the Presidency by a single revealing speech, given over the radio on the evening of March 2, 1930, when he said,

> "To bring about government by oligarchy, masquerading as democracy, it is fundamentally essential that practically all authority and control be centralized in our Federal Government ... The individual sovereignty of our states must be destroyed."

Centralism was one of the key words Communism. Lenin wrote of Marx,

> "Marx was never a federalist, he was a centralist."

Wilson, until the advent of Roosevelt, had been the most notorious perjurer to occupy the White House. In 1912 Wilson took his oath of office and swore to uphold the Constitution, when he had given his word ten months before that he would sign the Federal Reserve Act into law, which took the Constitutional right of issuing money away from Congress and gave it to the international bankers who financed his campaign. In 1916, after a campaign under the slogan of "He kept us out of war", Wilson again took the oath of office, when at that moment he knew that commitments had been made to London that we would be at war within a matter of weeks. He prematurely shattered his health in his campaign to give away the sovereignty of the United States to a gang as unprincipled and rootless as himself.

All this Franklin Roosevelt did, and more. Without shame he made the Treasury of the United States the headquarters to the gold merchants of the world, raising the price of gold to suit their needs, and enacting a law that Americans could no longer have gold in their possession, so that his friends could have absolute control over our gold supply.

The perjurer Roosevelt was never more than a shiftless, unscrupulous favorite son, a man born to every advantage, his birth in a free country, a famous name, a good education, and yet he was utterly incapable of doing enough honest work to support himself or his family. It is not recorded that he never spent one day of his life in any useful enterprise. He willingly became the intimate of the scum of the nation in Washington, and ever afterwards sought lower and lower levels.

A mortal blow was struck by Woodrow Wilson at the dignity of public office in America in the emergency of the First World War, when he gave away the highest offices in the Government to the Brandeises, Frankfurters, Baruchs, and Meyers, and that dignity was given its coup de grace by Franklin Roosevelt in 1933, when there swarmed into Washington in his wake, like sea scavengers following a garbage scow, a motley horde of misshapen degenerates and traitors. Roosevelt soon made it apparent that he was comfortable only in the lowest moral stratum, and he turned the White House into a free boarding-house for the wet-lipped crew of Hollywood pimps and Communist homosexuals who were his high priests and votaries. No one was welcome at the White House unless he had betrayed an empire, as did Churchill, or mortgaged his aged mother's home, as did Truman.

Roosevelt was the first American to establish a Popular Front Government, a method of administration which the Rothschilds had enforced in Europe. The Popular Front consisted of getting all of the lower elements of a nation, of whatever political complexion, to combine in an open conspiracy against the decent citizens. The principle element of Roosevelt's Popular Front disguised as the Democratic Party, was the national crime syndicate, which controlled the votes in the big cities, and competing for second place in Roosevelt's favor were the Communists and the Zionists. The Communists delivered the labor vote to Roosevelt, and the Zionists controlled public opinion and delivered the powerful Jewish vote. Often the Communists and the Zionists, as exemplified in Roosevelt's White House hanger-on, Rabbi Stephen S. Wise, were the same people. Whether Wise was a Communist posing as a Zionist, or a Zionist posing as a Communist, he was one of the more conspicuous of the wild-eyed crew who received free meals and a room by the month at the White House. Roosevelt's religious background may be surmised from the fact that he had a rabbi with him constantly during his years in the White House, while Christian ministers were never seen there. Eleanor Roosevelt, of course, had young Joe Lash in to live at the White House, but I have always believed that her attachment to him was purely a political one, and that she liked him only because he was a Communist.

At any rate, the invasion of Washington by these elements had its desired effect. Men of good character got out of the Government, and left it to the wreckers. More than one decent American, fearful of being sucked into the Communist vortex at the State Department, left public service forever.

Franklin Roosevelt found a fit partner for his shady intrigues in the person of Winston Churchill, who had crawled on his belly before the diamond merchants since 1898, when he went to South Africa to win the gold and diamond mines of the Witwatersrand for the Rothschilds, the Ecksteins, and the Joels. After the Boer War, Churchill returned to England to find himself the hero of a certain minority. He willingly accepted the role into which his character had delivered him, and entered upon a long career in the service of world Zionism. The peers of Great Britain, alarmed at the influx of the Mediterranean stock, and its accompanying-rise in poverty and crime in British cities, tried to pass an Aliens Act in 1903. For two years it was fought bitterly in Parliament, and finally defeated. The successful leader of the opposition to the Aliens Control Act was Winston Churchill. Naturally he was acclaimed in all of the Jewish organs. He cared nothing for the fact that he had betrayed his own race and taken the gold piece of another. In 1915, as First Lord of the Admiralty, he changed the British fleet from coal to oil, which meant an increase of some millions of pounds a year in the income of his good friends, the Samuel family, who owned the Royal Dutch Shell Oil Corporation. In 1916, when the Zionists were campaigning furiously for the Balfour Declaration, Churchill was the member of the British War Cabinet who spoke most strongly and effectively for it, nor has he lost an opportunity since to show were his sympathies lie.

Like Churchill, Franklin Roosevelt is a livid example of the moral depths to which a man must degrade himself in order to hold high public office in a democracy. However, a man must corrupt himself before he can corrupt others, and Roosevelt's disease, striking as it did BEFORE his political success, may be taken as evidence that he had succeeded in corrupting himself.

In his first Washington appearance, in 1916, Roosevelt learned from the Machiavelli of American politics, Bernard Baruch, the precept which characterized his administrations as President. Whenever he needed a particularly dirty job to be done, he tried to get the most respectable man possible to do it, and if he was refused, he went lower and lower until he found somebody who would do it. It was a method which the Rothschilds had practiced in Europe for a hundred years. They always went to the peerage when they had an especially odorous project in view, and they flashed their gold until they found a peer who would stand for them. Churchill, of the house of Marlborough, was their best find. He never talked at anything.

The presidency of Franklin Roosevelt has taught us an expensive lesson, a lesson we could have had free from the history of Greece. That lesson is the simple fact that the extension of the right to vote in a democracy is in exact ratio to the decreasing caliber and efficiency of public officials. As the suffrage is extended to each new group, the quality of the elected officials takes a notable drop. This has happened progressively in America until our government has become the ridiculous and disheartening farce that it is today. Although our bureaucracy on the lower levels is not openly corrupt, it is only because its personnel are too incompetent to devise successful methods of fraud. The higher echelons of the government, as investigations have disclosed, are almost one hundred per cent candidates for the penitentiary.

This condition, the result of the extension of the suffrage, has been aggravated by the procession of social misfits and professional rascals who have occupied the presidency in this century. Far more damaging to public morale has been the synthetic glory whipped up by the newspapers and magazines for these pulpy scoundrels. When a slob like Harding, a professional confidence man like Hoover, and a socially ambitious usurer like Franklin Roosevelt are held up as models for our youth, what can we expect but the cynicism and contempt which characterizes their attitude towards their parents, who actually fall for this nonsense?

The enormous sense of guilt which was typical of the low types whom the international bankers put in the White House caused a complete change in the atmosphere of our public administration. Beginning with Wilson, Washington was overcast with their neurotic fears and sleepless nights. Washington ceased to be a light-hearted Southern city, where cheerful and benign Presidents had resided; it was changed into the police camp of today, where a fearful President surrounds himself constantly with armed guards, dreading at every moment the stroke of death. Old-time Washingtonians can remember that they chased their baseballs across the White House lawn. The nervous and alcoholic wreck, Franklin Roosevelt, erected a high iron fence, so that the White House today looks like any other public place of detention.

When Franklin Roosevelt took his first oath of office, his mind was not on the suffering of the American people, or the widespread misery caused by the artificial depression which he had his cohorts had aggravated in the last months of Hoover's term. He was thinking most of his sacred mission, his pledge to recognize Soviet Russia. Arthur Upham Pope, in his book, "Maxim Litvinoff", writes on page 280,

> "Roosevelt had made it clear, even before his election, that he stood for recognition of Soviet Russia. During the summer of 1932, he had sent, as his personal emissary to Moscow, William C. Bullitt, who had already been there for President Wilson in 1919. Bullitt told the correspondents in Russia that 'Roosevelt will be the next President, and American recognition of Soviet Russia will be one of the first acts of his administration.' In January, 1933, eight hundred college presidents and professors addressed a message to the President-elect stating that 'the failure to recognize Russia has contributed to the serious situation in the Orient and prevented adoption of policies which might have frustrated the imperialistic ventures of Japan."

That list of eight hundred names would make interesting reading today. No wonder our universities turned out thousands of devoted young Communists during the Nineteen Thirties.

The Litvinoff story continues,

> "The chief factor in this sweeping reversal of opinion, however, was the economic situation, which was by now acutely dangerous. It was becoming more and more evident that a completely disorganized world market was among the main causes of the crisis."

It had been evident from the start of the depression, to those who had read Lenin or listened to Radek. According to Communist dialectic, a world depression would place all capital in their hands and give them absolute power. However, the blind disregard for human needs and desires which has condemned the Communist program to failure among developed peoples characterized their handling of the world crisis of 1929–1933. The Crash of 1929 had as its objective the wiping-out of the savings of the American middle class and thus creating a two-class system of workers and rulers, the many slaves and the few elite. This was the promise held out to the discontented young people who embraced Communism in our universities during the 1930s.

While the Communist parties of the world waited for Roosevelt to recognize Soviet Russia and become the spiritual leader of the Communist movement, the shifty politician lost his nerve. After his election, he postponed for month after month the fatal step, until at last, in November of 1933, he held the all-night conference at the White House with Henry Morgenthau Jr., Maxim Litvinoff, and the legal counsel for the Soviet Union, Dean Acheson. It was Acheson who provided the balance in favor of recognition. He assured Roosevelt of Wall Street support if Russia were recognized NOW, but he warned that further delay would mean the grooming of a man to take his place in 1936. It was the threat of losing support for his numerous schemes which forced Roosevelt to keep his promise to the Communists. This was the last time he ever hedged on his word to them. Now that he had crossed his Rubicon, and there had been no public denunciation of his action, he became a most fervent supporter of Communism. He filled the Government bureaus with long-haired Marxists from the City College of New York and from his own school, Harvard University. He made a special *protégé* of the brilliant young Communist leader, Alger Hiss, and kept near him Lauchlin Currie, a leader in the shadowy espionage ring in Washington. After Roosevelt's death, Currie slunk off to Colombia to avoid revealing his background to a Congressional Committee.

One of Roosevelt's first acts, after recognizing Russia, was to set up an Export-Import Bank, on February 12, 1934, which proudly announced that its mission was

> "the exclusive purpose of financing the trade between the United States and Russia."

We would send Russia goods, and Russia would write checks on the Export-Import Bank, which would be picked up by the American taxpayer. However, the swelling roar of welcome from the American proletariat to their Russian comrades failed to materialize. Indeed, the recognition of Russia brought little response from the American people, and the establishment of the Export-Import Bank at that time, when we were still suffering widespread unemployment and hunger, was overdoing it. Several Congressmen prepared to launch an attack on it, reminding the Government that Russia still owed us $150,000,000 which she had welched on in 1917. Roosevelt retreated in disorder before this opposition, and the Export-Import Bank hastily changed its mission to lending money to South America, where the investments of J. and W. Seligman had been affected by the depression. It took the Second World War to put the American citizen to work for Stalin.

The highlight of 1933 was the London Economic Conference, which mapped out the path for the democracies to follow into the Second World War. The international bankers saw their way clear to the planned slaughter which would culminate with their setting up of a

World Socialist State. The conference was poorly reported in the American press. It is almost impossible to find out who was there or what they did. From the Royal Institute of International Affairs we find that England was represented by Frank Ashton Gwatkin, Counsellor to the Foreign Office, and by the Lord Brand, the managing director of Lazard Brothers, London, and director of Lloyd's Bank, South African Railways, and the Times Publishing Co.

Likewise, the United States was represented by a careful selection from the members of the Council on Foreign Relations. The Harvard economist Prof. O. M. W. Sprague was placed in charge of preparing documents for the American delegation, and his assistant was Leo Pasvolsky, the Russian who figured in the birth of the United Nations. The delegation was headed by the team of Secretary of State Henry L. Stimson and James Paul Warburg, who had declined Roosevelt's offer of the Director of the Budget to accomplish this important mission. Dean Acheson's law partner, George Rublee, was there, and the Harvard economist John H. Williams; Norman H. Davis, then President of the Council On Foreign Relations; Leon Fraser, then vice-president of the Bank for International Settlements; and the Chief Technical Adviser to the U.S. Delegation, Stimson's economic Adviser Herbert Feis. Two of Baruch's brain trust, Raymond Moley and Herbert Bayard Swope were there. Swope was in charge of public relations for the U.S. Delegation, and he did such an excellent job that the negotiations still remain shrouded in mystery.

Pope's biography of Litvinoff points out on page 283 that

> "Litvinoff was undoubtedly the most important personality at the London Economic Conference, completely eclipsing Raymond Moley, Chief of the U.S. Delegation."

Litvinoff was there to bargain with the United States and England as to which side Russia would be on during the Second World War. His biggest victory was a promise from the Roosevelt Administration that members of the Communist Party of America would be exempt from arrest or hindrance in any way. This promise was kept faithfully until Roosevelt died, and Harry Truman did his best to live up to it, as witness his frantic efforts to help Alger Hiss, but he never enjoyed enough personal power to save Hiss.

The main agreement at the London Economic Conference was the conclusion by all concerned that they must stick to the gold standard, thus ensuring that no constructive changes would be undertaken to relive economic misery anywhere in the world, so as to make war the only possible course. Paul Einzig, in "World Finance 1935–1937", says

> "The Gold Bloc existed for a little more than three years, having been established at the London Economic Conference in July of 1933. The existence of the Gold Bloc prolonged the economic depression by at least two years. It was during these two years that the economic depression and the overvaluation of currencies led to the aggressive foreign policy of Italy and Germany."

The guilt of Roosevelt in prolonging the depression is shown by all of the evidence. Hoover, in the third volume of his Memoirs, charges that Roosevelt did nothing to alleviate the depression, and this is true. Roosevelt aggravated the depression, for, while devoted to a program of raising world prices, Roosevelt did not increase the amount of money in circulation, which meant less money to circulate the available goods. The amount of money in circulation, as shown by U.S. Treasury reports, stayed at seven billion dollars from 1933 to 1940, while prices were steadily increased. Hoover says that there were still ten million unemployed in 1940, and that it took the war to give Americans relief from the depression after seven years of Roosevelt had failed to do so.

It was not so much that Roosevelt FAILED to give relief. The conspirators at the London Monetary and Economic Conference decided that they would not give any relief to the people, and Roosevelt kept to that agreement. He was pledged to keep the people down. Hoover also charges that Roosevelt's action in closing the banks, by reversing an old and never-used statute from the First World War, was the American equivalent of burning the Reichstag, to create an atmosphere of emergency and to give the impression that Roosevelt was the savior of the American people. Certainly Roosevelt never missed a chance to imitate the dictators. In exact copy of his mentor, Nikolai Lenin, the ruler whom he most admired, Roosevelt burned tons of food while American children were undernourished, in order to further the collectivization of American agriculture. Like Stalin, Roosevelt sent large numbers of loyal American citizens to concentration camps, the Japanese-Americans of the West Coast, because they were "politically unreliable", which is a capital crime in Russia, like Hitler, Roosevelt encouraged aggression against small nations, notably against Finland when she tried to remain free of the Communist orbit.

Of Roosevelt's monetary program, Paul Einzig noted in "France's Crisis" Macmillan, 1934, that

> "The only hope for France lies in President Roosevelt's experiments. If he is unable to bring about a rise in world prices, on the basis of the present gold value of the dollar, he will resort to a second devaluation."

Whenever the French people may have ranked in Roosevelt's experiments, it is now certain that the American people ranked last. Einzig writes in "World Finance 1935–1937" that

> "President Roosevelt was the first to declare himself openly in favor of a monetary policy aiming at a deliberately engineered rise in prices. In a negative sense his policy was successful. Between 1933 and 1935, he succeeded in reducing private indebtedness, but this was done at a cost of increasing public indebtedness."

Roosevelt sympathy for the common man is proved by his success in raising the price of everything the common man has to buy. Wages were raised, but always after the price of goods had increased, so that the only people who benefited directly were the small loan sharks to whom the workers turned for money to pay their bills.

The pyramid-building program, publicized as the Works Progress Administration, was initiated by Roosevelt because it was government spending, or Socialism, as opposed to private or free-enterprise spending.

His Socialist Zionist backers, notably James Paul Warburg, turned their fury upon the first critic of the program. Dr. William Wirt, who was persecuted for years by the Roosevelt Administration.

The head of the WPA, which spent six billion dollars, and whose upper echelons were last estimated at seventy-five per cent members of the Communist Party, was Harry Pincus Hopkins, the ulcerated witch-doctor of the Roosevelt Voodoo Cult. Hopkins, who was wished on Roosevelt by his master, John Hertz, partner of Lehman Brothers, got his start with the Red Cross in New Orleans during the First World War, where he bravely campaigned for money. In the 1920s, Hopkins became mixed up in the fabulous Christmas Seal racket, the New York Tuberculosis and Health Association. Hopkins was an executive of this mob, which had a yearly take during the 1920s of more than four million dollars. New York City Health Commissioner Louis Harris stated in a letter in the New York Times on June 8, 1932 that

> "Not one penny ever went to a person with tuberculosis, or to any institution for such care. The Association acknowledged that all its money had been expended in salaries and overhead."

Such were the intimates of Franklin Roosevelt. While the Squire of Hyde Park settled himself in his easy chair, and ordered the microphone brought in, so that he could address the serfs, millions of Americans sat by their radios, fascinated by the magic incantations of the Fireside Chats. And what was the Great Phony's message? One of his first Fireside Chats was devoted to advertising a reprint of his dear friend Justice Brandeis's book, "Other People's Money", which had been ignored when it was published in 1913 and had been justly forgotten ever since. Roosevelt's advertisement of this hack work sold a million copies and brought Brandeis a profit of $150,000. Although Brandeis, as President of the Zionist Organization of America, knew plenty about other people's money, having collected millions of it for his Zionist racket, his only book was a vicious attack on those New York bankers who in 1913 were not yet under the influence of Kuhn, Loeb Co.

Perhaps Roosevelt's greatest talent was his ability to promote racial discontent for his own ends. The most unscrupulous racial agitator in modern politics, he turned the capital of our Republic into a bureaucratic Harlem, while the whites moved out to the suburbs to protect their daughters, and voted for Roosevelt again. New York had been his training-ground in racial agitators, as it was for his protégé, the Little Red Flower, Fiorello LaGuardia, the departed Mayor of New York. LaGuardia surpassed his contemporaries in his cynicism, making no secret of the fact that he flew plane loads of Puerto Ricans in from the Caribbean before his election and registered all of them on the city relief rolls. Democracy is fine if you know how to work it.

In his relations with minority groups, Roosevelt had the able assistance of his helpmeet, the sallow Eleanor. Known to columnists as the political One-Woman Band, Eleanor knew all the tunes, but the one she played the most was that of Marx. Like the hag-ridden cripple with whom she shared her life, Eleanor preferred any project which would keep her far from the unhealthy brood which she had hatched with the assistance of the Great Communist.

One of Eleanor Roosevelt's favorite projects was Howard University in Washington, a Negro school, of course, and one which has received year after year more Government funds than any other educational institution in the United States. The chief function of Howard University seems to be the training of a Negro intellectual elite for the Communist Party of America. Its President, Mordecai Johnson, who had been a Baptist before he discovered Communism, made no secret of his sympathies. The Chicago Defender printed a report of one of his pep talks on June 10, 1933 before an audience of Negro youths. The Defender said

> "Dr Johnson urged his hearers not to allow the words Communism and Socialism to blind their eyes to the reality that on Russian soil today-it makes no difference what mistakes are being made or what crimes are being committed-there is a movement for the first time in the history of the world to make available all their natural resources for the life of the common man."

This speech, and others like it, undoubtedly caused many Negroes to enlist in the Communist Party. Dr. Johnson is still President of Howard University, nor does his oft-avowed enmity for bankers interfere with his deep friendship for international banker Senator Herbert Lehman.

Eleanor Roosevelt uses her column "My Day", syndicated throughout the nation, to promote her favorite beliefs, such as atheism, the separation of church and state, and other Marxist ideals. She finds alcohol alright for young people, and is not prejudiced against it herself. Her penchant for driving while not herself caused her to get her famous buckteeth smashed in one evening. The American press clamped down on the story, but George Richards, owner of radio stations in Los Angeles and in other cities, let his reporters air the circumstances of this accident. His station license was provoked by the Federal Communications Commission, headed by Wayne Coy, who was personal assistant to Eugene Meyer on the Washington Post before becoming dictator of America's airwaves. For three years Richards fought this Marxist-inspired invasion of the constitutionally guaranteed right of free speech, without success, until his fortune was gone and his health was shattered. He died of a heart attack while still opposing the FCC. Sex, crime, and the corruption of American children met with no opposition from Meyer's boy Coy, but nobody could talk about Eleanor Roosevelt and get away with it.

Eleanor's years as First Lady were the heydays of some of the grubbier elements of the Communist hierarchy, including such acceptable persons as the social workers who went around the schools teaching children an oddment of sexual habits, all in the name of "self-expression", and "avoiding frustration". Sex has been one of the main weapons of the Communist Party. Nudist camps, converts who were nothing but prostitutes, and sexual "education" of children have been prominent in the efforts of the Marxists.

Eleanor Roosevelt has also mastered the Big Lie technique of Communism, and despite repeated exposures of her publicly printed falsehoods, she continues to twist the truth to suit her ideology. In the Congressional Record of August 12, 1952, Senator Cain on page A5003 goes into detail of her perversion of the facts in the veterans march on Washington. Despite a letter from former Secretary of War Hurley to Mrs. Roosevelt in January of 1950, her book, "This I remember", came out with the repetition of the Communist lie that General MacArthur had ordered the troops to attack the veterans, a lie in which she was upheld by John Gunther and Time Magazine. In his column of September 6, 1952, George Sokolsky took her to task for claiming that the proposed United Nations Covenants contained "no provisions which depart from the American way of life in the direction of communism, socialism, syndicalism, or statism." Sokolsky said that she was incorrect, and that he could prove it. In the November 1952 issue of See Magazine, Eleanor denied that there were any Russian spies at the United Nations. The day that that magazine went on the newsstands, the newspapers carried the announcement that Valerian Zorin had been appointed U.N. Delegate from Russia to succeed Jacob Malik, and identified Zorin as the mastermind of the Czech coup. As Pegler says, it is unfortunate that one has to accuse a lady of lying in public, but her vicious propaganda leaves an honest reporter no alternative but to expose her in all her treachery.

It is impossible to explain the Roosevelt regime without knowing the Communist Manifesto of 1848, from "The Official Version of the Communist Manifesto in English", printed by Kerr Co. Chicago, 1917. Its ten points are as follow:

> "In the most advanced countries the following will be pretty generally applicable:
>
> 1. Abolition of property in land and the application of all rents of land to public purposes.

2. A heavy progressive or graduated income tax.

3. Abolition of all right of inheritance.

4. Confiscation of the property of all emigrants and rebels.

5. Centralization of credit in the hands of the State, by means of a national bank with State capital and an exclusive monopoly.

6. Centralization of the means of transportation and communication in the hand of the State.

7. Extension of factories and instruments of production owned by the State; the bringing into cultivation of waste lands, and the improvement of the soil generally in accordance with a common plan.

8. Equal liability of all to labor. Establishment of industrial armies, especially for agriculture.

9. Combination of agriculture with the manufacturing industries; gradual abolition of the distinction between town and country by a more equable distribution of population over the country.

10. Free education for all children in public schools. Abolition of children's factory labor in its present form."

This Communist program, written more than a century ago by Karl Marx, the son of a Frankfurt banker, proves that we Americans already have Communism here, whether we like it or not. Part of it was enacted by Lenin's friend Woodrow Wilson, and the rest we got from Franklin Roosevelt, who was put into office in 1933 by such a dangerous group of revolutionaries that even Bernard Baruch was afraid of them.

Point One of the Communist Manifesto, the abolition of property in land, and application of rents for public purposes, means that the State will become the Landlord. In the United States, the government increases its land holdings every year, and the numerous attempts at socialized housing have the government as the rent collector or mortgage holder. None of the abuses of landlordism are to be remedied, but they are to be centralized. This point will be fulfilled when it becomes illegal to own property or real estate in the United States. If this sounds preposterous, remember that it is illegal to own gold coins in this country. Who in 1930 would have believed that such a law could be passed?

Before going further, it is just as well to define the State. The State is that particular gang of thieves which holds power at the moment. Nothing more, nothing less. Communism seeks to put in a gang of thieves and keep them in by exterminating all possible opposition. Our Republic is built on the premise that the people have the right to get rid of one gang and put another one in. Communism denies that right, which is the main difference between America and Russia. Communism capitalizes on the fact that most people dislike the responsibility of selecting Government officials by voting for them and would rather have a bad government than bother to vote intelligently.

Point Two, a heavy progressive or graduated income tax, was put into law by President Woodrow Wilson in 1914, after Otto Kahn and Jules S. Bache had written it for him, and the percentage of tax was increased by Franklin Roosevelt to as high as 98% of personal income.

Point Three, the abolition of all right of inheritance, which was achieved by the Roosevelt Administration through the power of taxation over inheritances, is a blow at the structure of the family, which is a principle target of Marxism. The father can no longer build a fortune or a home for his son without having most of it seized by the State. However, the families comprising the gang in power are allowed to preserve their fortunes intact, under the guise of "philanthropical foundations", such as the Guggenheim Foundation, the Rosenwald Foundation, and the Rockefeller Foundation. These foundations have been the main source of funds for Communists in America, through "fellowships", and "research grants".

Point Four, the confiscation of the property of emigrants and rebels, is done through legal persecution of the victim until his fortune is gone. The sedition trials of 1942 against thirty-three critics of Roosevelt, and the George Richards persecution by the Federal Communications Commission are instances of hundreds of cases under the "Liberal" Democratic Administration.

Point five, the centralization of credit in the hands of the State, by means of a national bank with State capital and an exclusive monopoly, gives the gang total power over the money and credit resources of the people. This is our Federal Reserve System of the United States, a successful conspiracy by Kuhn, Loeb Co. and the House of Rothschild which was enacted into law by President Woodrow Wilson in 1913, after they had elected him for that purpose. It is a monopoly which has the State capital, our Government's credit, behind it, and it is an exclusive monopoly owned by its shareholders. It is a centralization of credit exactly as prescribed by Karl Marx.

Point Six, the centralization of the means of transportation and communication in the hands of the State, was put over by Wilson and Roosevelt in each of two successive World Wars, under cover of war emergencies. The Communist publicity outfit, the Office of War Information, was an attempt at a Government monopoly of information, and other such agencies can be cited from either war.

Point Seven, Extension of factories and instruments of production owned by the State, has been put into effect indirectly, by making the Government the principal customer of heavy industry, which gives the State control without the headaches of management. The 1952 budget of the United States calls for Government expenditure of $65 billion, from an $85 billion national income.

Point Eight, equal liability of all to labor, is universal conscription. It means that the worker has no choice as to where he shall work or what work he shall perform. Roosevelt's Social Security Act created the bureaucracy to carry out this point. The Committee for Economic Development and the United Nations are both committed to full employment, that is, universal slavery and the equal liability of all to labor as the State decrees.

Point Nine, the combination of agriculture with the manufacturing industries and abolition of the distinction between town and country have been brought about by nationwide standardization of products, and more, directly, by the factories moving into the backwoods in search of cheap labor.

Point Ten, free education for all children in public schools, is an excellent program until the problem comes up as to what subjects are to be taught, whether they must revere the greasy slob who is the Chief of State and sit meekly in classrooms until they are old enough for the kill. The main point is that the child must be taught in an institution. This is a natural development of the atheist Marxist principle of the abolition of the family. The Communists want universal education so that they can achieve thought control over the child. They already have the teachers well in hand, as witness the treadmills which are sardonically referred to as "institutions of higher learning", the Rockefeller and Guggenheim endowed universities, which produced the eight hundred college presidents and professors who signed the plea to Roosevelt in 1933 to recognize Soviet Russia.

The Catholic parochial schools have been the worst thorn in the side of the Communist Party of America, and Eleanor Roosevelt has never missed an opportunity to attack them.

The most important provision of the Communist Manifesto, of course, has been the income tax. The possession of money is an independence, and the Marxist income tax is designed to take away all but money for the necessities of life, and particularly insuring that the citizen will not have any money with which to oppose the dictatorship of the State. Our State Bank, the Federal Reserve System, has been another useful development for Kuhn, Loeb Co. and the inheritance tax has been the third provision enacted by Wilson and Roosevelt which gives the State absolute control over the people's income. All three of these measures were enacted in an atmosphere on international intrigue by professional conspirators who knew that they were subverting the lawful government of the American Republic, the Constitution of the United States.

Nikolai Lenin issued a proclamation in October, 1917, declaring that

> "Banking is hereby declared a monopoly of the State; deposits of small investors will be protected."

Roosevelt imitated the politician whom he admired most, Nikolai Lenin, by promptly enacting in 1933 a Federal Deposit Insurance Corporation bill, which, after the many times his Wall Street friends had caused the banks to close with the life savings of thrifty citizens in them, provided a much-needed shot in the arm for the bankers by guaranteeing the deposits of small investors, a la Lenin. It set up a fund of $150 million to guarantee total deposits of fifteen billion dollars in America, so it could not have been very seriously intended. However, it did allow the U.S. Government to demand reports from and allow its supervisors entry into the small banks of the nation. For the Communists, anything which adds to the bureaucracy is a good thing.

Of the program published by Lenin in "The Threatening Catastrophe" in 1917, which was the cause of his rise to power (Chapter Seven), Franklin Roosevelt caused to be enacted the most important of its provisions, the compelling of laborers to join trade unions. Known as the Wagner Act, it provided for a closed shop, that is, no one could work unless he or she was a member of the union. It denied the American citizen the right to work and earn a living for his family unless he paid tribute to a shabby lot of union racketeers. That the union leadership depends heavily on habitual criminals, and that the union racket provided an occupation for hundreds of the thugs who were put out of the bootlegging business by Roosevelt's prohibition repeal, (after the liquor business had been swallowed up by the Jews which seems to have been the real object of prohibition in the first place), has been documented by hundreds of pages of testimony before Government Committees. The workers were threatened and beaten into accepting the new order in America, but occasionally they vented their feelings concerning their masters, as witness the parody of the Walt Disney tune from his movie "Snow White and the Seven Dwarfs", which still can be heard from the street in the garment factory district in New York,

"Heigh ho! Heigh ho!
We join the C.I.O.!
We pay our dues
To the goddam Jews,
Heigh ho! Heigh ho!

One of Roosevelt's unwritten chapters of history was his effort on behalf of the Baghdad emigrants, the family Sassoon, who had become known as the Rothschilds of the East. The Sassoons had a virtual monopoly on silver, which was the basis for monetary issue in the Far East, particularly in India and China. Roosevelt manipulated the price of silver so as to help the Sassoons wipe out the little cooperative banks which were springing up over the countryside in response to Gandhi's plea to the peasants to free themselves from the Sassoon gouge. Paul Einzig, in "World Finance 1935–1937" tells how this was done,

> "The immediate effect of the initiation of President Roosevelt's silver-buying policy was a sharp rise in the price of silver through speculative purchases. This rise was actually encouraged by the United States authorities, who gradually raised their internal buying price to show that they really meant to raise the price of silver to the statutory buying price of $1.29. In December, 1935, the Washington Treasury grew tired of supporting the market and allowed the price to find its level. There was a disastrous slump from over 29d to under 20d."

The Sassoons broke their peasant competition in India by getting Roosevelt to jack up the world price of silver and keep it there for a while, forcing the cooperative bankers to buy it at the high price to finance the harvest. Then agent Harry Dexter White (Weiss) silver expert for the Treasury knocked it down again, leaving the peasant bankers ruined. These manipulations caused widespread famine in India and China and greatly hastened the advent of Communism in the Far East.

The most abortive chapter in our economic history is the National Recovery Administration. Its origin is typical. Hoover gives its background in his Memoirs, volume 3. Hoover says that Gerard Swope, President of the Baruch-controlled General Electric Corporation, in September, 1931, made an address in which he took the lead in proposing the "reorganization of American industry by economic planning", and came to Hoover with the plan. Hoover comments that

> "I submitted the plan to the Attorney-General with my note, "It is the most gigantic proposal of monopoly ever made in history." The Attorney-General merely commented that it was entirely unconstitutional."

Hoover further terms the Swope Plan, which became the NRA, a "precise pattern of Fascism", the sordid story in its entirety is that Hoover was promised a second term if he would put over the Swope Plan, which came directly from the Baruch brain trust, of course, and which was given the billion-dollar-treatment in the press. Hoover, for reasons which he does not explain, feared this new racket, and refused to have anything to do with it. Its promoters went to Roosevelt, who agreed to it, as he agreed to anything in his sickly lust for power, and Hoover was through. Most of the dirt about him was made public, and Roosevelt slid in as the new champion of humanity.

The Swope Plan, a weird brew of Communism and Fascism, contained the provisions of the National Recovery Administration, with Marxist provisions for the closed shop and a complete "social security" and 'unemployment program. Roosevelt put the whole plan into law, every unconstitutional phase of it, browbeating Congress every inch of the way until he gave Baruch what he wanted. When the National Recovery Act went into effect in 1934, Baruch sent one of his inner circle down as its head, General Hugh Johnson, who remained on Baruch's payroll at $1,000 a month after he became Chief of the NRA. The NRA tried to set up a dictatorship over American business and industry, with price-fixing, wage-fixing, allocation of production quotas, all of Baruch's favorite police state controls, many of which he had put over during the First World War, and which he reinstated during the Second World War when his creature Byrnes was Director of War Mobilization. Baruch's argument for this dictatorship in 1934 was that it had worked during wartime, and it would help in peace-time. It had worked during wartime because the people were willing to accept a dictator for the emergency, but they did not want a dictator in time of peace. Also, war production is intended for destruction, and peace-time production is intended for constructive use. The requirements for war production and the necessities of civilian consumption could never be integrated into a single economic system. The NRA was a tremendous flop, and would have been a setback to anyone who lacked the unsurpassed gall of a Roosevelt. He never looked back, and if he had, he surely would have suffered the fate of lot, and would have been turned into a pillar of salt.

Carter Field, in his biography of Baruch, says,

> "Baruch was not only a valued advisor in personal contact with the Moley group of brain-trusters around Roosevelt, but he donated the services of experts on his payroll, notably Hugh Johnson, whose pungent and forceful speech-writing proved of enormous value."

Johnson, a $10,000 a year man from Baruch's New York office, continued to draw $1000 a month after taking over the NRA, which was interpreted by the press as a noble gesture on the part of Baruch so that Johnson could afford the pecuniary sacrifices of public office.

Carter Field writes of the London Economic Conferences,

> "Baruch's right hand bower, Herbert Bayard Swope, went with Moley, while Baruch sat in Moley's job during Moley's absence. Two former subordinates of Swope, Charley Michelson and Elliott Thurston, director and assistant director of public information for the American Delegation, had both worked under Swope on the New York World, when Moley returned, he found Benjamin Cohen in his place."

This was the Benjamin Cohen who had been legal counsel for the Zionists at the Paris Place Conference, and who later became the real chief of the United Nations. The Elliott Thurston was the Washington reporter for the New York World and public relations director for the Federal Reserve Board.

Field also tells us that both Wilson and Roosevelt offered Baruch the Secretaryship of the Treasury, but Baruch usually hired other men for jobs like that.

The literary Digest of July 8, 1933 simpered that

> "Bernard Baruch, super-advisor of the U.S.A., continues to hold this unofficial portfolio in the New Deal Administration. Each President since the days of Wilson has turned to this gray-haired giant for consultation. He has been the confidant of all leaders, in and out of politics, Republican and Democratic ... He is regularly yearly lecturer at the War College."

Like all internationals who dabble in foreign loans and the values of currencies, Baruch is above party politics. His visits to the War College each year give him the opportunity of inspecting the new crop of general officers to see which of them are potential Eisenhowers of Marshalls, who will not question the Baruch leadership.

Roosevelt failed to heed the warning of Col. House, and surrounded himself with a host of aliens. Like the Wilson Administration, the successive Roosevelt Administrations resound with the names of Frankfurter, Warburg, Meyer, Baruch, all leftovers from Wilson, as well as Benjamin Cohen, Victor Emanuel, Mordecai Ezekiel, Henry Morgenthau, and Leo Pasvolsky, as well as hundreds of Keyserlings and lesser creatures. Roosevelt was the first President to have a Zionist Inner Mission established at the White House, which, during the early 1930s, was composed of Justice Brandeis, Felix Frankfurter, and Rabbi Wise. With the lamented death of two of these things, it is now composed of Felix Frankfurter, David Niles, formerly using the name Neyhus, and Max Lowenthal. Lowenthal wrote a book which attempted to smear the FBI, and had it published by the leftwing house of William Sloane Associates. Six thousand copies of this $5,00 volume were distributed free in Washington, more than its total sales. It is interesting that the present Ambassador to the U.S. from Austria is Baron Max von Lowenthal.

Besides earning Brandeis a good profit on his old book, Roosevelt was a constant admirer of the great Zionist and Mosaic law-giver. Alpheus T. Mason, in his biography of Brandeis, says,

> "Rabbi Wise reported in a Memo of October 5, 1936 that the President said of Brandeis, "Grand man! You know, Stephen, we of the Inner Circle call him Isaiah.""

The Inner Circle, of course, was an Old Testament affair. Judging from its occupants during the Roosevelt regime, the White House must have looked to the casual visitor like a Near Eastern synagogue. Mason remarks on page 615 of his biography of Brandeis,

> "During the hectic one hundred days in the spring of 1933, and later, Frankfurter was tutor to the new administration. Several of the key administrators during the formative years were pupils of Brandeis-Tom Corcoran, Ben Cohen, A. A. Berle Jr., Dean Acheson, James M. Landis. Even after appointments had been decided upon, Frankfurter saw to it that the nominee was brought under Brandeis' influence."

Mason tells us that Brandeis was retired from the Supreme Court on Feb. 13, 1939, and was replaced by the Wall Street hack William O. Douglas, who has embarrassed Frankfurter ever since by being a more fervent Zionist than any Jew in Washington. Douglas, who had been kept out of sight on the Securities Exchange Commission, was evidence of Roosevelt's spite at the Supreme Court. By appointing Douglas, Roosevelt inaugurated the procession of non-entities which culminated with the sad visage of the Democratic water-boy, Fred Vinson, peering at us from the headgear of the Chief Justice.

Justice Douglas has been groomed repeatedly for the Presidential nomination. A synthetic applause for him has been appearing in the New York Times since 1950, when he was shoved forward as a sacrificial goat to test public reaction to recognition of Red China. The outcry of indignation from the American people sent Douglas scurrying back to the confines of the Court, from which he occasionally reappears to plug for some equally irresponsible goal. He had been joined in the recognition of Red China move by the same scurvy crew who had clamored for recognition of Russia in 1933, and who still dream of feting a Communist Ambassador from China while American boys are being slaughtered in Korea.

Part of the million-dollar-buildup of Douglas for President was the distribution of his book "Strange Lands and Friendly People" by Harry Scherman as a Book-of-the-Month-Club Selection, which is a standard item on such a program, as witness Eisenhower's huge profits from "Crusade in Europe", which contained such stirring sentences as "The din was incessant". Douglas gushes in his book that the biggest thrill of his life came when he sat on the Supreme Court of Israel. There is no reason to doubt his sincerity. There could be no thrill to sitting on the Supreme Court of the United States if your heart is in Israel. However, with the comforting presence of Frankfurter beside him, Douglas can pretend that ours is the Supreme Court of Israel.

Justice Brandeis understood the Marxist income tax. Mason tells us that this millionaire defender of the common man left his fortune to Hadassah, the women's Zionist organization, so that the Zionists got their money after all.

Felix Frankfurter, the Viennese importation whom Roosevelt appointed to the Supreme Court, had publicly declared on August 26, 1919 to a Zionist gathering that they were all animated by a common sentiment-the welfare of Israel and the good of Zion. His subsequent career bears out his statement of his allegiance.

Bundy's biography of Stimson notes on page 616 that

> "The labor of scouting for an Under Secretary of State was shared by two old friends, Felix Frankfurter and George Roberts." Bundy does not bother to inform us that Frankfurter, Roberts, and Stimson were law partners, but you can't get everything into a biography. On page 334, Bundy says

> "No discussion of Stimson's relationship with the administration would be complete without one further name, that of Mr. Justice Frankfurter. Without the least deviation from his fastidious devotion to the high traditions of the Supreme Court, Frankfurter made himself a continual source of comfort and help to Stimson. Although he never heard a word of it from Frankfurter, Stimson believed that his own presence in Washington was in some degree the result of Frankfurter's closer relationship with the President. Time after time, when critical issues developed, Stimson turned to Frankfurter."

Americans could sleep well, for their government was in good hands, hands which were devoted to the welfare of Israel and the good of Zion. Frankfurter's career as a professional Zionist, of course, did not interfere with his devotion to the traditions of the Supreme Court, for, it seems, you had to be a Zionist to be eligible for appointment to the Supreme Court. As far as Zionism is concerned, the 150 years of the Supreme Court are nothing compared to the thousands of years of tradition which Zionists claim for their ideology.

Rabbi Stephen Wise proudly reports in "Challenging Years" that

> "On Sept. 8, 1914, I first wrote to Franklin D. Roosevelt offering him my support in connection with the U.S. Senatorship."

From that day on, Wise was one of those rabbinical scarecrows fluttering in the breeze before the White House. We look in vain for a single Christian influence near Roosevelt in his years as President. Always surrounded by a horde of determined Zionists, Roosevelt never showed any sincere interest in the religion in which he claimed to have been christened, nor, in the dozens of books written about him by his fawning circle of Zionist adherents, do we find that he ever sought or accepted aid from ministers of the Gospel. When it became apparent that his time was short in the last months of 1944, Eleanor Roosevelt tells us in "This I remember" that he sought refuge in Baruch's South Carolina estate, Hobcaw Barony. His evil spirit had felt itself slipping away from the deformed body, and the Anti-Christ fled to his guide, Bernard Baruch, to gasp out his last days.

The malevolent old cripple, feeling the hand of death upon him, yet made one last attempt to sell his people into slavery. It was during these weeks that he approved the plans for the United Nations. The realization of this goal cheered him a great deal, and he moved on to the headquarters of his multi-million dollar charity racket, Warm Springs, Georgia. There, far from his family or anyone else who might have pretended to love him, he died suddenly under mysterious circumstances. At once the body was sealed in a coffin, and none of his family nor anyone else was permitted to view it. This was a strange turn, for his backers had intended to embalm him and exhibit him in a shrine at Hyde Park, in open imitation of the display of the corpse of Lenin before the faithful in the Kremlin.

Dr. Emanuel Josephson, in "The Strange Death of Roosevelt", has some interesting observations of this creature, to the effect that Roosevelt never had infantile paralysis at all, but another malignant disease which crippled his nervous system and affected his mind. Josephson's work is sound, and should be read by anyone wishing more information on this nightmarish thing which sucked away the heritage of the American people.

Franklin Roosevelt from the beginning surrounded himself with the warmongers and munitions-makers of international capital. His Secretary of the Treasury William H. Woodin, of Remington Arms Co. soon passed away and left that spot open for the son of the Harlem Slum King, Henry Morgenthau Jr. Young Morgenthau soon became the object of sly smiles in the Treasury Building. He had several times been the victim of some anti-Semitic starlings when he was stepping regally out of the Treasury Department. He rushed out, had his hat cleaned, and returned with a declaration of war. The ensuing campaign enlivened Washington cocktail parties for the next decade. Morgenthau tried everything. He set out balloons, he hired men to risk their lives to shoot the birds from their ledges, he set out poisons which, being sensible birds, they ignored, and for months he amused the birds and the Washington bureaucracy by his antics and his growing frustration. Finally admitting his defeat, he avoided the building for months at a time, and carried on much of the Treasury business in Roosevelt's offices.

It is unfortunate for our country that the birds did not claim all of Morgenthau's intelligence. He worked with Roosevelt on the Gold Reserve Act of 1934, which made it illegal for Americans to own gold, and his other manipulations may not come to light for several generations. His greatest piece of villainy, the demoralization of the Bureau of Internal Revenue, resulted in the scandals of 1951and the wholesale bribery of income tax collectors, an investigation which resounded with such musical names as Abraham Teitelbaum.

Morgenthau's direct responsibility for this corruption was disclosed by the *Washington Times Herald* of Jan. 18, 1952, commenting on Truman's comic remark that the Bureau of Internal Revenue should be reformed. This editorial brought forth a letter in the issue of Jan. 24, 1952, as follows:

> "Prior to 1938 the Bureau of Internal Revenue was by far the most efficient agency of the Federal Government. Since 1938 the Bureau has constantly deteriorated. What, if anything, was wrong with the administration of the Bureau of Internal Revenue prior to Secretary Morgenthau's reorganization of the bureau in 1938? What effect did Secretary Morgenthau's decentralization and reorganization have upon the fixing of authority and responsibility for the handling of tax cases? Was Dr. Yntema—who was the principle author of Morgenthau's decentralization reorganization-told in writing by almost every bureau official that the 1938 decentralization program would make it impossible for the Bureau of Internal Revenue to be properly administered and would lead to chaos and lack of control throughout the various decentralization field divisions? Until the efficient administration procedure as followed by the bureau prior to 1938 is restored, it cannot be properly administered."

This letter, written by a loyal Treasury Department employee whose name cannot be revealed, since it would involve the loss of his pension, mentions Dr. Yntema as Morgenthau's brain in this scandal. Yntema is an economist whose latest feat was the setting-up of the five hundred million dollar Ford Foundation. Yntema is the economic brain behind young Henry Ford. He is economic vice-president of Ford Motors and an official of the Foundation.

What was the reason for the demoralization of the Bureau of Internal Revenue in 1938? The gang was looking forward to the fabulous profits from the First World War. The Marxist income tax would take those profits unless the Bureau was wrecked, and wrecked it was.

With Roosevelt in 1933 was the scion of Kuhn, Loeb, James Paul Warburg, a Communist propagandist who describes himself as one of Roosevelt's original brain-trusters. Baruch saddled his personal brain trust on Roosevelt, the worthies Raymond Moley, Gerard Swope, General Hugh Johnson, Elliott Thurston, and Charley Michelson, who was Roosevelt's speech-writer during his Administrations.

Also at Roosevelt's side was the J. and W. Seligman employee, Norman H. Davis, the President of the Council On Foreign Relations. Sumner Welles, in "Seven Decisions that Shaped History" Harpers 1950, says on page 20,

> "Norman H. Davis occupied a unique place in the Roosevelt Administration, although his only fulltime office was chairman of the American Red Cross. Roosevelt and he had both been members of the Little Cabinet during the Wilson Administration. The President had great confidence in his judgment and gave some thought to appointing him Secretary of State in 1933. Norman H. Davis had already been named American delegate to the Brussels Conference on the Far East due to meet within a few weeks. Having served as American representative in innumerable other international conferences under Republican and Democratic administrations alike, he had an exceptionally comprehensive grasp of foreign affairs and had won to a singular degree the respect, the confidence, and the personal liking of Europe's leading statesmen."

Davis, who was unknown to the American people, died suddenly in 1944. A bipartisan, he never took any part in the politics of either party, yet he represented the United States at international meetings for twenty years. What did he say, What promises did he make? We do not know. We do know that he was for years an employee of J. and W. Seligman

Co. As the associate of known bribers and revolutionists, should he have made promises in the name of the American people?

In 1938 Roosevelt showed up the Red Cross for the farce it is by giving its Chairmanship to Davis, with a salary of $25,000 a year, chauffeur driven limousines, and a large expense account, while the collectors browbeat the workers of the nation into paying for it through "voluntary contributions" which, because of trade union deals, often were as voluntary as German contributions to the Nazi Winter Relief Fund.

Another mysterious figure of Roosevelt's circle was Mordecai Ezekiel, to whom Marriner Eccles gives full credit for Eccles' appointment as Chairman of the Federal Reserve Board.

One of the princes of Roosevelt's court was Victor Emanuel. Current Biography of 1951 informs us that

> "While living in England from 1927-34, Emanuel was active in stock market transactions and became associated with the London banking firm of J. Henry Schroder Co. Alfred Loewenstein, the Belgian financier who joined him in planning the formation of U.S. Electric Power Co., died before arrangements were completed, (he jumped or fell from a plane flying over the English Channel, but Emanuel, A.C. Allyn, and others succeeded in gaining control of an utilities empire stretching over twenty states, worth one billion, one hundred nineteen million dollars, according to Time Magazine, Oct. 7, 1946. Emanuel reorganized Standard Gas and Electric and turned the Chairman of the Board post over to Leo Crowley, who subsequently became Alien Property Custodian during the Second World War."

German property was in good hands, since Emanuel Crowley's master, was associated with the banking house of Schroder, Hitler's bankers. Emanuel's business address is 52 William St. New York, which, by an odd coincidence, is, and has been for many years, the address of Kuhn, Loeb Co. Emanuel, known as "the mystery man of Wall Street" has been President of Republic Steel and Chairman of the Avco Corporation, and director of many big industrial concerns. Emanuel was one of the favorites of the Roosevelt Administration, or should we say that Roosevelt was a favorite of Emanuel?

One of Roosevelt's aides was Tommy Corcoran, who, with his brother Dave of the Justice Department, represented I. G. Farben in America as late as 1941. Also basking in the light of the famous Roosevelt smile was Juan Trippe, head of Pan-American Airways and brother-in-law of J.P. Morgan partner Edward Stettinius.

Whatever may have been the vagaries of the mercurial Roosevelt temperament, which is attributed by Dr. Josephson to Roosevelt's "illness", his devotion to Communism remained constant. The Department of State's "History of Diplomatic Relations with Russia from 1933–1939" disclosed that Roosevelt ordered the State Department and the Navy Department to give "all help" to Russia's project for building battleships in 1938. A United Press review of this release, in the Miami Herald, May 25, 1952, commented that

> "The documents do not disclose Mr. Roosevelt's exact reasons for trying to help the Russians."

It should be obvious. Roosevelt wanted Russia to have as good a Navy as ours, or, in the light of what is known about him now, a better Navy than ours. One of the more notorious of the pro-Communist agencies in the United States, the International Association for Labor Legislation, had among its members, Frances Perkins, who was first heard from in 1916, when she raised her shrill voice in defense of Justice Brandeis. Roosevelt appointed her Secretary of Labor, a position which nobody but a professional Communist could have administered successfully during his Administration. Other members were Harry Hopkins, Leon Henderson, Eleanor Roosevelt, and the top officials of the Communist Party of America.

At Roosevelt's side throughout the 1930s was Sir William Wiseman, partner of Kuhn, Loeb Co. and head of the British Secret Service in the United States. Wiseman was never mentioned in the newspapers, and his presence at the White House was a well-kept secret. This writer had the experience of asking a well-known White House correspondent during those years if he had ever met a man there named William Wiseman. I watched him blench and stutter, and finally he said that he had not. Sir William, a director of the National Railways of Mexico and the United States Rubber Co., was written up by Lt. Col. Thomas Murray in "At Close Quarters", a book printed in England, which contains photos of Wiseman and Roosevelt on chummy picnics in the country in the late 1930s. It is possible that Wiseman carried too far the fanatical passion for anonymity which characterized the partners of Kuhn, Loeb Co., for his presence at the White House caused considerable conjecture.

For Franklin Roosevelt's last bequest to the American people, we have the statement of former Secretary of State Robert Lansing in 1950,

> "Franklin Roosevelt is the creator of the world Communist danger, by reversing the United States foreign policy towards Soviet Russia, which was laid down by me in 1919 and adhered to by every one of my successors until 1933."

CHAPTER 18

The history of the 1930s can be summed up in one sentence. It was a period of world rearmament. After the London Economic Conference of 1933, the modern industrial nations moved steadily and without a single deviation towards the Second World War. A number of nonpartisan observers, among them Congressman George Holden Tinkham of Boston, predicted step by step the events of that decade. Indeed, to anyone who understood the machinations of international finance, an obvious path was being followed.

Each of Hitler's annexations was accompanied by a chorus of Cassandras, a prearranged was hysteria created out of nonsense by the international news services. The publisher who capitalized most on this hysteria was Luee of the publications *Time*, and *Life*. On the air, Walter Winchell screamed a hymn of hate from B'nai Brith, and all of this hoopla was accompanied by such frenetic juggling on the stock exchanges of the world that it is hard to understand why the suckered did not wise up and get out of the game.

The Spanish Civil War, like Japan's war against China, provided a bull-fight which whetted the bloodlust of the industrial nations for a real world conflict. The newsreels and picture magazines were filled with the photographs of pieces of bodies flying through the air and the massacre of women and children. All of this had its effect in preparing the youths for their part in the slaughter. It is known to the sociologists as "conditioning".

Paul Einzig, in "World Finance 1937–1938", says

> "Experts are baffled by the fact that the Governments of both China and Japan appear to be able to finance the warfare."

It is difficult to understand why any economist should be puzzled by that. Both China and Japan had Central Banks, and, as I pointed out in

"The Federal Reserve", the principal function of a Central Bank is war finance.

The Spanish Civil War, a tragic affair marked by unspeakable atrocities against human beings, was at the time commonly reported as a preview of the Second World War. Events have proven that it was not so. It actually was a preview of the Third World War. The Spanish Civil War was a battle to the death between Communism and Christianity, and American "Liberals" have never forgiven Franco for the fact that Christianity won. The struggle so weakened Spain that she was barely able to resume her national existence, a fate likely to befall all of the participants in the Third World War.

The issues in the Spanish Civil War had little to do with the Second World War. Christianity was not represented in the Roosevelt war, for the Second World War was a battle between the Judaic National Socialism espoused by Hitler and the international Marxist Socialism led by Stalin. America, England, and France, fought on the side of Marx, and Germany and France defended the political philosophy of Syrkin. National Socialism fell before the allied forces of international Socialism, and the Third World War will be between the allied forces of Christianity and the Moslem world against the atheist doctrines of international Socialist Zionism.

Spain in 1934 was in a position much like that in which America finds herself in 1950. Spain's universities had been infiltrated by Communists after the First World War, so that she had reared a generation of professional people, school teachers, government officials, doctors of medicine, and lawyers, who were sincere Communists. They were no longer Spaniards, but devotees of the World Socialist State.

Against them were opposed the upholders of the status quo in Spain, the landholders and the priests. The conflict was complicated by the fact that England had to be sure of getting supplies from Spain for the Second World War, and Germany had to be sure that Spain would ship her supplies as she had done during the First World War. The House of Rothschild owned the huge iron works at Orconera and the docks at Bilboa, as well as the Rio Tinto Co., which was the largest copper mine in the world. The vast Pennaroya mining works had as their board of directors Baron Antony de Rothschild of Paris, his brother-in-law Pierre Mirabaud, former manager of the Bank of France, Charles Cahen, and

Humbert de Wendel, of the Suez Canal Co. and the Bank of France. (From Rucker's "The Tragedy of Spain" N.Y. 1945).

It was obvious that the Communists had enlisted many Spaniards who desired reform, and whose desires were a threat to the foreign domination of the hand of Rothschild, which was taking out the national wealth of Spain. The Rothschilds, seeing that the country was hopelessly divided, cried "Havoc!" and loosed the dogs of war. If the Communists won, the Rothschild properties would be nationalized, and they would manage them as before. If Franco won, nothing would change for the Rothschilds. Let the dogs tear each other's throats!

The cards were stacked for Franco, who guaranteed foreign investments. How he was backed by the Bank of England is described by Paul Einzig, in "World Finance 1937–1938",

> "Toward the end of 1935, British exporters were having to wait ten months for payment from Spain. The Spanish Government completed an agreement with the French Government by which French commercial credits were paid through the sale of gold. When the Civil War broke out, the amount of banking credits outstanding in Spain was exceptionally large. Even so, the revolt might never have materialized but for the support received from Italy at the very outset, the result of the Socialist victory in France. The Spanish credits were due in London in the early part of 1937. The Spanish Government transferred a quarter of a million pounds to the London account of the Bank of Spain with Martin's Bank. Martin's Bank refused to part with the amount. It is safe to assume that payments were made out of the gold reserve of the Bank of Spain. No definite information was available about the fate of that gold reserve. Mysterious individuals are said to have offered gold which nobody in the market was prepared to touch. A large part of it must have been spent on arms purchased abroad. Much of the gold must have disappeared in the hands of dishonest intermediaries in the armaments traffic."

Behind the Spanish Civil War were two factors, gold, and guns. Einzig continues with the revelation that Franco was picked to win because the Franco peseta commanded a higher price on the world exchanges. The fates of nations are determined by the rise or fall of the value of their monetary units on the exchanges.

> "The Franco peseta had all along been much more favorable than the Government (Communist) peseta, due to better economic

organization and industrial discipline, which enabled insurgent-controlled Spain to export freely. The Spanish experience provides a reminder that financial limitations to modern warfare are virtually non-existent. Modern warfare can be conducted on a large scale even in the absence of adequate financial resources."

Although Einzig does not explain his statement, the fact is that a nation can pay for everything she can produce. Gold nor any other form of money is used up by war. Goods and manpower disappear in the destruction of war, leaving behind the gold standard debts which arose from the credits extended to war finance by Central Banks. The impositions of "war debts" and the idea of "paying for a war" make up a gigantic system of fraud. The stockholders of the Central Bank, which, in America, is our Federal Reserve System, pretend to advance credit for war production, and this mythical credit, with adequate interest, is the war debt which they demand to be paid when the killing is finished, a circumstance which leads one to the observation that killing, a form of charity, should begin at home.

Franco won his victory because he carried on his war against the Communist Loyalist Government and at the same time, behind the front lines, he put the factories back into production and exported goods in return for armaments. In "World Finance 1938–1939", Einzig tells us that

> "At the beginning of the Civil War, the sympathies of foreign companies operating in Spain were entirely with General Franco, and the entry of insurgent armies was always warmly welcomed by the financial and industrial interests concerned in Spain ... When the crisis was at its height, three American warships paid a mysterious visit to Plymouth, England. It is understood that they collected the American gold held under earmark in London. The atmosphere on the stock exchanges was far from panicky. A dull tone prevailed everywhere."

The Spanish Civil War, although it was widely advertised as a potential World War, didn't sell too well on the exchanges. The presence of Russian arms and troops on the side of the Communists in Spain, and the presence of German and Italian military support for Franco caused little apprehension in London or in New York. By contrast, any move of Hitler sent the prices of stocks bounding up and down, a process which reached incredible proportions in the fall of 1938, when he annexed the Sudetenland of Czechoslavakia. Einzig, in "World Finance

1938–1939", described how the Warburgs and the Baruchs made millions in quick profits because of their inside knowledge of Hitler's moves.

> "On the surface a European way appeared almost inevitable. On Sep. 18, 1938, the tension in the financial markets reached its height. There was something like a landslide in the foreign exchange market, and the authorities allowed sterling to depreciate to 4.61 in the early afternoon. This was done with the full approval of the United States authorities. Notwithstanding the mobilization of the British Navy, sterling became remarkably resistant in the afternoon. Selling orders were still freely forthcoming, but they were easily absorbed by buying on a large scale. A very large proportion of these operations could be traced to certain banking-quarters, which were known to operate on account of a leading politician well in a position to know what was happening behind the scenes. From 2:30 p.m. onwards, dollars were sold on a large scale from that quarter. The rank and file of the market remained in suspense as the details of Mr. Chamberlain's statement came through. For an hour and a half, that statement appeared to indicate that there was very little hope of avoiding war. About half-past four, however, he made the dramatic announcement that Signor Mussolini was to intervene, and, very conveniently, the telegram announcing Hitler's decision to agree to a conference at Munich was also delivered at that moment, about two hours after well-in-formed foreign quarters had begun to act in the foreign exchange market on the assumption that there would after all be no war. Sterling jumped by ten points within a few minutes."

The farce of modern governments has never been more exposed. Navies and armies are mobilized, hundreds of commentators go on the air to add to the panic of millions of people, and seemingly omnipotent dictators jump when certain gamblers crack the whip, all this to make a few million dollars profit on the fluctuation of the British monetary unit.

Einzig continues that

> "Stock Exchange and foreign exchange operators, being hard-headed business men, were realistic enough to see that the most that could be said for the Munich Agreement was that it had brought a passing relief, but they nevertheless cynically cashed in on the 'peace in our time boom'."

More pre-war juggling is revealed by Einzig with the story of the Mendelssohn refinancing of the French railway bonds, carried through by M. Paul Reynaud, which, although hailed as a great financial success at the time, caused the press to face about a few months later, when Mendelssohn Co. went bankrupt. Einzig says

> "When the Mendelssohn Co. failed in Amsterdam following the death of its moving spirit, Dr. Fritz Mannheimer, several banks in France and the United States were involved to a considerable degree. However, owing to the French Government's policy of maintaining the Paris price of the Mendelssohn bonds, the banks were able to liquidate their commitments without disastrous losses. Paul Reynaud was blamed in certain quarters for having concluded the railway conversion loans with Mendelssohn and Co. It speaks very well for the remarkable change which has taken place in France that no attempt was made to attack Reynaud on this point by the French press."

To my mind, it speaks very ill of the French press. A Government leader concludes a huge financial conversion with a banking house which is so shaky that the death of one man is enough to throw it into bankruptcy and cause an international monetary crisis. The press kindly fails to take him to task for it, while the Government generously holds up the price of the defaulted bonds so that the banks lose nothing. The American people should take note of the fact that our Treasury has been doing the same thing for the private stockholders of the Federal Reserve System for years.

The Central Banks had excellent control in their respective countries by 1939. Einzig tells us that

> "The increase in unemployment was due to Mr. Montagu Norman's success in persuading Sir John Simon to authorize him to increase the bank rate. In his budget statement, Sir John quite frankly admitted that the object of his Draconian taxation measures was to reduce civilian consumption. The line taken by Norman and Simon on the matter of the surrender of the Czechoslavakia National Bank's gold to Germany caused intense resentment in official Paris. The French Treasury and the Bank of France were very anxious that the transfer of the gold should be stopped, while the Bank of England refused to take action."

The French bankers knew that Germany would spend the gold for raw materials to make guns which would be fired against France. The

French debacle can be traced to this gift of gold to Germany, which, of course, never went to Germany, but was merely transferred from the Czech vault to the English vault in the Bank of International Settlement. Moving a stack of gold bars a few feet in an underground cavern decides the fate of nations.

England was still playing Germany off against Russia. Einzig tells us in "World Finance 1939–1940" that

> "Representatives of the Federation of British Industries and the Reichsgruppe Industries met at Dusseldorf in March, 1939. A few days after, the Czechoslovak crisis entered its decisive phase. When the news of the occupation reached Dusseldorf, the Germans fully expected that the conference would be broken off. After consultation with London, however, the British delegates astonished their German colleagues by announcing their intention of proceeding and signing the hastily drafted preliminary agreement, it was actually signed on the day when Hitler made his triumphal entry into Prague."

The role of Franklin Roosevelt throughout the 1930s was disgraceful. He shamelessly played the role of the Great Peacemaker year after year while he was preparing for war. His Socialist program was a calamitous mistake. The immediate and farcical failure of the National Recovery Administration, the appalling waste of the Communist-led Works Progress Administration, the widespread resentment of his dictatorial attempts to beat the American farmer into submission to a Soviet form of collectivized agriculture of production quotas, all these fiascos left Roosevelt unmoved. He had a solution which would cause America to forget his complete failure as a President. That solution was the Second World War. Hoover, in the third volume of his Memoirs, caustically points out that Roosevelt had been a disastrous flop in every respect at the end of his two terms in the White House, and that his reputation was saved by the economic recovery of rearmament. Einzig, in "World Finance 1939–1940" says,

> "Whenever President Roosevelt announced an intensification of the rearmament drive of the United States, Wall Street responded favorably."

There were enough credits to allow the Government to purchase as many war goods as industry could produce. No wonder Wall Street was favorable. Einzig concludes with the verdict on Roosevelt which is confirmed by Hoover, Tinkham, and other observers,

"What President Roosevelt's New Deal and the reflationary policy was unable to achieve was accomplished in a few months as a result of the European War."

CHAPTER 19

The gloomiest comment on the failure of modern civilization is occasioned by the fate of small nations. Woodrow Wilson proclaimed that the rights of small nations must be protected, at the very moment when he was bludgeoning those small nations into accepting the terrible provisions of the Versailles Treaty which made the Second World War a certainty. As the armies of Hitler and Stalin deployed and redeployed across Europe, a tragedy was enacted which drew to its close the civilization of that continent. That tragedy was the systematic destruction of the decent elements of the European populations.

The enemies of the Nazis and the enemies of the Communists were the same people, the foes of tyranny. Those men whose strongest passion was liberty, those men whose creed as truth and justice, were marked for extinction when the Nazis marched into a city. If they survived the Nazi occupation, they were sought out and imprisoned or slain when the Communists arrived. This happened in Poland, in Czechoslovakia, In Austria, in all of Europe. The deliberate annihilation of the classes on whom the moral structure of these nations depended leads one to wonder, "Who is left in Europe worth saving?" Present events prove that there is no longer anyone in those countries to protest against corruption, brutality, and the ignorance of their leadership. The best of Europe is dead, and the odor of the remains is sufficient to quell our interest. The slave revolution which began in the Rome of the Caesars has reached its successful conclusion, and the next era of history will be written by the stupid and arrogant lower classes who have killed their masters.

The cause of the death of the small nations can be traced to England, which had borne the moral banner high in international relations, fulfilling the Pax Britannica. The Anglo-Saxon England which the small nations remembered as their standard-bearer, however, was gone. They trusted an England whose foreign policy was in the hands of

N. M. Rothschild and Sons. While decent Englishmen looked on in horror, the international bankers handed Poland over, not to one, but to both of her worst enemies at the same time. England was pledged to aid Poland, but when the German armies marched into Poland from one side and the Russian armies marched into Poland from the other, where were the English armies? One hundred years of the Rothschild dynasty had so debilitated England that she was not even able to save France, a nation which did not want to be saved, and which eagerly awaited Hitler's promise to deliver France from the Jewish international bankers.

Hitler seems to have been duped into the Second World War in 1939. He had been allowed to take much greater objectives, Austria and Czechoslovakia, without opposition, and the Munich Pact must have meant to Hitler that he could carry out his Pan-European Confederation without further interference, and conclude preparations for an all-out onslaught against Russia, as England wished. Therefore, England's declaration of war seem to have taken the Nazis by surprise. Paul Einzig, in "World Finance 1939–1940" writes that

> "One of the reasons why it was doubted that Great Britain would really embark upon a major war in fulfillment of her pledge to Poland was the thirty six million pounds in German short-term credits which would cause grave embarrassment to the London banking community. The authorities would have to support several banking houses. British banks remained as reluctant as ever to liquidate their German commitments. Their attitude was due to a sympathy and admiration towards German bankers and 'Germany in general'."

Hitler could take a very positive assurance that England would not declare war upon him, from the favorable attitude of the London banking community. Alas, in his most ranting speeches, he never adequately disclosed the duplicity of the international bankers. Col. Joseph Beck gives further confirmation of Hitler's attitude in "Dernier Rapport", editions La Baconière, Neufchatel, Paris, 1951. On page 211, footnote, we find that

> "On August 22, 1939, at a conference with his generals, Hitler expressed the conviction that Great Britain was not taking her obligations to Poland seriously, otherwise, he argued, she wouldn't fuss over a loan of 8million sterling to Poland, having invested a half-million in China."

What Adolf Hitler did not seem to know on August 22, 1939 was the fact that the World Zionist Organization opened its twenty-first World Congress at Geneva, Switzerland a week earlier, on August 16, 1939. It is significant that one week after that conference opened, Hitler and Stalin signed their nonaggression pact, and jointly invaded Poland. As one Jew remarked, anyone who remained a Communist after August 23, 1939 was really a Communist. Certainly many Jews did some soul-searching on that date, for they had vented hysterical invective on the Hitler Government for sixteen years, and they had been taught that the Stalinist Government was the only one in the world which guaranteed Jewish rights, with a death penalty for anti-Semitism. This sudden combination was a difficult one for Jewish nationalists to accept, but they accepted it.

The Nazi-Soviet Pact did not disturb the intellectual elite of the Council On Foreign Relations and the Communist Party of America, which formed an interlocking policy directorate of Hiss, Lattimore, Currie, and Frederick Vanderbilt Field. They knew that Hitler was being sabotaged by his Minister of Finance, Hjalmar Schacht. K.L. Treffetz explained in the March 1948 American Economic Review that

> "The explanation of Germany's failure to prepare on a much larger scale is essentially a financial one. The German leaders did not understand that 'a nation can finance everything which can be produced.' Germany could have rearmed on a much greater scale, had it not been for Schacht, who in 1937 advised Hitler that additional credits for rearmament could not be secured. He did get three billion more, but none after March, 1938."

This is the Dr. Hjalmar Schacht who correctly pointed out that "Money which is not issued against needed goods is merely paper." This could also be stated as "As much money can be issued as is required to produce needed goods." He also the Dr. Schacht who was not a Fascist.

March, 1938 is fixed as the peak of Hitler's power. After that, his international credits were cut off. He believed that he was strong enough to take what he needed after that, but he could not believe that America would ever attack him, and that was his fatal miscalculation. It is significant that Schacht was the only economist in the Nazi upper echelon. Hitler was an orator, Goering was a strategist, Hesse was a writer, Rosenberg was a geopolitician, Goebbels was a journalist, and Himmler was a policeman, but there was nobody to say how much money could be printed except Schacht. When Hitler came in with a radically new party in 1933, he retained the head of the Warburg-controlled Reichsbank, Dr. Schacht, as his financial brain. Everything was new about the Nazis except gold. It was the same gold, and it was borrowed from the same Jewish international bankers, sometimes known as international Jewish bankers, who were the targets of Hitler's diatribes.

When the bankers decided that Hitler had gone far enough, Schacht said, "No more credits", and this dictator, before whom all Europe stood in fear, accepted Schacht's verdict. Had Hitler continued to rearm on the scale of his preparations from 1935 to 1938, he could have finished Russia before American production was ready to save Stalin. It should not be forgotten that the only people in America who opposed Hitler were the Jews and their satellites. There were many Americans not in the for mentioned group who sincerely believed that Hitler was a bad man, but they did not believe that he constituted a threat to the United States, and they have been proven right. In all of the tons of captured Nazi documents, there has never been found so much as a single memorandum that Hitler contemplated or planned any military action against the United States.

England gave Poland away, half to Germany as a bribe to fight Russia, and the other half to Russia as a bribe to fight Germany. Then a propaganda campaign was started by the yellow liberal press in the United States that Eastern Poland had always been inhabited by Russians, and that the poles were anti-Semitic, which was probably true. This was the conditioning for the worst atrocity of the war, the murder of 10,000 captured Polish army officers by Russian Secret Police in the Katyn Forest. This is the worst <u>known</u> atrocity of the Second World War. Greater numbers are reputed to have been murdered by the Nazis. In 1942-43 the Advisory Committee on Postwar Foreign Policy of the Department of State, with Summer Welles as Chairman, advised the U.S. Government that all of Eastern Poland be ceded to the Soviet Government (From Post-War Foreign Policy Preparation 1939–1945, Department of State Publication 3580, pages 69–166 and 459–512.)

In April, 1943, Russia severed relations with the Polish Government in Exile, then quartered in London, and formed a Communist Government of Poland, called the Union of Polsi Patriots. In December, 1943, at Teheran, Roosevelt promised Eastern Poland to Stalin without consulting or notifying the Polish Government in Exile. If this news had been published, it would have broken Polish resistance to the Nazis. Anti-Polish propaganda in the Communist "liberal" press in the Unites States reached its greatest intensity at this time. It was claimed that the Poles were worse than the Nazis, that they were even more anti-Semitic, and so on. As a direct result of this propaganda, Russia's Communist Government was able to set up its offices at Lublin without protest from the United States or from England. In February, 1945, Roosevelt at Yalta, with the Communist Alger Hiss as his adviser, formally ceded Eastern Poland to Russia, and accepted the Lublin Government, thus rejecting the Polish Government in London. The callous delivery of Poland to the Communists was the climax of Roosevelt's career of treachery. The State Department, led by apologist George Kennan, still claims that Roosevelt gave away nothing at Yalta. Roosevelt condemned the brave Polish people, who had fought the Nazis and the Communists, to the hands of their most ruthless enemy, the Russian Secret Police, and Dean Acheson's law firm got them the loan to carry out that persecution. One of the strangest factors was the silence of the Roman Catholic Church. Poland was one of the largest Catholic nations in the world, but the Vatican let Poland go without a protest.

At once the Communist Government of Poland sent Oscar Lange, who had been an American citizen, and gladly renounced it to become a citizen of Communist Poland, to Washington as its Ambassador. Oscar Lange had been a professor of economics at the University of Chicago. His good friend and colleague there was another professor of economics, Paul Douglas, now Senator from Illinois. Lange subsequently became Polish delegate to the United Nations.

It seems profitless to write of the Second World War, because it is a repetition of the First World War. The same shady people who had been in Washington the first time, Roosevelt, Frankfurter, Baruch, etc., were in complete charge in 1941. We must record the names of some of the criminals who condemned themselves to history in this war, for they are still in power throughout the world. The following revelations about the Council On Foreign Relations should warn us against their members.

The machinations used to get the United States into the mess have no originality, or even ingenuity, to recommend them. The year 1941 was exactly like 1916. A Committee to Defend America by Aiding the Allies was formed in 1941, composed of the same old mob of international bankers and lawyers, including Henry L. Stimson, who was called in by Roosevelt to become Secretary of War. Stimson was a lifelong Republican, but Roosevelt made the adjustment.

The publicity machine was awning up. Walter Winchell was screaming war at the top of his lungs, and every Sunday night he raved against Hitler to an audience of twenty million Americans. Even more important was the fact that Luce, the publisher of Time, Life, and Fortune, had declared war on Germany in February of 1941. Bravely he stepped out on the front lines of warmongering, waving his slanted dispatches and ranted of Hitler's threat to America. He published a book in that month, "The American Century", Farrar, Rinehart, New York, 1941, which also was printed in full in Life Magazine in February 1941, ten months before Pearl Harbor. Luce said on page 25,

> "We ourselves have failed to make democracy work successfully. Our only chance now to make it work is in terms of a vital international economy and in terms of an international moral order."

Internationalist Henry Luce here proclaims the internationalist doctrines of Nikolai Lenin. Luce was Chairman of the Financial Committee of the Institute of Pacific Relations, furnishing the funds for the sellout of China. Luce was not slow to commit himself in print as a revolutionist. On pages 10 and 11 of his book, he writes,

> "We are in a war to defend and even to promote, encourage, and incite so-called democratic principles throughout the world."

In February of 1941, Luce was already at war, but it took ten months of steady and vehement warmongering by his magazines to get the American people to join him. Had he failed, Luce undoubtedly would have chartered a boat and sailed off to land and die on Festung Europa. On page 26 of this book, the Luce mind is revealed in all its pellucid depth and clarity,

> "Our job is to help in every way we can for our sakes and our children's sakes, to ensure that President Roosevelt shall be justly hailed as America's greatest President."

It is unfortunate that the present work so flagrantly disobeys the Luce mandate. However, it is not my fault that Roosevelt betrayed America and humanity at Teheran and Yalta.

When Germany, in fulfillment of all her political predictions, and in accordance with the published works of Hitler and the Nazi Party, carried out her policy of Drang Nach Osten (The Drive to the East), and attacked Russia on June, 22, 1941, a howl of pain and anger went up from world Jewry. It can be said that that date inaugurated the real Second World War, the battle against usurious oppression really began.

Russia survived the winter of 1941, and by that time enough American trucks and tanks were reaching her to enable her armies to hold the Hitler offensive.

Russia was saved by the holding action engendered by two men, Tito of Yugoslavia, and Averell Harriman of New York. In life Magazine, a forum for Communist writers, in the issue of May 5, 1952, the Communist dictator Tito tells his story, entitled "Tito Speaks". Of the German attack on Russia, Tito writes that

> "On June 22d the Nazis attacked Russia. We met the same day, and drafted a resolution calling upon the people to revolt against their enemies. We, the Central Committee of the Communist Party of Yugoslavia, designed a flag, the Yugoslav national flag with the Red Star superimposed."

While Draja Mihailovich and his gallant Chetniks fought the Nazis, Tito was hiding in Moscow. In the spring of 1941, Tito returned to Yugoslavia to prepare for a possible German attack on Russia. The Communists under Tito, according to his own story, did not begin fighting the Germans until Russia was attacked, although the Chetniks had been fighting for many months. When the war was over, Tito executed Mihailovich for being pro-American. At that time, Tito was shooting down American planes, and Mihailovich had sheltered many American airmen from the Nazis during the war.

Military strategists now agree that the Communist Army of Tito, a new and unknown force, caused the Nazis to divert several divisions from the Russian blitzkrieg, and weakened the German offensive against Moscow in the winter of 1941.

Stalin's other savior, Averell Harriman, is now Mutual Security Administrator. His partner from Brown Brothers Harriman, Robert Lovett, is Secretary of Defense, although it is not clear who is defending us from. In September of 1941, Averell Harriman flew on a Lend-Lease Mission to Russia. His Father was E.H. Harriman, front man for Jacob Schiff when Schiff acquired the Union Pacific Railroad for Kuhn, Loeb. Harriman himself held large properties for the House of Rothschild. The investment house of Brown Brothers Harriman is a useful liaison between Kuhn, Loeb and their insurance interests in England.

Harriman found out what armaments and supplies Stalin needed most desperately, and had them flown from the United States to Russia in one of the most amazing operations of the war, a project of which Harry Hopkins was in charge. These critical supplies reached the Russian armies at precisely the moment when they were most needed to halt the German offensive. The German General Staff had not calculated on Russia receiving any such material aid, and, aided by the Titoist diversion in Yugoslavia, Moscow and Stalin were saved from the Nazis. Tito and Harriman can claim equal share of the credit for rescuing the Stalinist Government from certain defeat. Yet both Tito and Harriman are publicized now as being anti-Stalinist. We must wait to see if they will be as determined foes of Stalin as they were devoted friends of his Government.

Now that Harriman had committed us to save world Communism, Roosevelt swung the industrial potential of America behind the Russian armies. The agency for this was the Lend-Lease Act, H.R. 1776, which might better have been numbered H.R. 1917, the year of the Russian Revolution. Its sponsor, who rushed it through Congress, was the Chairman of the House Committee on Foreign Relations, Rep. Sol Bloom. Bloom had qualified as an expert on foreign relations by his experience in managing burlesque theaters in New York City. How much Russia got under the provisions of Lend-Lease in unknown, but it has been estimated that of the total cost of the Second World War to the American taxpayer, three hundred billion dollars, Russia got one-third, or one hundred billion dollars. It is doubtful whether Communism is worth it.

Admiral Zacharias, former Chief of Naval Intelligence, writes in his book, "Behind Closed Doors", Putnams, 1950, on page 209 that

> "No instrument better exemplifies the gigantic scope of this cold war than a mysterious radio station called the Stalin Transmitter. It was built with Lend-Lease material shipped by the (David Sarnoff) Radio Corporation of America to Kuybyshev. It is by about five times the most powerful radio station in the world."

American taxpayers are now being gouged because they bought Stalin a radio transmitter five times more powerful than ours. Bundy, in his biography of the departed Stimson, remarks on page 360,

> "The Lend-Lease Act gave the President the power to 'manufacture or procure any defense article for the government of any country whose defense the President deems vital to the defense of the United

States, and to sell, transfer title to, exchange, lease, lend, or
otherwise dispose of, to any such government any defense article.'
It was another great Roosevelt triumph. Stimson called it 'a
declaration of economic war'."

I call it the greatest fraud in history. One man was authorized to give to
any government on earth any or all of the products of American heavy
industry, even if those products were needed by American troops.
Throughout the war, MacArthur's forces in the Pacific were starved for
supplies while General Marshall and Harry Hopkins shipped our
armament to Russia.

The members of Congress who voted for the Lend-Lease Act deserve
the honest contempt of every American citizen. Only one final
degradation remained for them, and that was the day the Senate
approved the United Nations Charter.

The operation of Lend-Lease was a comical exhibition of the Roosevelt
incompetents. Bundy writes on page 359 of the Stimson thing,

> "Through sheer inadvertence the final agreement with Britain, as
> published, omitted a part of the American obligation - 250,000
> Enfield rifles with 30,000,000 rounds of ammunition, and five B-17
> bombers. This of course was highly embarrassing. Throughout the
> summer and autumn of 1940 Stimson was engaged in labors to
> speed up the transfer of military supplies. British missionaries came
> in and out of the Secretary of War's office, and over the weeks a
> close and intelligent co-operation developed. The Treasury
> Department under Morgenthau was particularly zealous and
> effective in finding ways to finance these transactions."

It is the first time I ever heard of Morgenthau being zealous about
anything, although he is said to be quite an ardent Zionist. At any rate,
here is only one instance of the sloppy book-keeping involving the big
giveaway show of America's billions, the champion confidence game
of all time. Yet Roosevelt and his squirmy crowd flew into a hysterical
rage whenever anyone suggested that there ought to be some
supervision over Lend-Lease. Luckily, McGeorge Bundy has gone on
record with a bold account of the Roosevelt gang's contempt for
representative government. On page 360 of "On Active Duty in Peace
and War" we find an entry dated September 9, 1940 from Stimson's
Diary, as follows

> "These petty annoying checks placed upon the Commander-In-Chief do an immense amount more harm than good and they restrict the power of the Commander-In-Chief in ways in which Congress cannot possibly wisely interfere. They don't know enough."

The Congressmen are too dumb, sneers Kuhn, Loeb lawyer Stimson, who knows it all. Certainly Roosevelt did his best to keep Congress from finding out anything. Government by crony does not want to be questioned about what it is doing.

There had been some opposition to Roosevelt appointment of Stimson as Secretary of War. Bundy notes that

> "On July 2, 1940 Stimson appeared before the Committee on Military Affairs, to which his name had been referred. Four times before his name had been submitted to the Senate, and in none of those earlier cases had his fitness been seriously questioned. For nearly two hours they questioned him, with the assistance of two Senators not members of the Committee, Vandenberg and Taft. The majority of the Committee were sympathetic their few questions were simple and friendly.... Was he a member of Winthrop, Stimson, Putnam and Robert Well, he was listed as counsel. 'That is a euphemistic term for a gentleman who sits in an office without sharing in the profits.' (Laughter). Did this law firm have any clients with international investments? He didn't think so, but he didn't know, because he wasn't a partner. Did he have any such clients himself? No."

Stimson's name was on the door, but he didn't know what went on inside. He was one of the most influential Wall Street Lawyers in America, but he was not mixed up with international investments, nor was he paid anything from his own law firm. Perhaps he could have been arrested for vagrancy, since he had no visibly means of support. Certainly an arrest for perjury would have been in order. At any rate, the Wall Street vagrant became Secretary of War. The Hearings published by the Committee are of little help, since most of the discussion was off the record, a courtesy to the shy Stimson. Kuhn, Loeb partners and satellites are extremely retiring people.

One month after Hitler declared war on Russia, Roosevelt declared war on Japan. On July 25, 1941, Roosevelt froze all Japanese assets in the United States, a hostile action equivalent to sending troops against the Japanese mainland. Japan desperately tried to avoid war with America during the ensuing months, and then prepared the attack on Pearl

Harbor in the hopes that it would drive the United States out of Asia and let Japan develop her "Greater East Asia Co-Prosperity Sphere", a hemispheric economic and military alliance laid out according to the development of modern strategy known as geopolitics. It is significant that Japan never attacked the American mainland, despite Roosevelt's frantic come-ons. After Pearl Harbor, the nation's press for several weeks headlined stories that the West Coast could not defended, that we had only a few shore batteries, no planes or ships, and that the Japanese could easily take California. Man have been shot for treason for telling less than could be found on the front page of any metropolitan newspaper during January of 1942. Roosevelt wanted a Japanese attack on the United States mainland so that he could put our country under martial law and throw everyone who opposed his "government by crony" into the concentration camps which he was setting up in the deserts of New Mexico and Arizona. Hopkins later admitted that

> "Roosevelt would not have been taken aback by a Japanese attack on San Francisco. He believed that it would help unify the country."

Unfortunately for the Roosevelt dream of dictatorship, Japan did not want California. She wanted Asia, and her armies had only one purpose, to drive out the managers of the Rockefeller and Rothschild properties. Therefore, California remained undefended and unattacked. Bitter with disappointment, Roosevelt ordered all Japanese-Americans on the West Coast thrown into his concentration camps. This constitutes one of the most sordid chapters in our history. It was a vicious crime which was nothing but the evidence of the spite of one man against a racial group. Not one of these American citizens had committed any action hostile to the United States. Roosevelt's despicable treatment of these citizens is in shocking contrast to the manner in which the open and avowed enemies of our Republic, the members of the Communist Party, operated from the White House during the Second World War. Roosevelt was warned about Alger Hiss in 1941. He then made him his personal confidant and assistant. After two years, some of the young Americans of Japanese parentage were released from these concentration camps and enlisted in the Army. In Italy they distinguished themselves as the never-to-be-forgotten 442d regiment.

Another instance of Roosevelt's determination to permanently disgrace the legal structure of the United States was his arrogant persecution of thirty loyal Americans who had written or spoken against Communism. No sooner had Japan been inveigled into attacking Pearl Harbor, and given Roosevelt the chance to declare Germany as our mortal enemy, and atheist Russia as our sturdy ally, than he began a nationwide campaign of terror against anyone who had been opposed to Communist conspirators. The warrants of arrest for these patriots were sworn out the day after Pearl Harbor. The stimulus for this persecution is reliably reported to have come from the Government bond manipulator Eugene Meyer's Washington Post. One of his "reporters" gathered the so-called "evidence" against these foes of Communism, which evidence was finally thrown out of court. Meyer's Washington Post, of course, was loudest of all the yellow liberal papers in its campaign against these persecuted Americans.

It is significant that Roosevelt, on this witch-hunting expedition, placed the prosecution in the hands of those most favorable to Communism. Attorney General Francis Biddle has long been the star figure in the American Civil Liberties Union, which is devoted to the defense of Communist spies. The Government prosecutor was O. John Rogge. Herbert Philbrick, who exposed Communists to the FBI, wrote in his book, "I Led Three Lives" that whenever the FBI planned a raid on Communists, O. John Rogge tipped off the Reds that a raid was coming. Rogge's assistant prosecutor was that great American, T. Lamar Caudle, who was promoted as a result of his services in this persecution, only to have his Communist-inspired honors stripped from him when he was asked to resign from the Department of Justice in connection with his accepting a number of favors, which favors were linked to delinquent income tax cases.

In 1944, after two years of Government persecution, these thirty patriots went to trial. This trial ended with the death of the Judge, something named Eichler which Roosevelt had dredged up from the bottom of his Socialist morass for this particularly dirty job. Eichler's successor, Judge Proctor, declared that the Government did not have, and never had had, any grounds for a trial, and refused to continue the case. Appellate Justice Bolitha Laws in July, 1947 confirmed Proctor's ruling of a mistrial, and declared it a "travesty on justice". For six years and six months, these patriots had been persecuted by the government of their homeland. Most of them by 1947 were shattered in health and had spent most of their funds for legal fees. Despite this, they have since distinguished themselves by their continued fight against the spread of Communism in America. Senator William Langer sought for months to pass a bill which would repay them for their expenses in this mockery of justice, but the Senate refused to help them. Needless to say, the trial was never given any accurate reporting by the press. The news services collectively defined the defendants as "anti-Semites", which opened the doors to their systematic defamation by the creatures of the Anti-Defamation League, Winchell and Pearson. Pearson's staff member covering the trial was a known member of the Communist Party, Andrew Older.

The sinister motive behind America's intervention in the Second World War was soon apparent. Maxim Litvinoff arrived in Washington on Pearl Harbor Day to help Roosevelt run the war, and on January 1, 1942, one week after Pearl Harbor, Churchill, Litvinoff, and Roosevelt jointly announced from Washington the Declaration of the United Nations. We were no longer the American Republic.

With his successful involvement of America in the Second World War, Roosevelt called in the worst elements in the country to help him run the show, while our decent boys were being slaughtered to save Communism. When Litvinoff arrived on Pearl Harbor Day, he was met with open arms at the National Airport by Chief of Staff General George Marshall, who always seemed to get his instructions via the Kremlin. It took the courage of Senator McCarthy to expose this creature whom Truman termed "the greatest living American." Senator Jenner followed up by calling Marshall "a living lie", and "a front man for traitors". Marshall has never answered either of them. A court battle would probably expose even more facts in the sinister record of Marshall's collaboration with Communists. It is these collaborators, more dangerous than the members of the Communist Party, whom McCarthy has attempted to drive out of the Truman Administration, but their leader, Dean Acheson, former legal counsel for the Soviet Union, remains as Secretary of State.

In his book, "Retreat from Victory", Senator Joseph McCarthy says that one of the first events following Marshall's appointment as Chief of Staff was an attempt to destroy all Army records on Communist activities. Senator Styles Bridges learned of this treason, and stopped the Army Counter Intelligence Corps from carrying it out. How many of the files were destroyed will never be known.

Marshall had been appointed Chief of Staff by Roosevelt because of Marshall's deep-seated grudge against General Douglas MacArthur, the Commander of our forces in the Pacific. While Chief of Staff, Douglas MacArthur had refused to promote Marshall from Colonel to Brigadier-General after Marshall had proven his lack of leadership. Roosevelt needed a man who could stand off MacArthur. Litvinoff had convinced

Roosevelt that all available supplies must be sent to Russia for the next six months if Russia was to be saved, and this meant starving MacArthur of guns and planes in his battle against the Japanese armies. Marshall's dislike for MacArthur was such that he gladly joined in this conspiracy against our troops. While our boys in the Pacific were being bombed and shot by the Japanese Air Force, the planes which should have been protecting them were defending Moscow. The tragedy of our holding action in the Pacific in 1942 can be laid to the Roosevelt-Litvinoff-Marshall collusion to deprive the American Army of supplies in favor of Russia. Thus they condemned many thousands of American soldiers to mutilation, imprisonment, or death at the hands of the Japanese.

At the same time that Marshall was sending our armaments to Russia, he seems to have had a goal of getting as many American boys slaughtered as possible. In early 1942, Senator McCarthy says on page 19 of his book, Marshall and his assistant planner, Col. Dwight Eisenhower, completed their plan for a second front, and began urging Roosevelt to put it into action at once. Every military expert in the country, including Hanson Baldwin of the New York Times, joined in a denunciation of this plan. We could barely produce enough arms in the spring of 1942 to defend Russia, much less to launch an invasion of Europe. The second front was the official Communist Party Line during 1942 and 1943. Anyone who supported it during those months, when we were obviously unable to open a second front, was pro-Communist. Baldwin says that if we had opened a second front before 1944, we would probably have been thrown back and it could have taken years for us to recover from such a disaster. The Communists refused to listen to reason. Stalin himself had laid down the "second front" dictum, and Marshall and Eisenhower loyally seconded him. Perhaps this is why Dwight Eisenhower became the first foreigner ever to stand beside Stalin on Lenin's tomb during the Annual Sports Parade (Decision In Germany by General Lucious Clay.)

When any of his favorites, such as Averell Harriman, visited Moscow, Stalin's first question was always "When will you open the Second Front?" Not one word of gratitude for the supplies which had saved his government, for gratitude is a bourgeois and weakening emotion to the Communist. Lenin's first act, upon assuming power in Russia in 1917, was to denounce Helphand Parvus, who had gotten him safely across Germany, as an "opportunist".

The American people were not informed of the simple fact that Russia cannot be appeased. To publish any criticism of Russia during the war meant a possible charge of treason, and it was justified, since we were fighting to save Communism. Eisenhower had standing orders in his headquarters in London that no Russian was to be criticized, in the interests of "harmony".

General Marshall might well have been the military columnist for the Daily Worker during the Second World War, so closely did he follow the Communist Party Line. The most vigorous proponent of the second front absurdity, Marshall always loudly opposed a Mediterranean campaign, which would threaten Communist gains in Central Europe. He had little sympathy for the Italian campaign, which suffered continually from lack of supplies and sparse reinforcements. Italy was the scene of some of the worst slaughters of Americans in the Second World War, under the leadership of General Mark Clark, who drove them into the deathtraps at Anzio and Salerno. His own officers tried to have him indicted when they returned to the United States. This may explain why Clark has been placed in charge of the Korean blood rites. Clark's conduct of the war in Italy was characterized by the wholesale destruction of Catholic shrines and works of art. The worst crime was the deliberate destruction of the 16th century monastery of Monte Cassino by saturation bombing, a development of total warfare which took us back to the days of barbarism. After the bombing, German troops had a perfect fortress in the rubble of Monte Cassino, and it cost the lives of many Americans to dislodge them. Clark's mother and wife are both Jewish. We had no Catholic generals, of course, who could have been placed in command of the Italian campaign. As we moved up in Italy, Herbert Lehman was rushed over as Governor-General of the occupied territory.

It is interesting that the two great Catholic nations, Poland and Italy, were both scenes of such wanton destruction during the Second World War. Despite the administration of Herbert Lehman, Italy refused to go Communist after the war.

With Roosevelt's declaration of war in 1941, Baruch openly assumed power in Washington. At least he knew what he was doing. Seven years before, he had outlined to the Nye Committee his complete plans, step by step, for food and oil rationing, the draft of manpower, and other aspects of what became known as Roosevelt dictatorship. Baruch's stooge in Washington was his longtime favorite, Jimmy Byrnes of

South Carolina, where Baruch had his palatial estate, Hobcaw Barony. Byrnes had been one of the silent Congressmen at the Pujor Hearings in 1913. He is best described by referring to a toy popular with children, a black glove with the face of a monkey painted on it. The glove is placed over the hand, the fingers are moved, and the monkey grimaces and seems to speak. The face in Washington was Byrnes, but the hand was Baruch. The last time Byrnes was used by Baruch was in 1948, when Byrnes established the Dixiecrat Party to split the Democratic South and assure Truman's defeat. Baruch bitterly hated Truman at that time, and it is now generally accepted that Baruch's spite was aroused at a political shindig where Truman, in a moment of bourbon induced hilarity, jocularly addressed the great American as "hey, Jewboy!"

The vitriolic nature of the campaign against Truman in 1948 is said to have reelected him. Others maintain that the American people would never elect Dewey, even if he was called Ike, and that is probably true. However, Dewey can always retire to a good spot in the international narcotics trade, as long as Lucky Luciano is free.

Carter Field, in his biography of Baruch, says

> "As a young politician in South Carolina, years before, Byrnes had come to know and like Baruch."

Perhaps you have to know Baruch to like him. It has been said of Tom Dewey that you have to know him to dislike him.

Certainly Washington from 1941 to 1945 was filled with dangerous people in jobs where they could and did incalculable harm to our Republic. Bundy tells us that Stimson's three assistants were John J. McCloy, from Cravath and Henderson, Robert A. Lovett, from Brown Brothers Harriman, and Arthur Palmer from his own law firm of Winthrop and Stimson. Stimson always managed to find important jobs in Washington for his law partners. On page 494 of the Stimson masterwork, Bundy tells us that

> "At first it was Stimson's hope that Donald Nelson could be bolstered by the appointment of strong assistants, and he brought Charles E. Wilson and Ferdinand Eberstadt into the War Production Board in September, 1942. In February of 1943, when Nelson proved unable to drive so spirited a team, Stimson and other administrators joined in asking the President to replace him with Bernard Baruch."

Donald Nelson was a Sears Roebuck man, and Sears Roebuck, of course, is owned by the Rosenwald family, who kindly lent Nelson to the Government for a dollar-a-year.

One of the most abominable swindles of the war was the pay-as-you-go income tax plan, a product of the fertile brain of Beardsley Ruml, agent of the Strauss family which owns Macy Co of New York. Rep. Wright Patman denounced the Ruml Plan as having been designed expressly to protect the first crop of war millionaires, whose race we can well imagine. I. F. Stone noted in the newspaper PM, now dead of an overdose of Communism, that the Ruml Plan provided an excellent dodge for the get-rich-quick gang, because it did not tax undivided profits. To avoid the income tax, the partners could leave the money in the business. This, however, meant little to the worker who was getting hooked every week. The Ruml Plan was unjust in that it deprived the worker of his money as soon as he earned it. Before Ruml, the worker at least had the use of his money before the government took it. Now the government takes it when it is earned, and if too much is taken, as is often the case, the worker has an interesting struggle lasting from one to ten years to get it back.

The American Army picked up some interesting techniques from the Communists while General Marshall was Chief of Staff. It is not generally known that we too had our "political advisers" with our overseas troops throughout the Second World War. General Dwight Eisenhower at his headquarters in London had as adviser James Paul Warburg, organizer and director of the London branch of the Office of War Information. His cousin, Edward M. M. Warburg, of Kuhn, Loeb Co. was with Eisenhower with the official title of political adviser. Lt. John Schiff, partner of Kuhn, Loeb. And grandson of the financier of the Communist Revolution in Russia, was Eisenhower's Naval Attache. Judge Simon Rifkind was Eisenhower's adviser on Jewish affairs, which, of course, are extremely important. This staff formed the nucleus of the Eisenhower-for-President movement.

On the home front, the Communists reigned supreme. Roosevelt, insulated from the grubby American citizens by his sleek crew of Communist agitators, rapidly promoted Lauchlin Currie and Alger Hiss to the fore of his personal staff. The notorious Communist youth organizer Joe Lash often topped in for a quick meal and a shave at the White House between strikes and riots, and almost every day Soviet Commissar Maxim Litvinoff was to be seen going up the White House driveway in his chauffeur-driven limousine to have lunch with Roosevelt.

In 1943, Arthur Upham Pope had his biography of Litvinoff published by Louis Fischer Co. New York. This book explains some puzzling aspects of Russia's foreign policy. On page 451, Pope illuminates the Russo-German Pact of 1939 as follows:

> "Russia had one final hope; if she refused this military convention with France and England and if she made a non-aggression pact with Germany, the war might be localized between Germany and Poland and Europe would be spared the holocaust. The Russo-German agreement was the product of dire necessities which neither the urgency of the moment nor mutual interest could fully overcome. The Russians were wildly charged with double-dealing. As John Whittaker says: 'it was really the failure of the democracies to cooperate with Soviet Russia that had forced this mighty people to turn to isolationism and a pact with Nazi Germany. Walter Lippmann also defended Stalin in this case."

It is not surprising to find Lippmann defending Stalin anywhere. Certainly Lippmann would never charge the Russians with double-dealing merely because they reversed their entire foreign policy and made a pact with their worst enemy. Anyway, according to Pope, the democracies didn't cooperate with Russia.

The Non-aggression Pact caused some strange scenes. Russia's Ministry of Foreign Affairs had a completely Jewish staff, from Litvinoff on down, and now they had to wine and dine the anti-Semitic Nazis. One such banquet is described by Pope;

> "Lazar Kaganovich, Commissar of Railways, who is Jewish, did not appear at the State Banquet in honor of von Ribbentrop; but it was Kaganovich himself who declined to go, not Stalin who requested it; and another Jewish member of the Government, Solomon Lozovsky, Vice Commissar of Foreign Affairs, not only appeared at the banquet, but was seated next to Ribbentrop."

News photographs of this event never appeared. At any rate, these social tensions were short-lived. Russia also took advantage of the Pact to attack little Finland. Pope gives us the inside story of this event, on page 455;

> "On Nov. 2, 1939, Russia invaded Finland. The world in general knew little about the Fascist element in Finland and were not aware

that Mannerheim, a Swede who had been a Czarist General, and had a fearful record for cruelty, was, with others of the military clique, collaborating with Hitler. The public at large in the Western world was quite ignorant of the peril to Russia."

Under the leadership of the Czarist-Fascist-terrorist Mannerheim, says Pope, little Finland probably could have overrun Russia in a matter of days. No wonder democratic and gentle Stalin had to send his armies into Finland, before the Finns conquered Moscow. This idiotic argument is typical of the Communist propaganda with which the Communists flooded America while we were defending atheist Russia against Germany. The worst of it comes in Pope's description of the bank robber and mass murderer, Stalin. Pope writes that

> "Stalin has brown eyes, 'exceedingly kind and gentle', and beautiful hands. His demeanour is kindly, his manner almost deprecatingly simple, his personality and expression of reserve strength very marked, with a simple dignity. He has very great mentality. It is sharp, shrewd, and above all things else, wise. He has a sly humor, is well-informed on a considerable range of subjects and is not above doodling while he reflects. Quentin Reynolds quotes a British correspondent who once wrote of Stalin, 'He looks like the kindly Italian gardener you have in twice a week.' You couldn't find a better description of the Soviet Leader than that. His career has demonstrated perseverance, determination, patience, endurance, and courage, both physical bravery and the moral courage to admit his own errors, on which he lays special emphasis; and withal a certain flexibility that leads to the disregard of slogans or doctrinaire pronouncements which are more ideological than realistic. The collectivization of agriculture has been one of his major difficult achievements, made more difficult and consequently more cruel by the stubbornness of certain sections of the peasantry."

We quote at such length to emphasize the fanatical devotion of Communists abroad to their leader. Quentin Reynolds, formerly top foreign correspondent of Collier's, now edits United Nations World. This kindly old Italian gardener type managed to starve twelve million middle-class Russian farmers to death in order to collectivize their farms. Pope has drawn a perhaps over-sympathetic word-portrait of the most ruthless leader in the world.

In this classic work of Communist propaganda, "Maxim Litvinoff", by Arthur Upham Pope, we find little sympathy for American "reactionaries", thus

"Lindbergh's anti-Russian, anti-Asiatic, pro-Nazi views have since become obvious and are now discredited. In their reluctance to give up anti-Russian prejudices, Americans had by no means fully comprehended the change in policy under Stalin, a revised orientation that Lenin had favored from the start; the substitution for international revolution and its promotion in other countries, of a program for the full development of Russia's own resources, which was inspiring the Russian people to ever greater efforts, and laying the basis for a new internationalism which was making possible more cordial relations with foreign nations."

The past five years have shown us how true this is. Russia dreamed of replacing her illegal spies with legal ones at the United Nations, but at the present writing finds a combination of the two more satisfactory. Lindbergh, of course, was smeared because he opposed America's entry into the war to save Communism.

One of America's more indefatigable Communist propagandists is James Paul Warburg the scion of Kuhn, Loeb Co., and son of Paul Warburg. James Paul Warburg wrote "Foreign Policy Begins at Homes", Harcourt Brace, 1941, the publisher of the definitive edition of the Letters of Lenin, and other Communist books). On page 1, Warburg says,

"We are fighting not one but two wars, the military war against Germany and Japan, and the war against fascism, which is a worldwide civil conflict which crosses all national frontiers. The war against fascism will not end when the armies of Hitler and Hirohito have surrendered."

This use of the world "fascism" is a key word in Communist propaganda. It means all opposition to the World Socialist State. Communists label, all opponents "fascists".

On pages 19 and 20, Warburg tells us that

"Communism seeks to make the state the common steward of property and power for the benefit of all the people. Communism in Russia had its origin among an exploited and oppressed people which had enjoyed neither political nor economic democracy. It sought to establish economic democracy through a political dictatorship which it is now moving to abolish. Communism began in 1918 as a worldwide revolution of the working class against its exploiters. Russian Communism has abandoned world revolution and become a purely national experiment in state socialism.

Communism makes no distinctions of race, nationality, or religion. It stresses the brotherhood of man."

Although Warburg claims that Russia has abandoned world revolution, she has added China and Central Europe to her domain. He does not explain exactly how the political dictatorship is being abolished in Russia, nor does he refer to it in later works. Actually, of course, this fertilizer was not meant to be read ten years later. Like most propaganda, it had a temporary objective, the convincing of the American people that it was a glorious thing to die in the defense of Communism. Americans were somewhat reluctant to travel thousands of miles to defend an atheistic terrorist police state. It took Roosevelt to get them to do it.

The Council On Foreign Relations dominated the U. S. Government during the Second World War. Besides their hold on the State Department, their members comprised the upper echelons of the top secret Government agency, the Office of Strategic Services, as well as our official propaganda agency, the Office of War Information. The Office of War Information was organized by James Paul Warburg, who chose the tired newspaperman Elmer Davis as its front. The Pacific Branch of the OWI was placed in the hands of Owen Lattimore and William Holland of the Institute of Pacific Relations.

The Office of War Information provided a good place for such notorious fellow-travelers as Alan Cranston, who out of nowhere was appointed Chief of the Foreign Language Division of the OWI. Cranston is now President of United World Federalists, to which James Paul Warburg is the chief financial contributor. Cranston was the protégé of the professional Communist writer Louis Adamic, who was murdered in 1951 at his New Jersey home, presumably by Titoists. Cranston wrote for Adamic's magazine, Common Ground, a publication which also featured David Karr, also known as Katz, a writer for the Daily Worker who later turned up as Drew Pearson's chief reporter. Cranston was drafted into the Army, and wrote propaganda for the Army publication, Army Talk, which put out such useful Communist idea as Pamphlet 373, which suggested that the Panama Canal should be under international control. The Armed Forces Information and Education Service also provided a strategic place for the Communist vermin to hide while the fighting was going on.

Stanislaw Mikolajczyk, in "Rape of Poland", Whittlesey House, on page 25 writes that

"The Office of War Information followed the Communist line constantly, and was indistinguishable from Radio Moscow. The Poles were horrified to get nothing but Communist propaganda from the Office of War Information."

Mikolajczyk also pointed out that the Office of War Information stamped any report from the Polish Government in Exile in London as Top Secret, and buried in files, while the OWI carried nothing but Communist propaganda. This was also brought out by Hon. Charles A. Wolverton, Congressional Record, August 12, 1952, page A4963. The Office of War Information was reorganized by William Benton, now Senator, in 1946 as the Voice of America, and contains the same brand of creatures as the old Warburg outfit.

The Office of Strategic Services was completely dominated by Council On Foreign Relations members. The Wall Street Lawyer, General William Donovan was its Chief, and twenty-six of its top officials were members of the Council, such men as Allen W. Dulles, President of the Council, who met with German representatives throughout the war in the neutral territory of Switzerland, and Rear Admiral William Standley, who was with Harriman on the lend Lease Mission to Moscow in 1941, and who is a director of the Rothschild affiliate munitions firm, the Electric Boat Co., which recently got the Navy contract for the atomic submarine.

The Council was represented on every advisory group during the war. The U.S. Air Corps Strategic Bombing Survey which chose targets in Germany and Japan, had Elihu Root Jr. as its chief advisor, assisted by Elmo Roper, of Spiegel, Inc. and Theodore Paul Wright, all Council members, to choose industrial targets for our airmen.

Yugoslavia provided one of the saddest tragedies of the war. General Draja Mihailovich led an army of patriots against the Nazis from the beginning of the war. When Germany attacked Russia, Tito suddenly turned up with a Communist Army, and Churchill and Roosevelt refused supplies to Mihailovich, letting the Germans wipe out his patriotic forces, while they sent Military Missions and supplies to the Communist Army. Fitzroy MacLean represented Churchill at Tito's headquarters, and in his book "Escape to Adventure" he does not mention once the man with whom he ate and slept for many months, Col. Ellery C. Huntingdon, Chief of the U.S. Military Mission to Yugoslavia. Huntingdon and David Milton, John D. Rockefeller's son-in-law, together control the Morris Plan Banks and the Equity

Corporation, a vast network of holding corporations and banks. They also control the reinsurance business in America, on which they hold a monopoly. Insurance firms are required by law to be reinsured, and Huntingdon and Milton direct the General Reinsurance Corporation and the North Star Reinsurance Corporation, which interlock with the directorate of the Yugoslav-American Electric Co.

The World Zionist Organization worked steadily through the war for the establishment of the United Nations, which had guaranteed to set up the State of Israel, hence the Litvinoff-Churchill-Roosevelt Declaration of the United Nations one week after Pearl Harbor Day, Jan. 1, 1942. On March 21, 1944, Rabbi Wise led a rally of the American Zionist Emergency Council at Madison Square Garden in New York City. Wise said,

> "Our faith is in a tried and true friend of Zionism, Winston Churchill, and our faith is in the foremost democratic leader on earth today, Franklin Roosevelt."

In the trenches, the American boys were asking each other, "What are we fighting for?" but the Communist-front Office of War Information kept them from finding out that they were defending Communism and making it possible to set up the State of Israel. Instead, the Information and Education programs, loyally aided by American advertising men, wrote rhapsodically of the little red schoolhouse, Mom, and apple pie, and other symbols of their contempt for the intelligence of the boys who were being sent out to the profitable slaughter. In Hollywood, blonde-dyed movie queens rose reluctantly from the beds of Jewish film magnates, climbed into their limousines, rolled down to the U.S.O., where they kissed a sailor before a battery of newsreel cameras, got back into their limousines, and so to bed.

Douglas Reed, in "Lest We Regret", Jonathan Cape Co. London, 1943, writes

> "Max Ausnit was imprisoned in Roumania in 1940 for six year term for fraud and currency offenses. When the Germans came, they released him. Goering's nephew became a director of Ausnit's great Resitza Iron and Steel Works. Ausnit was released and officially cleared."

Nicholas Halasz wrote in the newspaper PM on July 26, 1944,

"Twenty-one persons flew from Hungary to Lisbon in three Lufthansa planes. This was the family and menage of the late Baron Manfred Weiss, the Hungarian armaments king. The party included Barons Eugene and Alphonse Weiss, Knight Oscar Wahl, and Baron Moric Kornfeld, the Chairman of the Board of the Hungarian General Credit Bank, which represents the Rothschild interests in the Danube Valley. The Weiss family owned the immense Csepel Armament Works, and reportedly has ten million dollars invested in New York real estate. The fact remains that despite the most stringent of Jewish laws in Hungary, the actual management of the Weiss interests remained the same without change, The Weisses were Jews under the racial theory. Many of them, however, are children of converts to Christianity."

The Weisses and Ausnits seemed to fare well under Nazi rule. Ambassador Dodd and George Sokolsky pointed out that the Warburgs were not bothered by Hitler. How anti-Semitic were the Nazis? At any rate, the Jews prepared a terrible vengeance on the German people. The Council On Foreign Relations in July of 1944 published "American Interests in the War and Peace", stamped Confidential, and declassified in 1946. It was authored by assorted personalities, among them Jacob Viner and Benjamin Cohen. It was subtitled "Postwar Controls of the German Economy". On page 1, we find

"In considering the economic measures to be applied to a defeated Germany, the victorious countries should have the following principles in mind:

1. To provide compensation for losses suffered by the victims of German aggression.

2. To supplement measures for disarmament.

3. To lay the foundations for recovery on an international scale, and for a durable peace.

4. Imports of food and materials as are in short supply should be allocated by United National Relief and Rehabilitation Administration to Germany with due regards to the needs of other countries impoverished as a result of the war. As long as shortages exist, UNRRA should not release scarce food and supplies for consumption in Germany except on license issued by the United Nations. The cost of the army of occupation is to be borne by Germany.

5.   All industrial and manufacturing installations which are designed for military purposes should be dismantled.

6.   There must be no government aid to Germany's synthetic industry."

This Confidential document, prepared by the Council On Foreign Relations, was actually the infamous Morgenthau Plan for wiping out the German people. It called for the dismantling of German industry, since almost any industrial plant could be classified as "designed for military purposes", and the denial of food to the German people, under Lehman's UNRRA organization. The Plan was first discussed at a dinner at Baron de Rothschild's home in London, where Israel Moses Sieff, head of the Political and Economic Planning Organization, the equivalent of our NRA, and Rothschild outlined the plane to visiting firemen Henry Morgenthau Jr. It was then publicized as the Morgenthau Plan. It was implemented by the Roosevelt demand for "unconditional surrender", which was broadcast to the German troops in the winter of 1944, when they were ready to quit. This infamous deed caused the deaths of thousands of American boys in the Battle of the Bulge in December, 1944, after the Germans decided to fight on, rather than to surrender unconditionally. Roosevelt's "unconditional surrender" extended the Second World War by at least six months.

The Morgenthau Plan would dismantle the entire German heavy industry and leave the German people with no way to support themselves or to maintain their high living standard. It was an abortive effort at genocide, or mass extermination of a racial group, which failed. Genocide has always been the specialty of the Jews. The great historian Gibbon, in his massive work, "The Decline and Fall of the Roman Empire", wrote in vol. 2, page 83, that

"From the reign of Nero to that of Antoninus Pius, the Jews discovered a fierce impatience of the dominion of Rome which repeatedly broke out in the most furious massacres and insurrections. Humanity is shocked at the recital of the horrid cruelties which the Jews committed in the cities of Egypt, of Cyprus, and of Cyrene, where they dwelt in treacherous friendship with the unsuspecting natives. In Cyrene they massacred 210,000; in Egypt a very great multitude. Many of their unhappy victims were sawed asunder, according to a precedent to which David had given the sanction of his example."

Americans have much in store for them.

The fate of Germany is intended as a warning to any nation which seeks national self-determination in the age of the World Socialist State. The web which holds together the fabric of internationalism was spun out from Frankfort to Amsterdam to Paris to London and to New York. At the conclusion of the Second World War, the spider hurried its subordinates into defeated Germany. A German Group Control Council was sent there in May, 1945, composed of the following Council On Foreign Relations members:

Wallace R. Deuel, Graeme K. Howard, Col. Thomas C. Betts, Calvin B. Hoover, who was the Group's Chief Economic Adviser, and Deweitt C. Poole, of the Russian Revolution. Other Council members in the Military Government of Germany were Maj. Gen. Lyman Lemnitzer, who handled the surrender negotiations (the United States was very anxious to have this Jew accept the German surrender, as if the Germans did not know who had beaten them); Raymond Sontag, who bore the title of Sidney Hillman Professor of European History at the University of California, in 1946 was in charge of all the captured German documents, as Chief of the German War Documents Project of the State Department; and Walter Lichtenstein, who out of nowhere came to be placed in charge of all German financial institutions from 1945 to 1947. This made him the supervisor of the records of the J. M. Stein Bankhaus, the branch of J. Henry Schroder Banking Co. which had handled Hitler's personal account. General William H. Draper Jr. of Dillon Read also was very anxious to be the first into conquered Germany.

The Military Government of Germany was under the command of General Eisenhower, who had made a wonderful record of cooperation with Stalin. Life Magazine of April 9, 1951 noted that Eisenhower had radioed Stalin through the U.S. Military Mission in Moscow that he would stop at the Elbe River and let the Russians take Berlin. Stalin reciprocated by decorating Eisenhower with the Russian Medal of Honor, the Order of Suvorov. No other American General was regarded by the Communists with such enthusiasm or so decorated as Ike Eisenhower.

Congressman Carroll B. Reece stated on March 19, 1951 that

> "We could have easily gotten to Berlin first. But our troops were first halted at the Elbe. They were then withdrawn from that river in a wide circle far enough westward to make Stalin a present of the great Zeiss optical and precision works at Jena, the most important

V-1 and V-2 rocket laboratory and production plant in Nordhausen, and the vital underground jet plant in Kahla. Everywhere we surrendered to the Soviets intact thousands of German planes, including great masses of jet fighters ready for assembly, as well as research centers, rocket developments, scientific personnel, and other military treasures. When it was all over a large part of the formidable Russian militarism of today was clearly marked 'Made in America' or 'donated by America from Germany'. But where Roosevelt left off Truman resumed."

Truman has indeed been a fierce contender for the title of the world's greatest benefactor of Communism, which was vacated by the passing of Roosevelt. The German people were in good hands at the end of the war. Fred Smith in the United Nations World of March, 1947, gives Eisenhower credit for implementing the "hard peace" plan against Germany. Eisenhower had with him throughout his months as Supreme Commander of the Allied Expeditionary Forces petite Kay Summersby, said to be his chauffeur. Whatever her duties were, she was with Ike night and day, while Mamie Eisenhower sat in Washington and endured the catty remarks of other Army wives whose husbands had male chauffeurs. Certainly no man could have been as cheering a companion to war-weary Ike as the warm-hearted Kay Summersby. After the war, she wrote a very interesting book, "Eisenhower Was My Boss", which is an account of how she and Ike amused themselves while American boys were being massacred in the war to save Communism. This book has now disappeared from the stores. It is a brazen revelation of drunken orgies and the contempt felt by Eisenhower's intimates for the grimy soldiers. On page 230, she quotes Ike on the pregift of Berlin to Russia as follows,

"The general idea, Ike declared, was to meet the Russians and split Germany in half. A message from Moscow quoted Stalin as in complete agreement with the Eisenhower directive; he promised detailed plans for coordinating the expected link-up."

General Lucius Clay was chosen by Eisenhower as the head of Germany's Military Government. Of course he took up his headquarters in the I. G. Farben Building, which had been undamaged by raids, and I. G. Farben continued to maintain offices a few doors from his own. He imported a choice collection from Kuhn, Loeb Co. to help him run Germany. Foremost was Max Lowenthal, the Lieutenant of Communist Sidney Hillman, and the man who swung the Vice-presidency to Truman at Chicago in 1944. Lowenthal moved in on Truman as head of the Zionist Inner Mission at the White House. The legal representative of Kuhn, Loeb's vast railroad properties, Lowenthal was accused of running the Interstate Commerce Commission to suit himself. He was a powerful lobbyist near the Senate Interstate Commerce Commission.

Max Lowenthal had a mission in Germany. He became Clay's assistant, and his own assistant was George Shaw Wheeler, who suddenly denounced the United States, and went to Communist Czechoslovakia to live. Lowenthal's assumption of power in Germany was marked by the sudden appearance of Communist agitator in West German cities, where they had previously been forbidden to speak.

Kuhn, Loeb was also represented by one of its partners, Assistant High Commissioner Benjamin Buttenweiser, whose wife, a niece of Senator Lehman, defended Alger Hiss at his first trial, Hiss was sheltered in the Buttenweiser's Park Avenue apartment during that trial. The U.S. High Commissioner for Germany was John J. McCloy, partner of the Law firm Cravath and Henderson, which represented Kuhn, Loeb Co. McCloy succeeded Eugene Meyer as President of the World Bank, and then was sent Germany.

Because of the kind intervention of Henry Morgenthau, the Russians had been given our plates for printing occupation marks, and they ran off a few billion extra, which further disrupted the economy of Germany. It was widely reported that plates for printing U.S. dollars had also been presented to Russia, and that many millions of dollars had been printed and sent to America in the possession of "refugees", who landed with fortunes in their luggage. This money was used to buy apartment houses. Liquor stores, and other profitable businesses, and gave the "refugees" a dominant position in the American economy over the luckless natives, who now work for them. This is an excellent example of how to conquer a nation by the power of the printing press. America has never lost a war, but we have an army of occupation on our soil, and that army has all the arrogance and power of the Caesars in Britain.

General William H. Draper Jr., partner in Dillon Read, the banking house which financed Hitler, was economic adviser to General Clay in Germany. In "Decision In Germany", Doubleday 1950, page 47, Clay writes

"It was to be followed shortly by Eisenhower's official trip to Moscow as the guest of the Soviet Government. The visit was made between August 10th and 15th. Eisenhower took with him an old friend from our days in Manila, General T. J. Davis, his son Lt. John Eisenhower, and me. Marshal Zhukov accompanied us in Eisenhower's plane to act as his escort. Eisenhower and Marshal Zhukov exchanged views on the use of troops."

Clay showed no sympathy for the sufferings of the German people, who had been led to war by a man foisted upon them by Wall Street bankers. On page 100

'I was shocked with a German recommendation to lower the ration of displaced persons to the German level. This recommendation came from the Laenderrat (Parliament).'

Clay was horrified that the German people should want as much to eat as the privileged class of displaced persons under the rule of Lowenthal and Buttenweiser. On page 235, Clay writes

"At my request our National Council of Christians and Jews has representatives in Germany working to prevent the regrowth of anti-Semitism."

On page 31 of "Decision in Germany" we find,

"To ensure that the property of Jewish people killed in Germany who left no heirs would not benefit German holders, a Jewish Successors' Organization, formed by reconvened Jewish organizations, was authorized to claim and receive their property."

Freda Utley wrote a piercing indictment of the American occupation of Germany in "The High Cost of Vengeance", Henry Regnery Co. pointing out that the American taxpayer has had to support Germany with billions of dollars because the Jews executed the plan of uprooting German industry and sending it to Russia.

The execution of the German Leader after the Nuremberg Trials so intimidated the Germans that only the worst slime of the nation dared seek public office since then, we have pledged ourselves never to let a Nazi-type government reappear in Italy or in Germany, which means that the first attempts in those countries to restrict the wrecking activities of the Jews will force us to declare war on them again. The Nuremberg Trials were conducted on those principles of justice which Stalin first showed to the world during the infamous Moscow Purge

Trials of 1937-38. Brutality and forced confessions marked the conduct of those trials. The man whose name appears and reappears in the horror stories of those torture-chambers at Nuremberg is then Lt. William R. Pearl, law partner of the late Senator McMahon, who was Chairman of the Joint Committee on Atomic Energy. The Nuremberg Trials were greeted with indignation by legal authorities all over the world. The law under which the Nazi leaders were sentenced was an ex post facto law, a law written after the "crime" was committed. Ex post facto law has never had any place in our legal code, but the Russians, sitting in judgment on their former partners, the Nazi, passed laws to fit the crime. They judged the Nazis for doing what the Russians had done and are still doing, aggressive acts against small nations. Montgomery Belgion and other observers wrote books condemning Nuremberg Trials. It is now admitted that they dealt a severe blow to our worldwide reputation for fairness in the administration of justice.

Freda Utley, in "The High Cost of Vengeance"[3] pointed out that we judged the Nazis on a "guilt by association" principle, that is, families and acquaintances of Nazis were sentenced and punished. Yet members of many Communist-front organizations in the United States, when they are exposed, complain that they are being attacked on a principle of "guilt by association".

The Chief Prosecutor at the Nuremberg Trials was General Telford Taylor, a partner in Judge Simon Rifkind's Wall Street law firm of Weiss, Paul, and Rifkind. Taylor is now Small Defense Plants Administrator in Washington.

The Nuremberg Trials, despite forced confessions by the Pearl, seriously obscured the charges that six million Jews were dead. The famous ovens, which have been the basis of Jewish hysteria ever since, were crematories which the Nazis used as a sanitary way to dispose of inmates who died in the concentration camps. No evidence was produced that any live persons were burned. The concentration-camp atrocities were shown to have been committed by Communist inmates whom the Nazis had placed in charge of the camps. Germans were needed at the front, and in the last two years of the war, the camps were under the direction of Communist trusties, who had a free hand in murdering anti-Communist prisoners. The prison camp atrocities at

---

[3] "The High Cost of Vengeance", by Freda Utley, Omnia Veritas Ltd, www.omnia-veritas.com.

Koje Island in Korea have been a duplication of what went on in German concentration camps. The Russians hurriedly passed over this portion of the testimony at Nuremberg.

The claim that Hitler killed six million Jews is belied by their own figures in the World Almanac. Immediately after Germany's surrender, a planeload of American editors and correspondents were flown to the concentration camps, where they were shown huge piles of bones. These were the remains of American Russian prisoners of war, but they were filmed and shown all over the United States as "Jewish bones", in one of the most revolting attempts to influence public opinion ever known. Many theater-goers became ill at this gruesome sight, and protests were made to the Loews and other owners of movie chains against showing these horrible things to women and children, but the Jewish propagandists were determined to spare no one this frightful experience, and for months afterwards, our newspapers and magazines were filled with the ghoulish bone-pictures.

The influx of more than six million Jews into the United States during the war makes it difficult for Americans to believe the charges against the Nazis. All restrictions on their entering the United States were lifted by personal orders of President Roosevelt. It is now estimated that from five to eight million Jews came into the United States from 1940 to 1946. They now create a serious economic problem because of their growing predominance in retail trade, forcing native Americans into less profitable occupations.

The background of the Nuremberg Trials is the same as the background of the Second World War, the identical international influences which plotted to put an end to the respect of one government for the officials of another.

On page 587 of Bundy's biography of Stimson, we find that

> "Stimson was skeptical about the trying of war criminals on the charge of aggressive war when it was first suggested to him by his law partner, William Chanler. He thought it "a little in advance of international thought" (Memo to McCloy, Nov. 28, 1944), and it was only after further consideration that he became an ardent advocate of the principle."

No doubt he conferred with that eminent authority, his former partner Frankfurter, who could find grounds for ex-post facto law.

Nuremberg law was considered a great advance in legal progress by the Council On Foreign Relations. In "Foreign Affairs", July, 1947, William E. Jackson wrote an article "Putting the Nuremberg Law to Work", quote

> "It would seem especially important that the Nuremberg principles, which establish a rule of law binding on all nations, should remain strong while the United Nations has not attained full command of its powers.

> The suggestion has for some time been current that the law of Nuremberg should be codified on the initiative of the General Assembly of the United Nations. A proposal to this effect by Mr. Paul Bul, American member of the International Military Tribunal, was approved by President Truman. What we must do, if we are to perpetuate the law of Nuremberg effectively, is not to direct our energies in refurbishing it but to set up, now, procedures to guarantee that it can be swiftly applied if ever again need should arise."

John Foster Dulles would be a good candidate for trial if the Nuremberg Law is to be invoked on the starting of the war in Korea.

The World Jewish Congress of New York City publishes a sheet called "Jewish Comment". The May 29, 1943 of this paper declared that

> 'It is generally agreed that the international legal definitions of war crimes, formulated before the Axis methods of "total warfare" were known, may prove an insufficient basis for penalizing some of the more flagrant German crimes against humanity. It is an altogether different matter if the whole question of retribution is considered in close connection with the tactics of warfare. If they are to play their part in the winning of the war, the trials and punishment of war criminals, traitorous collaborationists, and their accomplices, must be carried out at once in each newly conquered territory. Public trials should be held without awaiting the final general peace in each newly reconquered territory. An active United Nations Commission to try Axis and satellite criminals, as they are surrendered to the United Nations, should be established. Several similar bodies, more or less informal and uncoordinated, have already begun to work as a result of a Conference at St. James' Palace on Jan. 13, 1942. The Soviet Commission is even now conducting judicial proceedings.'

Under these principles of justice, at least 10,000 French citizens were executed by partisan 'Commissions of Communists in the closing months of the war, while the Soviet Commission is reported to have executed 1,500,000 victims of these United Nations provisions as it moved into Germany. Mussolini, the legal head of Italy, was brutally murdered by a gang carrying out these principles. Public trials held by advance troops, of course, were courts-martial which had no relation to civil courts of justice. The American and English armies refused to become party to these mass executions, and their prisoners were turned over to the United Nations Commission, which conducted the legal farce of the Nuremberg Trials.

The worst mass-murder of the war, the Katyn Forest massacre of 10,000 Polish officers by the Russian Secret Police, was hushed up at the Nuremberg Trials. This atrocity was greeted by "Jewish Comment", issue of May, 21, 1943, as follows:

> "After its sensational success with the story of the 10,000 Polish officers allegedly killed by the Soviets, the German Propaganda Ministry has evidently determined to explore further possibilities of splitting the Allies"

The Katyn massacre was hushed up in Washington through the efforts of Elmer Davis, who was Warburg's stooge in the OWI, and by W. Averell Harriman, according to evidence before the Senate Committee which belatedly investigated the story in 1952. The Voice of America, OWI's successor, steadfastly refused to mention the story until May, 1951, after repeated efforts by Congressmen to get them to use the Katyn Forest story to let Central Europe know what to expect from the Soviets. Indeed, the Voice of America has yet to use any strong anti-Communist propaganda.

General Clay finally tried to bring about some order in the economic chaos of Germany. The inflation caused by the extra billions from the Morgenthau plates made it impossible to restore a stable economy, but on August 2, 1948, the Americans introduced a currency reform, with the Western Mark B, which would replace the inflated Soviet Deutsche Mark. This currency reform, an open struggle between the Russians and the Americans for the right to issue money, caused the Soviets to set up the 'blockade of Berlin'. Clay responded with his famous 'airlift', which the press parlayed into a great achievement. When he returned to this country, Lehman Brothers gave him the Presidency of Continental Can, a directorship on the Marine Midland Trust, and a directorship of General Motors.

In the Far East, our generals knew by the spring of 1945 that Japan was defeated. American planes flew over Tokyo at will from airbases in Okinawa and from carriers operating off of the Japanese coast. MacArthur had done this with the few supplies sent him by Marshall, while the Soviet armies received priority over the Pacific campaign. Senator McCarthy, in 'Retreat from Victory', the sorry record of Marshall's collaboration with the Communists, says that Marshall strongly urged a land invasion of Japan, despite the fact that Japan was already beaten. Her oil supplies were gone, her fleet of tankers sunk, her heavy industry bombed out of existence, her cities rubble, yet Marshall expected thousands of American boys to die in a useless invasion of Japan. His insane insistence on this point continued in the face of opposition from General MacArthur and Admirals Nimitz and Leahy. At last, Marshall was forced to give way, with bad grace. Many Americans are alive today because Marshall did not gain his will. Leahy also advised Marshall that there was no reason for Russia to come in against Japan, but he might have saved his breath. Marshall and Truman, for reasons not yet explained, were determined to have Russia attack Japan, thus giving her a voice in the postwar administration in Tokyo. Russia attacked in the closing weeks of the war, after Japan and vainly sued for peace. A Japanese force of two million men was captured in Manchuria by the Russians and sent to Siberia for Communist indoctrination. The politically reliable ones were trained as revolutionists and repatriated to Japan to form the core of Communist agitation. The rest have never been heard from. Huge stores of Japanese armaments were captured and turned over to the Chinese Communists, together with American arms treacherously given to Mao's army through the influence of Stilvall's Communist advisers, these weapons conquered China for the Communists.

As the Commander of the Army of Occupation in Japan, General Douglas MacArthur was an outstanding success. Even the international news services were forced to recognize his fine administrative abilities. Nevertheless, he was almost recalled at the beginning of his service in Tokyo. He sent home two of the most outspoken Communist revolutionists then writing for the Tokyo edition of Stars and Stripes, and the resulting protest from the yellow liberal press encouraged Truman to decide to recall MacArthur. At that time, however, Truman was still unsure of himself, and he lost his nerve. Had he recalled MacArthur then, Japan would now be a Communist State. MacArthur's influence alone held down the Communist movement in Japan. It is noteworthy that as soon as MacArthur was recalled, there were widespread outbreaks of Communist riots in Japan, and attacks upon American personnel.

The Second World War failed to provide the attack on the United States mainland which Roosevelt so dearly desired as his chance to clamp down a military dictatorship and dispose of his critics. Roosevelt never gave up this dream, and he and Hopkins went so far as to have Senator Warren Austin sponsor a universal slavery bill, known as Bill No. 666, in 1944.

Also known as the Roosevelt National Service Act, this bill had its origin in Lenin's compulsory labor law for both sexes. It would have given Roosevelt power to draft all adult men and women in America and send them to work either on this continent or abroad. Senator Austin was paid off for this attempt at slavery by being appointed U.S. Representative to the United Nations. The bill, never seriously considered by Congress, was looked upon by some observers as evidence of one of the President's terrible hangovers, when he hated everybody, and by others as indication of the weakened condition of his mind. In any case, it was proof of his insane desire to see himself the absolute master of every living soul in America before he died, a vicious ambition which he never realized. Nevertheless, there was enough Government regulation of our lives during the war to satisfy any but the most insatiable Communists. The Office of Price Administration under Leon Henderson tried to get every American to spy upon his neighbor, and even attempted to introduce the old Communist custom of having children inform on their parents. Senator Benton defends such regulation in Fortune, October, 1944. On page 165, under the disarming title of 'The Economics of a Free Society', he said,

> 'Our government regulation has been necessary and in the interest of preserving free enterprise. After the war, the role of government-in-business will and must be lessened in many areas of the economy, transferred in others, and increased in still others. More adequate government skills must be devised, for example, to help stabilize the economy against the effects of the "business cycle" ... Labor, agriculture, and government, as well as business, must divest themselves of all practices that check expansion of production or that restrict out put.'

Benton says that 'free enterprise' can be preserved only by government regulation, an interesting argument which he does not develop. The expansion of production past all sensible needs is a favorite Communist goal. The surplus becomes an excellent weapon to wreck the economy. There is no denying the fact that the surplus production of heavy industry is the principal factor in our continued involvement in foreign wars. The 'business cycle', of course, is an old joke, still snickered at by the economists who teach it in the universities. In 'The Federal Reserve', I showed how the bankers started and ended 'business cycles' at their pleasure.

CHAPTER 20

With the establishment of the United Nations, it was revealed that the Second World War did have a purpose. The entry of the United States into this organization was brought about by a circumstance usually found only in sensational adventure novels, the seduction of a silly old man into the betrayal of a nation. The victim was Senator Arthur Vandenberg Chairman of the Senate Committee on Foreign Relations, a Michigan publisher and a highly respected man who for years had led the pro-American bloc in Congress during the era of Roosevelt's internationalism. He succeeded Borah as the 'isolationist Senator', and Vandenberg was the only Senator to vote against the recognition of Soviet Russia in 1933. In 1944, he fell into the clutches of an enchantress, the wife of a British commercial attaché. It was soon obvious that she had a single purpose in coming to Washington, and her association with Vandenberg became the subject of cocktail gossip in the salons.

At this time, in the fall of 1944, Vandenberg yet retained his position as the leader of the isolationist pro-American group. Congress had little interest in the formation of the United Nations. The politicians were bombarded with expensive brochures and the output of a well-trained and highly-paid publicity organization, the American Association for the United Nations, operating from the Council On Foreign Relations' address, 45 East 65th St. New York City. Samuel Untermeyer's law partner, Zionist Philip Amram, was its Washington representative. Because of Vandenberg's well-known opposition to these intriguers, the other Senators felt that the United Nations had little chance of being ratified.

The international bankers were also aware of this fact. Consequently, Vandenberg became the prime target for their influence. Evalyn Patterson arrived in Washington, and the rest is history. By November of 1944, the friendship was common knowledge, and in January of 1945 he shocked his colleagues and his country by making a speech in the well of the Senate vigorously urging that we ratify the United Nations Charter. The origin of this change in his outlook was no secret to anyone in Washington. The Washington Times-Herald repeatedly intimated that Vandenberg had been persuaded to ratify the Charter by the feminine wiles of Evalyn Patterson. Without implying that any impropriety took place between Patterson and Vandenberg, the fact remains inescapable that her gay charm was the deciding factor in changing him from a patriot and a decent American to a slobbering old man on his last pathetic fling. The price he paid was the freedom of his homeland. Senator Vandenberg had served his people for many years, but he ruined his name before he died. The sordid story hung over him at the Republican Convention of 1948, when the bankers wished to reward him by making him President in a certain victory over the hero of the Kansas City underworld, Harry Truman. The name of Evalyn Patterson was repeated again and again at those desperate and smoky conferences in the hotel rooms, before the friends of the Senator gave the word to the press that the Senator was not a candidate because he had heart trouble. Whether the pun was intended, I cannot say. Politicians are noted for their vulgar humor.

Although he could not collect the reward of the Presidency, Vandenberg did an excellent job of persuading his now-demoralized colleagues to go along with him on the ratification of the United Nations Charter. Senator Taft later hedged that he would have liked to see some changes in it, but only Senator Pat McCarran has had the guts to say publicly that he wished he had never voted for it. It is not improbably that every Senator who voted away the national sovereignty of the United States to an unscrupulous gang of international revolutionaries will be moved to make a like confession of error.

The authorship of the United Nations Charter is sufficient to condemn it to every America. Professor de Madariaga has long been one of the keenest European observers. In Spain during the 1920s, he was an official of the Spanish Republican Government, but with the coming of the Russian generals to Spain, he left the Communist Party. In his book, "Victors Beware!", he warned America against ideals of the United Nations, page 270)

> "The United Nations Charter in the main a translation of the Russian system into an international idiom and its adaptation to an international community ... The overwhelming mass of Russia's political influence has weighed down the evolution of world affairs and is now taking us back to an unholy alliance of Big Powers,

resting upon force and very little else. UN bare upon its brow from the very beginning the mark of Moscow."

To write the Charter, the State Department appointed a Russian Jew, Dr. Leo Pasvolsky, of the Council On Foreign Relations. The Chicago Tribune pointed out that

> "Leo Pasvolsky, Russian-born ardent internationalist, knows more about the new League of Nations to preserve peace than any other person in the world. That's because he wrote the first draft of the charter of the world peace league and attended its revision and amplification all the way from the first day of the Dumbarton Oaks Conference to the last day of the San-Francisco Conference. He bids for fame as the father of the Charter.. President Truman has appointed Stettinius the U.S. Representative to the capital of the league, when it is selected, to guide the American delegate through the maze of the Charter and provide him with the answers to the questions that will arise. For Pasvolsky knows all the answers can give them before the questions are asked ... He was brought into the department as an economist and successively advanced to the highest ranks outside of those positions filled by Presidential appointment subject to Senate confirmation. Pasvolsky, now a naturalized American citizen, was born in Pavlograd, Russia in 1893, and came to this country with his parents in 1905. He has published several works on Russia including "The Economics of Communism."

Pasvolsky of Petrograd was the director of international studies at the mysterious Brookings Institution, which advises our President on economic policy. It is another one of those tuxedo outfits without visible means of support and a lot of political influence. Its headquarters are just around the corner from the White House in Washington. Pasvolsky had previously prepared the documents for the American delegation to the London Economic Conference of 1933.

The lobbying for the United Nations began in 1943 with the formation of the State Departmental Committee on International Organization, headed by Sumner Welles, Acting Secretary of State. Other members were Senator Tom Connall Senator Warren Austin, Mrs. Anne O'Hare McCormick, one of those creatures from the New York Times, Myron C. Taylor of United States Steel, Hamilton Fish Armstrong, editor of "Foreign Affairs", Norman H. Davis, President of the Council On Foreign Relations, Dr. Isaiah Bowman, of the Paris Peace Conference and President Of Johns Hopkins University, and the Zionist Lawyer

Benjamin V. Cohen. Cordell Hull had nothing to do with this band of intriguers. He was so disgusted at being Secretary of State in name only, and having to read Eugene Meyer's Washington Post to find out what our foreign policy was, that he no longer had much to do with the Department. Most men would have had enough character to resign.

The United Nations Organization was patterned exactly like the International Secretariat of the Communist Party. Its arrangement and selection of Councils, the entire procedure and terminology, was that of Moscow, beginning with the head of UN, called the Secretary-General, which is Stalin's title in Russia, and continuing through every detail of UN, nor is this surprising when he consider that everyone who had anything to do with the birth of the United Nations believed with the fervor of fanaticism that Russia had the finest government in the world.

The American Delegation to the United Nations Conference at San Francisco in 1945 was composed of thirty-six members of the Council On Foreign Relations. They were John Foster Dulles, Philip C. Jessup, Hamilton Fish Armstrong, and thirty-three others who have figured largely in these pages. The character and allegiances of these men may best be recognized by the history of their leader, the Secretary-General of the San Francisco Conference, the imprisoned Communist spy and traitor Alger Hiss.

Every Communist in America beamed the day their hero, Alger Hiss, landed at National airport in Washington carrying the satchel with the signed United Nations Charter. Those were great in 1945, when the circle of devoted traitors carried on after the death of Roosevelt to fulfill his dream of Communism. The professional revolutionists had achieved the goal for which they had worked so long, a forum which would dictate to every country in the world. Alger Hiss was appointed President of the Carnegie League for the Endowment of International Peace, a twenty thousand dollars a year position with expenses. Hardly had Hiss settled down to enjoy the fruits of treason than his past began to haunt him. A former Communist named Whittaker Chambers had been going from office to office in wartime Washington telling government officials that Hiss was a Communist spy. These reports reached Roosevelt, who shrugged, and ordered that Hiss be promoted. Chambers continued his fight to get Hiss ousted from the policy-making staff of the State Department, but the only result was that Roosevelt made Hiss his personal secretary at the infamous Yalta conference.

Finally, Chambers got Hiss before the House Un-American Activities Committee hearing, where Hiss denied everything. After Chambers' story was corroborated by extensive FBI investigations, Hiss was tried for perjury. He was convicted for denying that he had stolen secret documents from the State Department for a Soviet spy ring. The international news services assumed from the beginning that Hiss was innocent, and embarked upon a vicious smear campaign against Chambers. The most prejudiced of the yellow liberal sheets in Hiss' favor was Eugene Meyer's Washington Post.

The Hiss case proved that you can't strike at a Communist without hitting a Jew. Hiss was a highly-paid confidential agent for the Communists, and behind him lurked the sinister figure of Benjamin Buttenweiser, partner of Kuhn, Loeb Co. New York. Buttenweiser's wife was Hiss' lawyer, and the Hisses made a nest in the Buttenweiser's Park Avenue apartment during the trial.

An impressive list of defendants and character witnesses appeared for Hiss Everybody but the official leaders of the Communist Party of America came down to vouch for him. Roosevelt was dead, or he would have appeared for him. The pompous Zionist, Justice Felix Frankfurter, whose brother Otto had been an habitual criminal, testified for Hiss. Gov. Adlaie Stevenson of Illinois swore for him. Stevenson got his start in politics through the Chicago branch of the Council On Foreign Relations. Secretary of State Dean Acheson, the former legal representative of the Soviet Union, came forward for Hiss, and said that he would never turn his back on him.

President Truman considered the prosecution of Hiss as a personal insult, and he flew into a rage whenever he was questioned about it. He denounced it as a "red herring", a phrase which was to haunt him. For some time, the Department of Justice, acting on orders from the White House, had no intention of prosecuting Hiss, and only the determined action of several Congressmen finally brought Hiss to trial. The arrest of Hiss was a great blow to the Zionist Inner Mission in the White House. Perhaps the American people were waking up. Many a traitor in Washington passed some sleepless nights before it became apparent that Hiss was to be a sacrificial goat who would appease the American people. Once Hiss was in prison, Americans settled down to their old routine of paying taxes to support Russia through the Marshall Plan and the Point Four program, and the Communists in government resumed their treasonable activities.

A case history of an internationalist can be found in the Who's Who In America biography of Clark Eichelberger, who has made a comfortable living out of the World State racket since 1922. The husband of Rosa Kohler, Eichelberger has been with the American Association for the League of Nations since 1929, which became the American Association for the United Nations in 1944, and which has always had its offices in the Council On Foreign Relations town house at 45 East 65th St. New York. Eichelberger lists himself as the director of the Commission to Study the Organization of Peace from 1939–1948. Before we ever got into the war, he was telling us what we were going to do afterwards. He is now Chairman of that Commission, and also Chairman of the Human Rights Commission of the World Federation Associations, he was director of the traitorous Committee to Defend America by Aiding the Allies, which gets credit for swinging the United States into the Second World War. Eichelberger has a number of claims to infamy. He was even a member of the United Nations Conference at San Francisco in 1945 with Alger Hiss.

The simple fact is that the personnel of the United Nations includes a gathering of top Communist revolutionaries from all over the world. This was proved on June 30, 1949, when Senator Pat McCarran wrote Admiral Hillenkoetter, nominal head of the Central Intelligence Agency, which was really run by Allen Dulles, to ask whether any Communist spies were coming into the United Nations as delegates. Hillenkoetter promptly returned to Senator McCarran a list of one hundred high-ranking Communist Party and Secret Police officials from various countries. Thirty-two of them were Secret Police officials, and all of these one hundred were known as lifelong revolutionaries. Shortly after this, Admiral Hillenkoetter was removed and sent to the Pacific for a tour of duty. Senator McCarthy brought this episode to light in "Retreat from Victory".

In the face of this and other published exposes of the United Nations spying, Eleanor Roosevelt continued her pro-Communist propaganda. In the November, 1952 issue of See Magazine, she denied that there were Russian spies at the United Nations, and insisted that intelligence agencies would find better places for their operatives to work. As senior U.S. representative at the United Nations, she ought to know whether there are Communist Secret Police there. On August 28, 1952, the day that issue of See went on the newsstands, AP dispatches announced that Valerian Zorin would replace Jacob Malik as Russian UN representative, and identified Zorin as the mastermind of the Czech coup in 1948.

Poor Eleanor has come a long way down since the passing of the Great Communist. Our slickest magazines formerly vied to print her articles, but now her propaganda appears among the scantily-clad beauties of See Magazine, a publication which is hardly slanted at an intellectual audience. Her lecture fees, too, are not what they were. Perhaps leftwing propaganda no longer commands top prices on the lecture circuits.

On June 22, 1952, the Washington Times-Herald carried a syndicated story that the United Nations had fired Eugene Wallach and Irving Kaplan, an economist, for false records of their former employment. A United Nations spokesman emphasized that they were not being fired because of subversive activities, because, said the spokesman, loyalty does not enter into United Nations qualifications.

Loyalty would certainly not be considered a qualification for entry into that world's greatest collection of traitors and revolutionaries, the United Nations. Any representative who showed a jingoistic preference for his homeland as opposed to the interests of Liberia or Israel would be sent packing. Kaplan and Wallach would never have been fired for subversive activities, because that is the actual work of the United Nations. It is devoted to subverting every government and religion in the world.

The Secretary-General of the United Nations is proof of that; the Big Lie is typical of world Communism, Comrade Trygvie Lie, who received that post as a reward for past favors to his neighbor Joseph Stalin. For instance, fat Lie, as Norway's Minister of Justice, ordered Trotsky deported so that Stalin could murder him further away from Russia. Trotsky said that he remembered Lie as a member of the Communist International. England had a candidate for the United Nations post, one Paul Henri-Spaak, an agent of the Amsterdam bankers, but, as usual, the superior wisdom of the ex-bank-robber, Joseph Stalin, prevailed, and the Big Lie got the job.

John D. Rockefeller Jr. gave a $1,500,000 site in Manhattan for the United Nations building, and the Russian delegation was housed at the J.P. Morgan estate at Glen Cove, Long Island, which should give some background on the farce of the United Nations.

Even before it was in operation, the United Nations had spawned a host of revolutionary organizations which had as their objective the continuation of Lend-Lease by other means, and chief of them was the United Nations Rehabilitation and Relief Administration. The world patriots in charge of this were now Senator Herbert Lehman, of the banking house of Lehman Brothers, and the Council On Foreign Relations agent Laurence Duggan, who went out of a high window in New York City before he could be questioned by a Congressional Committee.

Herbert Lehman, director of many corporations, and one of the founders and principals of the Palestine Economic Corporation, has been influencing the peddling of a $500,000,000 bond issue from Israel. This financial operation has not interfered with his Senatorial duties, nor has anyone questioned his propriety. He is also a director of the Woodrow Wilson Foundation with Alger Hiss.

Current Biography, volume of 1943, page 438, says of Lehman, then head of UNRRA, that he is

> "in a position in which he may take a part in reshaping the economy of the entire world."

This is an old Communist ideal. On page 439,

> "Lehman won as Governor of New York in 1938 through American Labor Party and Communist support."

The Communists usually support only those who are on their side.

The Hungarian patriot, Stephen J. Thuransky, leader of the anti-Communist movement in Hungary wrote in "How American Financed Hungarian Communism",

> "The Hungarian Communist Party made its first great gains in strength with American financial assistance rendered through the media of UNRRA, which dumped millions of dollars worth of goods and resources into the hands of the Communist Party. These funds and resources were not used to feed the Hungarian masses but to strengthen the Communist Party. Since only party members were eligible for UNRRA relief, the Communist Party circulated the following slogan: 'Join the Communist Party and get your UNRRA relief package.' America again helped the Hungarian Communist Party through the allegedly anti-Communist Voice of America. Their speakers pretended not to realize that when they glorified the victorious Russian Army and its Communist philosophy, they were destroying in the minds of the American people all respect for the

United States. Once in December, 1946, I had thirty guests in my home when to our horror the Voice of America program started with the Communist Internationale, which the announcer called the Hungarian anthem."

Now we have the Hungarian Jewess Anna Rosenberg as Assistant Secretary of Defense, while we are opposed to Communist Hungary. Is this intelligent?

Herbert Lehman marries Edith Altschul, daughter of Charles Altschul, a partner of Lazard Freres banking house. Lehman is brother-in-law to Frank Altschul, who is very active in a number of mysterious pressure groups, such as the Committee on the Present Danger. No one seems to know what these groups are doing or what they stand for.

Lehman's assistant in UNRRA, Laurence Duggan, was the son of Stephen Duggan, head of the bizarre Institute of International Education, which was one of the weird offshoots of the Council on Foreign Relations. Stephen Duggan was also partner of James MacDonald in pro-Russian propaganda in the 1920s. Current Biography in 1947 observed on page 181that

> "Laurence Duggan resigned from the State Department Division of Latin-American Affairs in July 1944 to go with UNRRA. PM noted at that time that 'His resignation is deeply disturbing to labor and liberal forces in Latin America, as well as in the United States. He was a champion of the Loyalist cause against Franco, an early proponent of fair-dealing with Russia, and an unequivocable opponent of the Vichyist and Darlanist policies of Secretary Hull.'"

This is a thumb-nail biography of a leading Communist collaborator in the State Department. The bright red of his views on foreign policy was noticeable even there. The evening before Duggan was to testify before the House Committee on Un-American Activities, his body was found on the sidewalk below his New York office. Sumner Welles said he did not believe that Duggan committed suicide, nor did anyone else who had seen him prior to his death, but that was the verdict. Like so many Communist collaborators, Duggan got his reward when the heat was turned on him, a helping hand out of a window.

Jewish Comment quoted the New York Herald Tribune of Nov. 30, 1943 saying,

"In distributing relief supplies, UNRRA is to make no discrimination on the grounds of race, creed, or political belief. However, those who have been the victims of the victims of Nazi persecution-Jews, and, to a lesser degree, other natives of occupied countries, will receive special consideration because of their extra needs."

There will be no discrimination, but Jews will receive preference. This is a marvelous statement. It seems that even Jews did not receive preference unless they were Communist. Perhaps Senator Lehman could clear this up for us. The American taxpayer paid for the spread of Communism in Europe through Lehman's directorship of UNRRA. New Republic complains on October 22, 1945,

"The success of world organization is in jeopardy today because the United States is behind with its bills. President Truman has told Congress that relief machinery will break down very shortly unless it appropriates the remaining $550 million we promised to pay in 1945. Forty-six other nations followed our lead in joining together officially to administer a cooperative program and agreed that uninvaded countries should pay one per cent of their national income towards the cost. The United States share on this basis came to $1,350 million. Purely from self-interest the United States stands to gain from UNRRA. UNRRA must be a success if real international cooperation is to have a chance. If it should fail, the whole idea of a world government would receive a tremendous setback."

The joker in the UNRRA agreement was that invaded countries, that is, Russia, did not have to pay a cent. In the end, the United States footed nearly all of the bill, just as we are footing the bill for the luxurious life of the Communist spies at the United Nations. The UNRRA agreement was a typical backstairs gathering where a few Council On Foreign Relations members got together and committed the American taxpayer to one billion three hundred and fifty million dollars for Communist expansion in Europe. Under Lehman's leadership, UNRRA was notorious for refusing aid to churches, schools and orphanages. It was strictly political.

The pathetic eagerness of the Democratic Administration to turn the government of the United States over to a lot of jabbering Zulus and Communist agents is evidence of that Party's unfitness to be placed on the ballot in America. It would be better to vote for Communists than for secret Communist collaborators. Mark, Lenin, and Trotsky together did not do as much to further world Communism as did Franklin Roosevelt. Consider the United Nations' pronouncement on full employment, a replica of Point 8 of the Communist Manifesto, the equal liability of all to labor:

> "All members of the United Nations are pledged to secure high levels of employment. Expanding world trade is impossible without full employment. To fail on this front is as great a breach of the United Nations Charter as to fail to reinforce the United Nations forces fighting in Korea. The maintenance of full employment in the United States and Great Britain would go very far to maintaining it elsewhere."

Full employment, of course, is universal slavery, regulated by the State. Thus, all Americans are to be put to work manufacturing tractors for Russia, which will be sent there through the Point Four Program, and other agencies which have extended Lend-Lease to Russia by other means. Despite widely reported accounts of Marshall Plan goods going to Russia, and whole power plants shipped to Europe under ECA (headed by Milton Katz), being sent across East Germany and into Russia, the American people continue to labor to rearm their worst enemy.

International Communist propaganda is always distinguished by certain key phrases. One of those key phrases, in constant use since 1938, is "collective security". The Council On Foreign Relations has set aside large sums of money for studies on collective security, and its foremost writer on that subject is Philip C. Jessup. The United Nations was set up to promote "collective security, and Jessup is alternate U.S. delegate to the United Nations James Paul Warburg, in 'Put Yourself in Marshall's Place', Simon and Schuster, 1948, page 8, writes that

> "From 1935 to 1938, Western diplomacy stultified itself by increasing appeasement of fascist aggression, while Soviet diplomacy, on the whole, stood firmly for collective security and resistance to fascism."

Russia's firm stand against fascism after 1938 was demonstrated by her own appeasement of Hitler, the non-aggression pact of 1939. This does not bother a Communist propagandist like Warburg, the scion of Kuhn, Loeb and the director of the Bank of Manhattan. On the same page, he writes that

> "Just as Russia's temporary alliance with Germany was for a time obliterated by the superb performance of the Red Army against the Hitlerites, so the Communist Parties of Europe redeemed their earlier sabotage of the war effort by their later courageous and effective contribution."

The United States never made a non-aggression pact with Hitler, yet the Communist party line is that we appeased Hitler, but Russia did not. Actually, Stalin was very much afraid of Hitler, and the non-aggression pact was his only salvation in 1939. This was a greater appeasement than any made by the Western nations, but this means nothing to James Paul Warburg.

The United Nations may be better understood by one of its more radical and lunatic-fringe offshoots, United World Federalists, of which James Paul Warburg is chief financial contributor. His cousin Edward M. M. Warburg, formerly of General Eisenhower's staff, is also a heavy spender in this cause. Why not? All of this money given to subvert the United States Government is taken off of the income tax by that same Government, and the Warburgs have incomes of such size that these things make quite a difference. United World Federalists is composed of Council On Foreign Relations members, and other such obvious Americans as A. Philip Randolph, the Union Czar of the Pullman Porters, who urged Negroes to dodge the draft until segregation was ended in the military services. I thought Eleanor Roosevelt put an end to that long ago, but apparently all of the Negroes are not yet officers, so there is much to be done toward reorganizing our armies in the Communist pattern.

United World Federalists also includes Justice William Douglas, the leader of the "Recognize Red China" movement. On May 14, 1952, Douglas addressed the CIO Amalgamated Clothing Workers at Atlantic City. As reported in the Daily Worker and the Daily Compass, he said

> "Revolution is our business. We want United Nations recognition for China and American aid for Mao (leader of Communist China)."

He also said that all Europeans should be kicked out of China, and other such sentiments. Douglas was a classmate of Bob Hutchins at Yale.

Other members of United World Federalists are a sordid assortment from the University of Chicago and Columbia University, whose files in the FBI contain much of interest to any student of the Communist movement. Congressmen Adolph Sabath and Emanuel Celler are members, (apparently it doesn't interfere with their law practice), as well as Norman Cousins, editor of the Saturday Review of Literature, whom the State Department recently sent to India to see how Communists were coming along. That chore has now been taken over by Librarian of Congress Luther Evans, on a different Government expense account.

The United Nations realizes that the next generation of Americans may show their dislike for working to support the backward races of the world in a style to which they would like to become accustomed, and therefore it is making a determined effort to "internationalize" the outlook of American schoolchildren. The United Nations Educational, Scientific, and Cultural Organization, known as UNESCO, published nine volumes of text books, collectively known as "Towards World Understanding", printed by Columbia University, and available at a very low price, to teach the advantages of the World Socialist State to our younger schoolchildren. Book Five, "In the Classroom with Children Under 13 Years of Age", says on pages 58–60

> "As we have pointed out, it is frequently the family that infects the child with extreme nationalism. The school should therefore use the measures described earlier to combat family attitudes."

If the father starts to tell his son that Abraham Lincoln was a great American, the son can report his father's jingoism, and the teacher will explain what a backward and narrow man the father is. This is in accordance with the Communist plan to end the authority of the father and breakup the family into a group of atheists who recognize no authority but the State. To educate a generation of slaves, it is necessary to "combat family attitudes", as UNESCO points out. Our Librarian of Congress, Luther Evans, is an executive member of UNESCO, and may be presumed to be in full accord with these goals, since he has never opposed them.

Page 16 of Book Five suggests that the teacher make every effort to explain

> "the methods for putting the resources of the globe at the disposal of all people."

This can also be described as putting the American national income at the disposal of Asia and Africa, as UNRRA and UNESCO try to do.

Book Six of this series is entitled "The Influence of Home and Community on Children Under 13 Years of Age", which says that Children ought to be questioned by the teacher on the sexual habits of their parents. This would discredit the parents in the eyes of the child and bring about a more international and inter-racial attitude toward sex by the child. Sexual education has always been a feature of the Communist program. Senator William Benton owns Encyclopaedia Britannica Films, which distributes films on sexual education to our schools. Reporters Lait and Mortimer were unkind enough to make a slanted reference to Benton's own sexual preferences in "U.S. Confidential".

The United Nations World is edited by the fervent admirer of Stalin, former Collier correspondent Quentin Reynolds. United Nations News is published by the Woodrow Wilson Foundation, of which Herbert Lehman and Alger Hiss are directors. Their editorial bias is quite transparent.

The United Nations has tried many times to pass a "Genocide Act". A proposed law binding on all nations, the Genocide Act provides that "persons accused of direct and public incitement to commit genocide shall be tried before an international tribunal." If someone accuses you of criticizing some race or group, you are without the protection of your homeland, and are tried by a group of aliens. An American who mentioned that an arrested Communist spy was a Jew would not be tried by an American court, but by a court composed of the Communist revolutionaries of the United Nations. Our Constitution, which formerly guaranteed the Life and Liberty of Americans, became a worthless scrap of paper when the Senate ratified the United Nations Charter. It was legal, including the seduction of Senator Vandenberg.

The Genocide Act says that genocide is forbidden only committed against a national, ethical, racial, or religious group as such. This exempts that nation most famed for genocidal crimes, Soviet Russia, which has systematically destroyed whole tribes in South Russia, entire classes in all of Russia, including first of all the aristocracy, then the middle class farmers who owned their farms, and the middle-class merchants and traders. However, these groups were wiped out in the interests of the solidarity and welfare of all groups in Russia. The argument becomes hazy, but any well-trained Communist can explain it to you.

CHAPTER 21

The most tragic development in American history has been the steady infiltration of our government by a shabby lot of Communist agitators and Zionist racketeers. With Tom Pendergast's boy Harry Truman as President, the Hungarian refugee Anna Rosenberg as Assistant Secretary of Defense, and former legal representative of the Soviet Union Dean Acheson as Secretary of State, to say nothing of Zionist Felix Frankfurter as Justice of the Supreme Court, decent Americans might well look to other lands to build their homes and raise their children. The story of Truman's lifelong loyalty to the Kansas City racketeer Tom Pendergast has been told many times, but the story of Anna M. Rosenberg has not been told, except in the Senate Hearings on Anna M. Rosenberg, Government Printing Office, 1950.

A Hungarian Jewess named Lederer who married a rug seller named Rosenberg, Anna M. Rosenberg originated in Hungary, the nation which boasted of the terrorist Bela Kuhn and his Jewish Communist police state. She was welcomed in this country, where she became a highly paid labor relations specialist. She also became prominent in Communist circles, according to a number of witnesses at these Hearings. On Nov. 8, 1950, the day when election news crowded everything else off of the front pages of the newspapers, and while Congress was in recess, Truman appointed Rosenberg Assistant Secretary of Defense, to aid the Communist Party Liner, Secretary of Defense General George C. Marshall.

Nevertheless, a few patriots noticed the appointment, and they were horrified. Among them was Benjamin Freedman, who for years has warned the Jewish minority in America that if they continue actively to support the Communist Party here they must inevitably draw upon themselves the righteous anger of the American people. Freedman is a Jew who does not believe that an American Jew's first duty is to Russia or Israel. He is constantly denounced by such creature as Winchell. In the Anna Rosenberg case, Freedman again exposed himself to the hysterical invective of the Communist camp-followers by going to Washington and demanding of the Senate that they investigate the Rosenberg. After a month of stalling, in the last week of December, 1950, the Armed Services Subcommittee held Hearings on the case of Anna Rosenberg. One witness pointed her out face to face as a member of the top secret Communist Party policy organization, the John Club. Others came forward to identify her, but the Senators were so obviously prejudiced in Rosenberg's favor, and so determined to hear nothing against her, that these witnesses regretted that they had come in to testify. The Senators had not wanted to hold the Hearings, and they did not like the witnesses who appeared against Rosenberg.

The most powerful influence operating in favor of Anna Rosenberg's confirmation as Assistant Secretary of Defense was Senator Harry Byrd of Virginia, a member of the Subcommittee. He made speeches against the "smear" of the Rosenberg, and here is one instance of his browbeating witnesses to get them to testify favorably towards Rosenberg. Page 296 of the published Hearings is as follows:

> "BYRD: There is evidently two Anna M. Rosenberg. Assuming this Anna M. Rosenberg didn't sign these statements, there must be another Anna Rosenberg. Do you have a file on the other Anna Rosenberg or know anything about her?
>
> KIRKPATRICK: We have no information on the Anna Rosenberg without the middle initial M.
>
> BYRD: Isn't there another Anna M. Rosenberg?
>
> KIRKPATRICK: I have no idea whether there is more than one Anna M. Rosenberg."

Under discussion were a number of Communist and pro-Communist manifestoes which Anna M. Rosenberg had signed. Theodore Kirkpatrick of the FBI testified that Anna M. Rosenberg signed these statements, whereupon Byrd Launched an attack upon him to get him to say that the FBI had another Anna M. Rosenberg, and that Byrd and Baruch's Anna M. Rosenberg was not the Communist under discussion. Byrd's point would have been bolstered if he had produced this other Anna M. Rosenberg or given some idea of where she could be found and how he knew her so well, but he failed to do this, nor has he done so since the Hearings. Byrd often seeks "advice" from Bernard Baruch, and in 1951 Lewis Lichtenstein Strauss, partner of Kuhn, Loeb Co., appointed State Senator Harry F. Byrd Jr. a director of the wealthy Industrial Rayon Corporation.

The international news services claimed that Anna Rosenberg's appointment was being opposed because she was a Jew. Anti-Semitic and reactionary force of Fascism were attempting to keep the liberal Anna M. Rosenberg from this high Government office; that was the story fed to the American people. Actually, the witnesses were ordinary American citizens who performed their duty and there was no reference in the published Hearings to Rosenberg's race. The press failed to inform the American people that Anna M. Rosenberg was identified as a prominent Communist associate in New York. She was well-known as a writer on the Communist-front New Masses, yet she denied at these Hearings that she had ever been a writer or written anything, leaving herself open to a charge of perjury. It seems that a person has to be a perjurer or pervert to get into the Democratic Administration. Otto Frankfurter got in by way of Anamosa State Prison. At any rate, Anna Rosenberg was definitely proved before this Committee to be pro-Communist, and then the Senate confirmed her appointment as Assistant Secretary of Defense. The press protected this treachery by covering up on Rosenberg's Communist background.

Anna M. Rosenberg, one of the original New Dealers, who became acquainted with Franklin Roosevelt when he was Governor of New York, in 1944 went to France as his personal representative to study conditions there. Seventeen days later she shocked our generals by issuing a statement that our soldiers overseas were unfit to resume their lives at home until they had undergone "reorientation courses". From her background, we can imagine what these courses would have consisted of Her vicious comments on our fighting men aroused such indignation among the troops that she had to be ordered home at once. Yet this creature was given the power of life or death over every American boy who was unfortunate enough to be past the age of eighteen years. She wrote the Draft Law, known as Public Law 51, passed by Congress on June 19, 1951, and she has since devoted herself to getting the Universal Military Training Bill enacted law, so far unsuccessfully.

Truman's astounding victory in 1948 was no mystery to the Communists, who re-elected him because of the Fair Deal program. It is not generally known that the basis and name of the Fair Deal program of Truman was "fair-dealing" with Russia. "Fair-Dealing" became a key word in Communist propaganda in 1946. Fair-Dealing with Russia was the reason for Dean Acheson being appointed Secretary of State. His assistant in this program was George Kennan, now Ambassador to Russia. Starting with the idea of fair-dealing with Russia, that is, continuing lend-lease to the Communists after the war by any means, Truman built up an entire Socialistic program of compulsory socialized medicine, fair-employment practices, collectivist farming (known as the Brannan Plan), and other un-American measures. The Communists were reassured, and they went out and re-elected Fair Deal Truman.

Which is more dangerous, a Communist, or a hired agent for the Communists, who has to deliver the goods if he gets paid? Secretary of State Dean Acheson was the paid legal representative of the Communists when we recognized Russia in 1933 and has served them since then. He refuses to state how much money he has received from the Stalinist government. He was proposed for UnderSecretary of the Treasury by Senator Millard Tydings, son-in-law of that outspoken admirer of modern Russia, Mission to Moscow Joe Davies. Tydings was defeated in his campaign for re-election to the Senate in 1950 after he whitewashed Senator McCarthy's documented charges of Communists in the State Department. Acheson has long been a partner in the Washington law firm of Covington, Burlington, Rublee, and Shorb, which specializes in representing foreign governments. Acheson seems always to have been delegated the job of representing Soviet Russia. His law partner George Rublee has long been a prominent member of the Council On Foreign Relations. Alger Hiss' brother, Donald Hiss, is a member of Acheson's law firm, and D. Hiss handles the Soviet account while Acheson is temporarily in Government service.

One of Acheson's closest friends in Washington was Communist Lauchlin Currie, personal advisor to Roosevelt. Currie was identified under oath by Whittaker Chambers and Elizabeth Bentley as a Soviet agent. A graduate of the London School of Economics, as is Acheson's brother, Edward Campion Acheson, Lauchlin Currie was appointed by the International Bank as financial adviser to the Government of Colombia at a salary of $150,000 a year. When his name began to figure in Congressional Hearings as a Soviet agent, he fled the country and now permanently makes his home in Colombia. However, he will be back after the revolution.

Acheson takes sole credit for protecting Communists in the State Department. Under his supervision, the State Department Loyalty Board has never found a single Communist, although creatures of various shades of red have been allowed to resign without publicity.

Some of our most prominent Senators include Paul Douglas, one of the more eminent intellectual rag-pickers from the University of Chicago, where he often talked world economy in that hotbed of Communism with his fellow professor of economics, Oscar Lange, now Communist delegate from Poland to the United Nations.

On page 540 of "Tammany Hall", M.R. Werner, Doubleday Doran 1928, we find that Herbert Lehman and Jacob Schiff financed the campaign of Governor William Sulzer, the only governor ever impeached and kicked out of office in the state of New York. Robert S. Allen, "The Truman Merry-Go-Round" says that Senator Lehman took a whole floor of a downtown hotel for his staff of fifty-seven when he came to Washington. Few Senators could afford such a staff, but few Senators have as many interests, such as the Palestine Economic Corporation, as does Senator Lehman.

Perhaps the high point in the cultural development of the brave new democracy was reached in 1950, when a prominent Negro evangelist quarreled with Truman. Typically, the evangelist took his revenge by cavorting down Pennsylvania Avenue at eight o'clock on Sunday morning, with a troupe of his gaily dressed followers, all shouting at the top of their lungs a ballad called "We're On Our Way To Haven". Truman was in no shape for such a disturbance, and he shrieked for his earpads.

W. Averell Harriman and his forty million dollars was the subject of a pathetic publicity campaign in the *New Yorker Magazine* in an attempt to build him up as Presidential timber before the Democratic Convention in 1952. Harriman's role in saving Stalin and his equally important part in hushing up the story of the Katyn Massacre can be better understood if we look at his family's close affiliation with Kuhn, Loeb Co. His father, a runty Wall Street speculator, was picked up by Jacob Schiff and used as a front man to secure the Union Pacific Railroad for Kuhn, Loeb Co. The biography of National City Bank President "James Stillman", by A. R. Burr, Duffield 1927, noted that

> "Mr. Schiff had been greatly impressed with Harriman's brilliant powers, and the association thus begun was to continue for many

years, to involve many large transactions, and to carry the firm of Kuhn, Loeb forward as Harriman's backers and bankers. Coincidentally with Harriman's appearance as a force was that of the Standard Oil capitalists, who were thus brought into alliance with a new power. The reorganization of the Union Pacific proceeded in a manner remarkably efficient. Financed by the resources of the Standard Oil interests and through the firm of Kuhn, Loeb Co., it was carried out with a thoroughness which brought confidence."

In "E.H. Harriman", by George Kennan, page 368, we find that

"Among the men who cooperated with Mr. Harriman in his various railroad enterprises, none played a more important part than Jacob Schiff, senior partner in the banking house of Kuhn, Loeb Co."

Much additional and bulky evidence is at hand to prove that Standard Oil, and the Union Pacific, as well as the Communist Revolution of 1917, were creations of Jacob Schiff and missions for Kuhn, Loeb Co.

CHAPTER 22

In 1945, all Europe lay prostrate and in ruins from the ravages of war, nor had any country suffered more destruction than Soviet Russia. It seemed doubtful, in that year, whether Russia could rebuild her shattered economy, her bombed cities, and her dynamited dams.

In 1950, all Europe was panicked with fear of Russia. The Central European countries had one by one become Soviet satellites directed from Moscow. Half of Germany was a Communist satellite, thanks to Eisenhower and Roosevelt. The Western nations were frantically rearming against the threat of Soviet aggression. How had this come about?

The forum of Communist diplomats in New York, known as the United Nations, had fought a protective rearguard action against anti-Communist political forces while Russia was being rebuilt with American money and supplies. A succession of conspiracies to restore the Soviet Union by American aid were perpetrated by Communists in our Government. UNRRA, the Marshall Plan, the Economic Co-Operation Administration, the Point Four Program, all of these well-advertised idylls of world peace had as their objective the indirect shipment of supplies to Russia to rearm her.

It was possible to get these programs into operation because they were not criticized by the American press. In 1951, after sufficient time had elapsed, some sensational disclosures were made of shipments of Marshall Plan goods to Russia, notably power plants, machine tools, and other basic equipment for heavy industry. By that time, the damage had been done, and Russia was rearmed, if we can believe the press's sensational stories about Russian tanks and planes, all of which have their effect on the stock markets.

Professional Communists, Communist collaborators, and paid representatives of the Soviet Union engineered this aid to Russia, nor was anyone more active than Secretary of State Dean Acheson, who for years had received large fees from Russia as her legal counsel in Washington. Felix Wittmer, in The American Mercury, April, 1952, wrote that

> "In 1946 the Soviet satellite government of Poland applied to the United States for a loan of $90 million. Acheson was then Undersecretary of State. And what law firm did the Reds retain to get the loan? The Acheson firm, with Donald Hiss assigned directly ... On April 24, 1946, Acting Secretary of State Acheson announced that the loan, to be made through the Export-Import Bank, had been approved. The fee paid the Communists to the Acheson law firm was $51,653.98."

This loan was used to equip the UB, the Russian Security Police, who then inaugurated their reign of terror in Poland. Wittmer also points out that

> "in June, 1947, over Congressional opposition, Acheson insisted that the United States deliver $17 million worth of postwar lend-lease supplies to Russia."

This was the so-called "fair-dealing with Russia" program sponsored by the Communist Party of America. Like other such stories, Wittmer's revelations were greeted with howls from the State Department. The familiar scream of "smear" was sent up. Facts are either true or false. The Communist collaborators never dare to deny that these published facts in a reputable organ are false, so they claim that it is a "smear", which they can do without being sued.

On Nov. 14, 1945, writes Wittmer, Acheson appeared at Madison Square Garden to welcome the notorious Communist propagandist, the Red Dean of Canterbury, England, who later made the newspapers in 1952 with his insistence that the United States was using germ warfare in Korea, his sole evidence being Radio Moscow. Such are Acheson's friends. Others who spoke on that program were America's most outspoken Communist collaborators, Paul Robeson, now repudiated by most Negroes, Corliss Lamont, son of a J.P. Morgan partner, Joseph E. Davies, who was honored by Maxim Litvinoff naming his grandson after him, and Dr. William Howard Melish, a Christian minister who approves of Soviet atheism. At that New York meeting, Acheson said,

"We understand and agree with the Soviet leaders that to have friendly governments along her borders is essential both for the security of the Soviet Union and for the peace of the world."

Acheson thereby gave notice to the captive nations of Russia that they could expect nothing but Communist enslavement. Speaking as a Government official, he warned that America would not help them.

The attitude of the Democratic Administration boards continuation of Lend-Lease to Russia after the war is best expressed by Naval Intelligence Chief, Admiral Zacharias, in "Behind Closed Doors", page 309,

"The arbitrary abolition of Lend-Lease was a blunder whose magnitude could not be appreciated then. It led to most of the ills of the postwar world, to be rapid alienation of Soviet affections."

By refusing to send more billions of goods and money free to Russia, we incurred the enmity of the Soviet leaders. A man who was a leader in our intelligence service commits himself in print to such an opinion. America is always wrong, according to these creatures. W. Averell Harriman was reported in the Washington Daily News, May 30, 1952, as saying at his public breast-beating over the Great Communist's grave in Hyde Park (Harriman was running for President from the graveside, a ghoulish performance) that he saw men and woman crying in the streets of Moscow the day Roosevelt died. He said

"They wept without shame because they regard the late President as a symbol of the nation that saved them from Nazi oppression."

The inhabitants of Moscow were weeping because the gravy-train was ended now that Roosevelt was dead, his personal triumph, Lend-Lease, would be terminated, and they would have to go to work. No wonder they wept. They still had a friend in Harriman, however. As Mutual Security Administrator, he has billions to throw away. For instance, he has made a number of large loans to Israel from MSA funds, in case you taxpayers wonder why you are paying higher taxes.

The devotion of the State Department to its Communists is illustrated by the staffing of its policy-making Committees. The Advisory Committee on Postwar Foreign Policy since 1942 had as its principal members Harry D. White (Dorn Weiss), Morgenthau's aide, who died suddenly after being identified as a Communist, and the self-confessed Communist, Julian Wadleigh. Alger Hiss was an operating officer of the Committee. Indeed, he was present in an advisory capacity on every important Committee of the State Department. Yet Warburg's stooge, Elmer Davis, claimed in an article in Harper's Monthly that Hiss was never of any importance in the State Department.

In 1943, twelve special committees of the Committee on Postwar Economic Policy were formed. The Special Committee on Labor Standards and Social Security was composed of Isador Lubin, who had been Baruch's right hand man during World War I, Herbert Feldman, David Dubinsky, and A.A. Berle Jr. Berle was on six of these committees. Alger Hiss, Donald Hiss, and Julian Wadleigh were advisory members to all twelve of them. Berle is now the head of the Liberal-Democratic Party of New York, which is represented by Senator Lehman. The Special Committee on Private Monopolies and Cartels had as Chairman Dean Acheson; its members were the mysterious Mordecai Ezekiel, Louis Deomartzky, Sigmund Timberg, Walter S. Louchheim Jr. from the Security Exchange Committee, and Moses Abramovitz from the Office of Strategic Services.

The State Department Special Committee on Migration and Settlement had as Chairman Arthur Schoenfeld, and members A. A. Berle Jr., John D. Rockefeller 3d, Herbert Lehman, and Laurence Duggan.

The devotion of the upper echelon of the Democratic Administration to the cause of world Communism was demonstrated in 1946, when a symposium of Communist propaganda, "The Great Conspiracy Against Russia", by Seghers and Kahn, was printed by the Steinberg Press, N.Y. Senator Claude Pepper wrote a glowing introduction to this Communist manifesto, Joseph E. Davies and Professor Frederick Schuman wrote paragraphs of praise which were printed on the covers. Many leading Democrats joined in peddling this openly Communist propaganda over the country. For instance, Woodrow Wilson was mentioned very favorably, and his messages of comfort to the Bolshevik regime were reprinted in this book, which leaned heavily on International Publishers, N.Y., and Moscow publications for its documentation. The Russian aristocracy, which was driven out or murdered, and their property seized by fanatical revolutionaries, was described as follows:

> "Whenever the White emigres went, they fertilized the soil for the World Counter-Revolution, Fascism. With the debacle of the White Armies of Kolchak, Yudentich, Wrangel, and Semyonov, the ruthless adventurers, the decadent aristocrats, the professional terrorists, the bandit soldiery, the dreaded secret police, and all the

other feudal and anti-democratic forces that had constituted the White Counter-Revolution now spilled out of Russia like a muddy, turbulent stream. Westward, eastward, and southward it flowed, bringing with it the sadism of the White Guard generals, the pogromist doctrines of the Black Hundreds, the fierce contempt of Czarism for democracy, the dark hatreds, prejudices, and neuroses of old Imperial Russia. The Protocols of Zion, the anti-Semitic forgeries by which the Ochrana had incited massacres of the Jews and the bible by which the Black Hundred explained all the ills of the world in terms of an international Jewish plot, were now circulated publicly in London, Paris, New York, Buenos Aires, Shanghai, and Madrid."

As usual, the Communists denounce the Protocols of Zion as a forgery, without going into any detail, for that might bear out Henry Ford's observation that "The Protocols of Zion explain twentieth-century history."

The Seghers-Kahn book, a fantastic compilation of perverted fact and impossible fiction, claims that Trotsky was murdered in a quarrel over a girlfriend in Mexico, that Hitler, Trotsky, and Trotsky's son Leon Sedov, engaged in a dark plot to overthrow Stalin, which forced Stalin to dispense justice in the Moscow Purge Trials, and that the House Un-American Activities Committee is a band of fascists. As usual, anti-Communists are dismissed as anti-Semites. It concludes in typical Daily Worker fashion:

> "The first great realization which came out of the Second World War was that the Red Army under Marshall Stalin was the most competent and powerful fighting force on the side of world progress and democracy. The alliance of the Western democracies with Soviet Russia opened up the realistic promise of a new international order of peace and security among all people. Yet, after the creation of the United Nations, based on the concept of the complete elimination of fascism, a new upsurge of anti-Soviet propaganda threatened the very foundations of the peace."

This is the best definition of the United Nations, an organization dedicated to the elimination of fascism. Since Seghers and Kahn earlier define fascism as the White Counter-Revolution, the United Nations' sole purpose is to wipe out opposition to the World Communist State. The White Counter-Revolution is the last-ditch stand of the white race to defend itself from the anti-gentile Marxists. Engels in "The Origin of the Family" explained that the Communists intended to destroy the gentile family.

This book was must reading for Government workers, and it received fantastically wave reviews in the nation's press. Senator Pepper was subsequently defeated for re-election to the Senate. There weren't enough Communists in Florida.

One of the most favorable propagandists for the Chinese Communists, Edgar Snow, suffered a change of heart after the Korean War began. I the Saturday Evening Post, March 7, 1952, he discusses the probably successor to Stalin, and decides it will be Malenkov, because Malenkov is the protégé of Jew Lazar Kaganovich, Commissar of Heavy Industry. Snow explains the Soviet as follows:

> "If you look upon the U.S.S.R. as a monopoly in which the state owns every branch of production and controls every market, the Politburo corresponds to the board of directors of a gigantic holding company. It holds the proxies of six million party members who may be considered the stock owners of the subsidiary organizations. They are, in turn, the managerial and steward class."

The foreign policy of the United States towards Russia for the past five years, and seemingly, for the next generation, was set by George Kennan, a prominent member of the Council On Foreign Relations, and Chief Long-range Policy Advisor to Secretary of State Dean Acheson, as well as Chief of the Long-range Policy Planning Committee of the State Department. In the July, 1947 issue of "Foreign Affairs", Kennan anonymously published "Plan X", which has been our policy ever since. Considerable protest was made by Washington correspondents that our official policy should reach the public through such a roundabout manner. Its author was the nephew and namesake of the world-famed Communist agent, George Kennan.

"Plan X" is the infamous "bipartisan" foreign policy sponsored by the Council On Foreign Relations. It is the policy of spend and give away our national wealth all over the world until we are bankrupt and demoralized, an easy prey for Russia. Not surprisingly, it fits in with official Soviet policy, Zacharias, in "Behind Closed Doors", writes on page 10,

> "According to the authoritative Soviet 'Estimate of the Situation',

1), the U.S. will experience a depression of major proportions between 1954 and 1956; 2) the U.S. will then go to war to stave off the cataclysmic effects of depression on her national economy and morale. Stalin expects to wag a final cumulative massive counteroffensive against a militarily, morally, and economically exhausted foe."

Kennan's program is exhausting us per the Soviet Estimate. It has already cost us more than one hundred billion dollars, and we have lost nearly two hundred thousand American boys as casualties in Korea, where Russia has not lost a man. Yet this was only a small part of what the collaborators intended for us. They had planned to involve us in a full-scale war with Communist China, which would bleed us down while Russia armed to attack us. This plan failed, but the policy of "containment" is going on as usual. It may be described as the Kennan Plan to bankrupt us and wane our strength in a series of small wars while Russia waits for the final round. Kennan successfully argued that we must maintain armies and send money and supplies to every nation towards which Russia MIGHT move. The nephew of Communist agent George Kennan wrote in the July, 1947 issue of Foreign Affairs,

> "It will be clearly seen that the Soviet pressure against the institutions of the Western world is something that can be contained by the adroit and vigorous application of counter-force at a series of constantly-shifting geographical and political points, corresponding to the shifts and maneuvers of Soviet policy".

Kennan's plan make obvious what had long been the case, that is, our State Department has become a branch of the Soviet Foreign Ministry. We rush our troops here and there, wherever Russia acts as though she might make a move, and we give large loans to countries which fear Soviet aggression. Our State Department officials blindly follow wherever the Politburo leads us. A more shameful, treacherous, and ridiculous policy would be difficult to devise.

Kennan's plan is particularly sympathetic to Stalin's cherished plan of building up Russia internally while revolutionists constantly promote outbreaks in other countries, at small expense to the Soviet Union. No wonder Kennan was received so well in Russia in 1952 as U.S. Ambassador.

It is interesting that Kennan's article setting forth "Plan X", in the July, 1947 issue of "Foreign Affairs" is followed by "Anglo-American Rivalry and Partnership-A Marxist View", by Eugene Varga, Russia's leading economist who is Director of the Institute of World Economics and Politics in Moscow. When he left the State Department to write a book defending his pro-Soviet policies, Kennan went to a similar Institution in America, the Institute for Advanced Studies at Princeton, where high-ranking intellectuals of the international elite, such as Emanuel Goldenweiser of the Federal Reserve Board, are put out to pasture.

Another sidelight on Kennan's article is provided by the fact that the entire back over of the July, 1947 issue of "Foreign Affairs" is a paid advertisement of Lazard Freres banking house of New York, London, and Paris. Known as Eugene Meyer's family banking house, Lazard Freres is one of the chief financial supporters of the Council On Foreign Relations and its affiliates. It has been pro-Nazi, pro-Communist, and probably pro-anything which has any chance of success. Politicians talk in generalities, but they deal in particularism, and so do the international bankers. That is why a banking house will contribute money to a movement with which it is in disagreement

The present Communist Party line is "co-existence". It is not surprising that George Kennan is a supporter of the co-existence theory, or that James Paul Warburg's latest book is entitled "How to Co-Exist", Beacon Press 1952. The idea of co-existence originated in Joseph Stalin's speech to the Soviet Congress on May, 17, 1948, and was published as a pamphlet, "For Peaceful Co-Existence", by Joseph Stalin, International Publishers, New York, 1952.

George Kennan, the State Department spokesman for the recognition of Red China, co-existence, fair-dealing with Russia, and containment, is probably the ideological leader of the Communist collaborators in America. In his book, "American Diplomacy 1900–1950", a whitewash of Roosevelt's aid to Stalin, which Kennan wrote in the luxurious surroundings at the Institute for Advanced Studies, he said,

> "The most vociferous charges of wartime mistakes relate to the conferences of Moscow, Tehran, and Yalta. Their importance has been considerably overrated. If it cannot be said that the Western democracies gained very much, it would also be incorrect to say that they gave very much away. The establishment of Soviet power in Europe and the entry of Soviet forces into Munich was not the result of those talks; it was the result of the military operations during the concluding phases of the war."

Thus Kennan blandly ignores the fact that Roosevelt gave Poland to Stalin at the Yalta Conference, with Alger Hiss at his side. It is Kennan's propaganda that everything Russia has she got by military operations, that she won by the strength of her armies. He does not mention that the Lend-Lease supplies from American gave her the power to overrun what nations she did subject. At any rate, Roosevelt was worth more to the Politburo than all the Russian armies. Kennan's book is typical of the well-dressed pulp which is thrust on our university students as a genuine critique of foreign policy.

President Truman, however, has not had to depend entirely upon George Kennan for his foreign policy. Truman's pet project is his Point Four program for developing backward areas of the world. The Point Four program follows exactly, step by step, the program laid down by Earl Browder, the Communist leader, in his book, "Teheran, Our Path in War and Peace", International Publishers, New York, 1945.

On page 256 of Zacharias' book "Behind Closed Doors", we find that

> "George Kennan prepared a political report published under the romantic pseudonym 'X' in July, 1947 issue of 'Foreign Affairs', amid unmistakable fanfare prearranged by a group of 'diplomatic activists' in the National War College, our top-ranking geopolitical institute, and in the State Department. There were supported by kindred spirits, such as the Alsop brothers the members of the Council On Foreign Relations, and the editors of Time and Life."

It may be understood why Baruch always chose to lecture before the National War College, which is not often revealed as our geopolitical institute. The fanfare raised for the Kennan Plan by the Council On Foreign Relations was considerable, since the Council includes among its members the publishers and editors of the New York Times, the Washington Post, Newsweek, Time, and Life.

Zacharias' book "Behind Closed Doors" gives other glimpses of Soviet activity in the United States. On page 85, he says,

> "It must be understood that Lomakin was ordinary consul. Certain information led us to believe that Lomakin was the head of the Russian political intelligence service in the entire Western hemisphere. He kept aloof from American Communists and their fellow-travelers. He preferred the company of Wall Street financiers, industrialists from Pittsburgh, Detroit, and Cleveland,

and other representatives of our big business who flocked to his cocktail parties in the New York consulate."

On page 216, Zacharias tells us that

"In his camouflaged post as envoy of Hungary in Washington, Sik was continuing the work he had begun for the Comintern, the study of Negro condition in the United States. His career typifies the planned infiltration of the Kremlin into the diplomatic apparatus of its satellites."

Yet Eleanor Roosevelt blandly insists that there are no Russian spies at the United Nations. Even more alarming is the aid given these foreign agitators by men in our own government. In this Negro agitation, for instance, Senator Herbert Lehman has been one of the lisping agitators for "home rule" in the District of Columbia, suffrage for the citizens who live there. The predominant Negro population could elect a Negro mayor for our National Capital city. The founders of the American Republic intended that our capital should be forever free from the cheap intrigues of party politics, and set up a Congressional Committee to govern it. Lehman, ably abetted by George Schuster of Hunter College, New York, has tried to change this to give Washington a city government as corrupt as other cities which have a large population of Negro criminals. The race issue always attracts a weird lot of self-promoters, for instance, the head of the National Association for the Advancement of Colored People, Walter White. Walter White, who claims to be a Negro, is married to a white woman. What he has done for Walter White is much more easily ascertained than what he has done for the American Negro. The lot of our Negroes has improved along with the steady and nationwide raising of our standard of living during the twentieth century. The Lehmans and Whites cannot claim the credit for it.

CHAPTER 23

Franklin Roosevelt did not live to see a worse crime than his sellout of the free nation of Poland at Yalta, but this, the last of his infamies, was soon surpassed by the sabotage of the Chinese Nationalist Government by the group of determined Communists which ran the Institute of Pacific Relations, and by their collaborators in the State Department. The result was that we lost our only strong ally in Asia, and Communism became the predominant political ideology of another continent.

At the Yalta Conference, Roosevelt opened the way for the Communists to seize China, by ceding to Russia the Dairen and Port Arthur Railways, as well as the Chinese Eastern and the Southern Manchuria Railways. Roosevelt also gave Russia the Chinese State of Manchuria, known as the Texas of China, its wealthiest province, which Russia had tried to win in the Russo-Japanese War of 1905. Now, as the result of a conspiracy, she won it without a struggle.

The Communist collaborators had their own way in the Pacific during the Second World War. General Stilwell seemed to be fighting Chiang Kai-Shek much harder than he was fighting the Japanese. This may have been due to the Communists and pro-Communists who made up his staff. As Commander of the China-Burma-India Theater, Stillwell was advised by Agnes Smedley, a Lifelong Communist whose ashes are now buried in Peiping; Dean Acheson's younger brother, Edward Campion Acheson, a graduate of the London School of Economics in 1936. Who's Who In American lists his as an economic adviser to the Lend-Lease Administration in 1943, financial adviser to Stilwell in 1944, and with the Office of Strategic Services in 1945. He is now a professor of finance at George Washington University; fellow-traveler John Paton Davies; the pro-Communist Marine, Evans Carlson, who was glorified in a Hollywood movie, "Carlson's Raiders", and Clare Boothe Luce, wife of Henry Luce. Even the unusually intimate friendship of Madame Chiang Kai-Shek and President Roosevelt could not repair the damage done to Chiang by this Stilwell crew.

Owen Lattimore was with the Office of War Information in the Pacific area during the war, and he got William L. Holland, editor of the Institute of Pacific Relations journal "Pacific Affairs", a job with the OWI in Chungking.

General Stilwell has recorded his hatred for Chiang in his diary, published as "The Stilwell Papers", which were hailed with delight by the Daily Worker. Stilwell diverted huge stores of American munitions to the Red Army of General Mao, and these, combined with the captured Japanese arms turned over to Mao by the Russians, enabled the Communists to take the field against Chiang's Nationalist Army. Simultaneously, Communist collaborators in the State Department, led by General George C. Marshall, shut off all aid to Chiang from the United States. This amazing story of treason in Washington is documented fully by the Senate Hearings on the Institute of Pacific Relations, by Freda Utley's book, "The China Story", and by Senator McCarthy's expose of General Marshall, "Retreat from Victory".

The Communists began their big propaganda drive against Chiang in 1946, with a three-day rally starting on October 18, 1946 in San Francisco, called the "Get Out of China, America" rally. The notorious Communist sympathizer from Stilwell's staff, General Evans Carlson, presided. Paul Robeson was Vice-Chairman, Gunther Stein, head of a spy ring in Japan, managed to get there, Joe Curran, the longshoremen's union leader, Bartley Crum, the aptly-named Wall Street lawyer who tried to revive PM as the New York Star, with the assistance of fellow-traveling Joseph Barnes, Frederick V. Field, now jailed as a Communist, Congressman Vito Marcantonio, since defeated Edward G. Robinson, Paulette Goddard, and Julius Garfinckel, known to the bobby-soxers as John Garfield, an actor who died mysteriously in some female acquaintance's apartment in New York.

In 1947 the Institute of Pacific Relations held its famous Far East Conference at which the plans were laid to finish off Chiang. The delegate from the United States for this important mission was the Communist propagandist James Paul Warburg.

Senator McCarthy, on page 171 of "Retreat from Victory", says that Michael Lee and William Remington of the Department of Commerce sabotaged the $125 million aid-to-China bill in 1948. Remington has since been discharged, amid much shrieking from the yellow liberal press. Lee, Chief of the Far Eastern Division of the Department of Commerce, has not been Lee very long. Arriving in the United States in 1932 as Ephraim Zinoye Liberman, his background was so shady that it took him nine years to get American citizenship.

The ground which Chiang Kai-Shrek had lost during the Second World War was rapidly being regained when his deadliest enemy in Washington, Communist party liner General George C. Marshall, cut off aid from America. Freda Utley, in "The China Story", tells the tragic story of General Marshall's mission to China in 1946 to tell Chiang that America was on the side of the Chinese Communists. Missionaries who sat in on conferences with Marshall returned to tell us that "Marshall sold Chiang down the river to the Communists". The Marshall Mission was the turning-point of the Chinese Civil War. After Marshall was lavishly entertained by Communist Chou En Lai, now Foreign Minister of the Mao regime, and when Marshall ordered Chiang to form a coalition government with the Communists, the Chinese people understood that Chiang had been betrayed by the United States, and they turned to Mao as their new leader. The State Department Coordinating Committee, composed of Dean Acheson, John Carter Vincent, and Alger Hiss, jubilant over the successful outcome of the Marshall Mission, recommended United States training for Communist troops and huge additional supplies for the Red Army, but this was too obvious, and after several Congressmen showed curiosity about the origins of this project, it was dropped.

Freda Utley and Senator McCarthy identify the Currie-Hiss-Lattimore team as the most potent behind-the-scenes influence working for the Chinese Communists in Washington, with General Marshall as the front man for these traitors. Hiss is in prison, Currie is hiding out in Colombia, Lattimore is very likely to go to prison for perjury before the McCarran Committee, and General Marshall has retired in disgrace. Such were the personal associates of Franklin Roosevelt.

On page 86 of "The China Story", Freda Utley says that the members of the State Department in Chungking in 1945 were unanimously for arming the Chinese Communists. They were John Paton Davies, John Stewart Service, and George Atcheson. She adds that

> "Atcheson later changed his views, and became political adviser to MacArthur in Tokyo, but he was killed in an airplane accident before his views could influence United States policy."

He shouldn't have changed his views.

Dean Acheson was trying to keep up with the Hisses and Curies by putting in his oar for the Chinese Communists. On June 19, 1946, he was asked by Congresswoman Edith Nourse Rogers if he saw any danger of a future attack on us by the Chinese Communist troops whom he so ardently desired to train and equip. Acheson was simply horrified by the idea. "Oh no", he trilled, "we can rest assured the Chinese will not do that."

On March 20, 1947, Acheson declared that there was not the slightest danger of a Communist victory over Chiang Kai-Shek. This testimony before the House Committee on Foreign Relations absolutely contradicted other testimony on the Chinese situation. After the debacle, writes Zacharias, in "Behind Closed Doors", page 288,

> "It was no secret in Washington that Mr. Acheson, urged by the British, was most eager to recognize the Mao regime, and that the White Paper was published to pave the way for recognition."

The White Paper on China issued by the State Department on August 5, 194 was such a startling tissue of lies that even the New York Times was constrained to admit that it was hardly impartial, and that it did not serve the truth. The chief fabricator of this tapestry of falsehoods was Philip C. Jessup, Chairman of the American Council of the Institute of Pacific Relations. Jessup had such a long list of pro-Communist affiliations that not a single Senator voted for him when he was nominated by Truman as our delegate to the United Nations. Truman sent him on to back up Eleanor Roosevelt as an alternate delegate from the United States to that focal point of Communist infection in America, the General Assembly of the United Nations.

A belated expose of the Communist spy ring in Washington came with the publication of "Shanghai Conspiracy", by General Charles Willoughby, Dutton 1952. Willoughby, General MacArthur's Chief of Intelligence in Tokyo during the period of MacArthur leadership, wrote of the Sorge spy ring, which operated in Tokyo throughout the Second World War. Its mastermind was the German Jew, Gunter Stein, who sent top-secret material to Moscow until 1944, when the Japanese police arrested his assistant, Sorge, and hanged him. Stein was taken from Japan by an American submarine and hurried across the Pacific to attend an important Institute of Pacific Relations Conference at Hot Springs, Virginia, in January of 1945. A desperate affair which decided the fate of Asia, this conference was a gathering of the principal Communist experts on Asia, and it was closed to the press. Edward C. Carter, Secretary-General of the IPR, presided. He holds the Order of the Red Banner of labor from Stalin.

General Willoughby tells us the story of Agnes Smedley. The Sorge Report was ready for release by the Army on December 15, 1947. It was held up by the War Department in Washington until February 20, 1949. No sooner did the War Department release it than its officials began to deny the entire report because it identified as a Communist spy one Agnes Smedley. Secretary of the Army Royall made a public statement dismissing the entire report as the error of a minor clerk, although it was based on years of work by the Japanese police and our own Counter-Intelligence-Corps. Agnes Smedley threatened to use General MacArthur, but she never got around to it. She even engaged the Communists' favorite lawyer, O. John Rogge, to handle it, but she never filled the suit. The yellow liberal press sprang yowling to the defense of Red Agnes Smedley. Harold Ickes wrote in his column in the New Republic that "Miss Smedley is a courageous and intelligent American citizen". She spent her whole adult life working for the Communists. In 1943 she was given a vacation at Yaddo in 1943. Yaddo, a fabulous resort set up by the Wall Street banker George Foster Peabody, a steward of Rothschild properties in Mexico, is at Saratoga Springs, New York. It is a luxurious free rest home for the upper echelon of Communist writers and artists in America, where they can relax from the tensions of international espionage.

Agnes Smedley, the intimate of Ickes, Wallace, Lattimore, etc., escaped from the United States in 1950 just before she was to be summoned to testify before a Congressional Committee. She went to London, and died suddenly in a "nursing home" there. She willed her ashes and all her possessions to General Chu Teh, leader of the Chinese Communist Army. Her ashes were buried at Peking in May, 1951, accompanied by worldwide ovations from the Communist press.

At the McCarran Committee Hearings, it was brought out on page 1217, 1236, and 1238, that the Rockefeller Foundation and Carnegie Fund had given the Institute of Pacific Relations more than two million dollars. John D. Rockefeller 3d, Alger Hiss, Frederick V. Field, Owen Lattimore, Edward C. Carter, and other such well known Americans were the guiding members of the Institute. After these damning Hearings were published, Baruch's boy Gerard Swope, Chairman of

International General Electric, wrote a letter to the trustees of the Institute condemning the Hearings as biased and unfair. Swope, the Chairman of the trustees of the Institute, expressed his satisfaction that the big Wall Street corporations were contributing just as much money to the Institute, despite its exposure as a Communist front.

The Communists always had plenty of favorable publicity in the United States. The newspapers, magazines and books vied in denouncing Chiang and praising agrarian leader Mao Tse Tung. Chiang was portrayed as a combination of Himmler and Hitler, while Mao, who is now engaged in murdering four million of his former opponents in China, was described as a harmless agrarian who sought a peaceful solution to the land problem in China.

Senator Brewster, in the June 4, 1951 Congressional Record, printed a table of dozens of books which showed how the New York Times Sunday Book Review and the New York Herald Tribune Book Review, the only two weekly newspaper reviews in America of any consequence, were controlled by Communists. This table, covering the period 1945–1950, shows that books on the politics of Asia were always given to notorious Communists or their spokesmen for review. Pro-Communist books received rave reviews, while books which did not toe the Party line were viciously attacked. Either of these Book Review Sections could qualify as the Daily Worker Literary Supplement. One of dozens of such instances was the reception accorded Israel Epstein's "The Unfinished Revolution in China", Little, Brown Co., 1947. Epstein's book was given a glowing review by Owen Lattimore in the New York Times Book Review of June 22, 1947. Elizabeth Bentley testified under oath that Israel Epstein has been a high official in the Russian secret police for many years. He is now the Daily Worker correspondent from the Red China.

Little, Brown Co. published Lattimore's book "Ordeal by Slander" in record time after Senator McCarthy exposed Lattimore as a Soviet agent. This publishing house seemed to be bidding for the position of official Communist publishers in America, a title now held by International Publishers, New York. Little Brown's chief editor, Angus Cameron, recently resigned in the face of publication of his Communist background.

Epstein's book was greeted by Samuel Siller in the Daily Worker with the recommendation that it be

> "placed at the top of the list of excellent books about China by topflight reporters like Agnes Smedley, Theodore White, and Annalee Jacoby."

Owen Lattimore was publicly accused by Alfred Kohlberg of being the top Soviet agent in America, in the hope that Lattimore would sue Kohlberg, but Lattimore has run from the accusation.

Another instance is offered by Brewster's listing of Gunter Stein's book, "The Challenge of Red China", which Stein wrote immediately after landing in this country, after we rescued him from the Japanese police in the winter of 1944. Stein's book was given a highly complimentary review in the New York Times Book Review of October 28, 1945, by Nathaniel Peffer, and two weeks earlier it had received the same understanding treatment from Owen Lattimore in the New York Herald Tribune of October 14, 1945. Gunter Stein had been the Christian Science Monitor correspondent in China. This paper has become less Christian and more scientific in its brazenly internationalist (per Lenin) editorial bias. Lattimore wrote of fellow-Soviet agent Stein in "Pacific Affairs" in 1939,

> "Gunter Stein is by long odds the best economic journalist in the Far East."

This economic journalist fled from the United States as soon as the Sorge Report was published by the Army in 1949. In 1950 he was arrested by the French police as a Communist spy, and he has since disappeared.

Whittaker Chambers, in his autobiographical "Witness", shows how difficult it was to get ahead in journalism unless you were a Communist. On page 498, he tells us that Time Magazine's staff of foreign correspondents, John Hersey, Charles C; Wertenbaker, Scott Nearing, Richard Lauterbach, and Theodore White, signed a round robin denouncing him for his editorial views as soon as he quit the Communist Party. This round robin declared that Chambers was unfit for his editorial position on Time Magazine and ought to be fired.

Scott Nearing is notorious for his Communist views; the others are more intellectual in their collectivism. Wertenbaker continues his good work for the cause in "The Reporter", a magazine which will never quit fighting Chiang until he is dead. This magazine cannot afford to be openly Communist today, but it is internationalist in the Lenin sense. It published a story by Wertenbaker, "The China Lobby", running in the issues of April 15th and 29th, 1952, attacking everybody who had ever criticized the Communists in China. On January 3, 1950, "The Reporter" devoted 24 pages to the urging of American recognition of Red China. The lead was written by editor Max Ascoli, who said,

> "In the case of Red China, the new rulers won their civil war because they have passionate popular support and because of the ineptitude of the previous rulers, whom unfortunately we have helped."

This new addition to the yellow liberal press has long way to go before it can match the leaders in the field, The Nation, and The New Republic. The Nation was financed to cover its losses for many years by Maurice Wertheim, senior partner of the Wall Street bankers Hallgarten Co., which originated in Frankfurt, Germany. Wertheim also was a director of the Theatre Guild, whose productions seem to be written almost exclusively by Marxists. The New Republic is edited by Michael Straight, son of J.P. Morgan partner Willard Straight. The Straight fortune pays for this Leninist rag. All of these sheets follow a consistent program of almost insane vituperation against Senators McCarran and McCarthy. McCarran is a Democrat, McCarthy is a Republican, but both of them are anti-Communist, and both of them are of the Catholic faith. Arthur Goldsmith, head of the B'Nai Brith Anti-Defamation League, sent large sums of money from New York to Nevada in a vain attempt to defeat McCarran in his last election.

The attack on the so-called "China Lobby" by The Reporter had its origins in a letter from May Miller which was printed in the Congressional Record.

May Miller is assistant organizing secretary of the Communist Party of New York. The letter, dated March 1, 1949, laid down the Communist party line of a consistent demand for an investigation of the China Lobby in Washington.

Wertenbaker's story on the China Lobby, printed in The Reporter, followed this Communist directive.

CHAPTER 24

L ies are many, but the truth is one. The very singleness of the truth sometimes causes it to be borne down by the weight of numbers sent out by the masters of the Big Lie technique, and this has caused our involvement in the Korean War. We are fighting those Chinese Communist whom Dean Acheson so fervently desired to arm and train, and it has come about through the cooperation of dozens of men, anyone of whom has surpassed Benedict Arnold a hundred times. They have betrayed millions of men and cost America hundreds of thousands of lives and billions of dollars in new debt.

In the *Saturday Evening Post* of November 10, 1951, Beverly Smith, its Washington editor, published an official propaganda version of how we got in the Korean conflict. Smith has the same educational background as Alger Hiss, an A. B. degree from Johns Hopkins, and a law degree from Harvard law school. Smith has the further advantage of being a Rhodes Scholar. He entered the Wall Street law firm of Chadbourne, Hunt, Jaeckel, and Brown, representing international bankers. Smith then discovered that as a lawyer he was a fine writer. He became a foreign correspondent for the New York Herald Tribune, a paper long noted for the number of Communist fellow travelers on its staff.

Smith says that our Ambassador to Korea during the outbreak of hostilities was John Muccio, born in Italy and naturalized in America after he was past his maturity. Smith says that Muccio wired the State Department of the Korean crisis on June 24, 1950, and our officials assembled to discuss the American position. They were Dean Rusk, Assistant Secretary for Far Eastern Affairs, John Dewey Hickerson, Assistant Secretary for United Nations Affairs, and Philip C. Jessup, our Ambassador-at-large.

Rhodes Scholar Dean Rusk previously had been in charge of United Nations Affairs. Hickerson had been a member of the infamous San Francisco Conference in 1945, and was on the advisory committee on international law at Harvard law School. Jessup, who had accompanied Kuhn, Loeb lawyer Elihu Root to the Hague Court in 1929, had been Lehman's Assistant Secretary-General in UNRRA, had represented the United States at the Bretton Woods Monetary Conference, and had been Alger Hiss' legal assistant at the San Francisco United Nations Conference in 1945. Jessup had been Chairman of the American Council and Chairman of the Pacific Council of the Communist-front Institute of Pacific Relations. The International Secretariat of the Institute published a book in the spring of 1950 "Korea Today", by George McCune, which says on page 180,

> "The Soviet civil administration kept well in the background and gave the Koreans maximum experience in self-government. Most observers agreed that the Soviet system quite readily adapted itself to the Korean scene, or at least that it was much more easily adopted by the Koreans than was the Western system sponsored by the American command."

This was typical of the Communist propaganda put out by the Institute, for which Jessup was the front man. A member of the millionaire Stotesbury family (Stotesbury was a J.P. Morgan partner), Jessup is brother of the millionaire Wilmington banker John Jessup, a director of many corporations such as Coca-Cola of Atlanta.

This was the group which gathered to stem the Korean crisis. America's interests were indeed in good hands. They needed only to call Alger Hiss from prison to make the fraternity meeting complete.

Smith says that this group conferred with Secretary Acheson by telephone. Acheson had qualified as Secretary of State not only as a paid legal representative of the Communists in America, but also of his submission to Zionist leaders, dating from his experience as law clerk to Justice Brandeis in the early 1920s when Brandeis was the recognized leader of Zionism in America.

The following day, says the Smith account, a telegram came from John Foster Dulles, who had returned to Tokyo from Korea a few days earlier. The telegram said,

> "If it appears that the South Koreans cannot repulse the attack, then we believe that United States force should be used."

This telegram is ample grounds for Dulles' prosecution as a war criminal, according to the Nuremberg law. Dulles had made several mysterious missions Korea just before the outbreak of hostilities, living up to Sullivan and Crowell's reputation of promoting revolutions and wars.

Smith says,

> "The President landed at Washington Sunday at 7:15." He was met by Louis Johnson, then Secretary of Defense, and Undersecretary of State James Webb."

Louis Johnson, a corporation lawyer, was President of General Dyestuff Corporation, a subsidiary of General Aniline and Film, the American branch of I. G. Farben, which Dulles' firm of Sullivan and Cromwell represented. Webb, prior to arriving at the State Department, had been personal assistant to Thomas A. Morgan of the international banking house of Lehman Brothers, President of Sperry Gyroscope, and director of Vickers.

When Truman met with his advisers at the White House for dinner that evening, among them was Secretary of the Air Force Thomas K; Finletter, formerly partner in Kuhn, Loeb lawyers Cravath and Henderson. Finletter, a member of the treacherous San Francisco Conference in 1945, was a trustee of the Communist nest called the New School of Social Research in New York, at which Anna M. Rosenberg had been a teacher. Smith tells us that at dinner at eight o'clock that fateful Sunday evening "conversation was general, and no notes were taken." The historian is often confounded by the fact that at conferences which shape the future of the world, the delegates talk about nothing in particular, speak in vague generalities, and take no notes. Actually, of course, precise courses of action are laid down, but for the sake of their own necks, these conspirators dare not let anyone find out what they have done even for generations after the event.

Of President Truman's decision to raise the curtain on the slaughter of American boys in Korea at this delightfully vague evening, Smith writes that

> "Practically every major newspaper in the country approved, with the exception of the *Chicago Tribune* and its affiliate, the *Washington Times-Herald*."

This is a terrible indictment of the American press, that only one publisher on this continent had the courage to oppose the senseless slaughter of our younger generation.

Congressional leaders with Truman at this crisis were Senator Scott Lucas who was later defeated for re-election from Illinois because of the scandalous tie up between Chicago gangsters and his organization, and Senator Millard Tydings, later defeated for re-election from Maryland because he whitewashed the investigation of Communists in the State Department which had been instigated by Senator McCarthy. Truman himself was the creature of Communist Sidney Hillman and his lieutenant Max Lowenthal, who got him the Vice-Presidential nomination at Chicago in 1944. As Chairman of the Senate Committee investigating war contracts during the Second World War, Truman had learned enough about the Rockefellers and Rothschilds to go on up to the top. His right-hand man has been George E. Allen, director of General Aniline and Film, and Hugo Stinnes Industries, as well as a dozen other giant corporations. Truman appointed Allen Chairman of the Reconstruction Finance Corporation.

Smith says that on the following Thursday, Truman again met with his advisers, including John Foster Dulles, just back from Korea, W. Averell Harriman, hastily summoned from Paris, Stuart Symington, and James Lay, head of the National Security Council. Harriman was then traveling about the world accompanied by the German Jewish oil expert, Walter Levy. Harriman's partner from Brown Brothers Harriman, Robert A. Lovett, is now Secretary of Defense. Lay's National Security Council is another of those mysterious Government agencies whose activities are a threat to every American. Operating in the utmost secrecy, it illustrates the fact that wherever security is mentioned in the title of an agency, it means the security of the international bankers who have financed and promoted world Communism.

Smith triumphantly concludes:

> "At 1:22 p.m., almost precisely six days after the fighting started, the orders were on the way to MacArthur. We were in."

In some 5000 words of his article, "Why We Went To War In Korea", Beverly Smith makes the point that we went to war to stop Communist aggression. The officials with Truman at the making of this decision, however, were the same individuals who for the past ten years had followed a consistent and well documented policy of pro-Communism, betraying China to the Communists, and sabotaging military aid to South Korea. This raises the question of whether our involvement in the Korean War benefits us or Russia. It can be answered by the number of our casualties there and by the fact that Russia has not lost a man in Korea.

That the main purpose of the present conduct of the Korean War is the slaughter of American youth is illustrated by Truman's steadfast refusal to let the Chinese Nationalist troops on Formosa be sent to Korea to fight the Chinese Communist armies there. As Freda Utley points out in "The China Story", Truman is helping the Communist Party propaganda that the Korean War is a war of Asiatics against white invaders. The aid seems to be intentional.

The international news services are unanimous in identifying American dead in Korea by the ignominious title of "United Nations casualties". The United States has furnished 96% of the soldiers and all of the supplies for the United Nations, but her dead are no longer Americans. Walter Trohan in the Washington Times-Herald of Jan. 25, 1952, writes of our butchered soldiers who had been taken prisoner by the Communists and brutally massacred, that

> "The prisoners' hands (at the Katyn massacre) were tied with a peculiar knot which became tighter if they struggled. Ten years later, in the snows of Korea, America hands were tied with the same peculiar knot in Soviet overrun territory. The Americans were found later, each with a bullet in his brain. They were executed in the same fashion as the Polish officers at Katyn Forest."

Arthur Bliss Lane, former U.S. Ambassador to Poland, wrote in the January 1952 issue of The American Legion Magazine that

> "Let us not forget that the hands of our Army officers, our military chaplains, our soldiers, when we found their cold bodies lying in blood on the Communist-overrun Korean soil, were found to be tied behind their backs just as the Polish army officers' hands had been tied at Katyn; tied with the same tricky knot the Communists used for the Polish officers."

Behind these atrocities against American prisoners of war looms the sinister figure of Dean Acheson, the former legal representative of the Soviet Union and Zionist adherent who sent our boys out to be massacred by his former employers, the ruthless Soviet leaders. Acheson and Lattimore had maneuvered to bring about the Communist attack in Korea, by assuring the Communists that we would not support the Rhee Government. In August of 1949, Lattimore, who has never had any official position in the State Department, but who seems to have directed our Asiatic policy for years, authored a top-secret Memorandum entitled, "For the Guidance of Ambassador-at-Large Philip C. Jessup", which recommended that we withdraw all support from South Korea and evacuate our forces from Japan. One of the most important behind-the-scenes influences in Washington, even more important than Alger Hiss, Lattimore had a half-hour conference with Truman before Truman sailed for Potsdam on August 14, 1945. On March 31, 1950, Truman paid a glowing tribute to Acheson, Jessup, and Lattimore at a press conference in his winter quarters at Key West, Florida, defending them against the exposure of their Communist affiliations by Senator McCarthy.

The *Daily Compass* on July 17, 1949 carried a note saying "The thing to do is to let South Korea fall but not to let it look as though we pushed it." This was signed O.L., since revealed to be Owen Lattimore. An indefatigable Communist propagandist, Lattimore wrote a constant stream of influential material for the journal of the Institute of Pacific Relations, "Pacific Affairs". Typical of his unswerving following of the Communist Party line is his attitude toward the Moscow Purge Trials of 1937-38. Approval of these trials is convincing proof of anyone's devotion to Communism, as is approval of the Russo-German Non-Aggression Pact of 1939. Lattimore wrote in "Pacific Affairs", September, 1938, pages 404–504,

> "The American Quarterly on the Soviet Union, published by the American-Russian Institute, April, 1938. This promising quarterly has developed from the Bulletin originally published by the ARI, and is a sign of the healthy growth of American interest in the Soviet Union. The first issue opens with an article by John Hazard, who studied Soviet law in Moscow for three years, on changes and controversy in the theory of law in the first country that is attempting to put the theories of Marx into practice. The subject is of very great importance, for it opens to laymen an understanding of the legal philosophy which guides the legal processes of the Soviet Union. The article is one more indication that the series of Moscow trials does not represent the climax of a process of repression, but, on the contrary, is part of a new advance in the struggle to set free the social and economic potentialities of a whole nation and its people."

John Hazard, America's outstanding expert on Soviet law, and a member of the Council On Foreign Relations, approved of the Moscow Trials, and fellow-Council member Lattimore seconded his approval. Another Council member Major General Lyman Lemnitzer, who handled the German surrender negotiations, admitted before a Senate Committee his personal responsibility for the sabotage of military aid to South Korea. He was head of the Office of Foreign Military Assistance. Newsweek of July 10, 1950 reported that Senator Ferguson demanded of Lemnitzer how much of the $10,230,000 of aid authorized by MAP for South Korea in July, 1949, had been delivered. Lemnitzer reluctantly admitted that two hundred dollars worth of obsolete signal equipment was all the aid we had sent South Korea.

In the conduct of this war, it has been difficult for the South Koreans to ascertain which side Washington is on. The yellow liberal press constantly castigates the "reactionary" Synghman Rhee, who is the legal head of the South Korean Government, and whom our state Department considers as a dirty fascist. The destruction of Chiang's army on Formosa seems to mean more to our State Department than anything else in Asia. William C. Bullitt testified before the McCarran Committee on April 8, 1952, that Acheson ordered the Seventh Fleet of the U.S. Navy to patrol the coast of Formosa and prevent Chiang's Navy from sinking Polish ships of the Gdynia Line which were sailing past Formosa on their way to North Korea with munitions for the Chinese Communist armies. Bullitt testified that Acheson's order released the Third and Fourth Chinese Communist Armies for duty in Korea and action against American troops.

The Voice of America propaganda against Rhee became so vicious that he closed down their operations in Korea in July, 1952, a great blow to Communist sympathizers in South Korea. The attack on Rhee continues from the New York Times, the Washington Post, the Christian Science Monitor, and their satellites, which seem to see only side of the news, the Marxist side.

The U.S. Army Information and Education Section, always a comfortable billet for Communists and fellow-travelers in the Army, furnished 80,000 North Korean prisoners of war on Koje Island with materials for making Communist flags and insignia, so they could express themselves without being frustrated. Atrocities against anti-Communist elements in the North Korean prisoners camps shed more light on the conditions in Nazi camps during the Second World War, when ruthless Communist bosses inside the camps systematically murdered all who opposed them.

The climax came in Korea when General MacArthur, who was being much too successful in his campaign, wished to bomb the North Korean power plants which made the Communist war effort possible. The Defense Minister of Great Britain, Emmanuel Shinwell, demanded that MacArthur be recalled, and Truman was happy to oblige him. Certain interests in Great Britain had done very well with sales of the Nene jet engine to Russia, so that their jets were outflying others on the Korean battlefronts. MacArthur seemed likely to win the war, and so Truman called him home and stripped him of his command.

For once, the hero of the Kansas City underworld, Harry Truman, had overstepped himself. The whole country was outraged by Truman's action, even though the influences behind it were not known for some months. The Senate held Hearings on MacArthur's return, and Marshall, the Communist collaborator whom Truman referred to as "the greatest living American", came to testify. He was in poor shape. The kindest commentators remarked that his memory seemed to have gone bad. His mind seemed to be impaired, and he was retired from public service. His assistant, Anna Rosenberg, bravely carried on in the Department of Defense until Robert A. Lovett could be summoned from the offices of Brown Brothers Harriman.

After more than a year of "peace negotiations", the slaughter of American boys in Korea goes on, much to the satisfaction of both sides. With the removal of General MacArthur, the war could be continued indefinitely, with the result that perhaps a million of our youth will find their last resting place on Korean soil. The peace negotiators are sometimes hard put to find an excuse to keep the war going, but at this writing, their ingenuity has sufficed.

This slaughter of American boys greatly weakens our power in the face of Russian rearmament. The suggestion has been advanced that, if our policy of killing Communists is sincere, it is not necessary to send our boys three thousand miles away to do it. Certain elements in America are much concerned over the possibility that our boys may get used to killing Communists, and that they may be desirous of continuing the habit when they return to America. To evade and postpone this issue, the Department of Defense has readied plans to keep the present troops in Korea for an indefinite number of years, should the peace negotiators fail to keep the war going

CHAPTER 25

An economy based on the barbaric sacrifice of youth upon the altar of war has little to recommend it to prosperity. Yet, under the Federal Reserve System, that is precisely the economy we have. The slaughter of American youth has been justified on Wall Street by the often-spoken but seldom published remark that if we did not rearm, our economy would collapse. Rearmament, of course, means war. There has never been an army which has not been used.

This remark on rearmament is so much fertilizer for more war. We have a monetary system which is operated for the benefit of a few international bankers and their satellites. That is the reason for Korea. No effort is being made to establish a peacetime economy, because the war economy offers so many more attractions to the gang which runs the show. An economy which had peace as its objective would not require that our young men be massacred in foreign wars.

Marriner Eccles, then Governor of the Federal Reserve Board, stated at the Bretton Woods Hearings in May 1945 that

> "An international currency is synonymous with international government."

The so-called "international currency", which is really the interbalance of various national currencies, is the root of the present monetary crisis in Europe. An entire continent has been stalemated in its recovery from the Second World War because the monetary structure depends too much on the supply of dollars from the United States. West Germany has made the most startling recovery because she has less interference from bankers who have investments to protect. England and France have been held back by the "vested interests" which could not adjust to the postwar economy. Admiral Zacharias, in "Behind Closed Doors", says on page 323,

> "Britain must be restored to power and influence. We must grant her at least $10 billion in cash with no strings attached."

Ridiculous as this statement may seem, it is true, according to the present international monetary structure. Great Britain is being strangled by her dependence upon the dollar supply, which is very good for those bankers who have dollars to sell on the exchanges. Why can't Britain help herself? The international bankers won't let her. The economic drool subsidized by the bankers is typified by the following propaganda from one of their highest-paid writers, Barbara West of the Rothschild house organ "The Economic", of London. Her book, "Policy for the West", Norton, 1951, is a defense of the containment policy, and claims that the defense of Western Europe is the defense of Western civilization. Why are we "containing" Communist aggression in Korea? She advises all nations in the Western orbit to curtail their non-defense spending. The national income must go into war production. This is the guns-instead-of-butter slogan which was so loudly denounced when the Nazis instigated it in Germany. War production carries a higher margin of profit than civilian production, and it is impossible to overproduce for the war market. Barbara West's mind is revealed in its mattress-piercing sharpness by these words,

> "A national debt is not necessarily inflationary. It does not involve a new burden on the community, but a redistribution of wealth within it. One set of people are taxed to provide the interest on the debt, another set receives the interest."

This brilliant female economist tells us that debt is not a new burden. Evidently she has never owed anything. 150,000,000 people are taxed to provide the interest on the debt, and a few members of the Council on Foreign Relations receive that interest. This is redistribution of wealth with a vengeance. Donald C. Miller, in his study "Taxation, the Public Debt, and Transfer of Income", 1950, notes that the net effect of increased taxation to service or retire the debt in the United States was to transfer income from those earning less than $5000 a year to a higher income group. This is taking from the poor to satisfy the rich. Three-fourths of the national debt is owned by the big trusts, banks, and insurance companies, which have interlocking directorates going back to the international banking houses. In May 1951, the U.S. Treasury that the taxpayers were paying five billion, nine hundred million dollars a year interest on the national debt, an average of 2.2% interest. Somebody is collecting six billion a year as profit for inveigling us into the Second World War. No wonder they can afford to endow universities to teach their gold standard Central Bank brand of economics, and to publish the drivel of dizzy Barbara West. Her "Policy for the West" offers an interesting problem in arithmetic, although her publishers have refused to answer queries about it. She writes,

> "There was an increase of general personal income from 72 billion in 1939 to 171 billion in 1945. These figures, incidentally, cannot be dismissed as mere monetary inflation. Real increases in consumption occurred. For instance, food consumption in America was eleven times larger in 1950 than in 1939."

Norton and Co. has failed to send me statistics showing that anybody in America consumed eleven times as much in 1950 as in 1939. Yet that is what she definitely claims. She specifically points out the actual consumption of food by Americans as eleven times increased, not what was stored, given away to other countries, or burned by a benevolent Administration to boost prices, but actually digested by the American citizenry. At least this gives us an insight into the value of Barbara West's pronouncements. A frequent contributor to the Atlantic Monthly and the *New York Times*, she is counted one of the more intellectual and valuable commentators today. So be it.

The manner in which the bankers spend millions to promote their shady plans is shown by the Lobbyists' Report to Congress, in which it is shown that the Council On Foreign Relations subsidiary at 45 East 65th St. New York, the American Association for the United Nations, distributed more than one million dollars in cash to three mysterious lobbying groups in Washington, $352,000 to the Committee for the Marshall Plan to aid European Recovery, $353,000 to the Committee on the Present Danger, headed by Senator Lehman's brother-in-law, Frank Altschul of Lazard Freres, and $353,000 to the Atlantic Union Committee, one more proof that all of these internationalist organizations stem from the Council On Foreign Relations, which is borne out by the interlocking directorates of their executive committees with the Council.

Prof. J.H. Morgan, K.C., in the *Quarterly Review* of January, 1939, tells how the bankers spend their money,

> "When I once asked Lord Haldane why he persuaded his friend Sir Ernest Cassel to settle by his will large sums on the London School of Economics, he replied, 'Our object is to make this institution a place to raise and train the bureaucracy of the future world Socialist State.' "

One of its graduates was Dean Acheson's brother, Edward Campion Acheson, another was Communist agent Lauchlin Currie. The guiding genius of the London School of Economics was the Communist propagandist Harold Laski. The administration of its funds was in the hands of Israel Moses Sieff, Chairman of the Political and Economic Planning Commission in England, and Managing Director of Marks and Spencer Department Stores.

The London School of Economics received more than one million dollars in grants from Rockefeller Foundation in three years, from 1926 to 1929. The foundations established by American millionaires interlock in the internationalist field. For instance, Julius Rosenwald, the Sears, Roebuck millionaire, was a director of the Rockefeller Foundation, while his own Rosenwald Foundation spent millions to promote racial agitation in the United States. After amassing three hundred million dollars in the mail order business, Rosenwald went into propaganda on a large scale, with grants to the University of Chicago, and with the purchase of the Encyclopaedia Britannica. He then set up the Rosenwald Fund, which, like the Guggenheim Foundation and others, made its grants available to Communist intellectuals to carry out their work, and financed the Leninist-Marxist doctrines of the world revolution by a constant promotion of class warfare, setting group against group. The clever and unremitting exploitation of the minority problems of the United States by these foundations was an essential step toward bringing about a Communist government in America. Setting minorities against each other, and against the Anglo-Saxon majority which built the American nation, these foundations spend one billion dollars a year for propaganda, and most of that propaganda is Communist. Racial agitation has become one of the most profitable professions in America, for these foundations pay up to fifty thousand dollars a year for an expert agent. When he was arrested as a Communist spy, Alger Hiss was President of the Carnegie Endowment for International Peace, a top Communist position paying $25,000 a year and expenses. There are dozens of such jobs provided by the foundations for the intellectual leaders of the Communist movement in America.

At present, the propaganda of the foundations is devoted to stirring up the Negro minority in America, raising more money for the State of Israel, and urging this country on toward bankruptcy through increased spending for "foreign aid", which, of course, all goes into the pockets of the most clever rascals on the other side of the ocean. The proposed

Fair Employment Practices Act, which tells the employer whom he must hire, is only one aspect of the continual class warfare carried on in America according to the precepts of Marx and Lenin.

Senator McCarthy listed dozens of prominent Communists who had been financed by liberal grants from the Rosenwald Foundation and the Guggenheim Foundation. Congressional Hearings turned up many others who were supported for years in their Communist agitation by fellowships and gifts of money from the Carnegie Foundation, the Rockefeller Foundation, and others. John D. Rockefeller set up the General Board in 1903. This board has made a specialty of granting funds to teachers' colleges all over the United States. It did not fully get under way until 1915, when its program was placed in the hands of Abraham Flexner, whose qualifications for determining the future of American education consisted solely in the fact that in 1913, he had written a book called "Prostitution in Europe".

The motto of these foundations has always been, "Millions for traitors, but not one cent for patriots." I have not found a single instance of any of these afore-mentioned foundations spending a cent for studies of the U.S. Constitution or the principles upon which our forefathers founded the American Republic. They present a solid front of Leninist internationalist One-Worlders. The moral sympathies of the Rockefeller Foundation may be surmised from the fact that it made no grants for religious purposes for many years, until 1947, when it gave $100,000 to the New York millionaires' nondenominational church, Riverside Church in New York City. The Federal Council of Churches of Christ in 1949 received $100,000 from the Rockefeller Foundation. This group for many years has been listed as a Communist-front by the Federal Bureau of Investigation. John Foster Dulles was a prominent official of this organization, which in 1950 changed its name to the National Council of Churches of Christ, because it was being mentioned so frequently in Congressional Hearings on Communist activity in America. The Congressional Record of August 17, 1935, page 13053, says,

> "The Federal Council of Churches of Christ in America: This is a large radical pacifist organization. It probably represents twenty million Protestants in the United States. However, its leadership consists of a small radical group which dictates its policies. (Quoted from U.S. Naval Intelligence Department Report: April 1, 1935)."

Not only is John D. Rockefeller 3d a contributor to and member of such Communist-front organizations as the Institute of pacific Relations, but Nelson Rockefeller also carries on the family tradition of promoting Leninist internationalism. Elizabeth Bentley testified that Nelson Rockefeller hired Bob Miller, editor of the notoriously pro-Communist Latin-American publication, The Hemisphere", as head of the political research division for Inter-American Affairs when Nelson Rockefeller was head of that State Department Division. When he left the State Department, Rockefeller took most of his staff with him as the personnel for his International Basic Economy Corporation, a mysterious company which is involved with the Truman-Browder Point Four Program for developing backward areas of the world.

The University of Chicago Annual Register for 1912–1913, page 4, says,

> "The incorporators named in the charter were John D; Rockefeller, F. Nelson Blake, Marshall Field, Frederick T. Gates, Francis E. Hinckley, and T. W. Goodspeed. In recognition of the peculiar relation of Mr. Rockefeller to the institution (he put up the money; EM) the Board of Trustees has enacted that on the seals and letterheads and in all official publications the title should read 'The University of Chicago, founded by John D. Rockefeller.'"

This university, the personal creation of Rockefeller, who was the creation of Jacob Schiff, has been for many years a focal point in the Communist infection of America. From its classrooms have come many of the most devoted revolutionaries who espouse the violent overthrow of the American Government, and its professors of economics have been particularly useful in promoting internationalism, since economics is a principal Marxist weapon. Fortune Magazine of April, 1947, page 2, reported that

> "A Commission on Freedom of the Press has been financed by grants of $200,000 from Time, Inc. and $15,000 from Encyclopaedia Britannica Inc. The Commission, appointed by Chancellor Robert M. Hutchins of the University of Chicago, was composed of thirteen Americans of high intellectual attainments."

Encyclopaedia Britannica is owned by Senator William Benton, as is its subsidiary, Encyclopaedia Britannica Films, which cooperates with the Twentieth Century Fund, left by pro-Communist Edward Filene, in the distribution of films on sexual education to America's schools. Benton, Hutchins, Henry Luce, and Paul Hoffman compose an interlocking directorate which controls much of our press and educational system. All four of them are on the board of directors of Encyclopaedia Britannica Inc. and the Committee for Economic Development, Luce and Hoffman are directors of Time, Inc., Benton and Hutchins are on the board of the University of Chicago, and Hoffman and Hutchins control the Ford Foundation.

The Commission on Freedom of the Press spent hundreds of thousands of dollars before reporting that there was too much freedom of the press, which was what its sponsors had wanted to hear. The Commission proposed a number of ways of indirectly muzzling a too-critical press, several of which Eleanor Roosevelt has tried to force on America via the United Nations, with the able assistance of Professor Zechariah Chafee, Jr. It is not likely that these recommendations will go into effect until the United Nations considerably increases its control over the internal affairs of member nations.

Current Biography, volume of 1945, says of William Benton,

> "Benton became Board Chairman of Britannica's English and Canadian companies (after Julius Rosenwald transferred it to him). The only change of importance announced at that time was that the University of Chicago faculty would become the official advisory staff of the publications, supervising the continuous revisions which the set of books undergoes. To insure extreme vigilance in reading for revision, the Britannica Co. established fellowships at the University of Chicago, to do the preliminary reading and make recommendations to the faculty members, who recommend revision by experts. Among the group, besides, Benton, who determined the policies of the Britannica project, were Robert Hutchins, Henry Luce, President of Time, Inc., and Paul Hoffman of Studebaker Corporation."

The standard reference work in all American educational institutions, the Encyclopaedia Britannica since 1938 has been undergoing revision in a hotbed of Communist revolutionaries, the University of Chicago, whose faculty furnished the present Communist delegate from Poland to the United Nations, Oscar Lange. Whittaker Chamber in a previously-quoted statement pointed out that most of Time's staff of foreign correspondents were Communists, nor was this accidental.

Time Magazine was founded in 1923 by Henry Luce and Briton Hadden. Bennett Cerf, in his column, "Trade Winds", in the Saturday Review of Literature, June 25, 1949, wrote,

"When they were graduated from Yale, Luce and Hadden had Time so well blueprinted that a June 1949 issue does not deviate more than 10% from the first prospectus dated 1922. While they were raising enough cash to float the magazine, Hadden took a temporary job under that great teacher, Herbert Bayard Swope, at the New York World; Luce meanwhile was getting experience on the Chicago News, under the knowing eye of Ben Hecht."

On page 1574 of the New York Co-Partnership Directory, 1923, E. L. Polk Co., the directors of Time, Inc. are listed as Briton Hadden, President, Henry Luce, Secretary, William T. Hincks, Harry P. Davison Jr., William V. Griffin, and William Hale Harkness, capitalized at $150,000. Time, Inc. was intended as the mouthpiece of the biggest interests on Wall Street. Haden's grandfather was President of the Brooklyn Savings Bank, Harry P. Davison Jr. was a partner of J.P. Morgan Co., Harkness was a member of the wealthy Standard Oil family, and William V. Griffin was a director of the Bank of Manhattan, controlled by the Warburg family.

Wolcott Gibbs, in the New Yorker Magazine, Nov. 28, 1935, page 21, named the persons putting up the initial capital for Time, Inc. as follows; Harry P. Davison Jr. of J.P. Morgan Co. $4000; Mrs. David S. Ingalls, sister of William Hale Harkness, $10,000; William Hale Harkness, their Yale classmate, $5000; his mother, Mrs. W. H. Harkness, $20,000; and other sums from J.P. Morgan partner Dwight Morrow, E. Roland Harriman, brother of W. Averell Harriman, partner of Brown Brothers Harriman, and backer and director of Newsweek Magazine, and William V. Griffin. The Harkness fortune came from Rockefeller's Standard Oil Corporation. Thus, from its very outset, Time was the spokesman for Standard Oil, J.P. Morgan, and Kuhn, Loeb via Griffin and the Bank of Manhattan. Needless to say, Luce and several of his editors are prominent members of the Council On Foreign Relations.

In 1923, Henry Luce was also a director of the Saturday Review of Literature, financed by Thomas Lamont of J.P. Morgan Co. to control the sale of books through favorable or unfavorable reviews. The Saturday Review has been notorious for its outspoken defense of persons involved in Communist activities, notably Owen Lattimore. Time Magazine struggled along for five years without showing a profit, a tribute to the genius of its founders, but, with these huge fortunes behind him, Luce couldn't go broke. In 1929, a year of disaster for most Americans, Time showed its first profit. It climbed steadily ahead, as its predecessors, such as World's Work, the North American Review, and the Literary Digest, fell by the wayside. The failure of the Literary Digest in 1936 left Luce an almost clear field. In the 1936 Annual Report of Time, Inc. Luce says that the corporation has $2,700,000 in Government bonds, and $3,000,000 in stocks of other corporations.

The directors of Time, Inc., publishers of Time, Life, Fortune, and the Architectural Forum, are listed on page 1210 of the 1952 Poor's Directory of Directors as follows:

Chairman of the Board, Maurice T. Moore, married to Elizabeth Luce, and partner in the law firm of Cravath, Swaine, and Moore, lawyers for Kuhn, Loeb Co. (formerly Cravath and Henderson). Moore was a special assistant to Paul Hoffman in ECA in 1948;

William V. Griffin, Vice-Chairman; director of the Yale Publishing Co., Bank of Manhattan, Continental Oil, Manati Sugar, Inc. and many others. Formerly director with Albert Strauss of J. and W. Seligman Co. in Compania Cubana, the Cuba Railroad, and the Consolidated Railways of Cuba.

Artemus L. Gates, President of the Union Pacific Railroad, one of the larger roads controlled by Kuhn, Loeb Co.; Roy Larsen, President of Time, Inc.; Henry Luce, Editor-in-Chief; Samuel W. Meek Jr., vice-president of J. Walter Thompson, New York's largest advertising agency; Charles Stillman, who was head of ECA's technical mission to China in 1948, and a director of the leftwing Foreign Policy Association with John D. Rockefeller 3d.

Last of the Time directors is Paul Hoffman, co-founder with William Benton of the Committee for Economic Development, director of the Federal Reserve Bank of Chicago, United Airlines, and formerly director of the Marine midland Trust. He was made President of Studebaker by Lehman Brothers, then he became head of ECA, then director of the Ford Foundation, and finally, head of the Citizens for Eisenhower movement.

As Assistant Secretary of State, William Benton inherited James Paul Warburg's Office of War Information, which he changed to the Voice of America. His advertising partner, Governor Chester Bowles of Connecticut, appointed Benton U.S. Senator from Connecticut in one of the most odorous political deals in the history of that state.

Benton and Hoffman founded the Committee for Economic Development in 1942, a top-level economic planning agency which exercises the dominant voice in our postwar economy. It is a book in itself.

Time, Inc. has steadily increased its political influence since the Second World War. It paid for the televised presentation of General Eisenhower's "Crusade in Europe" which built-up Eisenhower for the Presidential nomination, and also paid for the televised presentation of the Senate Crime Hearings to promote Senator Estes Kefauer, a spokesman for Atlantic Union, for the Presidency.

Hoffman and Hutchins together inherited the Ford Foundation, half of a billion dollars with the sole purpose of promoting world government. Robert Hutchins wrote a pamphlet entitled "The Atom Bomb and Education", published by the National Peace Council in London in 1947, in which he said, on page 5,

> "I believe in world government. I think we must have it and have it soon... A world State demands a world community, a world community demands a world revolution."

In the Ford Foundation, Hutchins has $500 million of what revolutionists always need, money. Fortune Magazine, December 1951, pages 116–117, describes the Ford Foundation as having assets of $493 million, mostly class A non-voting Ford stock, with liquid assets of $68.8 million. Paul Hoffman is Chief Director, the four Directors of Policy and Planning are Robert Hutchins, Chester C. Davis, who considered this position so important that he resigned the Presidency of the Federal Reserve Bank of St. Louis to take it, R. Rowan Gaither, Chairman of the Rand Corporation, and Milton Katz, former European Ambassador-at-large for the Marshall Plan while shipments were going to Russia. Working funds for 1951 were a $7million fund for the Advancement of Education, under Dr. Clarence Faust, Professor at the University of Chicago from 1930 to 1947, the Chairman of this fund being Frank Abrams, Chairman of Standard Oil of New Jersey; a $3 million fund for Adult Education, whose President is C. Scott Fletcher, formerly Hoffman's assistant at Studebaker, and director of Field Development of the Committee for Economic Development from 1943 to 1946, the chairman of this fund being Alexander Fraser, formerly President of Shell Oil; and an East European Fund, originally called the Free Russia Fund, with now Ambassador to Russia George

Kennan as President, intended to help Russian exiles adapt to American life, $200,000 granted to unidentified institutions in this field.

This was the Ford Foundation in 1951. It has been more reticent about its activities in 1952. Hoffman resigned to devote all of his time to securing the Presidency for Stalin's friend, General Eisenhower, and Robert Hutchins took charge of the $500 million. If one dollar of this fund is ever spent for any useful, patriotic purpose, it will only be after world revolutionist Hutchins and his Adler-pated gang of crackpots and One-Worlders have moved on to more fertile fields.

CHAPTER 26

Judge Simon Rifkind, Eisenhower's wartime aide, wrote in the World Jewish Congress Information Bulletin of 1946–1947, vol. 2, page 20,

> "The Jewish problem is not only a European problem but a world problem."

Adolf Hitler said the same thing. The establishment of a Jewish National Home in Palestine was achieved by the First World War. The establishment of the State of Israel was a principal result of the Second World War. Should we ask who would benefit by the Third World War?

No sooner did the Jews get into Palestine after the First World War than they began a systematic campaign against the natives, which culminated in their driving out 600,000 Arabs to starve in the desert while the Jews took their homes, under the authority of the United Nations. One instance of how the Jews waged war against the Arabs for thirty years is offered by this quote from the Zionist Bulletin, February 4, 1920,

> "The Arabic paper Beit El Mekdas has been suppressed. The following circular has been issued by the Government: 'I am instructed to inform you that the circular of the following newspapers is prohibited, and all copies found will be confiscated and destroyed. Al Ordun, Hermion, Al Hamara, Al Mufid Suria al Judida, Istikal al Arabi. Quotations in local papers from the afore-mentioned are also strictly prohibited, as the news contained in the papers referred to is inaccurate."

The Jews had won their first battle, the suppression of the Arabic newspapers. Since 1920, only one side of the story has been heard. The philosophic background of the Commission for Freedom of the Press is revealed by this chapter of history, that is, the suppression of all criticism on the grounds of "inaccuracy". Suppressed newspapers cannot be quoted from or circulated. In the United States, a similar war has been waged to suppress a number of patriotic newspapers for years, a vicious campaign of terrorism and intimidation of printers. Conde McGinley's journal, "Common Sense", published in Union, New Jersey, is a Christian American paper which has incurred the hatred of the Anti-Defamation League. Eight successive printers had to give up printing "Common Sense", and he finally had to have it printed in Florida. Other small weeklies, which fill the tremendous gap in the news suppressed by the international news services, have had similar experiences.

Although the Protocols of Zion are now denounced as a libel and forgery, not so long ago they were accepted by Jews as their plan of action. Herman Bernstein, in The American Hebrew, June 25, 1920, writes that the Protocols of Zion are the legacy of the great Zionist leader, Theodore Herzl. Bernstein tells us that the Protocols of Zion is the program which was delivered by Herzl to the delegates to the First Zionist World Congress at Basle, Switzerland in 1897.

Zionism and Communism progressed side by side from 1900 to 1950. Jewish Voice, issue of March April 1941, criticizes the conviction of Earl Browder on a charge of passport fraud as follows:

> "The leader of the only party which has fought for the outlawing of anti-Semitism in the world-the Communist Party—is Earl Browder, the greatest friend of the Jewish people in the United States. The imprisonment of Earl Browder is a direct blow against the interests of the Jewish people. The defense of the Communist Party, the movement to free Browder and Weiner, is a vital necessity for every Jew. The defense of the Communist Party is the first line of defense for every Jew."

The same issue, page 24, says,

> "The only way out for the Jewish masses in the capitalist countries is the socialist way-support of the peace policies of the Soviet Union and the struggle against the imperialist oppressors at home."

Jewish Voice of May, 1941, says

> "The Jews in the United States have been most active in the organization of the trade union movement and progressive organization. Despite the efforts of the reactionary and reformist social-democratic leadership the Jews have marched together with their Communist and militant brothers and sisters."

The May 1941 issue of Jewish Voice also contains an article by Rose Wortis, "Labor Is on the March", which says

> "We Communists have a special responsibility. It is the task of the Party and its members to draw the lessons of the strike movements to the workers in all industries. It is our task to show the workers that the militant policies of John L. Lewis and the progressives in the labor movement will bring victory to the workers. A particular responsibility rests upon us, the Jewish Communists, working in unions under social-democratic control."

Hundreds of similar quotations are available from Jewish and Marxist publications. I mention these to give the political background of the State of Israel, which is known as a Socialist nation. Admiral Zacharias, in "Behind Closed Doors", page 137, says

> "At the World Labor Conference in London, the Soviet delegate announced that his government propose to support a projected Jewish state; on Nov. 26, 1945, the U.S.S.R. made a formal proposal that the Big Five lay the groundwork for such a state. By late 1946, the Palestine policy was fixed in Stalin's mind and discussed in the Politburo. This was the decision which, when made, changed the course of Jewish. Russian-and possibly Anglo-American-history."

It has not been publicized that the proposal to set up the State of Israel came from Russia. It is actually a Marxist police state, modelled after its sponsor, Communist Russia. A police state is the only kind of government the Jews want, the only kind they can obey. On page 134, Zacharias says

> "At present, Communist parties may function openly only in Israel of all the Middle Eastern countries."

When the Jews, backed by the United Nations, began their war to drive out the Arabs, an Arab League was formed in Cairo of Moslem nations, and an Egyptian Army sent to fight the Jews. This Army was sabotaged at home by purchasing agents who sent inferior weapons or none at all, and the Egyptian Army was defeated. The scandals which caused that defeat finally unseated King Farouk's Government, and he abdicated. The Jewish conduct of the war was accompanied by some of the worst atrocities in modern history. One of the most shocking volumes ever published is one story of that struggle "The Revolt", written by the leader of the Jewish terrorists, Menahem Begin. Page after page is filled with a cold-blooded recitation of such acts as the bombing of the King

David Hotel in Jerusalem by his group, the Irgun Zvai Leumi, on July 22, 1946, in which two hundred civilians were killed or injured. To force the British officers in Palestine to accede to his demands, Begin tells us how he captured British soldiers and tortured and killed them, (sometime he only blinded them, and sent them back as a warning, at other times he hung them). Such cruelties have not been recorded since the American Indian wars. On page 274, Begin says that he

> "Published a communique announcing the setting-up of field courts-martial attached to every unit of the Irgun. Should any enemy troops fall into our hands they will be liable to die."

On page 314, of "The Revolt" distributed in America by the Jewish Book Guil Begin says

> "I met Quentin Reynolds after the conquest of Jaffa. He was an old friend of the fighting underground."

Reynolds, also an admirer of Stalin, is now editor of the United Nations World.

The Irgun terrorists achieved their victory on May, 14, 1948, when the State of Israel was proclaimed. Begin relates that he spoke over the Irgun radio station in Tel Aviv, "One phase of the battle for freedom has ended, but only one phase."

Of the State of Israel, born in Marxism and nurtured by terrorists, President Truman said to a Zionist audience,

> "On 6:12 p.m. on Friday, May 14, 1948, when I recognized Israel, was the proudest moment of my life." Even succeeding to the Presidency of the United States did not mean as much as the recognition of Israel.

No word of the Irgun atrocities was printed by the American press. Outstanding in its silence on the Irgun atrocities was Eugene Meyer's Washington Post. In *Fortune Magazine* of December, 1944, page 132, we find that

> "At the White House the Washington Post is one of six newspapers with which the President opens his day. He pays special attention to the Post's editorial pages. In Washington, the impression is widespread that President Roosevelt feels close enough to Eugene Meyer to telephone him and ask for editorial assistance on measures

dear to the White House. On occasions, the State Department has
referred reporters to Post editorials for illumination."

Most of the foul deeds of the terrorists waited for Begin's boasting to
give them to the world, but one atrocity even the Washington Post had
to report. This was the assassination of the United Nations mediator,
Count Folke Bernadotte, in Israel in 1948 by Jewish terrorists who were
never punished. He was supposed to have been killed because he was
slow to give in on some of the outrageous Jewish demands. Actually,
Bernadotte had been slated for assassination because, in the winter of
1944, he had been the go-between for the Hitler Government when the
Soviet leaders extended peace feelers to the Nazis in a bid for a separate
peace which would give them all of Central Europe. With the
impending collapse of Germany, Russia withdrew the offer, but since
then the Politburo had become increasingly nervous about Bernadotte's
possibly revealing these negotiations, and, when he went into the
warring zone of Palestine, he was set upon and murdered. He was
replaced by the Negro Ralph Bunche.

The former Communist propagandist, James McDonald, was rewarded
by being appointed the first U.S. Ambassador to Israel. In "My Mission
in Israel", Simon and Schuster, New York, 1951, McDonald writes,

> "The reason Dr. Weizmann was in Switzerland and not yet in the
> Jewish State was that the Israel Government wasn't prepared to
> provide from 400 to 800 men to protect Dr. Weizmann from
> assassination by Jewish terrorists."

Donald also writes that

> "We had a pleasant visit from the redoubtable Will Bill Donovan of
> wartime Office of Strategic Services fame. He did not disclose his
> mission, but he asked me questions more searching than were to be
> expected from a private visitor. I answered frankly, because I
> assumed that he was still close to the authorities in Washington." On
> page 263, he says

> "One of my personal favorites among the Israel Foreign Office
> officials was Reuven Shiloah. Trained by the British and active
> under them as an Intelligence office, Shiloah organized the excellent
> Intelligence Service of Haganah (Jewish underground). During
> World War II he won the confidence and affection of Allied leaders
> with whom he worked in Europe and the Middle East Gen. Donovan

told me four years after the War that he regarded Shiloah as one of his ablest aides and a trusted friend."

Menahem Begin says in "The Revolt" that his Irgun always received all the latest communiques of the British at the same time as the British troops, as well as their secret instructions. A scandal in the Central Intelligence Agency in Washington occurred in June of 1951, when two officials were discovered to be sending secret information on Arab troop strength to Israel. The scandal was promptly hushed up.

McDonald says on page 175 of "My Mission In Israel",

"The only Jewish-executed massacre of the war was the Irgun raid on Deir Yassin on April 9, 1948, in which the Raba village was destroyed together with its inhabitants, women and children."

On page 190, McDonald writes that

"The week before I saw the Cardinal I had lunch with two of his Monsignor one of whom expressed much concern because Israel had begun to turn Russian Church property over to its Soviet-controlled owners."

Christian missionaries have been given the not-wanted sign in Israel.

With the establishment of the State of Israel, its government was set up as a Socialist State with government-controlled trade unions, collective farm and nationally-owned land, all Marxist principles. Most of the government officials were Russian Jews, such as Eliezer Kaplan of Minsk, Russia, who is Deputy Prime Minister, and Golda Myerson. McDonald says on page 268,

"Like many of her Israel colleagues, Golda Myerson, Minister of Labor, was born in Russia. In her teens she had become an ardent Socialist and Zionist, and was active in the Poale Zion Labor Party." Yarmolinsky tells us that the Poale Zion was the Jewish Communist Party.

"The Jewish National Fund", by Adolf Bohn, published by the Jewish Colonial Trust, London, 1932, says,

"Land acquired by the Jewish National Fund may neither be sold nor mortgaged and remains the property of the Jewish people for all time."

This is perpetual communal ownership of land, Point One of the Communist Manifesto.

That the Rothschild interests in Palestine are not charitable is exposed by Henry H. Klein, a courageous Jewish lawyer of New York City, who for years has written about the Dead Sea, which contains literally trillions of dollars of mineral wealth, which is controlled by the Rothschilds. The biography "Edmond de Rothschild", by Isaac Naiditch, publishes by the Zionist Organization of America, 1945, says on page 68,

> "baron Edmond de Rothschild listened attentively and then said to me, 'The Dead Sea potash concession of the Engineer Novomevsky may well be one of the most beneficial things for Palestine. It is possible that the enterprise may bring in large dividends. That must be done through our bank."

Moshe Novomevsky is now head of Palestine Potash, Ltd., which reaps huge profits while Israel begs from the whole world, and she has browbeaten Germany into paying her more than one billion dollars for "claims" of nonexistent Jews. Continual requests for more and more billions for the State of Israel always meet with a sympathetic response from our Democratic Administration. The Zionist Inner Mission at the White House gives these requests priority, and Senator Herbert Lehman is a director of the Palestine Economic Corporation. Dean Acheson and W. Averell Harriman vie with each other in looking after the needs of Israel. Harriman's fortune can be traced back to Jacob Schiff, a Prince in Israel, and Acheson got his start as Zionist leader Justice Brandeis' law clerk. Boris Smolar, in California Jewish Voice, March 21, 1952, said,

> "The official Zionist leadership in this country is convinced that President Truman and the State Department will sincerely support maximum U.S financial aid for Israel this year."

Harriman, as head of the mutual Security Agency, sends vast sums of money to Israel. Franklin D. Roosevelt Jr. begs dollars for Israel, and looks forward to becoming President someday.

The *New York Times* on May 18, 1952 printed a story on the Israel debts, with a note that $65 million more had just been authorized Israel by Congress The Times story said,

> "American officials feel that with greater foresight Israel financial authorities could avoid the crises that recur every six months. To this, Israel replies that the nature of the greater part of the state's income, contributions and the sale of bonds, is such that it is impossible to budget accurately."

The State of Israel exists, not by the production of goods or by the practice of commerce, but depends for its national income on contributions and the sale of bonds which make good wallpaper. Consequently, the American taxpayer is being forced to pour billions of dollars into the Palestine desert, which the Communist administration of the Russian Jews has failed to transform into a paradise. Yet there is not one expression of gratitude from Israel for these gifts. Rather, there are strident denunciations of America by such as Meier Wilner, a Member of the Israeli Parliament who was reported by an AP dispatch dated March 6, 1949 as saying

> "Nobody in Israel will raise his hand against the Red Army if and when the world plunges again into war."

That the Jews cannot trust each other to handle their money was graphically illustrated in an Associated Press dispatch dated movement of supplies in combat. When we arrived at the Moscow airport we were met with appropriate honors by Soviet troops and taken directly to our Embassy, where we were to stay during our visit as the guests of Ambassador W. Averell Harriman. I am sure that General Eisenhower's invitation had been timed to permit him to see the Annual Sports Parade. It was at this review that Generalissimo Stalin invited Eisenhower to stand with him on the top of Lenin's tomb as the review passed by ... The warmth with which Eisenhower was received everywhere was encouraging, particularly at the stadium, where the audience gave both him and Marshall Zhuvok an ovation. We dined at the Kremlin at a state dinner given in Eisenhower's honor by Generalissimo Stalin during which Molotov was toastmaster ... It was a pleasant evening which seemed to reflect a desire by the Soviet Government to pay sincere respect to Eisenhower ... On our arrival in Berlin, Eisenhower and I agreed that we had enjoyed our trip and that we had found a sincere friend in Marshall Zhukov."

The often-discussed problem of Stalin's successor as leader of the world Communist movement has always leaned on the placing of Communist officials next to Stalin on Lenin's Tomb, so that Eisenhower's place next to Stalin during the Annual Sports Parade seemed very odd. Eisenhower himself boasts that he is the only foreigner who has ever been allowed to stand on Lenin's Tomb.

Clay's book contains other interesting items, a picture opposite page 62 showing Clay and Dubinsky grinning at each other, and a note that Dubinsky had his share in running postwar Germany. The caption says "Clay conferred frequently with American labor leaders." The Polish Zionist Dubinsky is a type which Americans have not yet learned to distrust. Clay built up the trade unions in Germany, nor were other Marxist precepts ignored by this American General. On page 294, he tells us that

> "The American Military Government established in the United States Zone a Central Bank, comparable to our Federal Reserve Bank, a State Central Bank."

This is point Five of the Communist Manifesto.

[Several pages are missing from the original manuscript. Editor's note]

Yet the United Nations World, edited by the admirer of Stalin, Quentin Reynolds, carries an article by Ellsworth Raymond in its issue of November, 1949, "How the Russians Got the Bomb", which does not mention espionage, but brazenly claims that the superior skill of Soviet scientists developed atomic energy much more quickly than we thought they would. American taxes pay for this Communist propaganda which is circulated in our schools.

However, atomic espionage had sanction from the highest officials of the U.S. Government. A man who was not a Communist could not expect to go far on the Manhattan Project. The authority for protecting the Communist spies and helping them get what they wanted came from the White House. Major George Racey Jordan was the former Lend-Lease Expediter at Great Falls, Montana, whence high-priority material was flown to Russia by the U.S. Air Force at a time when our own troops were being supplied by slow boat. Major Jordan appeared on Fulton Lewis' news broadcast and before a House Investigating Committee, with the information that Roosevelt's closest adviser, Harry Hopkins, had phoned him at Great Falls to expedite shipments of atomic supplies to Russia. On October 25, 1951, he reviews his experience before the National Society of New England Women at the Waldorf-Astoria Hotel, as follows:

> "In 1943 and 1944, when I was expediting these shipments to Russia, I had no idea what 'Uranium 92' was used for when I found a memorandum about it in one of the hundreds of patent leather suitcases which were being flown to Russia in a steady stream. The words "Manhattan Engineering Project-Oak Ridge" meant nothing to me when I found them on a blueprint. It was only because they were in a folder along with a letter on White House stationery signed by Harry Hopkins that my curiosity was aroused sufficiently that I copied these words in my diary, together with the phrase from the letter which read 'had a hell of a time getting these away from Groves'. (General Leslie Groves, in charge of the Manhattan Project)."

When Major Jordan declined to give a uranium shipment special priority because he didn't think it merited it, he says that "Col. Potivok, phoned Washington, and turned to me and said 'Mr. Hopkins wants to talk to you.' Harry Hopkins requested that I put this special shipment of atomic chemicals on the next plane to Moscow. I followed his instructions, for he, as Chairman of the President's Russian Protocol Committee on Lend-Lease, was my boss."

When Major Jordan objected to a planeload of films of our industrial plants approved by the State Department, being flown to Russia, he reported the matter to the Army Counter-Intelligence Corps. The CIC tried to stop it, but action was blocked and the matter was hushed up by W. Averell Harriman. Major Jordan was unexpectedly retired, and was replaced at Great Falls by Lt. Walewski Lashinski. When Jordan told this story on the radio, Drew Pearson got his notorious Communist assistant, David Karr, also known as David Katz, to inspect Jordan's Army record, and tried in every way to smear Jordan, without success. Jordan was even called 'anti-Semitic', although he had never mentioned any race in his exposes.

The husband and wife Rosenberg, smalltime couple sentenced to death for their part in the atomic bomb espionage, are still alive.[4] Another spy, David Greenglass, was defended by the Communists' favorite lawyer,

---

[4] The allusion was erased in the original manuscript but the written notes are unreadable. The author implies that the couple was in fact unharmed and vanished in a similar Epstein's fashion... [Editor's note.]

O. John Rogge. However, as Admiral Zacharias reminds us, no Soviet atomic spy of the first rank has yet been apprehended.

The Joint Congressional Committee on Atomic Energy was headed by the late Senator Brien McMahon of Connecticut. A freshman Senator, he was immediately given the Chairmanship of one of the most important Senate Committees. His law-partner, the former Lt. William R. Pearl, has been identified as one of the torturers who extracted amazing confessions from German prisoners of war at Nuremberg.

Walter Isard, in the Quarterly Journal of Economics, February, 1948, writes that the cost of electricity has been going down continuously, so that it is now costs one-half of what it cost in 1900. He says that if atomic power can generate electricity at one-half the present cost, it will not materially affect our economy. It utilization of atomic power can induce a general lowering of power costs, it is logical to expect an increased application of power and rate of production per laborer. Isard does not discuss the effect this would have on the present owners of electric power if they fail to control atomic power. If Victor Emanuel of the billion-dollar Standard Gas & Electric Corporation, the partners of J. and W. Seligman Co. who control the billion-dollar Electric Bond and Share, and the Lehmans and Schoellkopfs who own the vast power developments at Niagara Falls, let atomic power fall into Gentile hands, they would be ruined. That is why they kept control of the atomic project, and that is why Russia got the bomb. Once it was publicized in America that Russia had an atomic bomb, we would have to ignore the development of peacetime uses for atomic energy, and devote it entirely to war. Samuel Schurr wrote in the American Economic Review annual of 1947,

> "On the basis of comparative costs of producing electricity from atomic and non-atomic sources, it appears possible that atomic fuels may replace existing sources of power in some parts of the world at an early date. If an international arms race occurs, atomic power will result, if at all, as a by-product of the production of atomic explosives."

While our atomic program is devoted to war, the billions of dollars worth of stock in electric companies owned by the Emanuels, the Lehmans, and the Schoellkopfs is secure. The fact that the Lehman Corporation's economic adviser, Dr. Alexander Sachs, is the largest single figure in the atomic development indicates that no matter what course the atomic program takes, the Lehmans will benefit by it.

CHAPTER 27

Materialism is the religion of modern society. The Machine Age, with its tremendous increase in the material prosperity of all classes, and the multiplication of the amount of goods services, and money available to all the people, has clouded spiritual values, for this material wealth has not come about because of any ritual which requires gratitude to a god. As a result, Christianity, with its basic creed of denial of the self, and its historical overtones of asceticism, particularly its emphasis on the surpassing of material values by spiritual values, has been hard put to offer a suitable response to the new society. Communism, on the other hand, boldly asserts itself as the philosophy of materialism, and promises to distribute the vast increase in material goods to all of the people. The writings of Marx and Lenin preach a self-styled "scientific materialism" that glibly presumes to assure an absolute equality of distribution, together with their doctrine of atheism which is itself a religion aimed directly at the defeat of its most important rival, Christianity. This equable distribution is lacking in Russia and her satellites for two reasons. First, the Socialist State is inefficient, nor have any sound methods been offered to correct its deficiencies in production and distribution. Second, the Communists are fundamentally dishonest. They have no intention of making an equably distribution, which is advertising to secure support of the modern, materialist peoples. Communism actually intends the elimination of the conservative middle class and the creation of a two-class society, a class of slave farm and factory workers, and an intellectual elite ruling with despotic powers. This is the stake for which Alger Hiss played and lost in America.

In its attack on Christianity, Communism has subtly abandoned the direct atheistic onslaught with which it opened its campaign in the late nineteenth century, and is boring from within the church itself. The Nihilism of frank atheism of the early Communist intellectuals has been replaced by a new "universalism" in the twentieth century. Nihilism proclaimed its belief in nothing but "Universalism" proclaims its belief in everything, that all creeds are equally attractive, equally valuable, and, by a logical inference, equally worthless. The dominant position of Christianity in the religions of the Western nations has been greatly weakened by the infiltration of the "Universalists", by the formation of groups which claim to be spokesmen for Christianity, and which are definitely pro-Communist, notably, the Federal Council of Churches of Christ, one of the focal points of the "Universalist" infection. The National Conference of Christians and Jews is another stronghold of the "Universalists".

The increase in material wealth has some changes in our attitude toward the right of property. The old and static regard for property was a major item in the gentile society which Marx and Engels proposed to overthrow. Communism's principal attack on property is through the sovereign power to tax. Taxation has always been necessary to raise funds for conducting the business of government, and over-taxation was only an evidence of greed on the part of government leaders. Over-taxation in the Communist economy, however, such as the present exorbitant income tax and the inheritance tax in the United States, are punitive taxes, intended to break the citizens who have fortunes and possessions. The income tax is not necessary for the functioning of the United States Government. Even Truman's economic advisers admit that if they took all of the income from some groups, it would not raise enough extra money to take care of the book-keeping involved.

We are living in an age of inflation, the inflation of goods, monies, and populations. Because of the advances in the science of medicine and the increase of food supplies, world population has been doubling itself regularly for the past one hundred years. The slaughter of twelve million people in World War I and the massacre of twenty million people in World War II made no appreciable reduction in any population group. Despite the snuffing out of five hundred thousand lives in Hiroshima and Nagasaki with two atomic bombs, Japan's population has increased so enormously under the American occupation that she faces an economic crisis. The obvious solution to the population problems of Asia is to arm Japan and let her attack Communist China. The survivor of this conflict could then move on India. This has been the answer to population surpluses from Genghis Khan to the present day. The difficulty is that modern warfare kills of the most productive generation, leaving the lame and the old to be cared for by a greatly depleted younger generation. In past centuries, warfare served to raise the breed by killing off the slowest and the weakest, but modern warfare carelessly annihilates the very pick of the population, adolescents in their late teens and early twenties. Modern war is a war against youth.

To chart the pressure caused by these increases in populations, the Germans developed the study of geopolitics. This study gave rise to the German plan for the Drang Nach Osten fur Lebensraum, the drive to the East for living room for the German people, in an attempt to secure the Eurasian heartland, the rich agricultural section called the "breadbasket of Europe". Hitler announced that he intended to attack Russia to secure this section for years, the war he planned to make and the war he made. His declaration of war on England and France was an attempt to protect his rear from Communist sympathizers in those nations. When the Communist agents with Roosevelt tricked us into the war (and Pearl Harbor was only a minor part of this event), Hitler knew he had lost his war. The only thing that could save him would be a terror weapon, and he failed to get the V-bombs in mass production in time to prevent the Allied invasion of Europe to save the Communists.

The Communist traitors of Roosevelt's inner circle and in the State Department persuaded him to cede the Eurasian Heartland to Russia at the Tehran and Yalta Conferences. Yet George Kennan can write unblushingly that we didn't really give anything away at Yalta. We only gave away two continents, Europe and Asia. That isn't much for a day's work.

These same traitors continue to direct our foreign policy. The Council On Foreign Relations has improved its position by forcing both major political parties to openly adopt an identical foreign policy "the bipartisan foreign policy", while two members of the Council, Dwight Eisenhower and Adlai Stevenson, ran against each other in the Presidential elections of 1952.

The "bipartisan" policy proposes to defend Europe, although our own General Staff and Winston Churchill warn that we cannot hold the Russians back more than sixty days, George Sokolsky writes that we have poured more than one hundred billion dollars into Europe from the U.S. Treasury since 1945, and every dollar of it has been wasted.

One factor lessening the gift of the Eurasia to the Communists from Roosevelt is the shift from Europe as the center of world power. That center is now the United States. The Communists in Washington hope to shift it to Moscow, which can be done by our involvement in a Third World War. It is planned that we will lose that war, by the sabotage of our war effort, and by an early and treasonable surrender to Stalin. The result will be that the Unites States will become a province of the World Socialist State, run by the same old international gang, with headquarter probably remaining in New York, or transferred to Tel Aviv. The big trusts in America would be nationalized and run by the same people, just as they are now. The membership of the Council Of Foreign Relations, our leading international bankers and lawyers, would not have to go through the tiresome farce of electing stooges to run the country as fronts for them. The Council members would hold a more obvious and absolute power in America.

There are two examples which justify this prediction. Before the First World War, Germany was one of the great nations of the world, with a culture and industry second to none. When she suddenly surrendered to the Allies in 1918, her bankers and industrialists lost nothing by it. We also have the example of Russia and the Communist Revolution. When the dust settled, Baron Guinzberg's nationwide sugar monopoly became the Soviet Sugar Trust, under the direction of Commissar Guinzberg, and so it was with other interests.

The Third World War is not likely for several years. The Communist Fifth Column is not strong enough to sabotage our war effort, and America has not yet been weakened enough by the policies laid down by the Council On Foreign Relations to be beaten by Russia. The Council is directing the bleeding down of America through the policy of containment and "halting Communist aggression" by killing off the excess Chinese population. Aid to Europe and the slaughter of American boys in Asia are not reckless decisions. They are intended to exhaust our manpower and our financial resources, to cause an economic depression here and decimate our younger generation until we cannot offer serious resistance to the Russian armies.

Universal Military Training is one of the most urgent goals of the conspirators. We have Mrs. Anna Rosenberg to write the conscription laws for us. It was to escape forced conscription and exorbitant taxes that our ancestors came to America. The gang came out without their masks on March 4, 1952, when Eugene Meyer's Washington Post carried a full-page political advertisement, paid for by the National Emergency Committee of the Military Training Camps Association of the United States. It headlined "America Needs Universal Military

Training Now", and twelve men gave arguments for it below. The Chairman of this group was Julius Ochs Adler, publisher of the New York Times. Other names on this list were Paul Hoffman, General Dwight Eisenhower, General George C. Marshall, and Rabbi Rosenblum of Temple Israel, New York City. This group intends to make every American boy a corpse in uniform.

The sending of American boys in cattle-boats to the slaughter-pits of Korea is a violation of the fundamental principal of geopolitics, the doctrine hemispheric solidarity. This doctrine maps longrange political strategy in terms of continents, not nations. Japan employed this theory to develop her "Greater East Asia Co-Prosperity Sphere" which led her into war with the United States, because we protected Standard Oil's investments in China and Southeast Asia.

That Great Britain recognizes the doctrine of hemispheric solidarity is evinced by the fact that she abandoned all of her investments in China in 1952. Within a few years, Asia will be under the control of one power, Communism, because there is no alternative. It is generally supposed that Chester Bowles was sent as U.S. Ambassador to India on a mission similar to General Marshall's famed trip to China, to give the people of that nation proof that our government is pro-Communist.

Robert Strausz-Hupe, who adapted the geopolitical theories for Americans, wrote, in "The Balance of Tomorrow", Putnam, 1945, page 89,

> "Japan became a war country from learning the techniques of Western industry. Amid a host of imponderables only one near-certainly emerges; the introduction of Western techniques will within two or three decades make Asiatic manpower effective (in a war against the white race)."

That is the program laid down by Earl Browder of the Communist Party and carried out by President Truman's Point Four program, to train, arm, and equip the races of Asia and Africa for a gigantic onslaught against the Aryan race, in fulfillment of the command of Marx and Engels to wipe out the gentile society.

If our National War College were interested in defending the United States, we would not be wasting billions of dollars and American lives in Asia or in Europe; we would be arming Canada and Mexico and South America. The foreign aid program is a bitter joke.

Should the Council On Foreign Relations lose its control over America, how would our financial policy and foreign policy develop? The answer to that is found in the forces which are struggling for power, and in future trends in our economy. The two forces struggling for power on a worldwide scale are world Zionism and world Communism. They cooperate in destroying religions and nations because each one that is destroyed helps them toward their goal. Zionism, the dream of the Jewish race, is based on the Old Testament conception of the Jews as God's Chosen People, who will rule the world. Communism is based on a plan of a two-Class society of slaves and masters. However, neither Communism nor Zionism seem able to consolidate their gains, which they make by treachery and conspiracy. Unfortunately, as they have found out in Moscow and in Tel Aviv, conspirators do not make good administrators. Stalin had to liquidate the entire faction which brought about the Russian Revolution of 1917, and Israel will have to shove her Russian Jewish officials into the Dead Sea before she can hope to put herself on a sound footing. By 1940, Russia was suffering from such hardening of the economic arteries that Hitler almost conquered her in a matter of weeks. Israel, of course, exists on contributions and the sale of very doubtful bonds. When they drove out the 600,000 Arabs, there was nobody left to do the work or pay the taxes, effectively wrecking the economy of old Palestine for years to come.

The future economy of America will recognize that the industrial revolution is over. It reached its logical conclusion with the development of atomic power. This means that capital investment of funds must take a new turn. The next few decades should see the abolition of the stock exchanges and the end of the long-term method of financing industries and public works by the sale of bonds. This practice of finance has been the seed of most of the evil deeds of the twentieth century. Although this method served to finance the development of heavy industry and the modern centralized state, it has been used by the international bankers to wield more power than was ever held by any man, so that they have been able to precipitate monetary panics, wars, and depressions to gain their profits. With or without the Third World War, the stock exchanges and long-term bond financing will disappear in the twentieth century.

As for the forces of Zionism and Communism, each of them contains its own destruction. They are like mad dogs who can cause great suffering, but they will be destroyed. American has a Constitution which safeguards our citizens against such groups. We have only to live up to the political heritage which the founders of the American Republic bequeathed to us, and American will continue to be the hope of the world.

Other titles

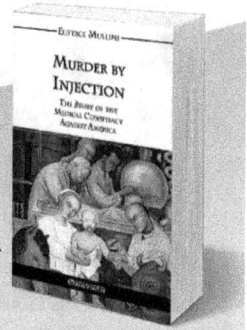

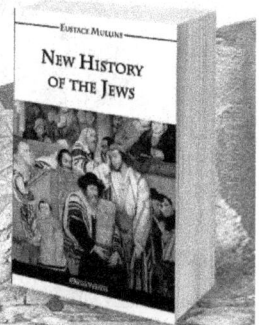

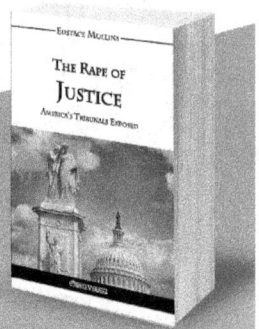

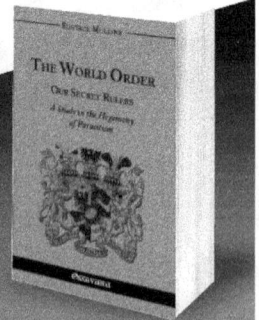

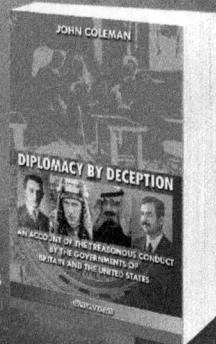

OMNIA VERITAS®
LIGHT-BEARERS OF DARKNESS
This book is an attempt to show, by means of documentary evidence, that the actual world conditions are under the influence of mystic and secret societies through which the Invisible Centre is seeking to direct and dominate the nations and the world.
LIGHT-BEARERS OF DARKNESS

OMNIA VERITAS®
THE TRAIL OF THE SERPENT
An attempt to trace the worship of the ancient Serpent, the Creative Principle, the God of all initiates of the Gnostics and Cabalists, emanating from the Hellenised Jews of Alexandria.
THE TRAIL OF THE SERPENT

OMNIA VERITAS®
www.omnia-veritas.com